*

Eld Religion Philosophy
Mysticism. Magicks
Invoking the Holy Guardian Angel

Books by Jason Wayn Persson:

**The Chronicles of the Black Winged Dragon
The Moonblade of Nuith**

First edition 2022

Jason Wayn Persson 2022
Cover art *Multraverse* (detail)
Oil on canvas. 36"x48". 2019

JWPersson@Protonmail.com

*

THE
MAGICKS TOME

Jason Wayn Persson

*

*

'I'm not perfect,' said the Master. 'But very nearly!'

Truth in itself is beautiful, and the best anchor of your ship; every truth fits all the rest of truth; and the most alluring lies will never do that.
Aleister Crowley.

The Magicks Tome

Imagine if there were a Book, a Magickal Book, writ by a Magus; a puissant talisman of wende and wonder. The Book would be as a window or portal onto and into universes other and strange; uncommon realities. It might be a key to a particular Magickal door. Perhaps it contains Magickal maps, with directions for the aspiring Magician, and the True Initiate, to find the paths of Wyrd & Doom.

Ah, it would be like as ne'er seen afore! Mysterious, mystical, beautiful, fascinating and powerful. A tome of weighty portend, wrought by the veritable Scribe of the Gods. What marvellous chapters we should expect! Why, each page would be a potent spell to shape universes! For every Word, when the will is sanctified and true, is a whirling star of God-force.

If the author were indeed a true Magus, called and anointed by the Divine, were who and what he claimed to be, in all truth, not a Pretender, then could he write such a Book.

Words are his Art. An if he so willed, then he could make every part of it pulse with cataclysmic Magicks, to quicken reality by an thousand years.

It would be a Book of Things. A tome of destinies. In it, each man would find his own Reckoning.

The false minds would encounter only jarring confusion, like sqiggledy nonsenses; because the Magickal Book is a mirror. For the shining hearted it is as a well of pure, clear waters. The pilgrims shalt therein come to lie in the bosom of the Goddess. The way shalt be strewn with celestial blooms, and scented with heavenly musks.

To open its leaves would be to step o'er an Elsewyr threshold. If the aspirant can approach with a genuine will to embrace the All, and with a heart free of wickedness, then each step along the path wilt draw him towards the centre, and an encounter with God. A holy tome of celestial treasures!

And, if such a Book existed, this would be its introduction.

Table of Contents

Bridge at Elsewyr

The Magickal Retirement

The Aeon Rasa

*

BRIDGE AT ELSEWYR

*

The Abyme

The Devil does not *buy* Souls, nor is he often interested in making trades. He won't even get out of bed and put his hat on for most of the useless broken-down wrecks that call upon him; what's left there to devour? He is not a creature of subtlety or sophistication. He is a parasitical megalomaniac who delights in perversions. In eld days he was known as *Disyful*: God of evil.

During my traverse across the Abyss, I encountered several guises. On one of the occasions that I met him face to face in the corporeal realm, I asked him what his name was, he replied: *There are no names here.* He is the Unnamed or Nameless One. It was a disturbing aspect; the overwhelming quality of his being was of utter loathsomeness. A being vile and degenerate, that revelled in every perversion.

I was haunted by the memory of it for a long time. Or, to phrase it in Magickal language: it took a year before I could cast that daemon down to its ruin.

Ah, but he is no longer the lustrous dragon that once he was. His sparkle is decidedly dulled. He is old now, and his power has been diminishing for centuries. He is desirite, decrepit, and his force is all but spent. His insanity broadens, and the fraying mind splinters and cracks, and is irretrievably drawn out into the void. On a good day he can still put on a little show; he has a few tricks and props left. But he has been drawing steadily away from the centre, and deeper into realms of void or chaos. The mind is delicately balanced, and even Gods can go mad. Insanity lends only temporary strength and power. Fury always abates.

There isn't a contract to sign, although there might be a symbolic representation close to hand. Instead, the Devil lures his dupes into surrendering responsibility, and abdicating reason. If men consent because they are weak and fearful, then they have turned their backs forever upon their own essential humanity and will. Such men become agents of evil, puppets controlled by an alien will, whose aim is to bring chaos to All. The very perfection of the Multraverses gives rise to the Idea of chaos. Order can be disturbed; at least in theory. Residing in the Idea of chaos, venturing far into its nefarious pits of unreason, and lingering there, delighting in the depravity of it, may result in the chaos becoming real for that mind. Like drug addicts they keep returning to the dark thrill. People slide into insanity.

'Many such people will deteriorate as regards their capacity to live meaningful lives in this world, here and now. They may feel they have found the key to all mystery, but we can judge their claim only by their zeal, their behaviour and their external symptoms,' said the Master. 'If you engage in Black Magic never lose sight of the ultimate penalty: the loss of your own Soul, or your individuality.'

When a mind turns to chaos the motivation is always arising from weakness; the nature of evil is weakness, never strength. It is the road of bitterness and de-generation. Only greedy, envious minds could make such a choice. An honest man can only choose that which is true, and he will not be seduced.

The ultimate aim of chaos is death to All. Its ambition is cold, empty void.

The mind is a very complex instrument, and is certainly little understood by the quacks modern. Every act is a *Magickal* act. Even *each thought* has consequence. First in the realm of the individual mind, and then out, into the oceans of unending tears. Health and well being, and sanity, are inextricably linked with our behaviours. The physical body is an extension of the mind, just as the mind is an extension of the Soul. A real morality strengthens will, and results in overall health of the Soul-mind-body. A lack of personal integrity conversely makes the man weak and vulnerable. Weak minds can easily snap, crack, and pop.

Pretence doesn't help. Pantomimes are not reality. We must choose. There is a fork in the road ahead. To reject the right and true and good, to oppose the Great Harmony, is to wilfully embrace evil. It is a threshold which one cannot re-cross. When we choose sides we have declared alliance.

Oh, but there is a price, o man. Listen for the galloping host: it is the Lords of Desolation which ride to meet thee.

*

Bridge at Elsewyr

*

And scribe these Words, Magus. Th'were a ryme upon a tyme, in a land of no-place. In the Wilderness minds are smelted and forged anew. The Lord of the Wild Places; I am the Reckoning. King of the Horns. KRNS the Hunter. I am the Arrow. I am the flight of the dart that never errs.

From *The Chronicles of the Black Winged Dragon.*

0 Parsifal, the Wandering Fool

At the Endless Lonely Bliss arises the sparking impulse of the
Original Genius. The Idea is the spinning point and it is the
Way. The Word is born from the Idea, expressed.
Yet recent to the Word is the Thought. Thought implies Mind.
In the moment whence the Way turned in the absolute
perfection of Divine All alone, the sparking force ignited, and
gathering momentum, it moves towards manifesting in absolute
perfection in infinite pattern. The impulse is Love.

Before the God Mind there was no thought. The Way escryd; it
saw all patterns, like a map of the Heavens. Finally it was sated.
It had comprehended the All.
Benignly the Way manifested Space and Dimension. It was a
small concentric force. It turned slowly in a dance of delicate
finesse, and moving in a spiral out into the void.
The Thought was forming. The momentum created by the idea
was like a whirling star. It had brilliance. The genius of the All
was the force. In the moment, the impulse and the Idea
collided, and the void was sundered.
At the spinning Point the Thought arose into the God Mind.
The Way expressed the Thought as Word: *All Will Manifest*, so
the Essence was ignited, and the Divine began to turn towards
manifested perfection in unending pattern.
The impulse originates from the perfection of the omniscient
All. Thus it must be pure, certain and flawless. The manifesting
of the All is the Great Harmony. The manifested All could only
be perfect in all its parts. Its Will was and is always towards the
perfecting of the whole, which is called the Great Work.

The Great Work is to bring Man, here represented in the first
Arcanum by Parsifal, the Wandering Fool, back onto his proper
path, which is the Royal Road.
The Great Work is not a revival; there has not yet been a
Golden Age of Humankind, so there can be no restoration of its
imagined conditions. When and where was Man on his True
Path? Somewhere in the era of pre-Monotheistic religions.

1 The Juggler

So begins the manifestation of the Eld Tome. It is her Religion, and it has endured the universal flux of events. It rises anew, refreshed, envigorated, quickened.

The Magician is the forming of the Idea, the whirling star of energies. He is the winged messenger, the herald of the Gods. He is the mind into which the thought arises. Beneath azure starry skies he transforms and becomes the Word incarnate. He draws the elements of stone and water, and imbues them with fire. He places his holy staff upon the mountain peak, and his declaration penetrates all the universes.

Within the All there are the Multraverses. Within the Multraverses are the multiverses, and contained within the boundaries of the multiverses are the myriad universes. Within the universe the Earth exists, and on the Earth Man exists. Man exists as a microcosm within the All.

The First Reality is the starting point; the prymordial point in this particular. The corporeal realms, the physical, material universes, are the first and pryme reality.

There is no part of Man which is not of and from the All. He is inseparable from the materials of which he is formed. Man has mind and awareness. Mind and awareness necessarily create an isolated intellectual realm. Each man is thus unique and individual, due to his isolated perceptions of the universe he lives in. His experience is individual. He grows and adapts according with his own genius and his immediate environment. There is nothing in Man which did not originate with the first Idea, from the Word of the Way. Ergo, because Man adjusts and grows, so too the universe adjusts and grows. As Man is alive and experiencing, so too is the All alive and experiencing. The universe has awareness and adjusts. Nature has intelligence. If the All were not aware then neither could Man be aware. Man is a microcosm of the All because every faculty and quality in Man originates from the first impulse of the All. It is in Man because it is in the All.

Each man has an isolated, unique intellect and perspective. He has his o*wn reality*. Ergo, the All has an isolated unique intellect and personality.

The Individual Mind and Personality of God is a difficult concept for those who worship their ego-mind, because it challenges their position as the ultimate intellect in the universe. *I am God!* they foam and froth. *There is no difference between the multifarious things.*
Incorrect. The All distinguished forms. Each intellect, each mind, even whilst we correspond, is isolated and unique. We are all from the same Essence, and we have many similarities, but we are not the same mind, and we are not God Mind; we never were, and we never will be. There is an Intellect older even than time. It resided in absolute perfection before the Multraverses existed. The finite human intellect of the pseudo-philosophers and pseudo-Magicians was never a part of that Original Personality. No man is God; he is a man, with a limited, confined perception of things. It is ego-mind that suggests otherwise.
They struggle with the concept of God Mind because accepting it would mean recognising the fact of billions of individual intellects existing simultaneously within the corporeal realm, equally valid and significant as their own. *Every man and woman is a star.* But, even worse, if the All has a unique isolated intellect, which ergo they themselves are not part of and cannot access, then they must recognise an Intellect and Mind inconceivably greater in every way than their own. That isn't an acknowledgement they are prepared to make. They don't articulate it, often even to themselves, but all their pseudo-philosophies come down to the same thing: their own ego-mind replaces God Mind.

The Eld Religion is, as the name indicates, the first religion. It is the *original* faith. It is Mankind's natural relationship with his environment, with the universe, and the Gods.
The Eld Masters were Druids. They taught in close contact with the aspirants, guiding them to the mountain, preparing

them for the climb ahead.

They recognised and revered the Goddess-force alongside, complementary to the God-force. The masculine and feminine aspects of the Divine apparent in all things.

Man swore an alliance with the Gods. He worked in harmony with the Will of All. He recognised his real position in the plan as the microcosm, and sought to co-operate rather than to contest or to dominate. Man was not a slave of the Gods, nor a puppet, for he had always free will. He worked in partnership.

The Eld Religion, which was called Occultism, is distinct from the multifarious philosophies and Practices which are generally considered to represent the Occult. The majority of what is presented as 'Occultism' is openly, or thinly disguised, Black Magicks, and sorcery.

The Aeon Rasa now brings the True Occultism into its final form. It is the Aeon of the Night. She is the Daughter; the manifesting of the Original Word: The Lovely Star, Nuit.

The Royal Road, which is the path followed by the Eld Druids, is the Way of the Noble Mind; the Beautiful Essence of Humankind. Their road leads even into the Heavens and beyond. The Gods declared the boundaries, the laws, and the Way. What they have set as the route to Divinity remains, and we may not change it. Truth endures, and fits perfectly with all other truth. The symbols and expressions may alter and adapt like modern colloquialisms, but the core is unchanging.

At its heart the Eld Religion is simple and natural. It is the Magicks of connection and harmony.

Its structure is like that of a great tree: the branches reach up into the Heavens, and the roots go deep into the belly of the Earth. The branches are the systems of ideas, stemming from the great trunk, the arts and the detail; and the broader concepts of the religion are the roots which feed and stabilize the tree.

The Magician erects his own Temple of Reality. He begins by laying the nine stones of foundation. These he sets upon the ancient earth. His Temple rises in sweeping curves and arches, lacing and weaving through intricate canopies of stone and wood. It is the graven image of the Great Tree that he builds, its branches raising up to the light. Perhaps he decorates the windows with colored glass, to represent his Gods and their Word, and to ignite the aelan of the sunlight.

When we work Magicks we are sending a call along those roots of the Great Tree.

The Master was a Druid who followed the Eld Religion. The teachings have descended eye to eye, face to face, since they were given by the Gods. His approach was starkly different from that of his father, Aleister Crowley. At least, at first glance.

'Our teachings on mysticism are more closely aligned than one might suppose,' he said. 'Perhaps I just express the same Ideas better.'

He didn't go in for false modesty; and he wasn't fishing for compliments or adoration. 'I am the greatest of Masters,' he said. Yet, he added that he was where Aleister would be now. He had no doubts about who he was, or why he was here, or of his direct connection to the Beyond: Crowley had used High Magicks to summon this homunculus, the Great Soul, to incarnate as the Master who would succeed him. Amado came in answer to his call.

Crowley had taken personal charge of the Magickal education of his illegitimate son. When the boy was fourteen years old he was made an Initiate. Or rather, he was presented to the Gods, who might yet reject him, for all the efforts of the aged Magician.

Despite the nefarious and sometimes savage imagery that Crowley employed in his Magickal Universe, according with the ambiguity of his mission, he was himself a Druid of the Eld Religion.

He passed the flame on to Amado (*one born out of wedlock*). The Master honed and sharpened his Magickal Tools. Of his methods, he said: 'I prepare the self to teach itself.'

'Why should we deny what the Gods have put in place?' he asked. 'Those who try to influence the Gods in any way are evil, and align themselves with the ranks of Black Magic and

Devilry.
A true Magician would never use magic for his own direct benefit.'

2 **The High Priestess. The God Mind**

The High Priestess Arcanum is the invoked Goddess. She who stands veiled by enchantments. She represents the sacred mysteries and initiations. At her Altar the Magician may uncover Divine wisdom and knowledge. Yet is she wrapped in shimmer and dancing starlights, and the dark night behind her, for she is the unknown as well as the revealed. She holds the Key of Mysteries, and thereby wieldeth a great power.
She is the Moon Goddess, and there is a darker side of her nature. She can represent hidden danger, death and lunacy. The pursuit of secrets and mysteries have lured many men into the pit.

The Magician learns to recognise hooks and bait, and is not seduced by trivia detail. He must be discerning, he must test out every Idea until he has full cognition. He is certain of every stone, else he lays it not.
Her Celestial Treasures are not to be found in secret Words or formulas. Ceremonies and Operations are of themselves incapable of producing a puissant effect; it is the rather the will of the Magician which is the vital component. There are not elevated Rites and Rituals, writ in angel-tongue, perfect in their geometry, like clockwork dances of cataclysmic gesture, which are properly unlocked with the rising through expensively attained grades. Truth will not be held back, nor is it available only to the materially affluent.
The true Mysteries of the Veiled Goddess are neither concerned with Magick Circles nor paraphrenalias, nor even angel or devil names.

It is evil that is eager to bind with debt and obligations. There are many ways to be indebted, and in a Magickal sense it is a kind of ownership. The pit covered o'er with chains. When knowledge and wisdom are dangled like unattainable golden carrots, then we must be chary.
The Magician should be generous in his actions, and mindful to avoid entangling contracts. The wise man ensures by remaining

firm and correct that his enemies are obliged to him.

She does not withhold from a man his due rewards. Her Secrets and her Mysteries belong to no man or organisation; truth must be accessible to all equally.

'Ignore this rule and chaos intervenes bringing down persons, organisations and even civilisations,' said the Master.

Obscurantism is the dominant philosophy of many Occult groups. With so many smoke screens and mazes one wonders if they actually have anything at all in the Inner Sanctum, or is it all an elaborate diversion? *We can not reveal these sacred mysteriums to the profane!* they might protest. Scientology does something similar. These organisations can become extremely rich from selling their golden carrots. But, even genuine pilgrims may be misled, and could forever lose the Way.

Catholicism advocates blind unquestioning faith, since, in their view, the Divine Mysteries are utterly confounding and dangerous to reason.

How would it benefit the Gods to hide their truth in mesmeric complications or indecipherable enigmas? Conversely, the truth is simple and clear, like pure, clean waters. It fits with all other truth, and can be comprehended by anyone. The Sacred Mysteries are not intended as the privilege of a select few: 'elites' is just another brand of 'chosen people.'

Some detail may be technical and complex, pertaining to arts; learning to play a musical instrument takes years of dedication and perseverance, and a modicum of natural talent. Not all of us are born to be musicians, but we can still find our right place in the scheme.

Classical Occultism is generally big on secrets and hidden knowledge. It's an endlessly fascinating field of study. One studies *oneself;* which is a subject few ever tire of.

Charlatans keep the music playing loudly: *What harm?* the Devil whispers. *Just one more dance?*

Despite every attempt to bury it, the Gods' truth keeps rising. And, if the Gods exist, we can have access to them.

Yes, she has layers of veiled mystery and wonders. She awaits in the Cave at the mountain's peak.

True Occultism is taught by the Masters who are chosen by the
Beyond for that specialised role. There have never been any
real *Secret* Masters. The true Master is accessible, and imparts
wisdom and Magickal empowerment through direct contact
with his students.
The Gods have already made arrangements so that we might
approach the Divine, to learn, to sustain and empower us. To
apprehend and reside in Reality. There is an absolute truth, and
we are capable of understanding it.
'Do everything in your power to show the better side of your
character, and then you will see that other things change too,'
the Master advised.

The first reality is the physical universe. The manifested All is
a stone for the floor of the Temple. This pryme reality, or
prymaeval reality, is immutable. It supersedes all other
realities. Awareness begins in the first reality.
The Multraverses within the All are endlessly perfect. The
motivation of the original Idea was towards the perfecting of
every pattern.

The Multraverses are alive. They exist, and have awareness.
They experience and grow. It is self-evident that they move
towards perfection, for they manifestly exist and have attained
perfected form in the pryme reality. The Will has fulfilled itself
and stands now as proof of the original motivation; and the
Multraverses continue to expand, distinguishing and dividing
themselves endlessly, from the protoplasmic cells of raw
materials to the clustered galaxies, moving forever to the limits
of dimension.
Were the original Impulse and Will that arose from the All
otherwise than to manifest in perfected endless pattern, which
is the manifested All, then the perfected Multraverses would
not exist. If the All tended towards death, chaos and emptiness
then it could not exist as the perfected form in the prymordial
reality; it would have collapsed in on itself long ago. Its Will to

death, chaos and emptiness would have been fulfilled instead; millions of years have passed since the first Impulse, and what we have existing now is proof of its motivation.

When we give a name to a thing we haul it out from the void and can begin to apprehend it. We attach an individualism to the thing, we distinguish it, by its name, from all other things. When the Magician comprehends the Individual Personality of the All, he begins to apprehend God.

The Word Logickal enables the Magician to see the patterns and the tides. He works backwards to the starting point.

The Goddess was the manifested All. He was the Genius, the pure Impulse that motivated her. *All Will Manifest in Great Harmony,* was the Thought, and the Goddess established God Mind to facilitate the Creation.

God Mind perceived the All. It witnessed the birthing of the multiverses. It was the Will of the movement. God Mind considered, and reached conclusions. Inspiration and intuition were the genius of God Mind. It refined its comprehensions. It expanded.

The Great Goddess is the Original Personality of God Mind. She is the Receptive All-Mother. *URCN* was her name in the Eld tomes. *DANU* was she hight by the Celts; the Divine Waters from which all matter and life was drawn.

God Mind examined itself. It reached to the limits. It challenged, and underwent the Ordeals of Mind. It Became.

3 The Son. The Crowned Will

Man perceives the universe within which he exists. His view is an individual one. This isolation exists as a (protective) barrier between his mind and his reality, and the universe and the divers realities of the Common World.

It is a haven whereunto he retreats and revives his energies. There he formulates his comprehensions and his secret machinations. There he views with a god-like vantage his own reality, and he refines his cognitions.

In the privacy of his Holy of Holies, he communicates with the All. It is there, the realm of his unique perceptions, that his rasa abides.

What is the purpose of the Magician? His role is to exist harmoniously with the universe. This impulse arises from Soul as a motivation, and it moves towards perfection. He is a part of the All, and his true nature is to align with the Will of the Way. He reaches towards perfection in unending pattern. The reality of the Magician seeks the Reality of God. Like concentric circles it closes in on the centre.

A mind can be helped to flourish, or enticed into disintegration. All religions attempt to exert influence upon the mind.

There are leaders, followers, and quitters. Let each man be judged by his intensions. Those who wilfully align themselves with negative forces must be left to reap their just harvest. Their anguish arises from their behaviours.

'My father taught me everything he knew about being a Magician,' said Amado Crowley, 'but there was not a single lesson on how to be a parasite.'

Some paths go downhill. When people find out they have been duped, that they have bound themselves to oblivion, they may be angry and disappointed; yet still they may become even more committed than before, as a self-protective response. Is the deluded man exempt from consequence?

The Magus of the Gods becomes the argent of the Way. He is then the active force working upon the physical universe. His

Work harmonizes his conscious will with his true will. He becomes the Word incarnate; the Scribe of the Gods. He is the spear tip which pierces the side of the Christ. His Word manifests in the pryme reality, for his Magickal Reality is woven through.

He enters into the Womb. It is the Cave and the Gateway. It is the Inner Sanctum, and an audience with the Gods.

He emerges cleansed and rebirthed. Now is he sanctified. Now art all his Works made true. He has connected directly with the Source. He stands erect and declares his Word. He announces the New Religion, and ushers in the New Aeon.

He is Vauteu, the Dancer Cosmiq, Lord of Tome. The *Staritz,* the Holy Madman of God.

His journey is idiosyncratic. His reality is unique, individual. His Star is held aloft in its orbit by his rasa. Each Magician will discover his own eccentric route. The Ordeals and the Rewards interlace. The Path is circular, spiralling to the centre.

The Magician works to actualise his being. He embraces the individual Soul.

The Material realm covers the Soul with consciousness. The Soul descends into the physical and is veiled. It waits whilst the conscious mind learns to think and to operate the body vehicle. It waits until the will of the conscious mind is to unite with Soul. It guides and prompts, according with its genius.

The Earth-realm is a temporary condition. There are restrictions which create frictions and tensions. The Magician has come to meet his wyrd. He can be of use to the Way.

The Soul extends into mind, and the mind extends into the body. The distinctions which we make between them are only intellectual. They are weaven, and can not be seperated.

The *Yi King* says that we can see a man's character in how he chooses to nourish himself. All our behaviours reflect and determine who and what we are.

If we reside in filth and our waters are polluted, then we will attract disease. Similarly, when the Soul-mind is contaminated with filth and perversion then it attracts disease; and it can attract strange forces like astral ticks and parasites. *Concubiti* are astral vampyres, and are identified in legends across the world. They can attach themselves to a human shell, and feed upon its vital energies by having sex with the human. These encounters will usually be experienced during dreams.

The integrity and balanced health of the Magician's mind can become an immunity to these types of psychic parasites. He will conversely attract positive forces.

Sex is a natural part of human life, and for healthy minds it brings an empowering charge. The Magician can harness the energies which he raises, and direct them into productive channels.

The impact of the sexual life will be significant upon the Soul-mind-body. There are, first of all, the occupying myriad complexities of a close relationship or partnership with another person; another mind and reality. Yet, in proper context, in love directed by a pure will, the union will fortify and strengthen, balance and protect the Soul-mind-body.

When a natural behaviour is focused upon negatively, as sex is in most areas of society, it leads to distortions, to shame and fear. These give rise to destructive behaviours and abnormal appetites. Perversions become normalised, as natural, and thus *healthy*, sexual activities which do not generate fascination or disgust, and don't need an instructional video, or safety goggles, are viewed as boring and old fashioned.

When the sexual life draws only negative energies, then the mind begins to topple into the abyss, and may become obsessed with sick and distorted forms of sex.

It doesn't take the online pornography addict long before he ventures into weirder and more deviant areas to find stimulation. Like the opiate addict, the 'hit' becomes increasingly elusive. It is a rabbit hole that leads to the loss of all restraint. The impact upon the mind will be a slow disintegration. It's one way to get to meet the God of evil; but there mightn't be much of anything left afterwards.

'An individual's sexuality does reflect the proximity of chaos in his mind,' said the Master. 'Almost every psychiatric patient shows some symptoms of disordered sexuality.'

4 The Daughter. The Individual Personality

The universes are very old. Yet, they are existing beyond time. Man is young. He has not yet stood and met his destiny. As a collective he is at odds with the All.
He is entrapped, and enslaved to shadow mind and ego. His civilisation and his societies are criminal, and philosophically juvenile or degenerate. He acts as though he were blind, deaf, dumb.

One difficulty we have when trying to construct our system of cognition is that we struggle to define and separate our projected realities, which arise from ideas of how things should be, how we would like reality to be. The Magician does not neglect to examine every quarter of his mind, and to apprehend all his motivations. We must *know ourselves* without flynching. Truth has nothing to do with opinions, popular or otherwise.

Time is a man-made system of records. It has no relevance other than to bureaucratic historians. Dates have no magickal significance; their use and power is literally in cataloging events. Time has no presence, no sapience. It is not a god, and it has no force. It is an intellectual fabrication.
We see in the world manifested cycles of change; these are real. There are the seasons, perpetually transforming into one another; yet they are not clockworked events; they flux and merge, overlapping, extending one into another, blurring, continuously shifting. There are High Days and Holy Days, such as the Equinoxes. This movement of cycles arises only from the Pulse of the All. The worlds turn. The galaxies spiral to a point. The multiverses sway in the aether winds. The cataloging of these events has no bearing upon the Will of the universes.
The only influence time has, consistent with all pseudo-philosophies and concepts, is upon ego-mind.
This Moment, stretching into Eternity, is the Centre. Tides and worlds turn, seasons change. The body of flesh is formed, grows old, and dies.

The Soul may precede conception, and it is released at the death of the body. Experience in the physical realms enables the Soul to expand. It grows, moving closer to God and absolute reality. Experience is the most valuable form of learning.

There were no previous human races that became so super-advanced that God had to destroy them. No, no, dears, that's never how things work. Neither are there alien super-beings that are conducting geological experiments with the Earthlings; those theories, and many similar, do not have sound logical basis. They are emotive speculations and False Myths, some of which are deliberately circulated, with intension to mislead, and to undermine the true will of Mankind. They are like malicious faery tales, and their motivation is avoidance of consequence (they all try to sell the Idea: it doesn't really matter what we do). This is Mankind's first experience. This point here is as far as we have gotten along the road of destiny. Rather than being insignificant or purposeless, Mankind is at the crux of the Gods' plan.

The corporeal realm, where we live and interact as humans, is the pryme reality; at least, it must be so for *us*. It is where the Magician begins when constructing his Temple of reality.
The Black Winged Dragon works the Magicks of Change. The Queen commands the worlds; yet, what are the worlds? In the name Death the Dragon devours, and reforms the Multraverse. The Magus details his Temple of absolute reality.

The Divine waters filled the Earth beneath the heavens. From the Eight Elements which were mixt within the waters, there sprang a seed. The light of the sun nourished the seed, and the waters fed the seed, and from it there issued its flower. The flower bloomed, and dropped its seeds. Then it withered and died. The seeds of the flower fell unto the end of the deeps, and there some rooted in the bed of the oceans. From one seed there issued a thin sprout. It reached up toward the light.

'Since the human brain invented logic,' said the Master, 'then it is capable of rising above the need for it. It has never been the aim to satisfy reason. First, there are many kinds of reason, and second, why be bound by the rules on how to use the tools? Let's put it this way: inside every mystic is a hidden artist.'

He sometimes would refer to a Magickal state of *no-mind,* or *not-thinking*. It is the state of mind freed from ego.

The Eld Religion can not be modernised or revamped, not at its core essence. Its truth must be eternal. This means the broad shapes remain true and unchanging.

It is not our task to provide a detailed map of the Multraverse, or a moment by moment history of everything. Superfluous detail may or might not satisfy bureaucratic quibblers. It is our approach to the Divine as an individual that matters.

The Gods put in place a system for Mankind to advance along its path to wisdom, knowledge, and perfecting; to communicate and work with the Divine. It is no point to object to the color of the tome's cover, or to ask for special exemptions from the bits you aren't that keen on. *That is how it works*, said God.

The Gods are the centre which Man must move towards; the centre does not adjust and move towards an embrace with *ego-mind*.

There is Absolute Truth. It is that which was, is, and will be. A man will live his life, and at some point he will die. That is an absolute truth; and one that carries sobering impact. No objections whatever can alter those original facts. Regardless of any sophisticated or devious argument devised, the man will live and he will die in this corporeal reality. Nothing can change those natural laws of life.

Death is an absolute for every man; therefore we are certain that absolute truth exists in the corporeal realms, and that it demonstrates an absolute reality.

The centre is named *Sooth*. It is the point of view of God Mind. The cognitions and perceptions of God Mind are the determining reality.

Yet, the aeons themselves shift and change. The Daughter is the synthesis of the conditions preceding. She is the Idea finally manifested as form. The aim of her Religion remains as it has always been: through *rasa* to reach to Union with All.

We are abled to communicate because our realities overlap to an extent. We share common experiences as human beings. I can talk about my cat *Blind Crow,* for example, and even if you have not met her, you probably have experience of cats, and so you easily comprehend the talisman.

The closer our realities align the more we move towards *mutual identification.*

The centre must always be the fixed absolute reality of God-Mind. Once we apprehend where the centre is, then we have placed a pin in the map. We can calculate our own relative position.

We seek to harmonise with the Way, with our environment. We move towards Union with All; we begin to identity with, and our reality overlaps with, the God Mind.

5 The Prophet of the Way. The Magus of the Eternal

Crowley recommended the excruciatingly painful Practice of Asana yoga for those who desired to attain to his Magickal Secrets. *It's indispensable for the serious Magician,* he would tell them with a sniff.

He chuckled to himself, sitting at the window of his room at Hastings, England, puffing at his pipe, gazing out over the dark promenade, and up at the twinkling stars. They, and all the followers after them, who would desecrate his Temple and spit on his Altar, would reap their due rewards. For some of them he might even take a personal interest, and lend a hand, just to make sure.

There were several ambiguous and dubious Practices he had recommended, or seemingly, with symbols and hints. At other places he was directly provocative; he was after all *the Great Beast whose number was six hundred an sixty an six.*

He wanted to make it easy for them, his band of treacherous knock-kneed freeloaders. He held the Magickal Mirror before them, and they could see only their own grotesque reflections. There was a particular Magickal Door or Portal that he invited them to enter. Beyond its threshold lay a deep nefarious pit that Crowley had labored long over.

Oh, but the dragon is not dead, my dears, he said in a breezy whisper, tobacco smokes writhing, curling out into the night. *It sleeps; and one great eye is always open!*

He was cognisant that they would betray him once he was gone. They would abandon all pretence then, and stab the Master's corpse in the back, whilst filling their pockets with the silver and gold of his Truth.

His true friends, and there were a handful, would tend the flame he had ignited, and keep their silence. He anticipated, and made arrangements as well as he could; a bit like knitting socks in the dark. True Pilgrims would find their way, faery-led if necessary, and True Initiates would comprehend. There were other matters, more pressing, on his mind.

These were his last days. Death was close.

Israel Regardie was forty years old in 1947, and a disciple of Aleister Crowley. He was popping in regularly, keeping an eye on his Master, and administering the injections Crowley needed to keep the asthma tamed.

Without the heroin to calm and relax his lungs the old man probably wouldn't survive the night. His body was entirely dependant on the opiate, and would react violently if deprived of it, likely triggering an asthma attack in his fitful sleep.

After a lifetime of managing the drug Crowley was expert at the finite adjustments necessary to keep a tolerable level of wellness; it had been very many years since he had used heroin to get high. Each dose was precisely calculated with regards to measure and timing, abling him to function and work.

He was *The Prophet of the Lovely Star,* and his obligations were to the Eld Gods. He was satisfied. He had perdured, even unto the veritable end.

There would never be enough days to do everything he wanted to, needed to. He was one man, and the Great Work was all-encompassing; the efforts of generations of Holy Men and Magicians, and Gods. He was not eager to leave, because there was always more that could be done; but he was ready.

Yet, the Completion of the Work was out of reach even of his mighty Magicks. Or, *was it not?*

It was a full moon that night, and he caught his breath sharply as he suddenly saw her: the azure lidded stooping starlight, bending to kiss him.

Regardie hadn't called upon Aleister Crowley that evening, although he had been expected, and he was perfectly aware of what the consequences to the Master would be when he didn't get his medicine at the allotted hour.

He spent a restless, excited night, and hurried to Crowley's apartment in early morning. He was full of cocaine and dread; the Master's Wand would pass now to him. He would ascend the dais as Magus, and no longer be just an also-ran in Crowley's giant shadow.

6 **The Lovers. The Mirror**

Rasa signifies our unique personal relationship with the Divine. It is our eccentric journey, and reflects our interaction along the way with the Divine. *Rasa,* in this *Sanskrit* context, signyfies our *wyrd*; the inescapable doom or destiny which follows our Star.

The Divine is the fixed centre about which every Star turns in its orbit. The centre may adjust, but it does not change.
The impulse preceded the God Mind, the individual personality of the All. God Mind formed so that there could be space within which the Thought could take shape. The Thought was conceived. The universe expressed the Word. The God Mind heard the Word, and felt the sound reverberating throughout every dimension.

The raw element of life is protoplasm. The Multraverses didn't appear instantaneously in perfect order. They grew from protoplasmic seeds. Life expanded out from the centre, moved by the Pulse. God breathed, and the Heavens sighed.
In the protoplasmic seed was the Word and the Idea.

The rasa of the Magician has value to the Multraverses.
The Magician connects with God, or with the Holy Guardian Angel, through his personality. He is a man, living an individual life in the world. The connection is expressed in his actions and his Word. He enters a dialogue with the Holy Guardian Angel.
The Angel represents God and truth. It is a cypher of the All, but it is far more than a collection of complex cyphers. Yet, so as to connect with and communicate with the man, the Angel must also express an individual personality. The dialogue between them will be in the way of two personalities embracing in friendship and mutual love. One comes down to the level of the man, whilst the man is raised up to meet it.

The ultimate aim of the Druid is a personal, direct encounter with the Gods. This may take divers forms, according with each individual character and wyrd. The Druidic path is a religious apprehension of the natural life. It reveres and co-operates with the God-Essence. It adheres to the Way. Yet, it has neither priests nor churches. Before the All, every man is equal.

The first task of the Aspirant is to uncover his true Self. Persevering in the Practices detailed in *The Aeon Rasa* he learns who and what he is, and creates an image or talisman of that which he was meant to become. From these two points, like pins stuck into a map, he can discover his present location on the road. He whittles the discrepancies between conscious mind and the Actualised Mind, and converges towards the second point.

The mind will persist with doubts long after the Magician has gained experience of working with Divine aspects and creatures. He is moving into realities strange and wondrous, and the mind is startled and dazzled. As his old realities are o'erthrown and dismantled he is disorientated and unsure. But this state will pass as he familiarises himself with conditions. Even doubts are helpful directors to him. Let him resolve them and find certainty.

If the Soul could not grow and endure, even beyond death of the body, then life itself would be meaningless. There must be a capacity for eternity. The Magician must prove this eternity. 'As we climb through different levels of being, our consciousness changes along with our capacity to think,' said the Master. 'If the aim is Union with All, then those roads climb the same mountain, though some may be slower and others may be faster.

'If you don't keep your shoulder against the stone it will roll back down the hill.'

7 The Chariot. The Seat of Power

Strangely, the Idea of the Way having a personality and
individual intellect, in a similar way that Man does, is often
disregarded out of hand. It is suggested somehow to be an
impossibility, and an Idea hardly worth pondering.

Yet, the isolated perception of Man, due to his individual
intellect, makes him the most potent force in the corporeal
world. It is via his individualism that Man has a god-like
vantage, and can form cognitions, that he can construct reality,
that he can shape the void and fill it with the lights of stars.
Religions postulate that the highest aspiration must be
dissolution into the All. The loss of the individual in Union
with Godhead, or ascending into Heavenly realms to become
some form of angelic mechanical worshipper of the Divine
Glory. The isolated god-vantage of individual perception is an
inconvenient consequence of life, such theologies suggest, and
should be transcended or abandoned as soon as possible.

The corporeal life is a temporary position, and it is the
trajectory of the Soul which is of prime value and importance
to the Magician. It is the Soul's journey, not the life of the body
and the ego, which signyfies. He aims not to extinguish his
own unique Star, but instead to follow the curve of its arc, even
unto perfection. If this were not so, then the Work of his
lifetime could be of only fragmentary value.

We are aware of the great value of the isolated mind. Why
would the All *not* assume an individual personality? Is there
reason to suppose that it could not or would not take on an
isolated mind and personality?

The opposition is an idea of ego-mind; that it alone possesses
the most valuable of treasures. How can the ego justify its
position of being the only real and relevant intellect in the
universes, or its claim to be exempt from any consequences,
when it accepts God Mind? When contrasted with the awesome
power of the God Mind intellect, even the brightest and
cleverest of human minds are demonstrably limited, finite in
scope, with muddled realities, and little real Magickal power.

Once we are cognizant of the personality and individual mind of the All then no mere human personality can challenge its supremacy. It brings the matter into a proper perspective; the microcosm and the *Macrocosm.* Seeing God in this way, to phrase it thus, allows us to approach a little closer.

Curious delusions pervade the collective consciousness of Mankind. All sorts of unjustified nonsense is accepted without being properly challenged by logic. The Magician is wary to test out the validity of every Idea before he accepts it as truth. Further, we can ask: if the Way wanted to, could it indwell a human body as a Soul?

We know that it can do so temporarily: as Beings of Light and Splendour share the Temple of the Magician. If this is so, and we can verify by our own experience, then arrangements could be made for a more permanent residence.

There may be restrictions that we are unaware of, but otherwise the general notion that God can not take on a fleshy body arises from ideas that, being entirely God, he can not confine himself within a corrupted state. But the premise is a lie: the human body is not corrupt; it is sanctified, and as pure and holy as God himself. If there are restrictions for the Divine, they are not concerned with sanctity of the flesh. Only the mind can be corrupted and degenerate.

It is common sense that the All will utilize every valuable asset at its disposal; of course it takes on individual personality. The Gods are facets of this personality. They are not cyphers or devas, but living personalities. They can be communicated with by dialogue.

If there is success or failure for the Soul, then we could fairly expect the consequences to be either continued progression of the Star along its trajectory, or a reduction to essence for the Star which has degenerated.

Is it a punishment if a Soul which was unable to progress during life is returned to the Cosmic Melting Pot? From this material new Souls are formed, and given the chance of responding to the Way.

A Soul might return to the world to further the Great Work; its mission will be first to actualise itself and Become. If the Gods send a messenger then they will ensure that he is appropriately equipt for his task. He dares to be himself.

Truthfulness is one quality that all spiritual teachers, since the veritable beginning of things, insist upon. Why is it so? If it is not that they fear punishment for 'wrongdoing,' what might be the reason?

8 Adjustment

Maat, Goddess of justice and truth. She is the Dancer, the Adjustment. The Arcana is the complement and the opposite of the first Arcanum, Parsifal. He is the conscious instinctive mind of the pilgrim, whilst she is the Divine mind.

As we have already observed, the All *must* assume God Mind in order for the Creation to be manifested. Thus God always has and always will have an isolated perception, and an individual mind and personality. Very similar to the mind of a human being, one might conjecture.
Objections to this Idea seem to arise from the fragility of ego-mind. For one thing, to accept the Idea means to acknowledge a Mind and Power infinitely greater, superior to our own isolated mind. This is where the shadow self baulks. For the shadow to accept God, it must give up its notion of I AM GOD. The shadow mind considers itself to be the Centre.

The Multraverses grew out from the centre. Very slowly they formed into planets and stars and elements, as the raw materials flowed outward, and winds and friction carved boundaries. They are very old.
The Mind of the Multraverses preceded the manifestation of the All. The Word is the expression of the Mind. The Thought was motivated by the impulse. It arose into the God Mind. *All Will Manifest* thought God. The original impulse arose from the genius of the All. It was an inspiration.
Creation, which we have direct evidence of in the established manifested Multraverses, *proves* that the All has individual mind. Genius. Impulse. God Mind. Thought. Word. Form.

The mind must keep thinking, or else it falls out of the sky. The ego-mind is an automatic function of the un-focused mind. When we take charge of the vehicle, the mind, ego-mind ceases. If we revert to previous behaviours, lazy or emotional behaviours, then focus may be lost, and ego-mind re-emerges. The shadow mind is not an auto function of mind in the same way as ego-mind. Yet it is not an individual personality that can exist beyond the realms of the mind. It is something like a ruthless, cruel antagonist. It is seemingly merciless and amoral. It is the mind adjusting itself.

It is the devil which whispers into the ear. Everyone has one. We are reminded of the old cartoon depictions of the devil and angel; the reality is not so dissimilar.

The shadow mind knows the mind inside out. Every experience of the man, every thought, desire, dream, every darkness and weakness, every secret corner. It is a natural part of the mind, and cannot be removed from the realm of mind. How then does the Magician approach it and subdue it, so that it will not intrude upon his Work?

Ego-mind has no coherence, yet shadow mind is calculated, and targets its assaults where they will be most damaging. The unresolved experiences and pains will perpetually arise, until the Magician faces them and resolves them, throws the off-switch. It will dig deep, deep into every shadow, crevice and nook. It will twist the dagger in the sensitive wounds. Unrelenting, it will harass and worry, giving no quarter to the mind. It can be heavy-handed; kill or cure.

Pain is a natural reaction. It is there as an early warning: we are meant to pull our hand away from the flames. The intellectual pain excited by the shadow mind might serve us in a similar manner.

A stitch in time saves nine.

The Magician transcends shadow mind by ascending from the hells in which it operates and holds sway. The Magician learns from his errors, and adapts. He finds his correct position and draws to the centre.

He can not destroy the shadow mind by direct assault. He apprehends it, and sees the route to perfecting mind.

9 The Lamp of Invisible Light

Before the manifesting of the All, the genius resided in non-being in the Endless Lonely Bliss.

It heard the Word quoth on the first breath. It watched as the raw materials of the All pulsed out from the centre, and expanded across millennia to become the living Multraverses. It perceived, and considered with flawless intelligence. Ages passed, and the God Mind, omnipresent and omniscient, abiding in perfection, refined its wisdom and its Magicks.

The God Mind comprehended the value of its position as perceiver. It retained its isolated awareness. It endured the ordeals and deaths of its Body and of its Mind, and as the All stretched towards the Limits, the God Mind had crossed the Great Void, and filled the emptiness with the flowering patterns of its imagination.

It experienced. Its personality was shaped by all it witnessed and by every Thought that arose from its holy genius. It acted, the God Mind, and expressed its Will.

It distinguished within itself forces and aspects, and formed these into Souls. Each Soul was isolated from the All by a mind and an individual awareness. These Souls were the First Gods. They were FORMS of the God Mind and its personality; they were imaginative projections. The Souls experienced, and adjusted. They waxed in wisdom and power.

They were distinguished from the All in the realm of God Mind, as in a dream the First Gods were conjured to appearance. It was the mightiest Magicks that God Mind had wrought, dividing the original personality into forces and powers and qualities.

They were Eight, and the God Mind called their names: Spirit, Earth, Water, Fire, Air, Metal, Wood, and Stone.

The Gods are ancient Souls of infinite power and wisdom. They are the Way, the Truth, and the Light. They are the Guardians, the Laws, and the Boundaries.

Drawn from the original impulse, they are pure, manifested from and in perfection. Their nature is the Great Harmony, being vivid aspects of the All. They are Light and Dark, but all tend towards the perfecting of the All.

Evil and chaos do not tend towards harmonious perfection. Such qualities, originating not from the Great Source but from degenerate mind, are at odds with the movement of the Multraverses, and lead to putrefaction, madness and death. They are a weakness, a brokenness. The Original Gods, pure, flawless, and holy, could only be moving towards the perfecting of the All.

There are no evil or broken Gods; but even Divine minds could conceivably degenerate; do the Gods not have free will? If they are free to make choices, they might forsake the Great Harmony. Such is the lay of the Pride of Satan and the Fall of the angels. There are pools of unholy power which are the worship of deva, but these are not sapient Gods. They are not Gods at all. They are cyphers; elaborate collections of intricate symbols; talismans. They are given a semblance of life by the worship of their devotees, but they have no existence of their own. They do not experience. They are objects, not sapient Souls.

They can be classified amongst the realms of the Lower Intelligences. They may exist as denizens of the shadow realms and the Labyrinth. Heaven and Hell and demons and angels are all very real to Doris at number 47.

10 **The Whael**

The Magician begins to construct his Magickal Universe. The
Centre is the Point whereat he establishes the foundations of
the Temple Absolute. The stones fold out from the Centre.
There are Eight Foundation Stones, and one Central Stone.
It is the Crux.
The Magician must place the stones, beginning with the one
Central Stone. Everything which follows after the Eight Stones
shall be a consequence of the Reality that each represents.
The Centre is the Perfected Reality, the All.
In the Magician's Magickal Universe it is the hub of the engine.
It is the Impulse and the Motivating Force. It is the Whael.
The Centre Stone is a symbol of God Mind. The Eight Stones
represent the First Emanations of God Mind.

Spirit: The Will to Manifest. Evident from the Perfection of the
Multraverses.
Earth: The Word. The Will expressed as Intension.
Water: The Manifested Multraverses. The corporeal universes.
Air: Motivated Towards the Perfecting of All through Harmony.
Fire: Awareness. The consequences of God Mind. Intellect,
Intelligence, Inspiration.
Metal: Genius. The Impulse arose when the Way was Alone.
Wood: The Way. The Path Absolute.
Stone: Individual Personality of God. Of Goddesses and Gods.

Words are Magickal Talismans. They are whirling stars of
force. They convey Ideas. They can be seeds that will yield up
great fruits. They can be used as a bitter weapon, or like a
healing, nurturing balm.
We attach meaning to each symbol, and thus individual words
become more or less potent, depending on our interpretations.
When the Black Hats read the word 'God' it disturbs them.
They are opposed to Divinity, howsoever they articulate the
objections to themselves and others, and every time they
encounter the concept there is a jarring. They may even take
the trouble to mentally invert such symbols to lessen their

direct impact.

When they encounter such talismanic symbols as 'sincerity, truthfulness, integrity, grace, holiness, noble' they are liable to feel quite uncomfortable.

Their relationship to these whirling stars may be one of denial, aversion, or avoidance. For the Black Hats, the words contain Ideas that are improbable, impossible, bewildering, dangerous to their status, painful, damning and company.

Legion only likes to read about legion, commented Aldous Huxley. They don't like to read about Divinity, sainthood, or integrity; they don't comprehend the concepts. Their definitions will be vague. It upsets them to hear that some people are sincere and truthful, because those are unattainable qualities for the Black Hat minds. It upsets them that *anyone* should have *something* which they can't have.

The mind will then begin to gloss over the symbols which otherwise are like stabbing daggers in the belly, twisting sharp pains to the brittle ego. The meaning of the words become blurred, half-forgotten. It flies then from the symbols of truth, reality, absolute. The mind inverts its own reality, denies the common realm of truth; and good becomes bad, beauty transmutes to disgusting, and God is a moron.

The type of mind drawn to chaos is self-centric, narcissistic, greedy, immature, stunted and selfish. Those are just some of the weak man's qualities. They bethink themselves unique, and very special and entitled, because they deem their own intellect to be Supreme, but their behaviours run along common themes of parasitical intensions.

They reshape their reality to resemble the chaos which they see as the only fitting revenge upon a world which has failed to recognise and acknowledge their supremacy. They cut the threads which tether the mind in solid sanity, and are adrift then in a delusive realm of their own constructing. Right and True, those potent talismans, are just faint echoes in the void.

And, what is it that these sinking minds are actually trying to achieve, on a personal level? They destroy their own Soul and mind in a petulant show of arrogant temper, like children smashing their own toys.

To climb the peaks takes a rare mind. Few have the character and talents needed. Acquiring the wisdom of a sage is difficult. 'The better you understand your own motivation, the easier the climb will be,' said the Master.

If every human mind were turned to the Way, and all human society became harmonious, would evil still exist?

11 Magick. The twin-headed Beast

There is a single main definition of the object of all magical ritual. It is the uniting of the microcosm with the Macrocosm. The supreme and complete ritual is therefore the Invocation of the Holy Guardian Angel; or in the language of Mysticism, Union with God.
Aleister Crowley.

A lot of what Crowley wrote was elaborate and deliberate detailing. He was trying to sell books, and used poetry as filler. Some of his published works were calculated and constructed with the intension of leading the Hunt astray. The broad symbols that he used are where the truth of his Magick remains. *The Book of the Law* is usually considered the synthesis and the peak of his magickal work. He himself declares it so, and writes extensive commentaries on it, and claims it as the pivot of Thelemic theology. In its Qabalah, he claimed, was proof of an Intelligence that existed beyond Man. Yet, in private he admitted it was not much more than High Poetry.
The purpose of its publication was to deflect his enemies from his real work. *The Book of the Law* was meat thrown out to appease the ravening wolves at his door. The imagery that he uses in the second and third chapters is particularly difficult; dark and Fascist. Often, he is selling rope for the Hangman; Crowley says in *Confessions* that when he realised the task the Gods had called him to he was appalled. Yet, he says, he gritted his teeth and persevered.
All the secrets of Magick are in its sublime Qabalah; far deeper and more delicately wrought than the mere Scribe could ever have conceived possible. It is a Qabalah only a Divine Intelligence could have written. Its pure mathematics remains still far beyond his apprehension.
'That should keep them entertained for awhile,' he said aside, with a wink.
He had many enemies, like all soothsayers, all true prophets of the Divine. His talents provoked envy. He also did not tolerate fools but was plain in his contempt of them. Worst of all, from

their viewpoint, he exposed the dearth of their intelligence and their lack of power. He laughed at their mysteries and magick, scoffed at the paper dragons. Weak men hate the man of intellectual strength and creativity, especially if they perceive him to be somehow a threat to their incomes.

The Qabalah has use as a memory frame, a system of symbols neatly linked, but otherwise it is mysterious waffle. An *endless* maze that ultimately leads no place. Trying to work magicks and construct realities in such a dubious realm is a fast track to the collapse of the mind. In *Magick in Theory and Practice* Crowley states clearly that 'the magical language is nothing but a convenient system of classification to enable the magician to docket his experiences as he obtains them.'

Shadow magick and ego magick can 'work,' but they rely upon the gullibility and co-operation of their victims. Such magick is always about manipulation and domination, control and ownership of people, and as such belongs to the realm of accursed magick, and is always black magick, opposed to the Harmonious Way. Pseudo-realms may be created and shared in, but only by mutual agreement. They have no power to reach to and effect Common Reality.

The Old Crone may curse you, but if you only pity her miserable state of madness, then all her bitter spells have no power over you.

Satan and the princes of Hell are weaklings with no real power outside of the universe of Jehovah. The Devil is real, but he isn't a Jew.

Mathematics are the building blocks of the universe, but God is not an equation. Its truth is the truth of one angle. The symbol is never the thing itself.

We delineate the virtues of the higher man, and the behaviours of the lower man, because we intend to make clear the proper conducts. We aspire towards improvement, not deterioration. It is helpful to have a clear understanding of the qualities of both. The universe's first principle is Harmony.

The Goddess is the Manifested Multraverse, limitless and unending. The atomic yet omnipresent Point is called God.

From the prymordial Point arose the sparking agent which was the Idea. The union of the Goddess and God was the birth of their child, the Word. The Word is the Father of Thought. It is intelligence and the realms of the intellect and reason.

Aleister Crowley provides a detailed map of the magickal universes which the Magician can work in. He demonstrates his own experiences vividly, and in doing so he throws light on the path. The broad symbols are useful pointers.
He makes clear that each true Magician, should he attain to the loftiest Grade of Magus, as defined by Crowley's system, must formulate his own Word, and prove this by establishing his own religion. Crowley's Word and religion were *Thelema*, or *The Will.*
Of course; because we are each of us unique individual Souls experiencing our own true universe. We must make sense of it ourselves. We are responsible for the coherence of our own comprehensions. The real relationship between Man and the Multraverses is *rasa*.
Crowley built through his public persona and his extensive published writings a complex Magickal World. The Magician must emulate the spirit of this feat rather then residing in the universe Therion crafted, perpetually picking over the bones of it. He presented the Thelemic Universe as an absolute reality, and for him it was; in the magickal and unique realm which he was creating. He dwelt on the minutia detail, and from his attentions arose wide and beautiful mazes, deep dungeons, and imperturbable mountains. He built towers and keeps and cities. He traced coastlines and borders, identified Gates and Bridges. He called upon ancient Gods to indwell his worlds, and Angels and daemons. He dug lochs and dolve valleys.
He chose the Gods of the Egyptians to represent his archetypals. He resonated with the pure mathematics of the Hebrew Qabalah, and found the Tarot to be a convenient collection of images and symbols upon which to hang his truth.

Like the wood and the trees sometimes we see only the cyphers. All things may have use and purpose for us in the universe we are creating, yet we should be circumspect in our choices. Crowley performed public rituals, for example, Ceremonial Magicks of high drama and poetry. They worked for him because they were a true expression of his universe and who he was. These Ceremonial Magicks were an integral facet of his magickal fingerprint and his intimate rasa with the Divine.

We may conjure Gods and spirits but really the process is more of a creation than a calling-forth, said Crowley. It is the imagination which is the active force. The word 'magick' is derived from image and imagination, as in 'magi.'

The only true points of relevance for us when considering realities which originate outside of ourselves are the broad shapes, colors and symbols. The detail is personal. Without magickal experience the symbols are more or less meaningless. With experience we begin to comprehend the subtleties.

12 The hanged God. Self sacrifice

His road is not slow, but long and intricate, deep and broad. There is a larger plan. Conditions in the Material Realm are isolated from the Greater Reality. It is a temporary condition that will eventually be resolved.

The Gods are Individual Personalities and Souls; vital and energised Aspects of the All. They perceive and have personal perspective. Some of them are as old as the Multraverses. They are the Argent Actives of the Forces of the All, expressed in myriad forms.

Degeneracy comes only from perverted mind. It is only Man that is capable of this perversion and insanity. There can be no Degenerate Gods, not real ones. There is little semblance between Gods and the demons of the Lower Intelligences. The demoniac forces are cyphers and symbols. Satan and his crew, along with all the Fake Gods, are gaoled within the Labyrinth. Demons, or tormentors of men, exist in the Intellectual or Astral Realms. The demons of the mind and psyche, of nightmare and horror, of bitter regret. They are creatures of delusion, despite their popularity in common reality. The Accursed Gods are devas or sentient forces. They may have the appearance of life but they are not Actualised Beings or microcosms.
Or, perhaps the legends are true, and some Gods go mad.

A cursory study of historical Egyptian hieroglyphic texts reveals the insidious influence of Monotheistic thought across centuries. Five thousand years ago, the Egyptians recognised God the Creator, the Eternal All-Father; and alongside the Great God they distinguished the many Gods that were aspects of the All, divers expressions of the Divine personality. The themes of Osiris as the One-Father begin to converge during the age of Middle Egypt. They bring with them corruptions and devilry. At some point the Egyptian Religion breaks away from natural partnership with the Gods. Instead of harmonious supplication, and identification with the Divine, many scribes now try to coerce, to wheedle, control, and dominate their Gods.

Towards the end of the Great Civilisation, around the time of the coming of the Son of Man, as the Aeon shifts, the legends which are being inscribed on tablets, and tombs, are of cruel, sadistic, warlike Gods of revenge, punishment, and retribution. These aspects must be appeased with blood sacrifice.

Many of the extant texts can only be classified as sorcery or Black Magick.

Now the One-Father closely resembles Jehovah: *By their works you will know them.* He is *jealous* of his name. He *hates* disobedience. He demands that fathers raise their sons in his worship. He complains of blasphemy. He is irritated by men, and slaughters them in their thousands.

Jealousy, rage, punishment, retribution, vengeance, murder, bloody sacrifice, hate; these are standard qualities of the ego-mind and the Lower Intelligences.

The One-Father was always a devil-god.

13 Death. Victory over one's enemies

Though they fade quickly, O have no sorrow!
There will be others new-born tomorrow!

The Master leads his true sons out into the Wilderness.
'I hear words or phrases,' he said. 'Some passages I must keep,
even if I object. They use my body, like a hand slipping into a
glove. It's quite disconcerting.'

Leonardo's pencil work is exquisite. He draws with *tenderness.*
His is the perfection of technique, yet he remains approachable.
He dresses the Divine in rough rags, disguises his Angels as
mortals. Thus can we apprehend the perfection clothed in flaws.
We can aspire towards such masterful technique, such deep
beauty and compassion. We can learn from Leonardo.
Raphael is pure perfection. We cannot aspire to emulate or
approach his technique without a lifetime's efforts. And only
ever a poor reflection of his utter mastery. The beauty Divine is
overwhelming. The sublimity of his icons makes us feel a bit
queasy. We are quick to leave Raphael's Perfected Altar, and
loth to return there.
Vincent was interesting in every part of his paintings. His brush
strokes, and the patterns he makes with them, are skilfully
wrought fascinations.
I was about seventeen years old when I first saw his painting
The Chair. I was amazed that he had produced this beautiful
image from such an ordinary item. The colors were brought
from the walls into the chair, and then out into the wooden
floorboards. Although it is all distinct, everything seems to be
formed from the same stuff. His skies and trees look as though
they are made out of mud.
'When I was younger, I sometimes wondered if he painted them
with his cock,' said the Master.
Goya dealt with very dark subjects in a remarkable way.
So often when we see images of the degenerate aspects of
Humanity and the psyche there is a certain perverse pleasure of
the artist apparent; he enjoys displaying his effluence; he

delights in disgusting and repelling the viewer. In a sense we are attacked by the artist's perversion; he is wallowing in the depravities. We can't view the talisman without absorbing the negativities.

Goya though was able to represent his highly charged images of monsters and lunacy in a detached, scientific way; as a study in psychology perhaps. He isn't perverted, and he isn't wallowing in the filth. His work is the eye of a benevolent master who wants to instruct. He presents astounding images, and we recognise the faces of strangers, and faces from our dreams. We are not under attack by the depravities and the monsters he shews us, but instead we can observe them safely, unmolested by perversions, and thus apprehend them.

14 The Magickal Art

I remarked that his book was probably the strangest book I had ever read. 'It may be *even stranger* than you think,' he replied.

'You go straight through barriers,' Amado said to me, 'not over or around them.'
What do you know about Magick? He asked me.
I was twenty five years old. I had applied myself to the study of Occult philosophy for the past eight years. I had a natural aptitude for the art. I was a gifted student with a mind of genius. His question demanded an accurate, tangible response. What did I actually *know* about Magick?
I considered deeply, but eventually I realised that all my study had been more or less instinctive and intuitive. Much of the learning process was in other realms, and rarely brought to conscious synthesis. Now that I had thought about it, I wasn't *certain* of much. I was working in a general direction, towards the Great Centre, and my comprehensions and philosophies were unrefined.
I considered numerous alternatives, but at last, the only answer I felt I could give with sincerity was: *I understand that every act is a magickal act.* I was quoting Aleister Crowley, but that succinct phrase expressed my comprehension completely.
It is a broad statement, yet its core is deep and wise. The whole thing was a part of the magicks, every aspect and facet.
Working magicks was a process that properly should occupy every moment of the Magician's conscious life.
It was a good answer, he said.
It was a well timed question. With it he enabled both me and him to define where I was on the Magickal Path. We knew where our starting point was.
Under his direction, I made swift, tangible progress. He drew me towards the centre, and things became clearer and sharper. Now I knew how to work Magicks. He did not overburden me with theory, or with exercises. 'Someone like you doesn't need those pacifiers,' he said. 'You don't even need books, really!'
His teaching, in my experience of it, was a Magickal process;

a lot of it was slow, and unspoken. He planted seeds, and tended them so that they would bloom. He transferred power. He unlocked doors, and brought me into Magickal realms. He introduced me to the Gods; the rest was up to me. 'I don't want to be too much of an influence upon you,' he said. He pointed me in the direction of where I may find my destiny and truth. He removed obstacles from my path. He balanced me; soothed my pains, strengthened and encouraged me. He cleansed my Soul-body-mind. 'I have filled you up with gold,' he said. 'Now, just don't do anything stupid!'

I don't think I ever heard him mention the *Holy Guardian Angel.* 'Abra Melin,' he said pointedly. 'Standard stuff.' His approach was a *religious* interpretation of the Occult. He started by disentangling the aspirant. He brought them to a calm, safe harbour, where they might think more clearly. He forbade his students from ever performing the *Lesser or Greater Banishing Ritual.* 'Do you even know what it is you are supposedly banishing?' he asked. 'And what if *it* objects to your attempts? You are far more likely to attract malign entities and forces with your activity than to repel them. We cannot *command* the Beyond. We may not enter that other world there and then without consent, and we may not use its powers unless some entity over there is glad to aid us. There is no question of force.'

The Master encouraged a reverent, humble approach to the Gods. Occultism can be very slap-dash and improvised, but he insisted that there was a proper way of doing things, and a proper order of progression to Truth.

He was a Druid, but his students were never compelled to accept his reality or to follow his path. He allowed them to uncover and express their own truth; be it through Shamanism, Witchcraft, or Nature Worships; but it must harmonise on the broad shapes. It was a religion, in the sense that there were Gods to appeal to and work with, and a route to Union with All; but there was never a book of strict rules of conduct. He didn't teach yogic meditations. There wasn't a lingo to learn, nor were there secret handshakes, or special advanced techniques awarded with grades. Yes, sometimes he published rituals and ceremonies, and recipes for Magicks, for his students; else might they stumble. It was more about the old ways, common sense, harmonising with the plan of the Gods, developing love directed by true will, and finding your own unique role in the scheme. Yet, he added more than a dash of Magicks.

'If you follow my path, you will be struck by the wonder of it,' he said.

He recommended sensible practice in all things. He didn't drink, smoke, or take drugs. It wasn't his style to forbid, except in any kind of Devilry, but instead to point out the reasons one might want to avoid such actions. If something was harmful to health, and if it might undermine true will, then it would probably be wiser not to indulge. His patience was not unlimited, but he allowed each student the space to come to these progressions themselves.

In his book *Quest Magic* (Diamond Books 1997) he writes:
Reality is very deceptive and almost impossible to define. No evidence is totally reliable. Let us harness our confidence and do everything possible to gather truth even by unfamiliar means. Neither Nature nor the Gods would tease us with occasional hints of truth, if we could not apprehend it. Our fine minds were not made in order to be so terribly thwarted that they slump in despair and invent negative, ruinous philosophies.

He spoke of 'Our Lady,' but rarely ventured into specific delineations of Eld Theology. He used broad brushstrokes to paint his canvas. He spoke of God, and of the Devil.

He taped lectures on cassette, and sent them to his groups of students. The idea was to listen and discuss. Periodically he would visit in person. He treated each individual, and each group, according with their needs. He would not accept a person as a student unless he could guarantee their success; if they followed his guidance. One must put into Practice.

His teachings were systematically progressive, leading the pilgrim one step at a time to the foot of the Sacred Mountain. His aim was to bring those capable to Adeptship.

In some ways he was like a gardener attending the flowerbed.

He was tired. He sighed. 'Well, now I must go and *perform* for them,' he said. Is that how you think of it? I wondered. 'Yes,' he said heavily. 'They expect it.'

His voice and his presence stilled the ego-babble of his student's minds. He allayed their fears and comforted, warmed them. He made them laugh. They slowly stopped spinning like out of control tops. They blinked through the daze, as they absorbed a Magickal teaching that drew them towards the centre.

15 **The Devil**

Now Jak was idling, and he had come unto the High lands. He sang his melancholy blues, and he was strumming an old dreadnought guitar. Winds blew cold down o'er the tors and crags and chilled the stream, and the trees trembled. The winds sighed low into the town and crept through the streets, past windows and under doors.

Dusk fell, as Jak hit a steady four beat, and his lamentations stole across the town below. He swooned as he sang, and swayed and rocked gently, and slapped the sole of his foot against the stone.

He sang of dire and drear and dreaded. He sang of death and he sang of woe. He sang of endless tears, and he wept into his songs, and a melancholy air arose about him, and gusted down o'er the bleak hills and into the streets.

And the ravens came unto that place, the high place, and broad winged shadows they settled nearby. Their raw cries and sharp caws wove a melody over the blues of Jak.

Midnight, and the morninglym stars flade a thin light. The moon was o'ercast with stormy clouds.

A weeping murmured in the streets, and from houses came the cry of the blues. The town slept fitfully, and sobs broke in dark quarters. The ravens rose then like a cloud and passed o'er the wood, and their shadow wrought gloom. They swooped silently, yet their wings fluttered gusty beats, and they called their laments. Gloaming shades slipped betwixt the alleyways. Crow alighted at the rock. He was grim and dower. He saw the ravens and the melancholy airs, and he harked Jak's blues. He spoke with a hoarse soft voice: *In the seed is its harvest.* Creatures crept in those last hours of night, and witches astrode and wailed, and screamed for their twisted delights. Madness bellowed from deep darknesses, like cattle lowing in the dark rains which had begun to fall. Lunacy stalked, his blade aflash in street lamps' flare.

He tore at his flesh crying: *It is not I! It is not I!*

The rains fell upon Jak, and he sang no more. He watched the darkness across the town far below. The raindrops rolled upon him like tears. He slung the dreadnought guitar upon his back, and descended.

There was a mist o'er the town like a shroud that morning. The echoes of the night's song clung to the mizzle. Jak, the Great and Eld, walked in the suburbs.

They were stirring from their slumbers when he passed by beneath their windows. His boot heels rang gently on the cobble stones.

He wore a Comanche hat. It had a long feather through its band. The feather was half black and scarlet red.

He came to the marketplace. He drank from the well of cold waters. He sate and regarded the merchants as they began to set up their stalls. They erected tables and covered them with brightly colored sheets. Soon the tables displayed their wares. The goods were vibrant, and the merchants were easy in their labors. They smiled and laughed and shouted across to one another whilst they worked.

Jak took up his dreadnought guitar and began to tune its strings. Soon people were ambling into the marketplace, and they browsed the stalls and made their purchases. He watched them, and they grew into a busy throng. He thought about the rhythms of their movement.

He started to sing a melancholy song, and the tap of his boot toe was a persisting drum.

16 **The Blasted Tower**

The Aelinor Rasa swiftly replaces the Aeon Thelema; one
hundred years, the Aeon of Horus. The Goddess whom doth
rule o'er the present, and so she shalt, is the Lovely Star Nuith.
Nu is Nuith, in her aspect as the Daughter, the Night. Nuith is
the Great Sky Goddess. She is the foreverlasting vaults of the
firmaments. She is the starry night skies, and the infinite
universes. She is the primaeval feminine element, as her
counterpart, named 'Nau,' was the masculine force within the
Divine waters and the aethers.
She is Artemis, the Huntress, the bride of the Great God Pan.
It seems a strange symbolism, that she is now manifested as the
Daughter; but the Gods each have many aspects and forms,
every peculiar facet expressing their nature in a particular way.
Nuith must manifest as the Daughter, so that she can ascend the
Throne as ruler of the New Aeon, and once there she reassumes
her identity as the Mother Goddess, Nuith. She is Nu and Nuith,
and Nuit, and Nut, and Neith. Hathor and Isis blur with her.
Nuith is the shape with which she comes back from the deserts,
through the Gate, necessarily wrought to fit the aetheral locks
with her Talismanic form.
The procession of the Aeons begins with the Great and Terrible
Goddess Isis, the Magician. She is the daughter of Nuith and
the Earth-God, whom the Egyptians named Keb.
Her brother and husband, Osiris, follows her, and it is then the
Aeon of the One God. Ancient Egyptian texts shew a record of
this gradual transference of power. The Well becomes polluted
and poisoned. Osiris is the Slain God, who is resurrected into
the celestial abodes. The Aeon of Osiris gives way to the Aeon
of the son of Isis and Osiris, Horus, the twin.
These Gods follow the four-fold Idea of Magickal Hieroglyphs;
they are the Mother, Father, and the Son. Their concluding and
resolution, and their explanation, is expressed in the second
child of their union, the Daughter. The Daughter is the
culmination of everything that has gone before, and she is
everything that will follow on.
She is young, fertile, and points to days ahead, everlasting. Yet,

it is her natural role eventually to ascend the Throne in her own right as the Mother.

It is called the Aeon of *Aelinor Rasa.* The Aeon of Horus, quickened an thousand years, was expressed by the Word *Thelema,* which is, according to Crowley, *The Will.* We shall look more closely at the meaning of the Word Aelinor Rasa. In ancient Egypt the hieroglyphs meaning *the will,* were synonymous with those of *the heart.* In *The Book of Knowing the Evolutions of Ra,* the self-created God, Khepera, tells that he: *khut-na em abt-a; worked a charm upon my heart.* A little further on he reiterates: *senti-na em abt-a tches-a; I made a foundation in my heart my own.* Or, as E.A.Wallis Budge suggests in his transliterations: *by means of my own will.* The heart of Khepera is the Great Goddess of wisdom, Maat. The will of the God thus arose from a pure and true motivation, since Maat is wisdom, truth, and justice personified. It was the *true will* of Khepera's being; his *heart,* his will, from the centre of his being, from his Soul.
With this in mind, the meaning of the Thelemic *Do what thou wilt shall be the whole of the law. Love is the law, love under will* is perhaps somewhat clarified.

The Word *Aelinor* is of English, Anglo-Saxon origin. Its literal application is *bright or shining one. Rasa,* as discussed in *The Aeon Rasa,* is a Sanskrit word, meaning our unique position in the scheme of things, and our direct relationship with God. If *rasa* were to be considered instead an Egyptian word, and herein we see all the Romany threads delicately tie, then we might separate it into its forming components of *Ra* and *Sa.* *Ra* is the mighty Sun-God, the All-Begetter. *Sa* means *magickal power.* The Maa-Kheru: Aelinor Ra-Sa; the Word: The Great Shining God of Power.
Sa is also the name of the Egyptian God of knowledge, who is the son of Ra.

17 The Star. The Muse

The *Order of the Lamp of Invisible Light* was established by
Aleister Crowley during the later years of his life.
Crowley had been installed as the Head of the English O.T.O.
in 1912, by Theodor Reuss. He was twenty three years old. At
forty years old he ascended from the Abyss as Master of the
Temple, and soon claimed the grade of Magus.
He was a genius, with a natural flair and aptitude for his Art.
He was also thoroughly serious and dedicated. He was
unflinching and utterly determined. Even in his early career as
a talented mountaineer we see all of these characteristics, and
great courage and strength, and creativity, exhibited in his
personality. The Magickal Motto that he took on as an Adept
was *Perdurabo: I will endure to the end.*
By the end of his life he was experienced and wise. His
Magickal Force waxed; e'en though his mortal flesh was
weakened by age and asthma, and by the drugs he needed for
its treatment. As a Magician he was unrivalled. He was the
Flower that had bloomed and scattered its seed.
He wanted to get it right this time, and to pass the flame on. He
wanted it to endure, free from corrupting influences.
It was not open to any and all-comers. Rather it was a Secret
Order, whose members were few in its Inner Sanctum.
After the death of Aleister, the responsibility of the Order fell
on the young shoulders of Crowley's son and Magickal Heir,
Amado. Eventually he assumed the mantle as Master.
The truth is alive and adapting, constantly in movement,
refining itself. The flame still burns and dances.
(*See The Riddles of Aleister Crowley. Amado Crowley.
Diamond Books 1992.*)

Ecstasy and madness can both mean stepping outside of
oneself, or the Soul or essence being displaced. At such a time
there may be room for other beings to move into the vacated
space. They may be drawn, either to the shining light, or to the
wailing darknesses.
For the Magician, the energies that can be raised and

channelled through the ecstatic experience are of Magickal significance.

The physical aspect of sex is secondary to its spiritual or mystic quality. These energies, if he can only properly harness them and direct them, can empower him to Become.

The orgone energies, as they have been called, are the shining energies of the All, and the process of drawing them to oneself Magickally begins with a stable natural approach to sexuality. Contrarily, a deviant or broken sexuality betrays a mind in freefall. It is evidently not functioning as it should be, and so will not attract to itself the shining energies. There would be no resonance between the twain that might attract. The wailing darknesses draw to themselves only their kind.

The Druid aims to harmonise with nature, thereby to resonate with her qualities. For him, sacred ecstasy is a key that can unlock his potential and power. Love, under the direction of the true will of the Soul, as Crowley intended.

Ah, there are love and love, says Nuith, in *The Book of the Law.* 'The power which really motivates sexuality is also capable of drawing you closer and closer to the Creator,' the Master said. 'One becomes, at least temporarily, a vessel for the Divine principal.'

The Magician employs the energies that he is able to harness to raise his consciousness. He expands upward and outwards. He rides upon the waves of the tides, and they abear him to a distant shore, and perhaps an encounter with the Divine.

If the force were potent enough, the Soul might leap from the body, spiralling into the embrace of God.

Similarly, if the light generated by the Magician were bright and pure enough, he might draw to himself Beings of Light and Splendour.

This encounter with the Divine Principle is the underlying purpose of all the Magician's labor.

If he can cross to *that place* then he will have, at least temporarily, left ego and shadow mind behind with his common consciousness. He will thus have been reduced to his basic raw elements. His awareness now is centred in the Higher Planes, and is stripped of all adornment and artifice. Here, he will *see, know, and apprehend.* His perceptions will be sharp and true, and he may start to directly adsorb a mystic or Divine learning. His progress will accelerate. His cognitions become deeper, clearer, and profound. His whole being will respond with health and vitality. His path is clear of obstacles. The self is purified and enhanced.

It is to be possessed by the Divine.

'We must not be craven cowards but heroes,' he said. 'We must not be slaves to mere biological urges, but the Master of them. The man who is able to exercise control over his own physiology is already using magic.'

18 The Moon

Strange creatures walk the night, and in the shadowy places. Wise and Eld, nimble and unseen. There are also dark shadows and ghosts that lurk vampyric and ravenous.

The dead must cross o'er the bridge to what is now their proper environment, the Land of the Dead. Some do not have the courage to cross. They remain amongst the living as ghosts. This status is contrary to Cosmic Law; they have become outlaw or criminal. It is likely that they are weak minds that fear punishment or consequence for the life they led. There are other possibilities; they may be Souls that have been so shocked and disorientated by death that they become stuck, trying to return to the world of the living.

The notion of ghosts is not a popular one amongst Occult philosophers, unlike the Eastern systems, where ghosts are frequently acknowledged to be intruding upon the living. They are considered antagonistic and dangerous by the Eastern Magician.

The European mind can't help but think of some poor chap carrying his head under his arm, or a lady in white drifting like a flickering projection through the corridors of a stately home. In the West, the concept of ghosts, the spirits of the dead, is very often trivialised and dismissed as silly nonsense. People may see spirits and visions of the dead occasionally, we accept, but dead people just hanging around for eternity, moaning and rattling chains? What would be the point?

It is not a subject that is addressed frequently in Occultism. The closest one might get to it is probably amongst the grymoires of necromancy.

Demons are far more exciting to the Occultists. Yet, much of what we might attribute to demonic influence may actually have far more to do with the dead.

The dabbling or misguided Magician, dependant on the nature of his activity, may well attract the attentions of ghosts. Ghosts can be drawn to weak and troubled minds, emotional turmoil, and may attach themselves to a living mind which is vulnerable from anger, guilt, shame, despair. They bury themselves deep inside the mind, accessing its thoughts and influencing its dreams. Usually they will remain passively hidden, parasitical, but some do attempt to usurp the living mind and take control of the body.

To do so it must communicate directly to its host as a 'voice.' It may pose as an angel, a demon, or a god. If it can convince the living mind to accept it, and perhaps even to worship it as a god, then it will drive the mind into lunacy, and settle in for the ride as it directly manipulates the course of its victim's life. Much of what we see in the realm of schizophrenia, those lonely drugged-up incurables wandering our streets, might be attributed to this root cause.

Depending on the peculiar individual mind of the ghost will be its intensions. These obsessions are found amongst practitioners of Shadow Magicks, and those strange men and women who operate as low level vampyres. They are easy targets; duped by flattery and the promise of a kind of power, they co-operate with their own inevitable destruction, embracing the alien mind and surrendering to its direction. They may take on the reality that the ghost presents, and having done so they are easily manipulated and become its puppet.

19 The Sun. The Great God Ra

What is evil? Does it exist outside of the minds of men? Is
there a force which is evil? Are there evil entities?
The answer to the last question is apparent; yes, we know that
there are evil minds; those of men and ghosts. It is the same
type of microcosmic mind under different conditions. We might
thus rephrase the question to ask if there are evil entities other
than the mind of Man?
There cannot be evil Gods, but is there an equivalent force of
dark power? Equivalent or equal in force and potency, no. If
there were, perhaps a parallel Impulse, the motivation of which
was towards chaos and emptiness, then it would have achieved
its end, and extinguished itself, returning to void, long ago.
Evil cannot endure. It cannot attain perfection.
The Multraverses are inconceivably old. Perhaps the Way tied
up all the loose ends and cleared the workspace, before
proceeding with Man and his dramas.
The universes are calm and ordered. They turn without efforts
in perfection unending. The Multraverse is not divided against
its Self. God is not at war with God. The universe is sane,
rational, exact and logical. The aethers sigh, and the All
manifests in beautiful Great Harmony.
We therefore see no evidence of evil existing as a force beyond
the realm of the Earth. The manifested All, outside of the
Earth, which is the first and prymaeval reality, exhibits no
evidence of evil Gods or forces of Chaotic Destruction. There
is no evidence of insanity in the endless perfection. Contrarily,
the All is perfected and harmonious, and reaches ever towards
greater perfection. It refines and adjusts so that the whole
echoes and moves with the Pulse and the Impulse.
If we could search every universe within this Multraverse we
would find only calm rhythm and harmony in every pattern.
There are no wars; there are no evil Gods clashing perpetually
with the Forces of Light. It's just quiet, serene, beauteous,
endless space.

Whatever its original cataclysmic cause may have been, evil is a deteriorated mind. Only a broken mind is evil; evil is amoral, self-centric, narcissistic, and nihilistic. It is always degenerate. Its effects are limited, and ultimately it consumes itself.

If there were in fact evil Gods or extremely powerful entities or forces of evil *their works would be apparent*. They would be wreaking mayhem and havoc throughout the universes, inciting destruction and chaos. Upon the Earth they would actively pursue spiritually advanced men, and those aspiring to Truth, and slaughter them. They would be aggressive, merciless, violent and sadistic.

We see no indication of such activity on a God-level; we see all those scenarios, but only on a small scale, a microcosmic level.

There are then the celestial and spirit creatures.

The Magician is more likely to encounter entities or forms that are ambiguous in their morality, rather than evil, since evil cannot maintain itself. It does not often exist in an enduring form.

If there are celestial and spiritual creatures and entities, having no physical bodily presence, which are inclined to wickedness and maliciousness, then they are self-evidently confined in power and effectiveness. They do not display Magickal powers that might tangibly effect the corporeal world. Their influence is subtle and narrow.

Even if spiteful and wicked spirits exist, they must work upon the individual minds of men.

Men have long worshipped and sacrificed to dark Gods. What of them? Are they all devas? It seems likely. Yet, devas are just pooled energies. They cannot be sapient and cannot respond to appeal. They are blind, deaf, and dumb to their devotees. They are only empty idols. Something else might pose as the 'voice' of the deva, of course. A ghost mind, for example.

The God Set is known as the *God of Evil* in later legends and myths, but his origins are non-antagonistic. With his female counterpart, Nefytiti, he is the necessary symbol of darkness against which the mythical legends of the Gods must contest. Osiris and Isis were the Light, and Set and Nefytiti the darknesses. In this sense the myths are not lies, but they are using allegory to express elusive concepts.

In Egyptian Theology Horus and Set are called the *Two Fighters*. We could interpret this as the Higher Mind of the Soul, and the antagonistic Shadow.

Daemons is a more accurate description for the Occultist than 'demon,' since it refers principally to spirits of nature rather than microcosmic entities; and these are not generally evil. They are performing a certain role, the reasons for which might be obscure, and some may display personality and characteristics belonging properly to the Lower Intelligences.

Gods might degenerate, but if so they could not endure. If a degenerating mind cannot stabilize itself and return to its centre, then it ends in death of the mind. It is a mind that has fallen from the natural course of its Star. Without aligning with True Will mind does not expand, it contracts. Even a God could not endure the loss of its mind.

20 The Aeon

After the Son, who is represented by the sun, there comes the culminating of all forces and factors in the Daughter. She represents the Three Prymordial Forces combined and manifested in a Fourth Independent Form: the Aeon Ra-Sa. She is the resolution of those talismans, the perfecting and completing of them. Her symbol is the moon, and she is the stooping starlight.

She is Nuith: *'I am the blue-lidded daughter of Sunset; I am the naked brilliance of the voluptuous night sky. To me! To me!'*

Thelema was the Aeon of The Will; this means the *True Will of the Soul*. It is the Will of the Higher Man, the Magician united with his Angel. *Do what thou wilt shalt be the whole of the law,* says Nuith, in the *Book of the Law.* Follow the True Will of the Soul, is what she intends. In the 66 verses (re the Great Work) of the first chapter the Goddess speaks; the rest of the book is perhaps only smokes and mirrors.

The phrase *Do what thou wilt* is ambiguous, allowing diametrically opposed interpretations. For the Magician it does not mean: *Do whatever you want!* Where would such a philosophy really fit? It is the ambition of ego and shadow mind; there are no consequences, so we can indulge every whim and impulse of the scattered puffed up ego-mind. But how could such a philosophy be fruitful? How could allowing the ego-mind to dictate *every* action, for that is what it must mean, ever be conducive to Magickal Potency? It is the suspension of intellect and reason, and the aligning with the life of the ego; the will of the ego-mind is not commeasurable with the True Will of Soul.

To abandon all semblance of moral compass, must mean to abandon one-pointed concentrated energy and any hope of ever Becoming. Always we seem to arrive back at the same core motivation when we consider the Black Hat philosophies, in all their divers manifestations: it is always a justification, an avoidance of consequence for action.

Fools! Even as an Aspirant I understood that *every act is a*

Magickal act. You can not and will not avoid consequence. What then does Nuith really intend when she says: *Do what thou wilt shalt be the whole of the law*? 'Love is the law,' she elucidates, 'love under will.' What *will* is she talking about? Does she mean: Love is the law, love under the direction of the will of ego-mind, under the control of shadow mind? Is that what the Goddess recommends for the Magician?

Perhaps she means to say: do whatever the shadow mind prompts you to do? Follow every whim of ego?

Is to be a blind, deaf, dumb slave a freedom, an Actualising?

There is an old legend of selling one's Soul to the Devil in exchange for seven years of wealth, fame and power. At the crossroad one finds the Devil's beaten up old guitar. Incredibly, some are tempted by the offer; seven years of whatever it is they want seems more than worthwhile to these pitiful Souls.

In the blink of an eye it is over.

The seven years refers, from an Occult perspective, to the life span of a man. It is seven times ten, or three score and ten.

We are all free to live whatever life we choose, within the environmental boundaries of our peculiar situation. Selling one's Soul to the Devil in this context means to live life under the direction of ego and shadow mind. In an extreme, psychopathic case, it would mean becoming a demon, an active agent of evil. It isn't possible to 'sell' the Soul, but it might be traded in.

I am the Crossroad, boy, says Jak, the Great Eld. *I don't think you comprehend how this works.*

21 **The Universe**

The Tome Lord moves from the centre, accessing every point. He works beyond puny time, in the Eternal, moving through the Inbetweens. What is this life I am born to? he asks.

The Aeon Ra-Sa is the Manifestation of Nuit. The Daughter, who is the explanation of the Father, Mother, and Son. It is the Aeon of Love, for she is Love. It is a Flowering of the Great Work.

There is a New Religion established, and it is called the RASA. It is the unification of the conscious mind with the Soul and its True Will. The Magician Becomes; he crosses the Wild Places and descends into the Pits of Hell, so that he may at last Ascend, phoenix-like, into the unending skies. Every battle and testing, if it does not break him, makes him stronger.

Carefully, delicately, the Soul leads him one step at a time, shielding him, knowing the correct moment for each advance. She is Love, she is the All, she is the Holy Guardian Angel, she is Divine Soul. Long was she bound, and cast into the Desolate Places. In deserts she wandered, arid and barren became her dreams. Perpetual gloams shrouded her from her people, and her light and her truth were veiled. Seeming lost, she slept until the appointed moment. And dreamed.

The New Religion must be the re-shaping and re-forming of the Eld. That which is true remains true, and fits with all other truth.

With experience of the Three Prymaeval Forces, represented as Isis, Wisdom, Magick, All-Mother; as Osiris, the Sacrificed God, the One-Father; Horus, the vanquisher of evil, the sun, the Impulse; and finally as Nuith, the moon, the Daughter, who transmutes all that has gone before into her own perfection.

There are many Gods.

*

The Magickal Retirement
or
Preparation for the Ascent

*

The Magickal Retirement is employed for a number of purposes. First, the Magician uses the discipline to fortify and train his mind. He may be preparing for an important ritual or Ceremonial Magick. He may need to revive and replenish. He may want to withdraw from society and isolate himself so as to work at his creative projects. He may need the separation so that he is free to cross the worlds. Or perhaps there is a knotty equation that he wishes to resolve, and so he intends to venture deep into the contemplative realms to discover its answer.

The Magickal Retirement should be set for a definite period, such as multiples of eight days. The Magician must commit himself to complete each part faithfully. Once begun he must not abandon the practice under any pretext. Death of the Magician is the only acceptable excuse.

That may sound like some hyperbole, but we must approach the Gods with due respect. If we ask them to engage with us in a Magickal Operation, such as the Retirement, then we must commit to our end of the deal. A slack attitude in any area will not assist.

Keeping the Retirement to manageable divisions of eight days allows for the inevitable intrusions which life will make. After each eight day period the Magician rests for one day, and attends whatever pressing business has arisen during the time he was secluded.

Each Retirement will necessarily be idiosyncratic, depending on the pressing details of the Magician's situation.

As his focus will be demanded during the entire duration of every day he can only plan for general activity. This applies even when he is working towards a very specific purpose, such as a Ceremonial Magick. He must still be flexible and adapting. He should arrange his days into periods of Work, Study, Meditations, Magickal Work, etc. These, and other activities such as recording his experiences in the Magickal Journal, should be attended each day, but not by an hour of the clock, rather intuitively, when the Magician is properly inspired for each.

One

Ascending Dancer Cosmiq:: mirrors shattered. Astral works
confined to the mind. Objective reality intrudes. Do what thou
wilt, thyself, a slave to none.
An Intelligence outside of the consciousness of the Self;
apparent from the presentation of a new and startling idea. The
God Voice. Construct an universe, using a book as the raw
materials. Constricting as though throat and vocal chords were
trying to twist and form strange shapes and sounds.
Exhilarating and powerful. They were deaf to it, intent on their
silly testing.

Where does it begin? With the Impulse and the Word. The Idea
is the flaming spinning pulse. *All Will* says God, and the light is
distinguished from the darkness. *All Shalt Be* says Goddess,
and the Multraverses form about her.
I am proof that God is alive. Breath:: *be alive!*
Wiselier. It did. It did not. Every thing has some impact.
The Magus is delicately balanced, astride realities. He can, like
an expert tightrope walker, pirouette on the knife edge at the
Inbetweens.

The power of Disinterested Truth is greater than all these
obstacles.

I lifted like a dragon into the unending skies.
A thousand times a thousand angels upheld me, enrapt me with
their song. They were obsidian black, and oh, so beautiful.
My own daemon had not forsaken me. He led the host in a
dizzy dance. His wings were like dark rainbows or the deepest
folds of the night.
'Now you will be beautiful always,' he said. 'Even unto forever.'

Custard Creamiers. Galaxiam.
The Wedge only needs a gap or crack to enter and bring down
the tower. When it is driven in, with all the weight of the
universe supporting it, it is Unstoppable Force.

I've already defined everything they will need for the journey. But, they await the sequel.

The Magickal Memory is a weapon the Magician can reach to, once he begins to resolve every issue within his psyche. The ego-mind constantly dredges up old bruises and knocks. The wounds fester, never allowed to heal or forget. All these memories have an unresolved element. The mind retrieves them in the hope of attaining a conscious resolution.
The memories are usually incidents that hurt us in some slight way, or perhaps one in which we made an error of some kind, and would like to have acted differently. The variations being endless.
When the Magician finds a general or specific solution to the roots of these memories, coming to some conscious conclusion, then the mind no longer seeks a resolution. The anecdotal recollections surrounding the bruised point cease.

Completed *The Word Logickal.*
Battle fatigue. Crafting Multiverses demands energy. Mood has been irritable since Ascending. Anger. Incongruous and unusual. Tired today after ten days' work. Tomorrow should be energising.
This vantage has adjusted everything. A great amount to process. Mind has been centred on work at hand.
The Gods came to me, to bring blessing and encourage. It was terrifying and beautiful.
External affairs rapid transformations. Changing appearance, attitude, clothes. Clearing out and bringing in new.
The view is clear, and he is able to make sense of all things. He must begin by reviewing his journey, and re-assessing his path across the Abyss. For him, now everything is True.
New shoes. Little wonder. Wore a long Jackdaw feather in my hat. Shoes seem Magickal. Was pronounced. Buoyant. I used to have a hat which did that; it was so potent, and being headwear, concentrated in the area of mind, that it took me to the edges of a strange madness whenever I wore it. Eventually I had to dispose of it, having achieved my ends, as it was too

volatile. The Queen. Change is afoot. The Tome Lords. Dance Steppireprise for e'ersolong. Without the gates at lofty vantage. Coz towers tumbling.

An Universe 257 was formed and manifestly. Deosil we twirlyed the Way. Goddess 'twere said with strangeness. With twists and barely words. Beautifully sown and sewn. All sensibles, making logics. The smokes of the incense like clouds disperse. Thrice, nobly victorious. Here is Goodness. Pure. Holy. Sanctified. Sword. Shield.

The Tome Lords arising dance the Swirlitwyrl and The Word Logickal. Leaves of gold. I'll craft thee one as ne'er seen. Beauteous we'll shape it, with sparkling gleams agleam.

Ascending as Black Winged Dragon. Then descending down, down, down into the Nether Depths, whereat the Old Cruel Gods dwell. Imagine my astonishment to discover that they are nothing at all except overblown devas; literally paper tigers. The Old Great One I sought. I drew him into the fiery pit. Wisps of smoke, for he was dry and weak, just a paper image. Devas are not immortal.

Womb. What of his enemies? they asked. Pity them, he responded. His road is open. Desired. Who could abear this hell without soothing companions? Who can stand above the fire which illumines the Way and endure? The Magician crosses the Wilderness and lo! he discoverth unending deserts. He is the Serpent which consumes itself.

He follows the perfumed breeze. The towers crumble. Cave. The Magician begins the day by asking the Celestial Angels to bless and keep him. He hails Phra, Lord of the Sky, the Creator. He hails Ra, the Sun God. He enters into the Temple Room and attends the Altar of the Gods.

He breaks his fast. *High days and Holy days.* He ponders the tomes of the Eld masters. He records his Acts in the Magickal Journal. At the Altar he makes his prayer.

The Gods send him a letter; it is a contract, and awaits his signature. To witness a Star. She wraps him in folds. She assures him, courages him. The cavalry have arrived. The warrant. The license. He casts the yarrow sticks of the Yi King. His debts are cleared, the shackles slipped. A year to work. Two canvasses to paint. Three books to write. He turns himself into a stranger.

Business brought to clusion. Shadow identified yesterday, and today silence. Extreme change in tension.

Withdrew forces from field. The Pit remaineth.

Cathar: *Being capable of doing, having done.* A person who is Absolute. All traces of impurity cleansed away. Not perfected, but the heart and will are proper and right. On his way, rather than having arrived. Like God, but not yet One with God. Preparing for next step. The Alchemic Wedding into which a Third Substance is born.

The Master said: 'She is not dead, only sleeping. Let us walk in whispers, so we do not awaken her before her due time.'

Whereat the Book?

Implemented *ricochet.* 254 stamped it. The purpose of this ritual protracted becomes a little clearer; its Scope unfurls! It is mine, at least on loan, if they have given it to me.

Creates fascination, intrigue, excites imagination. We all love stories about wizards! Reality of role. Absolute. One with God. Startly satori. A pinnacle lofty and remote. Yikes! don't look down. Logics and sensibles.

Perfected work. Ceremony begins from a pure starting point. The Temple is cleansed and fumigated. Proven True. The Work of each day is in the Consecration of the Prayer.

'If I were the only one, yet I had proof, I would not be worried,' he said.

In the Wilderness one loses everything, forgets everything. Reality is necessarily reformed.

Let us pause at the Threshold, to be certain that all patterns align. To step across is to die.

The dragon is in the field. Completed sketch for painting *The*

Chronicles of the Black Winged Dragon. Title page, background will be yellow. The dragon represents coiled energy and force building to the point of explosive demonstration.

As he walks, the dragon flies low o'er the town.

High winds and hail. And sunshine. We are up in the clouds here, in the High Peak. Difficult mood. A coming back slowly to Earth. Like being on a battlefield.

The *Chronicles* painting progressing. I will use pastely colors on the body of the dragon, to suggest white iridescence.

Don't read too much into it.

The distinctions of ego/shadow mind from one-pointed attention seem clearer. The shadow mind is greatly weakened. Remaining in one-pointedness as the intrusions of shadow mind seem ridiculous. Once we know our enemy he cannot so easily deceive us. We can bring the ego programme to nought, but the shadow mind is of a subtler quality, and cannot be extinguished because it is cast from the core light. It must be brought to heel instead, tamed and subdued. When we regard these aspects of mind as natural functions, never as sapient beings, then we can dispassionately do what is correct with regard to them. We shut them down, turn them off.

Ricochet Magick works much like that of Zebedee Boomarung. There can be no Magickal power inherent in a man-made system of records. Dates have very little occult significance. What is relevant from an Occult point of view are the changing seasons, the equinoxes and solstice, and to an extent the moon phases.

The idea of 'unlucky days' is false.

For that is writ. Rejoice.

Union with God must mean dissolution in Godhead. It is the loss of individual Self and perceptions. It is the death of the Self. How is the All enriched by the sacrifice?

Moving the individual personality towards perfection is the correct way to Union with God. The Self retains awareness, and its perceptions and unique genius continue to be of value to the All. The *Absolute* translates as Magus in Crowley's system.

Recalling several conversations with the Master. They seem rather innocuous, but I will write them down. They will lead onto other recollections.
How Magicks really work. Don't be afraid of the symbols.

Keep coming back to centre, gently. Unstoppable Force. Easing into new reality. The rest is idiosyncratic to his Star.
Our Lady of the Stars, the Stooping Starlight. Nuith.
He takes over the reigns. It is a Lamp of Reckoning Fires.
Probably will include the Multraverse. This is just the beginning. Did we come all this way for naught?

Goddess indwells. Realism continues on its long trajectory.
Blissful kisses. Historic. Anniversary of Jehanne's death.
Stress and worry sap energy. Incense ordered from A-man for Sunday. One appreciates the chemistry when using these raw ingredients.
Energies calm and subdued today. Languid and sensual.
The general fashion style these days, apparently almost across the entire world, is very scruffy and loose and baggy, like pyjamas and sweat pants, trailer trash, or crotch crushing tight trousers, that a nice hat seems extravagant to them.

Now we reach a plateau which they can not perceive. Perilously close to entanglements, but now we are clear. The Unstoppable Force of the Universe pulses out from the Centre, implacable.
Dispute with guitar dealers.

Two

Peace. He returns to his Temple and rests.
Small rug for Temple, and a light shade.
I anticipate a protracted Retreat, perhaps a year. Refine now
and perfect. It seems that, having crossed this Abyss, the order
is adjusted. The Magician shatters the Mirror of the Delusion
Reality as he leaves that reality.
I squish Tetragrammaton like an irritating bug. He has no
power here. Since Tetragrammaton is himself a Deva of ego-
mind, which is a False God, thus all his minions are demoniac;
even his angels.

Bruce Lee said: *if you are injured by words, then you are at the
mercy of every man you meet.*

The Temple, which extends to the wider space occupied by the
Magician, is cleansed. Obstacles and impediments are removed.
Intrusions and contaminants art deflected. The perfumes are
ignited and burn in the braziers.
He closes up the gates and barres the passages. Lookouts are on
the walls, archers at the windows. The keep is fortified against
invaders.
The dragon leaves the field desolated. Fiery winds blow across
the dead. The towers fall. The Looking Glass is shattered. He
works his Seal. The wedge is driven home by the force of its
momentum. The Magus retains the key. The Guardian of the
Gates is the Way.
Swiftly the tension is broken.
5 Like being on a battlefield. Twin-headed dragon.
6 Energies calm and settled.
7 The dragon leaves the field desolated.
8 The Magus turns inward.

Ceased ricochet. Useful, low level. Evil returns to the hand that
begat it.
He Practices being one-pointed in his encounters outside of the
Temple building. Behaviours are modified, adjusting after

small blunders. Better to allow the small error, and then to take measures to properly align, than to continue in error wilfully. Placed incense. Gorgeous perfumes. A brantub of assorted memories. God enters the Cave. Horned like Antlers. Centaur. Movement, beast-like; horse's body. Cerenos, Lord of the Wilderness. The Arrow. The Hunter. Remained a while. Seemed high spirited and joyful. Humility and gratitude. oz.

The Aeon Rasa arrived yesterday. The front cover image, *The Word Logickal,* is still coming out very dull. One more try with it. *The Chronicles of the Black Winged Dragon* painting progressing. Will complete in a couple of days.
Deliverance. Victory complete, says *Yi King.* The dragon expands, accumulating energy. Dispute with guitar dealer settled. They returned my guitar fully repaired. Drawing in the threads. Should I paint Kerynos? Friends arrive.
The *Multraverse* painting from 2019 represents that section as it was at that moment, like a photograph. We have moved on since then. Feels calm. The breeze benign o'er the tors. Now ride the very Gods! Ample signs of victory well won. Started *Master and Magus. Transported.* Coming back was slow and protracted. Closing up the passes, but fill the golden quiver!
Aeon Rasa is, in a sense completed, few minor corrections here and there. I might change the cover. We ended with a nice version; it works well with the two main books, and then the extended dele.
Tired today. Woke very early after a few hours. We turn inward and seek the Divine. I can feel the shift.

I had ceased all other Occult studies when I became a student of the Master. I submitted myself to learn at his feet. This is the correct approach; we must try to have a clean slate to begin, so as not to impede his work.
The Master gives of his great experience and wisdom, but he receives little apart from love in payment. Amado did not charge for the service he was providing. A meal, and a bed if he would be staying overnight, was all he expected. The student must be grateful and respectful; he has not much to offer the

Master in return for the gift of his teachings. What would please him most is the student's success.

'I do have a *few* adepts,' he confided to me one afternoon.

The Master came to visit his students at Brighton whilst I was there, descended into Hell. It was a few weeks before I would leave, and the wide Wilderness was yet ahead of me. He was pushing me towards it, urging me to make the leap.

A meeting was held in the function room upstairs at one of the local pubs. About twenty students perhaps. Amado looked somewhat unsteady as he climbed the stairs, but he caught my eye as he entered the room, and gave a mischievous smile. We sat on our chairs in a wide semi-circle, with him facing us, at the centre.

'You are the figurehead, or the mascot, on our ship,' he said.

I asked him the question my Angel said I should ask; which was about Realities. *You'll have to think about a good question,* she had advised me. *It will show him where you are, and it will prompt him too, energise him. You must ask it.*

I was only beginning to tackle this complex Idea, which I did not fully grasp until after I had ascended, and probably not even fully then. The main points were formulating though: we each have our own reality, I said, how we see things and interpret things, shaped by our experience, our prejudices and opinions, and we overlap to an extent in a common reality. Yet, the Absolute Reality is God's reality; how he perceives the universes and all things. That's how things really are. Is it possible for us to share, even temporarily, in God's reality; see the Truth from that central point? Can we move from where we are to align with God's reality?

He liked the question, and it did prompt him into his lecture. He was on good form, and had us all laughing.

Except one young man, who had grabbed the seat next to me, to my slight annoyance. He was some kind of vampyre, I wasn't sure exactly, but parasitical, posing as a potential student. I would rather he had sat somewhere else, but that didn't worry him.

He seemed to be very uncomfortable on his chair whilst

the Master was talking. The young man squirmed, fidgeting and grimacing. It was the first time he had met the Master, being a realitively new member of one of the groups, which he had attended infrequently, and lamented over how he was so torn about Occultism, and didn't know what he should do. But now he looked like a rabbit about to get squished. He must have realised he was way out of his depth, but politeness kept him bound to the chair, unable to interrupt the Master's sonorous flow.

Do you think I would stand aside and allow you to crucify my only son? he was saying, looking directly at this young man, and slowly ploughing the zipper of his jacket pocket. The Master met my eyes afterward, and I raised my eyebrows a little in surprise at this uncharacteristic demonstration.

There was a break after half hour or so, and the young man excused himself, claiming (quite ridiculously) that his chair was so uncomfortable he had to leave immediately. He fled into the night, never to return.

And seal it at the top.

It will be like Abra-Melin on a grand scale, she said. It was, curiously, since I hadn't been thinking about the protracted ritual much during the previous fifteen years. I had long since abandoned my intension of performing it. *These are the themes you have chosen. You travelled along the Occult path. That imagery appealed to you.*

I'm wondering whether or not to include *Prelude* with dele. It would make it neat and tidy, all those collated pieces. It may make the book too long for the formatting.

Propriety, the state of being proper. Justness, fitness, consonance with established principles and customs.

Unwavering, unswerving, focused on the Point for each day of sixteen years. Refining, polishing, perfecting, honing our magicks.

At this moment he can only be. He has been climbing out of the Abyss. It is the Labors and Ordeals of many years. Long, slow, arduous, lonely the Ascent. Fatigued and enhungered he arrives at the summit exhilarated but exhausted.

It is now that everything makes a clearer sense. His eyes are washed, and he is born anew. He must re-assemble his realities. He walked on the low lands; now after the labors, he is enabled and can soar. THESE forces operate in the corporeal world and the common reality.

At first the Magus is numb. He has destroyed himself. Death does not move him. Then he feels anger, frustration. He is irritable. Then shalt he sink in melancholy awhile.

He is still emerging from the Womb. When he at last rises above the clouds of gloom he alights upon a new shore.

Conditions are wholly altered for him. He must now take stock, recording his Ordeals and Triumphs in his Magickal Journal. He shall take on his Role and comprehend it.

It is a long, complex Ceremony. Concentration must be fixed. He makes his ablutions and burns the perfumes at the Altar. His talisman receives an extra charge from the Gods.

I have enough incense now to last several months. Not happy with the flowery one though, not what I had hoped for. But it is a cheaper alternative. Now we have the real one. These ablutions seem to be a necessary part of the intricacies. Without them it probably wouldn't have materialised. A bit like placing stepping stones to cross the stream.

Magick is a slow, thoughtful and painstaking process. With explosive demonstrations.

Mood calm this evening. *Chronicles* will be completed tomorrow. Worked on *Prelude* for inclusion with *Aeon*. Perhaps I can find those other few pages too.

Three

The Word.

Legal matters, to phrase it thus, coming to completion in successful manner. DL acknowledged today, and request further documents. That will be settled in a week or two. Still awaiting final word on the key. I'm considering my coffee consumption.

It may not be possible soon.

It is necessary to take attention for these entangling details. By observing the minimums we avoid the greater snares. The common legal system piles weights upon a man like heavy chains, until he breaks and sinks. If they can they will cage him, enslave him.

Approaching order now with no loose threads.

Will mark inside of book with 'Occult Philosophy, Mysticism.' The true born wait, watching. He navigates. He views the consequences. He continues to expand. Began reading AC's *Diary of a Drug Fiend.* I've only read it once before.

Meat balls with peppers for lunch. Mood moving to settled. Completed *Aeon Rasa* edition. I hope the printing of its cover is improved. Extended to 270 pages. Now includes *Prelude* and *Clear as Custard.* Title page now lists previous books: *Other Side Up, Something Incongruous & Jarring, Chronicles of the Black Winged Dragon.*

Obtaining the real incense for the Altar was a symbol of success. It has been a long time coming.

Training one-pointedness when out interacting. Excellent exercise starting to yield results. One must avoid the automatic social mode, rambling nonsense. It is an unguarded state, which should be reserved for trusted friendships. One becomes open to subtle insults and manipulations, sophisms and false realities, and perhaps vulnerable to malicious Magickal attack. Being one-pointed avoids any difficulties.

It is to walk with the Gods. In one-pointedness the Magician retains his vantage. His power flows unchecked. Walking along the High Street the strength of magnetism was palpable. Now each venture out, even to do some shopping, has become an opportunity to Practice. We work towards the state of permanently fixed attention.

One wing left to paint on *Chronicles.*

The key six. Blood.

When the Magician is fixed in concentration then shadow mind does not intrude. It is not when shadow mind is directing the thoughts and memories that he is fixed in his Angel.

It is the victory of perseverance. Little by little he wrests power away from his enemy. Like Gandalf and the Balrog they tumble down into the endless falling. Yet, slowly, slowly, shadow mind is weakened, and the Magician grows incrementally more powerful.

It is the Point, the Centre, the Pulse.

He examines his heart. Whereto does his course lead? What is the truth of his Soul?

She comes. She manifests. It shifts. She is calm and centred. She is certain. It is what they worked towards. We, the Queen. Only at the Point does the Queen reside. Once he can rest there, then his Dialogue can develop.

He manifests his Word. Through his Art; through prose, painting, song, martial arts, dance, Magicks, and by his movement. His talisman is a whirling star. It is constant flux as he refines and adjusts. He purifies and updates. He moves to new realities and leaves the old.

He called to his Soul sincerely, persistently. Eventually the Holy Guardian Angel came with conversation and kisses.

Magnetism. Small rug for Temple. Will complete the *Chronicles* painting today. An hour or two work left. Need to distribute books. Keep hard backed copies. Donate copies to library. Five copies of *Universe 257. Many Tears Ago, Aeon Rasa.*

But the effect was simply to dazzle us.

'A spoilt child is most hurt by being ignored,' said the Master.

Completed painting. Art Nouveau style sort of, with a yellow

backdrop and a lot of black on foreground figure, and lettering. Nice picture.
Mood a bit erratic today, but tending to calm.

'One must be Divine to comprehend Divinity. The passions of the pit find outlet only in bestial noises,' he said.
Mood vastly improved today, as though the storm has finally passed over. I have been fatigued for the past few days. Energy expended. But, today I am not tired. I feel settled. Collected some real incense today, burns lovely.
It is the centring, finding balance.
After all there was only one seed, not three. Now there is no need. The subconscious mind takes its cues from the conscious mind and the Higher Mind of Soul. It is not that somehow physical energies are exerted whilst the Magician works in the Astral Realms, but that the Magician's *Magickal or Vital* energies are expended. This can result in otherwise inexplicable fatigue. It is the Magickal energies that need to be replenished.

The talismanic impact of an image, perhaps a painting, has divers forms. From the position of a mind its main power is in its first impact, when, during the first few seconds, the viewer absorbs the image and makes his judgement upon it. He opens himself to the talisman in a kind of innocence. This he does so that he can see the image clearly. He takes in the whole image and its affect so that he might comprehend it. The viewer can then file and catalog the talisman.
The husk falls away, and she emerges, reborn. She spreads her wings, and they are glittering with starlights.
Thereafter the effects of the talisman upon the mind are of a secondary purity. The impact will depend entirely on how much fascination the talisman contains for the particular mind. Whilst the impact can be profound and transporting if the image has potency, these secondary effects and affects are generally fleeting and slight.
The mind is constantly beset with images, so it files them swiftly and efficiently, without direct involvement.

Returning to look again at the talisman, its impact will be mostly benign. The mind reads different stories in the image, enjoys the colors and shapes, the skill of the artist. But all this is after the fact of the talisman's Magickal impact.

We are aware that images are often used to manipulate the ego-mind. The techniques employed belong to the arts of manipulation and hypnotism. These images are not Magickal Talismans. They are perverted symbols whose mesmerism is confined within bland repetition.

The life, and the most potent Magickal impact, of a Magickal Talisman that has been expressed as an intuitive painting or drawing, is mostly in and during its creation. The energy will be swift and the Magician works accordingly. He is concentrated, all his energies directed to the task. As he completes the final brush strokes the Virtue of the Talisman is at it whirling peak, and thus its impact upon the universe. It blazes briefly, brilliantly.

The secondary impacts cannot be considered Magickal effects since they belong to the common reality. A more or less clever artist could work with such symbols.

The power of the Magician is in the Act of Creation, in all its complex parts, from the first idea to the established Work. What happens in the 'life' of the created talisman afterwards doesn't have much relevance, except on a sentimental level.

It has nothing to do with how many books did he sell, but did he write the Book? It doesn't matter if his paintings are sold or not, but did he create the images that he was born to create? The wheels of Commerce have no bearing on Magickal efficacies.

Did his Magicks work or not?

'The inequality of wealth and all the trickery of commerce arose from artificial restriction,' said the Master.

The Temple has transformed with the slow additions and changes made. The sofa is a big impact. As are the three large canvasses on the wall. Plus rugs etc. Character materialising strongly to inhabit surroundings. Very much like not knowing who you are after the regeneration; the Ascent.

The Trance of Perfected Wisdom. Matters arranged so that we may work quietly undisturbed. The handbrake is released, and Spaceyship leaps o'er the voids.

The key has become a corporeal symbol of this adventure; beginning with the dream of the six key. I am impatient for it to conclude matters neatly. Perhaps the license will arrive in synch?

Resolved issues with cover. Now it has its proper snap. The image was repellently dull on previous copies. They print with an extremely dark red. The layout is clean.

Moving into deep contemplative moods. Centring reality. One must delve deep for these Ideas.

To build an universe, which is to build an reality, the Magician must proceed logically with reason and care. He doesn't begin by erecting towers and mountains and bridges: instead he creates space and dimension to contain the abyss. The broad, wide gyrders of construction are more or less fixed, for they are the Reality of the Multraverses, overlapping into common reality.

These foundations are not a matter of choice. He doesn't forget that he is a man living in the corporeal world. Without those structures he cannot hope to produce a sane universe. The crux, which we can consider to be the first nine stones, must be Absolute.

Delusions, lies, shadow mind and ego-mind vanities, if placed as the First Foundations of a reality can only lead to failure. If your central stone is *I am God* then everything that follows is brittle madness.

God Mind is the whirling point. Without this stone the Magician's realities will always falter and deteriorate.

The raw materials are formed in seclusion. The first talisman is those raw materials. Now he begins a new form. Refining, expanding upon the impulse.

7 is the Chariot. The appetites. We come back around, honing our skills; perhaps we will get it right this time. Yi King advises, wait a little. Began the second talisman of *Chronicles*.

Ah, but from such a height! The protracted Ceremony, she manifests with increasing realism. Queen manifesting in perfect bliss. It is a period to assimilate, review, and make cognisant.

Will save remainings. About a week or so. Surprisingly, after having left it untouched for about two months, this incense is pretty good. Quite a mellow relaxed perfume for the Altar. Now it makes more sense, and I can save the golden perfumes for more appropriate use. Useful, because I have probably six months supply, and won't ever be able to get any more of this nature. Haven't quite settled on the alchemical mix with the emeralds. If I can find the correct combination, it would stretch to about a year. That would work out to a sound investment. After this I will change it up. Considering appetites.

Strangely agitated today. Restless. Had a walk about forty minutes. The fires were burning. Mind is rebelling against the discipline of the Retirement. It is asserting itself, demanding stimulation. We are twenty days in now. No 'entertainment' or distractions for the ego-mind. The Magician Works: he writes, paints, makes musics, Magicks, meditations, reading. The mind reaches the point of repugnance towards the work. We adjust and circumvent the objections.

The ego-mind regards the Practice as a waste of time. It would sooner revel in distractions. What does it mean to conquer the ego-mind? We cannot remove the ego from the mind, because it is a function of the natural mind. It cannot be killed because it has no sapient existence. It is conquered by fixing the attention. Ego-mind only exists in the uncontrolled streaming of thoughts, desires, and memories.

The common man associates 'ego' with puffed-upness and narcissistic self aggrandisement, but these are qualities of a weak mind, not ego-mind. Like the charioteer, the Magician brings the mad flight of his team of horses under calm control. He directs his own course.

The weak mind does not enjoy being alone with its thoughts. It seeks noise, distraction, stimulation, company. The coward flies from the Long Dark Night of the Soul. The man does not want to be tortured by the unresolved memories, or the deepening shadows. To be introspective is an agony for him. He has no control over these functionings of the mind, and is entirely at the mercy of ego-mind's dispassionate loop. It has neither cruelty nor mercy, but it will perpetually focus upon each and every unresolved issue in the man's psyche.

The Magician turns inward towards bliss, not tortures.

Four

I was in an unsettled state of temper yesterday. I veered betwixt morose and listless, to agitated, to joyful, to focused. I was released somewhat from my agitations by spending the evening ceremoniously consecrating the talisman. A couple of trifles to adjust, but otherwise completed.

I expect the hardback copy to arrive today. Whittling out all the tiny format errors and co from these three books has occupied about six months. I have had numerous hard-copies. It's quite amazing how these small errors persist.

My mood *today* after a late and refreshing sleep is light and cheerful.

Although I had not read the Tarot for many years, still those 22 archetypal images of the Major Arcana are emblazoned upon my mind and my subconscious. My Angel or my Soul will often use those symbols to communicate with the conscious mind.

Now that the Ordeal has reach its perfecting, having been represented by the number six, the lovers, which is the 'official' marriage or union, now the number seven naturally follows. We also consider the correspondences with the eleventh Arcanum. It is in the Alchemical Wedding of the Art Arcanum that we meet the resolution.

Now is he winged. Now does he feast wi' the Gods, and tarry, familiar with Angels. The flames burn at the High Place, forever fed. It is the Beacon. True pilgrims will be filled and refreshed.

That's the trouble with slimy bureaucrat types.

'Where are the Occult stars of today?' the Master lamented.

Thoth Tarot. Funny, I have been contemplating them for months. They are newly printed, and reasonably priced. But I have no interest in reading Tarot, which is why I have been resistant to their purchase. However, today I felt convinced that they would aid Therion to operate and comment.

I shalt divide the deck. Making a deck of 44 cards.

This evening my mood is settled, calm, contented. It was a

turbulent year. Come through to clarity.

Chair of Kings. He is the Way, the Truth, and the Light.
The Multraverse aligns with the common reality; not the
common *delusions*. The Queen adjusts.

Air remains clear. Considering nourishments. Got shoes, as
advised. DMs back tomorrow. Ordered Blakeys online. Got
jacket, hand tailored wool. Thin, summer jacket.

This is the Image of the Tome Lord. It all aids the transition
into the role, the notion of being a different person, re-born.
Re-generated. Our clothes directly impact ourselves and
everyone we encounter. Dressing in well made attire buoys us.
Wear fine jewels to me!

As a musician I can seamlessly move into the new role. For this
phase I have so far acquired four trousers, DMs and four shoes,
two wool jumpers, thin leather jacket, five wool jackets etc. I
have more or less all I need in that regard now. A couple of
decent waistcoats would be welcome.

Found Great Tree box for Impulse cards. Dome lidded. 17 The
Star. The Master strong today.

'Aleister was unable to experience real love. I am forbidden the
love of women. I wonder what your sacrifice will be?' he
mused.

The Lighthouse Keeper. Max Bolton? The Book. The Impulse
(fire). The Wand (pen). The Magus returns to the Temple.

The fourth period of the Magickal Retirement seems a peculiar
duration. It feels long and testing. Of course, we are almost a
month in now, so there is mental weariness and fatigue. Mood
has been slowly adjusting, and moving towards a centred and
calm repose. The adjustments have often come in spikes and
troughs; it hasn't been smooth sailing.

The exercise is yielding good fruits. The Book. The Impulse.
The Will. The Magus puts to sea in a pea green boat. When he
crosses into the oceans beyond there is nothing remaining to
despoil. The wedge driven in.

Significant connecting (as yesterday) with Exeter. Poignant
tears. Rally to me. The seven pointed star blazes and throws

back the darkness. Carry the light in your eyes. He loved you always as a daughter; you were his *favored* one.

Having been aware of the symbols for the Tome Lord for some years, it is interesting to see them finally coming to manifestation. I always thought it only an amusing sub-plot. The mind is still apparent in habits of thought and behaviours. Lazy opinions jar more. We pick apart and re-thread the tapestry one stitch at a time; and our work encompasses an universe.

Still more Temple items. Confirmation later this week. We must buy whatever is needed, without quibbling over the price of goose eggs. That was the ablution. Now is the sacrifice.

I think we must be approaching completion with furnishings. A few more rugs. The Temple is also a working studio. And a living space for cat. Sometimes we must allow members of the public access, workmen and such. We can't be too precious about it. It's not those details which are significant. We navigate and adapt. Reality must be accommodated. For all that, it is no less the Holy of Holies.

The real Temple is not in an object, such as a building; it is the fleshy body and the purified mind. The Cathedral is in the heart.

I purchased a second small pair of binoculars, oddly enough. The other was a pocket type from the Sixties. I'm not sure when they'll find a use, but *she* wanted them. Success is thy proof. God Mind has no thought. Ego-mind has been silenced in No Mind. There are no babbling nonsenses. The Magician must step aside, allow space for her to dance.

Never again. Cleaned Kitchen space.

The Magician must discard as much of the old mind as he can, the self-defeating and negativities. They are persistent mantras of opposition. *You can't, you aren't, that isn't true* etc. The shadow mind has its arsenal of favorites. The day is brief, we cannot afford to *reside* in doubt.

It is my nature to move forward, towards the light. I cannot turn aside from the path. I am driven to resolve and uncover truth. I will keep going, always straight ahead, until I get there.

The Magician trains himself to be the Light. In his eyes is the Fire of God, like a beacon. He throws back the darkness. He must be the Truth. He is proof, united with his Holy Guardian Angel. It is the Great Harmony. The truth is alive in the Magician. He draws to the centre, echoing the truth of the All. The Magician trains himself to be the Way. In the Actualised Man the Way has found perfect expression. He adheres firmly and correctly. Nothing can sway or move him from following the course of Heaven. He learns to embody the Path.

Above the starry firmaments she dips and bows, spins and whirls, and from her skirts spin dazzles and sparkles. She leaps and steps in silhouette, all at the arc of her wrist. Her cascade curls tumble and unfurl the stars.

Fingers & thumbs.

Our way is easy. See them weep. See them moan.
Our way is beautiful, and leads us home.

Moonchild was a Prologue. To what? The main theme of its story is *The Butterfly Net.* This alludes to the protracted Magickal Ceremony designed to draw a Great Soul to the Earthly realm, and for that Soul to take on a body. Why? Because the Plan of the Gods reaches crisis point. What Great Soul might Crowley have been thinking of?

He led me out into Wild Places. 'I wish you well,' he said, abandoning me to the darknesses which arose as clouds of thunder and rains. I tumbled down into nefarious realms. 'I guess it is the way of things,' I replied. 'You don't have to worry; I've got it now. Thank you.'

There is a famous photograph of Aleister Crowley, in which he is older and thinner, near the end of his life. His raised hand is casting a shadow behind him on the wall. I have seen the black and white image on the covers of a couple of different books about him. It could be considered to be a bit of a spooky photo, and they are using it to represent something wicked and evil.

They all think he is making a Diabolical Magickal Sign; the shadow his hand casts bears a fleeting resemblance to the Devil. But no, he is an Englishman at heart, and it's just his quirky sense of humour: he is actually invoking the Great God Punch.

Now he returns from the Wild Places.
And, what have you been doing all this while? He does not come to save, but to hold to account.
The outmoded behaviours and thoughts clash. They are anomalies. It is a tedious process, having to deal with each individual thought as it arises. He is whetting and honing his concentration. They are all useful reminders. He brings his life to a constant meditation or prayer. He becomes sharp and one-pointed.

The Magicks Tome is probably the greatest book ever writ on the theme of the Holy Guardian Angel and Holy Magicks. Simple naivety, hidden in absurdities, is its veil. I had Wilheim and Jung's translation of *Yi King*, thankfully, but would have been glad to have had such a treatise available to me as a young pilgrim searching for the centre of the Labyrinth. One would not require another. The rest is detail. Yet, the details do add interest.
With perseverance the Practice yields up its fruits and its secrets. But, few seek absolute truth. They want all kinds of different things instead.
The Magician should read from the first to the last page in proper order, and with concentrated attention, to properly charge the Talisman. If he does so he may then dip in and out, and still draw Magickal impact therefrom.

Couple of days early. Air settled. Once clouds disperse one notices they were there. Moved into manifested centre. Blakeys arrived. Try on Jak. Might have to take care not to lose them. See how it goes. Memories have distinctly changed type and flavor. Memories of the Master, and younger years, but scenarios I have not recalled for a long time. Not the same old pains! This 'novelty' adds some interest. There is a lot of material to write up.

Her perfume like burning wood, musky.

Aeon Rasa enters into the Collective Consciousness. I acquired another rug for Temple floor. It is strong and tightly woven, yet it can be rolled or folded as though it were just thick material, the colors are soft lime green, beige, golds, flower patterns. It makes me think of the *Raj* for some reason; it would be ideal for trunk travelling.

Settled and paid. Making great progress on songs. Finally settled in comfortable keys. Bought a lot of fruit from stall. Apples, bananas, blueberries, strawberries, satsumas.

Good exercise for the regenerating processes. Blind Crow likes the new rug quite well. She has been stretching herself blissfully upon it.

I have cleansed Temple, purified the space that it might be holy.

Perhaps I need to paint that canvas. I have no clear image. I have envisioned complex flower patterns, and feel obliged to paint the God, but somewhat reluctant.

Perhaps an image just arrived: an angelic female within a large frame, twisty vines and flowers. Robe and skirt etc.

Auto-mind. A new Idea, proof of Higher Intelligence.

Auto-mind is the ego-mind or shadow mind producing random content; not wilful. Mind without concentration.

Magickal musings; they are not real in the sense of physical reality, but they are Magickal musings. They closely resemble an reality, they seem very real, but they are day-dreams. The Magician explores these realms, and works to comprehend the symbolism of events there. A large part of my journeyings was through those musing realms.

She tested me today, and thereby led me to cognition. She awarded me the KEY.

In the evening deep samadhi. Angel reveals the Key of the Muse. It illuminates all the journey. The realms of the Muse. Now may he employ them Actualised. C. was the light that I followed during my first ventures into the Wilderness. Like a

Soul of Monroe; in the mirror with a red rose. She was most certainly the catalyst that first ignited me. The Master had brought me to the Gate. His work was complete, he bid me fare well, blessed me.

The Muse represents archetypal images of the God Mind. She appears in precisely the role that will quicken him. The Lovers is a mirror.

Ah, but *he* was a saboteur; a manipulative narcissist, shaped by the bloated spider. You were an object he owned, and he would not stand *any* rival.

Did I know you were there? I sensed. And, I did send you a sweet kiss. For *us*, that remains a victory.

The painting will complete the collection. I have drawn the borders, both of which I will paint first, before drawing the main piece. The space between them will be flowers and vines, central, the Muse. There are nine stones, the radiance, and this one is the Key.

I saw a painted fabric of the Star Tarot image today.

It is clearer to regard ego-mind and shadow mind as auto-mind. Ego and shadow affords them too much personality and wilful intension. The Magician is liable to personify them, imagining them to have a kind of sapience.

Auto-mind is the streaming of memories, thoughts, once ego has been quietened. Instead of a babbling stream of nonsense auto-mind is pragmatic and selective.

The shadow mind seems very much like an antagonist. It is almost like a dark muse. The shadow is a devious and cunning foe, but the Magician learns how to shut it out, and minimise its influence. It is a shadow, and shadows are destroyed with light.

The Practice is doing me well. Conditions after Ascension are wholly altered. I am adjusting to the new laws. The Keys are uncovering so much. It is overwhelming. As yet I cannot formulate it all coherently. In due course I hope I shall, but for now it is a storm of information. I must approach methodically, and be faithful in my arrangements.

The three Magus cards.

To define the role of Muse.

Like a thousand Ideas whirling about a centre. Somehow the Magician must decipher them, and make his selections in good order. Each Idea seems fleet as a wood nymph, and fragile as a snowflake. Yet must he stand astride realities, juggling universes, whilst engaged in the most delicate and intricate Ceremonial Magicks.

It is easier to watch the prettiness of the imploding stars, and to languor amongst pleasing philosophies, than to hold the mind alert, judicial, correct.

The Magickal Journal proving useful. We are able to pin these iridescent butterflies. It has probably become indispensable. Angel strong and powerful, extended dialogue. Ate a lot of fruit.

Five

Rose very early, before 5 am. His earlier notes throw light on current experiences. The Word declared. His pursues his Work to his own satisfaction. The long strange path led to this moment.

Dreamt of shadow being cast out. It is broken, like the Balrog upon the rocks. We meet in the open field, and swear death. Puf the Magick dragon! Thank you, dear. Last rug for Temple. Nice dark blue, greens, aztecy colors and shapes. Large. Detailed graven steel (?) cigarette box. For keeping Tarot. The Masters arrived today. Handmade chessboard. Picture frame. Acorns. Tree represents. Start small. Seeds. Try keeping. Don't mix different elements. Love & hate would cross contaminate. The *Reckoning* is a name or title of an Eld God.

Awaken! The moment eternal.

Thou joineth the song. Instead of careering uncontrollably through life, or crashing headlong into the sun, a Magician elects to glide on the ship with silver sails; the one that soars through the heavens towards a crescent moon.

Aeon 20 closure. Resolution. Definite action. The next step. Dolven. She seems quite chirpy about it.

Second frame on *Muse,* outer border. I may begin the sketching today. 37 days in.

Corrupted intelligences. Sometimes one does get a sort of thank you. The wayward, outcast, sanyasin. Completed words and names. Master brought Key to language. Book arrived to seal it. Manifesting. Full day's work.

Delve is very narrow in its application nowadays. *Delve into* is almost its only common usage. So we lose many other poetic words, such as *dolve, dolven.* Modern language does not aim to improve upon. It's been a dumbing-down. The Black Hats are pushing towards English for Idiots. Maybe Kurt was right, and illiteracy will prevail.

'Be heard on other planes. Be forceful. Cause other voices to compound with yours so that the resultant sound can be sculpted into power,' the Master advised.

He delivers the answer to the enigma in spectacular fashion. Now every part makes sense. Spent day doing first pencil work, detailed and intricate, then began painting. Began with green. She was strong, with Keys.

She walks in beauty, like the night of azure skies and clement climes.

Deosil with sun.

The personality continues in a 'pure' state, retaining much of its experience as memories. It digests and meditates upon its experiences, extracting every lesson therefrom. It retains the art and the beauty.

The librarys of the Tome Lord contain books writ in divers realities, and they are reverently transcribed and translated.

In some realms the eyes of the Magician are blind. *The Blind King.*

After poignant signs and pauses, I arrived with exquisite timing. I worked on *Muse* painting day and evening. Delicate and intricate detail. Looking gorgeous. Explain what attitude towards Master is correct. He is going mad, they tell me. Master strong today. Suddenly every mystery is resolved. One doesn't lose one's Soul in a moment. It is an intricate Magick wrought across a life.

St John of the Cross. The Dark Night of the Soul.

'Occultism is the autochthonous religion of Mankind. It sprang from earth itself, before civilisation. True Occultism is the authentic path of Nature and Life,' said the Master.

What does Murgator do when he meets the Goddess at the Endless Stair? He tries to fight her, using ego as a weapon.

The shadow does not have sapience. It is auto-mind. When the mind is scattered, sunk in delusions, at the mercy of ego-whim, then the honing and whetting functions of shadow can be overwhelming and painful. It is to work on a faulty instrument. That can lead directly to the collapse of the mind. For a healthy balanced mind the shadow hone and whet mode is helpful.

Little Buddha crossed over and stayed there. He made the pact.
You were aetheral-like, barely there.
I would go onto the little hills and be unconcerned in my own
company. I wanted to be left alone. Then they would come; in
the trees, the squirrels, the birds. Faery. I was deeply emersed.
I prayed to the stars, the sky.

Dream of Bedlam. Significance of license. Casting bread upon
the waters 06. 16. DVLA sent me a PO for 3$; they refunded
postage. It returns to me in this moment this space, and it is a
license. It symbolizes the completing of the circle.
E'en the wher'dtheybaens and the verylongagos. We come to
Work. One less enemy.
The perfecting of the Magician does not mean that he aims to
transcend all emotion. On the contrary; because an
emotionless, un-feeling person will struggle to have empathy,
and will tend towards psychopathy. It's a strange
misconception, that the Holy Man should lose his sensitivity
and his humanness in his Perfecting. What he has transcended
is ego.
He is no longer at the mercy of tumultuous emotions, but they
are reined in, held in control, and thus do not overwhelm. This
is what it is to be Master of the Temple. It is not a strained
position; emotions are comprehended in their proper context.
He does not soar and fall as he once did. The common joys are
tempered, he concedes, but the griefs are now fleeting.
It is not a loss of personality or humanness. Perhaps he appears
remote and unreachable, but he is engaged with his Work. He
has risen above the tides and swells of emotion, and resides in
calmness. His nerves have not transmuted; yet he has control.

Day forty two. License arrived, unexpectedly early.
I feel calm and quite happy today. My energy feels settled and
healthy. Apple pie hot.
Called upon her. Empowering all my arts. Strong, blissful,
silken mythil.
He stands at the Inbetweens, reshaping. The acorns represent

Ideas. The Ideas are conjured, like Princesses. They manifest and yield up their meanings. This may be swift or protracted. Continuing with typing. Mirror Fire.

All signs point to successful completion. Fires are burning hot. Goddess manifesting with strength and power. *The Muse* progresses. It is another large painting 48" x 36", and the intricate detail means the entire surface is small brushwork, so an inevitably slow process. I expect and hope to finish before the end of this Magickal Retirement.

The Practice of the Magickal Retirement intensyfies with each moment. When we are concentrated in our attention then time is expanded, stretched.

Creativity at peak. Writing unchecked, and 4 large paintings completed during 6 weeks.

The fires and blisses are her stooping kisses. The Butterfly Net was the pivot of his Works. Is it like a treasure map? *My joy is to see your joy.* Intense orgone. The key is in how to retain that energy, and to put it to work. Robin, and family, as the envoy. The *spiralswirls* will occupy most of today's Work. And drawing the fires into the heart.

The moral compass. Pen has served well, but the moment comes when it must be replaced by a new pen. Cheetah from BSTT. Good progress.

Main figure to paint today on the Gorgeousy Gate. Still undecided on colors. The Ceremony gathers momentum. All the stories are true. The Goddess manifests. Bastet is midnight cornelian blue. The jigsaw pieces fit into place. Like a set of three Battle Cards. Writing up Magickal Retirement. The Master will be in it a fair amount. That opens a door upon some interesting topics and recollections. I have freedom now to write without any confines, having detailed the main points already in *Aeon Rasa*. What I am doing is presenting my experiences, and the conclusions my journey has led me too. It is philosophy, for the value it has. It is the Word of the *Holy Madman*. It has meaning, for it works under rare and extreme conditions.

I am Magus; therefore these Tomes are also Magickal

Talismans. We are synthesising our Occult Wisdom and Knowledge, shaped by our experiences. We are drawing a map of the Cosmos. The Aeon Rasa is represented by the Daughter; she is the Lovely Star, Nuith.

Worked on *The Muse*. Painting main figure. Settled on colors finally. Silence, Love, Great Harmony. Holy oil.

Some sea-sickness as the universes tumble.

I am not concerning myself with reproducing day by day entries here. Dates have no significance, although they can be helpful in proper context. It is May 2022, and we are upon the island England.

Six

The Regeneration is becoming more solid. There are many
residue behaviours and emotions that linger, and it is a process
of patience to weed them out. In themselves they are negatives
arising from shadow; anxiety, tension, anger, irritations and
company. Also incorrect habits of self care and nourishment,
being detrimental to physical well being and vitality. Still not
resolved properly.
BT. Singing beginning to manifest. Put aside everything except
your direct experience. Hold the concentration and watch and
record what the mind does. Flow around, like water. Queen of
Fire. The watery part of fire; its fluidity and color. 8 tomes.
Present: *chronicles*. Painting on schedule to complete with
Magickal Retirement.

The moon. Midnight. How splendid is the adventure!
Anubis: *the Watcher in the twilight.*
The threshold of life and death.
Rust, orange, gold, muted green. Making progress on songs,
finding better keys, fine tuning. A lot of resistance but
beginning to break through.
Feel good. Health and vitality, well being. Singing brings joy.
Dust settling and smoke clearing. What remains?
The Gods galloping.

Will complete *Muse* tomorrow. Gold detail, cuffs, small details.
I feel a bit exhausted with it. Heya!
Does evil exist outside of the minds of men? Is there a force
which is evil? Are there entities that are evil? There are
certainly evil minds; those of men and ghosts. It is the same
type of mind under different conditions. Apart from the mind
of man, does evil exist as an entity or intelligent force?
There can not be evil Gods. It is a contradiction of terms. But
are there equivalent powers that are evil?
Well, what do we mean by 'evil?' We intend a mind that acts
without caring for consequence, malicious, and devoid of
empathy and reason. We consider evil to be cruel, sadistic, and

psychopathic. It is insanity that tends towards disintegration. Could there be an evil power, equivalent in force to the power of the All? If there were such a power, perhaps a parallel impulse, towards chaos and emptiness, then over the course of millions or billions of years it would have fulfilled its aim, and extinguished itself, returning to void; if its power were ever *equal* to the power of God.

The power of evil is not commeasurable with the power of Great Harmony. Evil can not endure. It must become insane and destroy itself. It can not reach perfection.

The Multraverses are very old. Perhaps the Gods tied up all loose ends and cleared the workspace before proceeding with their plans for the Earth and Man.

What level of power does evil then possess?

The multiverses are calm and ordered. They turn without efforts in perfection unending. We see no evidence of a war in the universes; no clashing forces of darkness and light on a God-level. God is not divided against God. The Multraverse is sane, rational, and exact. The aethers sigh and the All manifests in Beautiful Great Harmony.

If we were able to search every universe we would discover only *unending perfection*, stretching into *Infinity*, the Macrocosm of God. If there *was* a war between Good and Evil reaching to the manifested universes, then the evidence suggests that the battle has been over for a long time, and that the good guys won.

Yet, the very fact of order implies the potential for chaos. Even so, that is no reason for the Cosmos not to impose order and pattern.

We can not claim evidence of powerful evil entities existing beyond the realm of the Earth, because we see only calm order. It is only here upon the Earth that we see evil manifested in the minds of men. Extending from the Mind-Ego are dark gods and 'devas.'

Evil is a deteriorated mind, or a broken mind. It is without morals, entirely self-centric, narcissistic and nihilistic. It is always degenerate. Its effects are limited.

An enemy only keeps itself hidden when it wants to lure its prey, or because it is weak and cannot survive a head-on encounter.

If the forces of evil had the means and power to attack and destroy every person who was motivated towards the light, then it would do so. We don't see evidence of violence and aggression against decent people on a God-level. We see it only on a microcosmic level.

If there are evil entities upon Earth, other than the mind of Man, then they are constricted, and the effects they might cause are narrow and limited.

We must consider the Celestial planes and the Astrals. If evil minds could exist independently, then we might reasonably expect to find them here.

The Magician is more likely to encounter entities that are ambiguous in their morality rather than evil. Evil consumes itself, so it rarely exists in an enduring form.

Men have long worshipped and sacrificed to dark gods. What of those gods? Are they beings on the astrals, or only ever devas? Devas are pooled power, yet they can not be sapient nor respond to appeal. They are blind, deaf and dumb to their worshippers.

If the dark gods are beings, then perhaps they were not always insane. Or, perhaps another type of entity is drawn to the pooled power of diabolical worship. Something might even pose as the voice of the deva or god.

Whether or not evil exists as entities or as a force, it seems apparent that upon the corporeal world it must work its influence upon the minds of men.

That idea makes some sense; if these Astral entities or intelligences do not have corporeal bodies, then influencing the Material Realm, unless they have the powers of Gods, is naturally difficult. Influencing the mind of a man may be the only way they can impact this realm of the physical in a meaningful way.

How do the *Gods usually* impact this realm, if not through the minds of men?

Daemons are not generally evil. They are performing a certain obscure role. Some display characteristics and personality consistent with the Lower Intelligences.

A God could degenerate, we assume, since it possesses a mind. All minds are subject to imbalance under certain conditions. If a degenerating mind can not stabilize itself and return to the centre, then it must end with insanity, and the death of the mind. A degenerating mind has fallen from the natural course of its star. Mind does not expand without aligning with the True Will, it contracts instead. Even a God could not endure the loss of its mind.

She manifests.

O rise Great Moon! Let the night come!

Day 48. Completed the *Muse* painting. Prettiest face! Unusual combination of colors. Powerfully transportive. Collected incense from A-man. Bit stronger, reduce. Images of gorgeous BST.

Here endeth the Magickal Retirement.

*

The Aeon Rasa

Invoking the Holy Guardian Angel

*

0 The Mirror of the Gods

See the circle rippling into the centre. Your choices have
brought you to this very moment. How could you go back?
Destiny is an intricate magick wrought across a lifetime. Your
reflection is already upon the surface of the looking glass.
What is it that you bring to the Gods as an offering?
It is like a mirror because it reflects. What does this mean?
Why do we use these images to express our Idea?
When we meditate upon the images and the symbols we draw
closer to the Idea, and are introduced to associations and
correspondences. We might ask: What is it that the mirror
reflects? How does it reflect?
Consider Aleister Crowley's Fifteenth Arcanum of his Thelemic
Tarot, so beautifully painted by Lady Freda Harris: 'The Devil'
card. What do you see when you look at it? This is how
Magickal Talismans Reflect.

The pilgrim wanders the gloaming Labyrinth, and its passages
are set with traps and obstacles. Strange daemons and monsters
are guarding the path. He does not seek an escape, because
beyond the walls of its maze there is only void and death. He
must press onward. At the Labyrinth's centre is the well of pure
clean waters, and a door.
Is the Labyrinth a place? Is it marked on the map?
Crossing the threshold of the door is to step out into the
wilderness realms, where Gods and angels and devils abide.
There are no exemptions, and no get-out clauses. Each shalt
reap just that which he did sow.

1 Of the brilliant core

We reach towards the Divine Reality by turning inward and apprehending the core. Reality is not found amongst the nonsenses of ego-mind.

The core is like a star that shines against the dark firmament, reflecting the brilliance of the sun. We cannot see the pure source which is God, the sparking impulse, but we can see the Divine radiance reflecting upon forms.

We begin our Practice by finding the centre of balance. The centre is not the destination, it is the starting point. Here, we uncover the pulse. We aim to resonate with and echo the pulse.

The Tao is harmonious and tends to growth. The motivation of the universe is towards perfection. From the flawless impulse to perfection arise every good quality in Man and in the universes. Only a will towards harmony could result in the endless structures of intricate and perfect patterns which we see in all the universes. If the universe were motivated towards chaos instead of perfection, and if the Tao was disharmonious and tending towards decay, then the universe could never have attained its perfect form. It would have collapsed in upon itself long ago, because that is where tendencies towards chaos, disharmony, and decay would lead.

The man is like a talisman drawing to himself powers, forces and virtues. The talisman is shaped by what he does and by how he chooses to nourish himself. Every act and even each thought have consequence, and each is indelibly etched.

When we join an organisation we are aligning ourselves magickally with its talisman, and all that it represents. We are making the statement before the Gods: *I stand with these men.* The Magician is a charged talisman, and for him such alliances are more potent than for the common man. Every symbol he adds to his magickal talisman is heavy with portended doom.

The ego-mind is without focus. It is scattered, lurching from one desire for gratification to the next. It is a babbling stream of nonsenses. Confusion and delusion are compounded when one's life is lived in ego-mind.

We make the distinction of ego-*mind*; there is an old sense of the word 'ego' which refers to the physical life, and a 'natural' uncomplicated approach, such as skilled craftsmen, farmers, stone masons, even dancers and musicians; those who live and work through the body, the hands. Why would such a life be 'wrong'? If it is the man's true will to follow such a path, and if he flies from delusion, then he is in perfect harmony with the All. The Magician keeps in mind that most are not called to be mystics and workers of wonders.

When we discuss *ego-mind* here we are referring to the specialized Work of the mystic and the Magician. They are narrow disciplines, just as Ballet as a pursuit is only suited to certain individuals.

We must be circumspect when venturing into the realms of intricate speculation on obscure points of theology or philosophy.

In a sense everything around us is an illusion, because ego-mind is responsible for perceiving and interpreting reality, unless and until we are ourselves in the seat of power. Many of the things which seem real in this life, such as time and wealth, are intellectual fabrications. Consider the vast amount of books written across ages which amount to nothing but the passionate bleating of ego-mind.

The Sanskrit scriptures call this universe of delusions the *Body of Maia*. They intend that all is constructed from and by the Essence of God; the notion of separation is illusionary. The world of ego-mind, and its ambitions and philosophies are delusions.

Yes, yet it is not a logical continuation that thus All is Illusion. Time is an intellectual construct, but we cannot conclude that therefore this moment that we are experiencing in and existing within is not real.

We must dare to draw only accurate conclusions.

The universe is real. It exists. It is unaltered by fancy philosophical speculations. The material world is a solid reality.

It is dense and heavy, and it is the veritable realm of consequence. Nothing can change that absolute reality. Not even a popular vote.

The ego-mind flies from truth because therein is its destruction. Ego-mind will tend towards philosophies in which there are no consequences for action. If the universe doesn't really exist then what difference could there be between virtue and degeneracy? Everything is excused as a valid experience, and the world falls into chaos.
The universe rolls out from the centre, implacable.

The ego-mind has no sapience of its own. It is a function of the natural mind, very much like an autopilot, or a default setting. When the mind is without a fixed concentration then it is ego-mind which is directing the course.
The ego-mind is re-active. It responds to external stimuli. It has neither judgement nor insight, but tends to distractions, to repose and pleasures and oblivions, to sensuous gratifications. It is a formidable and relentless foe. Yet once we grasp how to wrest control away from it its power diminishes.
The mind and the body are the vessel, and it is the will of Self that must seize the seat of power and take control.
Some rise to the surface of clarity, and then sink back into ego delusion, like a drowning man. If they apprehended the truth they would strike for shore instead of remaining where they are, treading water.
We are not insisting upon lives of saintly austerity. The Magician leads a natural life. Remaining in a state of clarity needs neither ablutions nor sacrifices. It demands only sincere application and perseverance.

2 Of the Holy Guardian Angel

In the late eighteenth and early nineteenth centuries Joseph Wronski was postulating the idea that knowledge obtained by reason alone can lead to the Absolute Reality.
He was friends with Eliphas Levi, who is renowned within the literary world of Western Occultism as a great Magician. Apparently, Levi regarded Wronski as his spiritual teacher.
It was Levi who first suggested a correspondence between Tarot cards and the Hebrew alphabet and the Qabalah. He wrote a nice book about it. The idea was expanded upon by Papus, and has become an accepted and rarely questioned part of occult lore.
Henri Cornelius Agrippa, in his 16C works on Occult Philosophy makes no reference to Qabbalistic correspondences with the Tarot. He most certainly would have done if any had existed in his day; he collated every piece of existing occult lore into his three books.
It is an amalgamation of folk recipes, sympathetic and contagious magicks, ceremonial and mathematical conjurations, opinion and superstition. It makes a fascinating and beautiful document. The third book is predominantly Qabbalistic, and we should have expected to find a discussion of the Tarot there, if it were, as Levi claimed, part of occult tradition.
Interestingly Francis Barrett's updated version of collated occult philosophy, borrowing directly from Agrippa's idea and work, and published in 1801, *The Magus, Celestial Intelligencer, a complete system of Occult Philosophy*, likewise does not even mention Tarot.

Joseph Wronski was the original author of *The Sacred Magic of Abra Melin the Mage.*
Eliphas Levi added the parts about the Qabalah.
The French manuscript was later translated by Mathers, and the work was brought into the public consciousness and given validity by Aleister Crowley. Indeed Crowley based his magickal system, at least publicly, around the idea of

communicating with the Holy Guardian Angel, as described in *The Sacred Magic of Abra Melin the Mage.*

The original manuscript is in the Bibilotheque d'le Arsenal at Paris (ms 2351). It's full title is: *La sacree magie que Dieu donna a Moyse Aaron David Salomon, et a d'autres patriarches et prophetes, qui enseigne la vraye sapience Divine, laisse par Abraham a Lamech son fils, traduite en hebreu 1458.*

Crowley had embraced the idea of the Qabbalistic Tarot, which similarly features extensively in his symbolic systems.

One curious thing about it all is that whilst the presentation of the work *Abra Melin* is fiction, it being writ by Wronski not Abraham, and then embellished by Levi, the essence of the idea it presents is sound.

'Once one has received instruction and guidance from the Holy Guardian Angel what other guide does one need?' remarked Crowley.

3 Of the Universe

The Universe is motivated towards harmonious growth and co-operative existence. It will resonate with the parts of its Body that similarly tend to growth, harmony, and perfection. Those parts will flourish, as though receiving the blessing of God. Aspects or parts of the universe which are contrary to the Divine, and thus are tending to degeneracy and decay cannot endure. They will not resonate nor flourish, and the Divine Essence will be drawn from them. They will perish. This is certain; they are anomalies. In God's universe of beauty and perfection neither insanity nor evil nor chaos can endure.
It is a perfection which is in constant movement. God is experiencing, and that implies that he must also learn from experience and change, and continue to grow and expand. The universe is alive.
The will of the universes continues towards Divine Purity. All parts of his Body shall strive towards the perfection of the whole.

The path of the Superior Man is nefarious and obscure. Only a rare mind sincerely seeks the Absolute Truth. The delusions of the external world, and the delusions of the scattered mind are persistent. Few men truly bring the ego-mind to nought.
The Trial of the Adept reaches to the further edge of the Abyss. It is first into the Wilderness, where he finds the Gate. He lays down his body and his life for the Gods. They will consider him, and if he be fit they will call him to his task.
If he has prepared his way in resonance and accord with Self and God, this his true identity and destiny, then his Angel shall meet him at the Gate.
The Angel is the shield to his small flame, and without its guidance and protection the chasm will not be brooked. It is the long slow falling into deepest darkest horror.
To become Adept, one having mastery of his craft, he must descend, traverse, then climb from the pit.
He emerges reborn, rising like the phoenix, a crowned and conquering king. Now may his work begin in earnest.

To be overwhelmed by darkness means to fall prey to the delusions of the world and of ego-mind. When the mind ventures far into illusions and does not resist, but accepts for its reality lies and the nonsenses of ego ambition, then it is tending towards madness and insanity. The measure of sanity is not emotional, nor is it popular opinion, but how near our reality is to the *Sooth* of the universe.

Whether sophists like it or not, reality begins and ends with God. How the Supraverse perceives and interprets the universes and all phenomena is the crux of what is and what is not.

The ego-mind contrives a thousand plausible and implausible theories, compounding errors. Yet the realities of ego-mind, which are postulated, pursued, and violently imposed upon society by inferior men, are castles of delusion. The Towers of Abaddon rise from the deeps of the abyss. They are structures raised by degenerate and twisted minds. Their theories and philosophies veer far from truth, and really they are the ramblings of the insane.

The universes remain true and enduring, held close to the rhythm of the Pulse. They reach towards perfection, motivated by the original will to life.

The universes exist, and that is a cornerstone of God's reality. They are real, solid, and perfect in their form and pattern. They prove the success of the Essence: that it has through the division and union of its forces, through active energies and yielding energies, with light and darkness, with the full and the empty, with pattern and synchronicity, become the established living Multraverse.

4 The Devil in the details

It is always the case that when we consider the works of Initiates we will jar with some aspects, and resonate with other facets. This is inevitable because we did not compose the particular work ourselves. How could any spiritual or magickal view of the universe align exactly with our own?
This is why we need large sweeping symbols to properly communicate. The minutiae is our own concern, and we can not expect to find those details perfectly cataloged anywhere else. They are the small differences that make individuality fascinating. We must compose that work ourselves.
We are existing in this moment, and every truth has been modified and transmuted by its experience leading up to this moment. The space we are occupying now is unique, and its truth is individual and personal.

For example, if we approach the Old and New Testaments as records of accurate history, and further as the pure Word of Almighty God then we are heading for trouble. That is a reality which cannot be sustained. We may get hung up on the errors of the Bible, and furious at the way it has been employed to manipulate and deceive Mankind, but of what use would that be to our immediate work? Instead we should approach it as it is, a collection of allegories, fables and faery stories. Then it has quaint interest. Further, as meditations upon the Infinite. This approach does not lead us into harm, but we are able to extract that which is of use to us, and fits with our universe. Instead of dwelling upon errors, which are misalignments, we seek resonance. We look for the golden wheat amongst the dross. We comprehend where our universes overlap, and then we find elucidating examples of experience.
This dangerous task can only be properly performed by a Master of the Temple.
Crowley's attention to detail is helpful for the Magician. He provides a fine example. One of his most useful contributions are the elaborate descriptions of the stages of the Magician's journey: from the aspirant's pilgrimage, across the Wilderness

to Adeptship, to eventually become Master of the Temple, and ultimately Magus of his own Universe.

Crowley really *was* a Magus; he knew what he was doing, and he put in the great efforts required. It was correct for him in the field of his magickal aura, to phrase it thus.

That doesn't imply in any way that to follow his footsteps would be the right way for Doris from number 47, or for anyone else. For one thing she isn't a Magus, and never will be. She might call herself a High Priestess if she wants to, but then she might equally bethink herself to be the Queen of Sheba. Is it reality? is the question. Is this truly her unique magickal fingerprint?

What is reality in that context? We mean how closely does the expressed 'truth' align with the Absolute Reality of the universes. Does God agree or disagree that Doris is the Queen of Sheba? Or, as Crowley had it: is it the True Will of Self?

5 Ill met by moonlight

Here is the destiny of the Magician revealed: he swears his
terrible oath as Master of the Temple. He has ascended unto the
High Place. He is sate with the Gods in power and majesty.
Yet he is not free from the Ordeals.
It is here, when he has ascended to the Plateau, if he does not
rest in easy retirement, languid in this Heavenly Paradise that
he has hard won, but takes upon himself the Mantle of Light,
so as to aid humanity at its struggle, then must he surrender his
accomplishment. His magickal weapons are destroyed. The
Wand has been shattered. The blade of the Dagger is blunted
and ruined. The Cup is o'erturned, and the Pantacle clove
asunder.
He is cast down from the High Place. The Gods abandon him
to the Wilderness, wherein long ago he was first formed as
Adept. His Angel, always the faithful and truest friend, is silent.
It is the Descent into Deepest Endless Falling.
He is cast down, down into the utter abysses. Alone and
powerless, he awakens on a strange shore. Now is the Ordeal of
the Magus.

It is far easier to not comprehend God and the Universe than to
commit oneself to the long and gruelling road of spiritual
purification and consecration. The individual work of raising
ego-mind to power is very simple indeed, and takes absolutely
no effort at all.
The man of mathematics replaces the idea of God with his own
intellect. I am so clever, he thinks to himself, that I have
transcended God. Yet it was God that was the sparking Idea that
ignited into life all the perfections of the Multraverses.
The ego-mind gets so caught up in its self-flattering that it
forgets that it is powerless to bring about any effect soever
without the support of the universes.
The Magician is aware that every effect is produced, never by
a solitary will, but always by a great number of converging
factors. To remain correct in his Magickal Stance the Magician
says: *My Act was probably a factor in that effect.* Thus does he

regard the Gods, and their vital role in all his Magickal Arts. We can not sensibly remove the universe from our study of the universe. We may concentrate our attention on one small area of the universe's truth, but doing so can never prove that the universe does not exist in a real tangible material sense.

God and the universes are inseparable. They are one and the same thing. The limitless multiverses are the Body of the Divine. The original Point is God. Everything that extended from there is the Way. How then could we logically say that God is ever unnecessary or redundant, or not real, or dead? Neither does the harnessing of electricity prove that lightnings do not exist.

The universes continue. We are alive at this moment, in a physical body in the corporeal realm; that is proof that the universe is a solid reality. It exists; ergo God, which is the limitless universes and all things, exists unendingly.

When the premise of who and what the Divine may be is incorrect, it follows that every conclusion drawn from that premise is likely to also be fundamentally incorrect. 'God' is a very large, broad and deep Talisman. We cannot express its symbol in full, only in parts, like concentric circles moving in to a centre. The mind can tremble when facing such vast and awesome power, so we must take care.

A man who has devoted all his study to number has no other experience of the Divine. His conclusions will always be expressed in number.

It is correct to say that Father Christmas isn't real, but Father Christmas was never the Divine Limitless All.

The first task of the Magus, once he has found a stable corner within the ever shifting realities of his Ordeal, is to establish his Word and his New Religion.

Let us first clarify our meaning when we are referring to these various grades and stages, such as Aspirant, Adept, Master of the Temple, Magus. They are borrowed directly from the maps drawn up by Aleister Crowley.

Just as he quickened and invigorated the realms of Western Occult Philosophy with his opulent vision, so too he was called upon to salvage the wreckage that was Freemasonry.

He discusses in his *Confessions* how he rewrote the Masons' woeful sacred magickal texts, brought meaning and coherence to their rituals, and introduced a tiered system of meaningful spiritual instruction. Later, he would establish his own Orders. Crowley took his work as a Magician seriously. He was dedicated and thorough in establishing his New Religion. The canvas upon which he painted his Universe of Magick was broad and wide; he transformed and cleansed the entire environment of Occultism and Magick.

He deftly and delicately integrated and firmly established techniques and meditations of Eastern Mysticism as essential tools of the Magician.

He is also, almost incidentally, one of the fathers of modern Witchcraft, according to Amado Crowley. He was paid for his services by Gerald Gardner to write the Book of Shadows. Armed with this grimoire Gardner went on to set up the modern Wiccan religion.

We have already made reference to the Magician whom Crowley believed to have been a previous incarnation of his Soul, Eliphas Levi, and his involvement with the authorship of *The Book of the Sacred Magic of Abra Melin the Mage.* Occult authors have frequently employed such embellishments or devices; it makes their books more appealing and exciting. It appears to lend an authenticity to their claims. Perhaps they have been given instructions and secret tomes by Hidden Masters, or they found an ancient manuscript in a cave somewhere in Tibet. It's all very poetic and impressive. But it's just theatre, darling.

The Pilgrimage of the Magician, the True Holy Man of God, begins humbly, and his road is long and beset with obstacles, trails and ordeals. It is a journey that encompasses his entire life, passing through stages until it reaches its destination. Thus, if they are in some wise common, tangible and recognisable, we might broadly define the peaks and the depths of that journey.

From his own direct experiences as a Magician and mystic, and from his experiences through teaching his magick, Crowley drew the details of his map. He established the system of Magickal Grades to mark the spiritual progression of the man from his beginnings as a Neophyte or Aspirant, through to the Grade of Magus. The hieroglyphs are large and vivid enough that we can resonate with them. Then the images and records can be signposts pointing our way. They can reassure, clarify and elucidate.

The sense then in which we refer to the Magickal Grades are as the signposts which mark the twists and turns in the long road of the Magician's journey.

We don't seek after grades as compensations. They have scant relevance outside of Freemasonry and Magickal Philosophy. As pointers they give a general direction to pursue, and an approximate location on the Path.

6 The Master Therion

As I began writing parts of *The Magicks Tome* I returned to Crowley's *Magick in Theory and Practice*. I hadn't read it since my early twenties. It was interesting and illuminating coming back around to it.

At twenty years old I loved Crowley's High Prose, and I loved his angelic and daemonic themes, all the Grand Magicks of his theatre. Yet I found him often obscure, and studying his works was a labyrinthine process.

Reading *Magick in Theory and Practice* again, I was pleasantly surprised with the correspondences between it and my own work. From the top of the Sacred Mountain the view is panoramic, and how one arrives there, whichever widdering route, is of small consequence. Much of what in youth was boggling and baffling is now clear and apparent.

I wrote most of *The Aeon Rasa* during winter 2021. I acquired a copy of *Magick in Theory and Practice* and read it in February 2022. Had I come back around to it before writing *The Aeon Rasa* then my book would have doubtless been quite different; I would probably have avoided many of my themes as being repetitious of Crowley's work.

I have expressed these Ideas very differently from Crowley, who wrote from the view of High Ceremonial Magick; my approach is perhaps predominately a Mystic Meditative Invocation of the Holy Guardian Angel. Yet it is really the same essay.

I had stopped reading and studying Crowley's work completely since about 1992. Much of what I express in this book I didn't comprehend whilst studying Crowley's Thelemic Universe.

The Aeon Rasa is an introduction. It is the ground level of the Magickal Universe of Rasa. I have introduced the broad shapes and colors. I have begun to delineate ideas and forms. It is the outline, the overview. It is only later, when we start adding details, that correspondences become subtler.

I have discussed Crowley quite a lot in these opening chapters. That is because, as I have demonstrated already in small part, we cannot properly look at Western Occultism or Magickal and

Mystical Philosophy without acknowledging the great efforts in recent times that Crowley made. It all leads back to him and his work.

As we have already pointed out, Crowley's work underscores the entire genre of Magickal literature. He is the Light amid the dross. He brings structure, insight, imagination, reason, clarity. He brings authenticity to the Realm of the Magician.

We have useful and helpful contributions to the Magickal Path from varied sources, antiquated and modern, yes, but it is Aleister Crowley who synthesised the whole mess of it into a coherent route to the spiritual perfecting of the Man. There are very few authors who are genuinely writing from the point of view of an Occult Master and Magus.

Every Initiate's truth must be unique and personal. The trick of it is to make your unique truth align with the Multraverse's as closely as possible. We are moving towards the Light not away from it.

The Magickal Universe which the Master Therion constructed is bona fide, and it will aid us in forming and distinguishing our stones. It is nefarious and deep, elaborate and inspired, infinitely complex. He raised it on solid stomes, and it is gyrded with broad beams of reason and logic and beauty. It is a working model of God's Reality. It remains a close approximation of the Reality of the Multraverses. The detail is unique and personal but the sweeping brush strokes are general. He writes with wisdom, humour, and intelligence. He maps out the spiritual journey and that is then a Key. We recognise our own experiences in his universe. His light brightens the Way, and points us home.

Students of magick suspect that all the best secrets are hidden in the fine details. It is fair to say that the study of magick is very much about solving riddles and puzzles. But, as Bruce Lee said: *Don't concentrate on the finger which points to the Moon, or you'll miss all that heavenly glory.*

I am not the same Star that Aleister Crowley was. If I am Magus, then I must build my own Universe. His Magickal Universe, although a fine example of how these things should be properly done, is not perfectly fitted for my unique and personal truth. Of course not. How could it be?

The first matter of Aleister Crowley is that he was, and remains eternally, an Occult Master. This means that being a Teacher of Magick was his job, and his employers were the Gods. It is a very specified role. It comes with heavy responsibility. The Master is fixed then in his position. He must abear the burden of his disciples, he must guide them to Truth. His life is dedicated to instructing Humanity.

In a world of fools, we must teach! said Crowley.

He is compensated for his personal sacrifices. He is given the Keys of Magick. He accesses knowledge and wisdom of Divine profundity. Yet is he specialised, and narrow in his scopes. He cannot veer from his sworn task.

Since I am not an Occult Master how then could the necessary conditions of the universe of my own True Will align perfectly with Crowley's Magickal Universe? The Universe of Thelema is fitted for a Teacher of Magick, with all its connotations. Consider also that Crowley took on the mantle of the *Great Beast 666.* Alongside being a Teacher of Humanity, that is another extremely polarized position.

These distinctions between myself and Crowley, and they are only the very tip of that iceberg, must produce conditions of a radically different order.

The surest way I could enter into and accept his Magickal Universe as being true in every regard would be to enrol as his student. Since he died in 1947 this is not easy to accomplish. Were it possible, then therein he remains in his role as Teacher and Guide, and as his pupil I submit to learn at his feet. For the disciple the Master is God; he is father, mother, brother, lover, friend.

Only in this capacity can I safely and beneficently take on the reality of the Universe of Thelema entirely as my own.

The Master is responsible for the student. Yet, a student, a disciple, an aspirant... these are all temporary positions. The natural conclusion of them is in progression. At some point the student must graduate. The aspirant must Become. What then of the Thelemic Universe? We progress beyond it, blossoming into the gardens of our own unique universe.

If we were a disciple of Crowley and Magickal Philosophies generally then our environment will continue to be shaped by his Ideas and direction. They would be painted from the same palette. We will recognise the themes, the language, the images. But if we are a Star true to our own course, then even with every highlighted correspondence, we need create something new and individual.

One must occasionally inject the reminder that the universe we create must be as close an approximation to God's Reality as possible. It simply isn't going to work if we are lazy about it. The standard is always and forever: does the Multraverse agree that this is Absolute Reality or not?

Perhaps you might want to say that in your Magickal Universe the sky is orange and all the houses are actually built out of cheese. Perhaps you'd like to plant bushes in your front garden that bear blueberry pies as fruits? Well, you can say so, but we can all see that it is not Reality.

When we refine the Truth, getting at the minutiae details, it becomes very much more difficult to be certain of where reality is. The Ideas and concepts can get quite complicated, and matters easily become clouded.

7 **Of the Aeon RASA**

Do I then bring an ending, after an hundred years, to Crowley's Age of Horus; Thelema. The Word of the New Aeon is like a star shining in the dark night. The Word is *Aelinor Rasa*. And the religion which must stand in truth is the Eld Religion, and new woven, and it is in the Word.

Its Name is RASA; which, in one interpretation of its symbols, means: *The Seeing Mind of God.*

In his *Thoth* Crowley says, in relation to the Twentieth Arcanum, the Aeon: *The old card was called The Angel, or The Last Judgement. It represented an Angel or Messenger blowing a trumpet, attached to which was a flag, bearing the symbol of the Aeon of Osiris.*

The card represented the destruction of the world by Fire. This was accomplished, Crowley says, in 1904, *when the fiery god Horus took the place of the airy god Osiris in the East as the Hierophant.*

He continues: *At the bottom of the card we see the letter Shin itself in a form suggestive of a flower; the three Yods are occupied by three human figures arising to partake in the Essence of the new Aeon. Behind this letter is a symbolic representation of the sign of Libra;* (the Eighth Arcanum Adjustment) *this is the forth-shadowing of the Aeon which is to follow this present one, presumably in about 2000 years: 'the fall of the Great Equinox, when Hrumachis shall arise and the double-wanded one assume my throne and place.' The present Aeon is too young to give a more definite representation of this future event. But in this connection attention must be drawn to the figure of Ra-Hoor-Khuit: 'I am the Lord of the Double Wand of Power; the Wand of the Force of Coph Nia; but my left hand is empty, for I have crushed an Universe; & nought remains.'*

He finishes his notes on the Twentieth Arcanum:

The time for the birth of an Aeon seems to be indicated by great concentration of political power with the accompanying improvements in the means of travel and communication, with a general advance in philosophy and science, with a general need of consolidation in religious thought. It is very instructive to compare the events of the five hundred years preceding and following the crisis of approximately 2000 years ago, with those of similar periods centred in 1904 of the old era. It is a thought far from comforting to the present generation, that 500 years of Dark Ages are likely to be upon us. But, if the analogy holds, that is the case. Fortunately, to-day we have brighter torches and more torch-bearers.

As Horus has as his symbol the blazing sun, so the Goddess who represents the Aeon of Rasa has the moon as her symbol. She is the Daughter, the Night, the Lovely Star, Nuith.

8 Crossing the Wilderness

Let us look at an example, taken from 'Appendix III. Notes on the nature of the Astral plane.' Crowley briefly discusses each of the grades of his Magickal Order.
Within this passage I find details that I 'disagree' with, or that do not fit my Universe, yet the main points I align with perfectly.

10. The Grade of Adeptus Minor is the main theme of the instructions of the A. A. It is characterised by the Attainment of the Knowledge and Conversation of the Holy Guardian Angel. This is the essential work of every man; none other ranks with it either for personal progress or for power to help one's fellows. This unachieved, man is no more than the unhappiest and blindest of animals. He is conscious of his own incomprehensible calamity, and clumsily incapable of repairing it. Achieved, he is no less than the co-heir of Gods, a Lord of Light. He is conscious of his own consecrated course, and confidently ready to run it. The Adeptus Minor needs little help or guidance even from his superiors in our Order.

So far I am in agreement with Aleister. The vital and essential work of the Magician is the Ordeal of the Adept. Until then his magicks are narrowly confined. It is the crossing of the Wilderness, which the Magician must do so that he can emerge Adept, and it is the Union with God, expressed by Crowley as the Knowledge and Conversation of the Holy Guardian Angel.
This Union is the vital step to empower all our magicks.
Without it the Magician remains on the far shore of the abyss, and becomes increasingly ineffectual.
There comes the moment when all the universes align for him in absolute harmony. It is then that he must strike out, at exactly that point, committing himself to his Angel, and following it across into the void.
If he miss his timing or his footing slips, then tides turn, and the boat sails. There cannot be another.
The Uniting with the Angel is the first theme of the Work. The

Practices in The Aeon RASA are all to this end. It is the first crux of the Magician's journey. It can not be avoided.

Once he has experienced the Knowledge and Conversation of his Holy Guardian Angel then he will have his own True Guide, and he will be fixed resolutely upon his destiny. The Angel will bring him the keys to real magicks, and lead him out into the Wilderness.

It is impossible to lay down precise rules by which a man may attain to the knowledge and conversation of His Holy Guardian Angel; for that is the particular secret of each one of us; a secret not to be told or even Divined by any other, whatever his grade.

It is the Holy of Holies, whereof each man is his own High Priest, and none knoweth the Name of his brother's God, or the Rite that invokes Him.

Crowley makes an astute observation very neatly. He continues:

Every Magician possesses an Astral Universe peculiar to himself, just as no man's experience of the world is conterminous with that of another. There will be a general agreement on the main points, of course; and so the Master Therion is able to describe the principle properties of these 'planes' and their laws...

Aleister here specifies the unique 'Astral Universe' of each man, and reiterates for us the resonance of the broad shapes. He continues:

...the Magician will be grateful to the Master Therion for the Compass that guides him at night, the Map that extends his comprehension of his country, and shows him how best he may travel afield, the advice as to Sandals and Staff that make surer his feet, and the Book that tells him how, splitting open his rocks with an Hammer, he may be master of their Virgin Gold. But he will understand that his own career on earth is his kingdom, that even the Master Therion is no more than a fellow

man in another valley, and that he must explore and exploit his own inheritance with his own eyes and hands.

The Magician must not accept the Master Therion's account of the Astral Plane, His Qabalistic discoveries, His instructions in Magick. They may be correct in the main for most men; yet they cannot be wholly true for any save Him, even as no two artists can make identical pictures of the same subject.

More, even in fundamentals, though these things be Truth for all Mankind, as we carelessly say, any one particular Magician may be the one man for whom they are false. May not the flag that seems red to ten thousand seem green to some one other? Then, every man and woman being a Star, that which is green to him is verily green; if he consent to the crowd and call it red, hath he not broken the Staff of Truth that he leaneth upon? Each and every man therefore that will be a Magician must explore the Universe for himself.

I am in accord with Crowley on these points. I selected these passages from Appendix III because they closely echo my own thoughts and experience on this matter. Crowley's statements help to elucidate my own, throwing light on the subject, approaching the same theme from a different angle.

The Magician can not take on the universe, the reality, of another. He must instead adapt its truth to properly fit his own True Universe. He will align more or less, depending on where each truth aligns with God.

Crowley confirms our premise that each Magician must construct his own Temple of Absolute Reality, and raise his own unique Magickal Universe, integrated seamlessly with his corporeal life. In harmony and perfect accord with his rasa.

We have begun with *The Aeon Rasa* to lay the foundations of our Divine Temple. It is imperative that we outline these broad shapes and symbols to begin. We must give a general overview of the Work and the Path. Only then can we describe the details of the Magickal Universe, and thereby offer Maps and Signs, and the fruits of our own unique experience and genius.

These details are not so essential as the broad symbols. Within the work *The Magicks Tome* is everything the aspirant and the

Magician needs to ensure their own successful journey to
Union with God. The details are elucidations, refinements, and
peculiar insights. They are the unique progression of the Star,
to use Crowley's term.

We have been diligent in laying our ground. For the Magician
we have also given several extensive examples, collected in
other books, and we shall append some few here, of the
working processes of divers facets of the Crafting.
We have lain our foundations and covered the base of the Work.
Now we can move on to other points of particular interest.

My friend, I did walk the desolate Wilderness, and the Devil with his hounds was always dogging my steps.

I gave up everything I had, and everything I was. All bridges were burning behind me, so that returning to who I had been was not possible. I descended into Hell, and I was alone. It was deeper and more horrifying than any terror I had ever glimpsed or imagined. It was a long dark road, and only my Angel could guide me.

I crossed the Wild Places, and I descended into the Utter, and built a bridge to span that nether realm. The Gods are witness to my trails and my deeds.

'Seeing you as you are makes it all worthwhile,' said Amado, 'all these long lonely years of being Master.'

'My name is a secret name, which all men fear; except the wise. I shall come as the Black Winged Dragon, to devour all the Worlds,' I told him, in response to his questioning.

'You are the Queen,' he said, bending his knee to offer me his Sword in Service.

'Any that come against you come also against me,' he swore.

These are Stones of Truth. It is for you to find their application in the Crafting of your own Magickal Universe.

Here shalt the RELIGION of RASA be established. Yea, shalt it be ESTABLISHED.

Now is the Aeon of Night.

*

The One Father

9 Of the singular strangeness

When a written work claims Divine inspiration above common creativity we must be sceptical before accepting that it really does come from God. Every scriptural document was initially filtered through the mind and by the hand of a man. Even the purest inspiration is diluted via the process.

We must scrutinize the material to try to find out whether or not the claim of Divine authorship is justified. An active scepticism is particularly necessary when someone (or a group of people) claims a work to be the unadulterated Word of God Almighty.

If it is God's Pure Word then of course we must pay close attention to everything that he said. But if it is the work of ego-mind masquerading as Divine then we must undeceive ourselves.

It is to state the obvious, yet people gamble their Souls on far less than certainty.

Samson and Delilah was probably my favorite out of the Old Testament Bible stories I heard as a child. It's a great story. Samson was the strongest man in the world, for a start.

There are many incidents described in the Biblical book of Judges, chapters fourteen on, concerning the life of Samson which are miraculous. They are very bold statements for the author to have made. It is precisely these points which we should first examine when looking for truth. When they describe events contrary to the natural laws of the universe it should make our Spidey senses tingle.

We shall briefly consider just a few examples of the miraculous events described.

The story opens with Samson's barren mother being visited by an angel with news that she will soon bear a child.

This is a familiar scene recurring throughout the Bible. It might seem that the mothers of saints are always either barren or virgin? Angels are frequent heralds. It tends to the realm of myth. Which is not to say it could not have been a real event, accurately related. But, we must take note. If true, it is a miraculous occurrence. The angel returns on the following day, so as to meet the father of Samson.

When Samson is a young man he encounters a lion, and tears it apart with his bare hands. Young, unarmed men aren't ordinarily capable of killing lions. It's an extraordinary deed. Again it tends to myth, presenting Samson as a hero who wouldn't be out of place amongst the Greek and Roman legends: as the great warrior, blessed and favored by the Gods, performing wondrous feats of strength and dexterity. A bit like Achilles, perhaps?

Hmm, and we later discover that like Achilles' heel, Samson also has a fatal flaw of singular strangeness.

A few days after he has killed the lion he discovers a bee's nest inside the carcass' belly. There is enough honey that he carries some away with him and eats it. I'm not a bee-keeper, but as far as I'm aware it takes bees quite a bit longer than a couple of days to draw the raw materials for the comb, to form a hive, and produce a crop of honey. Which places this event in the realm of magick.

Jehovah has here flouted the natural laws of the universe apparently just in case Samson might be hungry.

Samson is still just a young man without any demonstration of especial spiritual purity, he has done nothing remarkable to win the Gods' favour before he tare the beast. The subtle suggestion is that he was born favoured and followed by the angels, the son of a favored people.

We are only a chapter into Samson's story, glossing over and highlighting the main scenes. Already we have enough details to challenge credulity.

We might ask who is it that claims that the books of the Bible are the actual Word of God? Many of the Old Testament stories seem fantastic and mythological. It might be more rational to consider them in the same way as legends and symbolic allegories.

It is unclear who the human author of Judges was. The book is considered to have been written between 1400BC and 1050BC. It describes numerous incredible events; already we have seen a barren woman giving birth, people talking with angels, super human feats, miracles, and magicks.

Why was it included in the collection of books of the Old

Testament?

It describes events which are outside of the natural laws of the universe. Things that can't happen in this reality. Usually we classify such stories as fiction or fable or faery stories. What was it that identified the story, in the minds of the ecclesiastics, as being from the pen of God Almighty himself?

Whoever compiled the books into the collection of the Jewish scriptures surely must have been cautious and diligent when sorting the chaff from the wheat. We would hope for and expect integrity and honesty and spiritual purity from the team that brought us the Bible, right?

If we don't know who the author of Judges was then we don't know whether he was a saint or a madman. Why should we trust his version of events? We therefore can only weigh the authenticity and value of the book by its own content.

Judges Fifteen takes the story into bizarre realms, where after strange adventures Samson slays a thousand warriors, armed only with the jawbone of an ass.

That didn't happen in this corporeal reality.

The beam is overburdened and the house collapses.

10 Of the serpent and the rod

Now Moses was a young man, and was out for a stroll on the mountain pathways. He came across a flaming bush, and a voice addressed him.

'It's me, God,' said the voice, seeming to come from the burning foliage. 'You'll like this one. Throw down your staff, go on.'

So Moses throws his rod down, and Kaboom! it turns into a serpent.

'What the heck,' says Moses.

'Now grab it by the tail,' says God.

And lo! the serpent becomes a rod once more.

The voice directs Moses to go to the court of the Pharaoh, to persuade him to release God's people from bondage.

'Throw down your staff and I will turn it into a serpent,' God commands him.

Moses goes before Pharaoh and says: 'Take a look at this, Pharaoh! Rod serpent, serpent rod! Pretty neat, huh?'

Then the court magicians are all like: 'Oh, that's so last season. We can all do that.'

That never happened.

The subtle point the story seems to be making is that the court magicians, who are presented as devil worshippers and sorcerers, have real magickal power and can perform miracles equal to the Holy Men of God.

11 Of nefarious machinations

Perhaps we should ask where and when and by whom was the Old Testament compiled? Does anyone know?

We have computers and internet access, so of course we can find out. We discover that the Jewish scriptures (the term Old Testament being a Christian perspective) were compiled somewhat haphazardly across centuries. The 49 books were apparently collected in the time of Ezra around 400BC, but this date is disputed.

We can't really be sure who decided that those books were the ones which should make up the Jewish canon.

The majority of the books, including the Torah, are thought to have been written around 600BC to 535BC, during the Jews' Babylonian captivity. Again, this attempt at dating the scriptures seems somewhat dubious and uncertain if one examines the detail and fine print.

The origins of the collection are nefarious and ambiguous. We don't know who the original authors of many of the books were. If Moses didn't write the Torah, the first five books of the Jewish canon, who did?

Should we trust that this hap-hazard process has resulted in a collection of scriptures that are the unadulterated Word of God Almighty? Regardless of their content, it would be naive of us to do so.

The Jews' position, supported by those scriptures, is that they are God's First Children. They are his chosen ones, thus superior and favored and privileged above all other races.

Those other non-Jewish races are referred to throughout the Bible as 'heathen' or 'Gentiles' or 'the uncircumcised.' They are outside of God's law, and do not have his blessing. They are without Divine Soul, and for them there is no paradise afterlife. They are not worth much more to Jehovah than the beasts of the Earth.

The God of the Old Testament seems to be a god of war and conquest. The books are a catalogue of barbarous slaughter and rapine. Jehovah is irritable, petty, vengeful, and obscure. He leads his people via his prophets through centuries of bizarre and often murderous adventures.

His people never seem to get it right, or get to anywhere worthwhile. Despite the constant performing of miracles by Jehovah and his prophets, the Jews are perpetually at odds with their God, and he continues to punish them. He is a God of conflict and retribution.

Have we not seen that the impulse of the Divine is motivated towards harmony? Contrarily, Tetragrammaton, the Mighty God of the Bible, is all about Division and Punishment. Monotheistic philosophy sets the Creation in opposition to the core. Humanity is a brotherhood. There is not one race amongst Humanity that has been elevated to a special status by the universe. No one group of people receive extra credits by default. The universe's favor or displeasure has nothing to do with which religion our parents followed, not which corner of the planet we were born on. The Gods are not interested in ego-mind books of rules of conduct, nor are they impressed by nationality. Library membership cards won't be much use either. The universe sees who we are, and everything that we do.

On further investigation we discover that the Jewish canon of books was joined with the New Testament sometime during the second century AD.

This was arranged by the Catholic Church, those fine fellows who would later bring us the Church Militant, the doctrines of Hell and Eternal Torment, and the torturous Inquisitors, and become the traditional bedfellows of Political Corporations.

What conclusions can we draw from this about the Bible, and in particular the books of the Jewish scriptures?

It is not our purpose here to analyse every incident of the Old Testament. We have highlighted only a few examples of where the scriptures are dubious, and appear to venture into fable, and thus challenge its claim to be the Holy and Pure Word of Almighty God. Rather than being exceptions, the highlighted incidents are typical of the entire collection.

We might easily proceed with the analytical investigation of the material, and in doing so we would be likely to accrue a mass of evidence of similar quality and kind.

When we approach the work looking for absolute truth every page of the scriptures raises serious questions. As a history of factual events it is highly dubious.

In light of our conclusions regarding the Jewish scriptures, the Old Testament, we should be likewise cautious in dealing with the New Testament.

The same group of Catholic ecclesiastics that determined the books which would make up the 39 books of the Old Testament also had charge over which books would be included in the New Testament. The Vulgar version of the Bible, containing sixty six books in all.

We must conclude that their judgement was doubtful, since the Jewish scriptures are mostly fables and propaganda rather than the unadulterated Word of God Almighty. If those priests were 'led by the holy spirit' as is claimed by the Church, then they probably would have spotted that the Jewish scriptures were of doubtful origin and validity, and rejected them. They were of course led by political machinations instead.

It is no surprise that corporate and political bodies would be directly involved with the publication and distribution of such a powerful document. They are the overseers of state religions.

The books should never have been presented as accurate history, or as a book of rules which must be obeyed.

The Old Testament is given credibility by being bound with the New Testament.

The New Testament at least shows a little more coherence in its structuring.

It begins with the Gospels, which are ostensibly eye witness accounts. Then we have a couple of books attributed to John, the favoured disciple who reclined on the Lord's breast. The book of Revelation, also by John, concludes the canon. There are a few short epistles claiming various authorship, and the bulk of the twenty seven books are the letters of St Paul to the congregations. As a collection of books it makes sense, more or less.

We have evidence to support the fact of Jesus Christ's life in this world; not least the Roman accounts referencing him. It seems likely that he was a real person, a teacher and a prophet of God.

Jesus' message was direct and simple. He didn't complicate things with unnecessary bureaucracy and rules of conduct. *Try to be a good person in all that you do*, was more or less what he was getting at. *Love God with your whole heart, mind, and soul*, he said. *This is greater than all the rules of Law.* The quality of genius is in its ability to simplify; it finds the quickest, easiest solution. Christ reveals himself to be an Initiate of Great Power. His teaching is characteristic of genius; it is deceptively simple. In that phrase, *love God with your whole heart, mind, and soul. This is greater than all the rules of Law,* he gifts every man a Supreme Key of Magick, if only they can heed him.

Some people live their lives believing in the Corporate Religion, and they do their best to follow every guideline. Many are sincere, and this type of religious devotion is for them the highest plateau of worship. They will live their entire lives in the Church, and their body will eventually be buried in its graveyard. For the Magician, manifested as a man, the way is somewhat different, and his religion is instinctive, vital and alive. He must erect a temple of Absolute Truth, and shun every form of delusion and self-deception.

The circumstances in which the Bible was compiled are cause for concern. It is quite clearly a work motivated and manipulated by inferior minds; regardless of the integrity and excellence of some of its authors. Therefore we must be careful to extract the chaff from the golden wheat when we contemplate its theology.

It is not the unadulterated Word of Almighty God.

It is on par with most other spiritual texts in that it contains truth and beauty, and it contains ego-mind nonsense. There are also deliberate lies and fabrications.

We cannot include it as a stone for our foundations.

However, we can draw the pure essence from the New Testament, which is apparent depending upon our own proximity to the centre. Jesus was a real person, after all. Most likely.

We can still resonate with his spirit and his wisdom, despite the embellishments of the Bible. Let us be cautious and sceptical of the miraculous events described. Like much of the Old Testament, they tend to myth and propagandas.

12 Of the Great Work

Rather than regarding scriptures as the unadulterated Word of
God Almighty, and therefore immutable, inflexible and
unchanging truth, we would be wise to approach them only
with caution. We can find beauty, poetry, and truth there.
They are the works of men, and the origin of their inspiration
is self-evident.
The truth of God is alive. It experiences and grows. It adapts
and is motivated to perfection. It will not be constricted by, nor
entombed in, systems of ineffable rules. Trying to confine it
into narrow spaces, one size fits all, is a mistake.
What are we left with when we step aside from the corporate
versions of who and what God is?
When we put aside the scriptural definitions what remains is
that which we see and experience of Divinity.
The ancient masters of the Way used abstracts to describe the
Divine. This is helpful, because we resonate easily with broad
symbols.

Man has been violently coerced away from his natural life.
Can he raise himself from the pyre before he has lost
everything? Somehow he must get himself back onto his true
path.
The ancient masters spoke of the Great Work. They labored to
bring about a Golden Age for Humanity.
As civilisation staggers towards complete collapse, one may
conclude that the Great Work has come to nought, and that
perhaps the Will of the Gods was not with them.
The masters of antiquity, who have passed their teachings on
both through scripture and by word of mouth, eye to eye with
their disciples, worked in harmony with the motivations of the
universe. They invigorated and quickened the Way. When we
distil their lives and philosophies into simple broad symbols
we see that they were the agents and the prophets of the
Essence. They urged Man to raise himself up, and to become
like the Divine. Because they resonated with the Way their
works were fruitful.

Did they foresee the rise to power, in every seat, of the inferior minds which control the global criminal organisations and governments? What happens to a society in which the political and bureaucratic systems operate only for the benefit of the criminals? It is a situation which can only lead to great evil for the common man. Civilisation will fall, and Humanity has entered a Dark Age.

The collapse of civilisation will not be an act of Divine retribution. Instead it is the logical consequence of criminal management.

Cowards do not have the wherewithal to move in a contrary direction to ego, and they will not find the narrow road of truth. The Magician, the Actualised Man, is a rare bird, like the Bird of Paradise obliged to fly against the wind. He is always driven to the edges of society, since he is an oddity. His true work shall be in nefarious quarters, unsung and unseen. There have been true masters of the Way, and prophets, and pure holy men of God. The Divine personified in them. It was through these men that the Essence worked.

13 Of the Antagonist

Outside of scripture, what do we know about the Devil?
The Western concept of the Devil is almost entirely derived
from the Old and New Testament accounts, and the character
apparently originates there. We should probably look at the
scriptural description of Satan.
He is ambiguous and obscure. There is not much detail.

The term 'the Devil' is not used in the Jewish scriptures. 'Devils'
and 'unclean spirits' are frequently referenced however.
Possession by these spirits is a common occurrence. The word
'demon' isn't used in either the Old or New Testament.
In Genesis there is the serpent, who is the Beguiler and the
Antagonist. The serpent is not identified as the Devil or Satan,
although we see echoes of the character in the serpent. Instead
it is referred to as the 'most subtle' of the beasts God has made.
The serpent is capable of speech, and beguiles the woman.
God says that there will always be enmity between the seed of
the woman, and the seed of the serpent. The suggestion may be
that the Jewish race is born from Adam and Eve, and the
Gentiles are born from the serpent.
The author of Genesis does not expand on this strange
description of the serpent, who acts as the Antagonist to God,
and Adam and Eve; he says nothing about the nature of the
serpent or its motivations. Once it has beguiled the woman, and
God has cursed them all, the serpent is not directly mentioned
in the scriptures again.
Isn't that rather peculiar, and convenient? The serpent, created
by Jehovah, is indirectly responsible for the 'Fall of Man,'
having deliberately coaxed the woman, aware of the
consequences of the deed it enticed her to. Surely the serpent
will prove to be a pivotal character as the plot unfolds? Who is
the serpent? Where did it come from? Where did it go? Why
did Jehovah create it, and allow it to tempt Adam and Eve?
These questions are not raised by Yahweh's prophets, and the
serpent dematerialises back into the aethers, or something,
never to be seen again.

'Satan' is only directly mentioned in three books of the Jewish scriptures: the Book of Job, 1Chronicles, and Zechariah. Besides those three appearances of Satan, there are also brief references to Leviathan, Behemoth, Beelzebub, and Lucifer. We might take these entities as symbols of the forces of darkness and evil. They form a conglomerate personification, and their distinctions blur. Later Gnosticism would provide a detailed catalog of their proper hierarchy.

Isaiah 27:2 *In that day the Lord with his sore and great and mighty sword shall visit Leviathan, that piercing serpent, even Leviathan, that crooked serpent, and he shall slay the dragon that is in the sea.*

Isaiah also makes the only reference to Lucifer in the Bible, at Isaiah 14. We have further mention of Leviathan in Job, where Jehovah describes Leviathan as a magnificent creature, bejewelled and living in the seas. Behemoth is similarly described.

1 Chronicles 21 begins: *And Satan stood up against Israel, and provoked David to number Israel.* That is the first appearance of Satan. Chronicles is set during the days of David and Goliath. Next comes the Book of Job, and this book elevates Satan in numerous ways. Here is he seen in the role of every man's tormentor and antagonist.

Satan is revealed to be one of the 'Children of God,' or angels. He appears to have a special relationship with Jehovah. There is no enmity apparent between them. Are they working towards the same end? is the unarticulated question. Jehovah delivers Job up, and allows Satan to work his worst.

Satan is accepted amongst the Children of God. His work as the tormentor of men is an especial role, neither good nor bad in itself. Jehovah does not expel him from his presence. He doesn't destroy him. He doesn't view Satan as an enemy, but as the executor of the Divine will, as the Bringer of Woes and the Tester of men.

In Zechariah he appears only in a vision, at the right hand of Christ, to resist him. He is there reproved by God. Zechariah 3: *And he showed me Joshua the high Priest, standing before the Angel of the Lord, and Satan stood at his right hand to resist him. And the Lord said unto Satan, The Lord reprove thee, O Satan: even the Lord that hath chosen Jerusalem, reprove thee. Is not this a brand taken out of the fire?*

Who the author of the Book of Job was is unclear. It is attributed to Ezekiel and also to Moses (and, why not?) but there is no direct evidence of its having been written by either. What are we to conclude from these three references?

First, we notice that Satan is not a prominent character in the Jewish scriptures. He is not the Israelite's antagonist. Not that is, until he suddenly appears in 1Chronicles in that very role, as he stands up against Israel.

Besides the Book of Job we have only two slim references. A total of three verses. Is it possible those verses were added after the fact? Without them Job's version of Satan is a total anomaly. Even with them, the character described in Job is almost entirely incongruous with the rest of the Jewish canon. Where was he during all the adventures of the Jews? Where was he in the days of Samson? Why wasn't he there tempting Moses?

It is the Book of Job which establishes Satan's role as the Tempter. It is in Job that we learn that he is an angel, and that he has an especial role in God's work. This is the idea of Satan as the Devil in Western consciousness.

Is the Book of Job a work of Satanist propaganda? It prepares the way, supported by the brief mention in the vision of Zechariah, and with the New Testament Satan has become the Antagonist. He is the Father of Lies, the enemy of Christ, God. He is now the opponent of all men.

The only solid connection between the Satan of the Jewish scriptures and Satan as the Devil in the New Testament is the link provided by Job.

We must be sceptical and ask: was the Book of Job added to the collection of Jewish scriptures in the Old Testament specifically for the purpose of continuity, with a view to establishing the character of the Devil? To create a solid link from the old to the new, in which the Devil was ready to become the tormentor of the common man. It seems likely.

We might add that incidentally Satanism and divers devil

worship cults hinge on the postulated reality of the Book of Job.

Satan makes his appearance proper in the second act of the
Bible, in the Gospels, as he tempts Christ in the desert.
Christ clearly identifies Satan as the enemy, the Antagonist, and
that idea is at the crux of Christianity. Now, in the Gospels, we
see him in the role of the Devil of Western consciousness. He
is the Deceiver, and the Devourer of Souls.
1 Peter 5:8 *Be sober and watch: for your adversary the Devil
as a roaring lion walketh about, seeking whom he may devour.*
Since the book of Job, Satan has led the revolt in Heaven, and
he and a third of the angels have been cast down and bound to
the physical realm of the Earth. He is now actively at war with
God.

The Jewish scriptures are generally about Jehovah leading his
chosen people from bondage to their promised land. They are
not an accurate history of events, but a collection of myths and
fables and legends.
We might bear in mind that even today the Jews have not
accepted that Christ was the Messiah their scriptures pointed
to.
Conversely the New Testament references the Jewish scriptures
extensively. The writers are Jewish, and their society lived by
the Law of Moses. They revere the prophets of the Old
Testament. Christ himself is well versed in scripture, and
identifies with the Jewish prophets, but claims to have brought
an end to the Law of Moses.
The writers of the New Testament bring a lot of legitimacy to
the Jewish scriptures. They write as though the fables and faery
stories of the Old Testament were all proven realities. They
accept those scriptures as the true Word of God Almighty. The
Torah is a holy and sacred collection of texts which describe
real events, and was written down by Moses: the Jews are the
First Children of God, his Chosen People.
Jehovah, vengeful, petty, war-like, a nefarious god of conquest
and retribution, is God Almighty.
It all smacks of deliberate propaganda.

It opens the way for the Catholic doctrines of Hell and Eternal Torment, and of the corrupt state of the Soul of man, born an irredeemable sinner, whose salvation can only come from Christ and the Church.

It opens the way for the Church Militant, whose word can never be disputed, having come directly from God. And for the Pope, God's incarnated representative on Earth.

The God created by the myths of the Old Testament is supported by the new religion, even though it breaks away from the Jewish Law of Moses. The Jewish God in return supports the fearsome doctrines of Catholicism; we have seen already that Jehovah is a wrathful God of punishment.

Priests were intermediaries between the Divine and the common man, who was often illiterate. The Church soon became very rich and influential.

After trying to tempt Christ in the wilderness Satan does not make another appearance in the Gospels. Yet he is referred to continuously throughout the New Testament, in his role as the Enemy of God and every man. It is Christ who establishes Satan in that role. He says he saw Satan falling from Heaven like lightning.

In John 13 it describes Judas being possessed by the Devil: *and after the sop, Satan entered into him. Then Jesus said unto him, That thou doest, doest quickly.*

Possession by unclean spirits and devils is frequent throughout the New Testament. Jesus, and his true followers, are able to cast the spirits and devils out. They are also able to cure blindness, leprosy, heal the lame, and even raise the dead back to life. In the book of Acts they are able to strike men dead with a word.

The New Testament sells the broad ideas: firstly, Jehovah is God Almighty. The Jews are the First and the Chosen people. The Divine can only be approached through the Church. Man is base, worthless, corrupted, and Jehovah is a God of punishment. The Devil is actively pursuing every common man, and intends to devour them all. Only the Church can protect the common man from the Devil's wrath. The Bible is the absolute truth of God, written by God Almighty himself, through the pure and holy scribes.

The character of the Devil was then elaborated upon outside of the Bible, as the figure entered the collective consciousness. Details were embellished or imagined, in scripture and lore and literature, and in colloquial interpretations. He assumed various roles, and his powers and legends waxed and morphed.

We have an overview of the Devil, and his Biblical origins. It tends to fable. Only the book of Job describes Satan as in an especial position, working as Jehovah's henchman. With the Gospels he is firmly established as the enemy, at war with God, and has been attributed all sorts of powers. He has become the

Prince of the Earth.

Our cursory investigation of the material has revealed the New Testament to be almost as dubious as the Old Testament.

We conclude that it cannot be the Absolute Truth of Almighty God, and ergo neither can any philosophy founded upon it. From what we might logically surmise, it appears likely that the Bible was deliberately constructed as a political weapon. Its probable intension was to establish Christianity as a dominant religion.

Christianity was built upon the pyre of the rural and druidic faiths that were natural to Europe. It all but wiped them out, persecuting their practitioners and followers as devil worshippers. It absorbed into itself much of the colloquial detail and imagery, the festivals, and even the Gods, adapting its mysteries to suit local tastes.

The old religions were forced below the surface.

We cannot consider the Bible as an accurate source. Yet, the prevalent Western idea of who and what the Devil is is based entirely on those scriptures. Everything that followed was an elaboration or an invention.

The Devil may not have been the creation of the New Testament authors, but they launched his career, and secured his position. He was a Bogey Man to subdue the common man into thraldom and servitude.

That is not to say the Devil is not real or does not exist at all; any more than the Bible's dubious origins and functions should prove that God does not exist. Those are not logical continuations. But the scriptural version of him is not reliable, and must therefore be disregarded. The Devil which exists in the collective mythology of the Western mind is drawn entirely from this unreliable source. It likewise must be disregarded. If the Devil is real we need to look elsewhere to discover the truth about him. Perhaps only direct experience is reliable.

Similarly, the corrupt source of the material, and the criminal intentions which probably motivated its publication, have no bearing on the reality or unreality of Jesus Christ as a human being.

Jesus was a teacher and a prophet, and a powerful one. His essence resonates still, two thousand years later. The Gospel stories contain timeless wisdom, and the story of Christ is beautiful and moving.

Christ is the little piece of chocolate for the discerning palate. The jewel of truth buried in the mire of falsehood. His light makes everything look brighter. He brings authenticity. Even the numerous miracles attributed to him, and in his name, seem plausible.

Once we attempt to look beyond the Bible's reality we see how insidious it has been, how far reaching its impact. The Western mind has been shaped by it.

Without the scriptures there is only the silent wilderness.

15 **Of the New Religion**

All these numbers are of course parts of the magician himself considered as the microcosm. The microcosm is an exact image of the Macrocosm; the Great Work is the raising of the whole man in perfect balance to the power of Infinity.
Aleister Crowley.

Once we conclude that the Bible is a book of mythological propaganda, then, regardless of its content, it follows that its purpose was to sell the new religion: Christianity. The new religion was a reinvigorating of Jehovah. It was Monotheism for the masses.

Christ was probably a real prophet, but not in the way the New Testament writers claim. He is unlikely to have performed public miracles. It doesn't make sense for him to have done so, on a magickal level. Instead, the accounts of his miracles are more likely to have been fabulous embellishments of his career. True men of God usually shun magickal displays and public demonstrations of power. What good did any of those miracles do for Christ and his work? According to the Gospels they brought him a lot of troubles. They were mostly petty tricks, if we might phrase it so. Turning water into wine, healing random people he met of blindness and leprosy, cursing the fig tree. They would have been frivolous displays of power if he had really performed such magicks.

We are reminded how the Old Testament makes similar claims to the frequent miracles powered by Jehovah. He is the God of miracles, we might say.

If Jesus was working frequent miracles then he must be sanctioned and supported by the Divine. His power to work startling magicks proves the power of Jehovah. Christ later bequeaths his magickal abilities to his disciples, and they become workers of miracles too.

Those miraculous acts do not conform to the natural laws of the universe. We must be very cautious before accepting any claim which if true would involve the suspension of natural laws. It is reasonable to suppose that God wouldn't suspend natural laws unless it were *vital* to do so. A very rare occurrence in other words. Or, never.

Not that magicks cannot happen, but that's not how the universe usually works. It's how Jehovah works in his universe, yes. Yet, frivolous usurping of the natural order is not the Act of an Almighty God; Jehovah often reminds one of a petulant teenager.

The Universe lays its plans at the Beginning.

The powers later attributed to Christ's disciples, especially in the book of Acts, are equally unlikely. That is not to dismiss them as impossible, because, again, God could transcend natural laws if he so willed, but it would be a more logical progression to conclude that, as with the Old Testament, the scriptures of the New Testament tend to myth rather than being an accurate record of events.

The Qabalah is a Jewish system of numerology. Western Occultism is heavily influenced by the Qabalah, and particularly in the arena of Ceremonial and Ritual Magick. The Goetia, the Book of Evil Spirits, is a catalog of Jewish demonology. The princes of Gnostic lore are demons drawn directly from Jewish scripture, as are the angelic names, with elaborations and embellishments and inventions.

Satan and his cronies are all Yiddish demons.

Why was the idea of Satan as the Devil so important to the ecclesiastics who financed and produced the Bible? Perhaps because they wanted to sell the idea of an antagonist pursuing every man, seeking to devour him, to destroy his Soul and damn him to an eternal torment.

The purpose of the new religion was to control the world. And the world's resources and wealth, of course.

The old religions which had existed since pre-history were outlawed and violently suppressed, their practitioners branded as devil worshippers. Druidism, nature rites, faeries and folk remedies, natural magicks and goddess worship were all viewed as sorceries by the Church, and were aggressively persecuted.

The violent suppression of opposition is a tactic representative of Fascism. Could the Holy Church of God Almighty be raised on such a foundation and retain God's blessing?

Dark and vicious gods sanction murder and violence and domination. On the contrary, the Divine Force is harmonious, tending towards perfection.

By their works shall you know them.

Women, who in the old religion were magickal embodiments of the universe's yielding energies, the companion and complement of the man, goddesses, high priestesses, muses and seers, were now degraded to the role of slaves with the New Religion.

We must reject any theological system which fails to recognize the Goddess alongside the God, a perfect combination of harmonious complementary energies. We must reject it because we see the overwhelming evidence of its error. The manifested multiverses are first Male and Female. God is the Manifested Multiverses; it is the Body of the Divine, formed from the distinguished powers of God. He is those energies, virtues and powers. To claim there is no Goddess equal with the Masculine God is to deny the First Principal of the Universe.

Humanity as a whole was degraded by Christianity from its position as the Glorious Microcosm, the living reflection and embodiment of the Divine, to the role of the wretched sinner, born corrupted and worthless.

You shall have no other God than me, demands Jehovah. In this one phrase Jehovah reveals himself to be a False God.

The One Father of Monotheism is a god of Ego-mind, and his philosophies are eloquent sophisms.

The Law of Moses excluded non-Jews so a revamp was necessary if the new religion were to control the wider populace. They had to be extended salvation; denied to them by Moses' Law. They also had to be dependant on the Church and its clergy, so only through Christ is redemption possible.

*

SOMETHING INCONGRUOUS & JARRING

*

'Why don't you write about your Pilgrimage?' suggested the Master. 'That's always interesting.'
'How about 'The Eldritch Garden' as a title?' I asked him.
'Too archaic,' he responded. 'You should try for something incongruous and jarring.'

Book the First

It is, of course, ironical that I, a psychiatrist, should at almost every step of my experiment have run into the same psychic material which is the stuff of psychosis and is found in the insane. This is the fund of unconscious images which fatally confuse the mental patient. But it is also the matrix of a mythopoeic imagination which has vanished from our rational age. Though such imagination is present everywhere, it is both tabooed and dreaded, so that it even appears to be a risky experiment or a questionable adventure to entrust oneself to the uncertain path that leads into the depths of unconscious. It is considered the path of error, of equivocation and misunderstanding.

I am reminded of Geothe's words: 'Now let me dare to open wide the gate past which men's steps have never flinching trod.'

The second part of Faust, too, was more than a literary exercise. It is a link in the Aurea Catena which has existed from the beginnings of philosophical alchemy and Gnosticism down to Nietzche's Zarathustra. Unpopular, ambiguous, and dangerous, it is a voyage of discovery to the other pole of the world.

from *Memories, Dreams, Reflections* by C.G. Jung

Prelude

It defines both the goal and the route to attainment. Striving to be connects one to the beautiful Divine and pulls towards the radiant core. Innocuous and unassuming it is a key to perfect magick.

We might create an image of glorious perfection that we hold forever ahead, unattainable, that draws us always onward, inspiring us further and higher, reaching towards the peak of the Sacred Mountain and an encounter with God.

The image begins far off and vague, but we refine it, as we adapt ourselves. We delineate it with each step so that it gradually becomes clearer, gradually becomes something we can see and grasp.

Our obligations are to truth and divinity. The gods are prescient. They wait, watching, and only fools deny them their just dues. All realities are linked and merged. I exist in this physical universe as all human beings do, and my actions here, and my thoughts, have consequence. The effects ripple out into the unending ocean of tears and are cataclysmic.

Even gods share in the collective consciousness. They are its Guardians, the Keepers at the Gate.

One

I am rising slowly to the brink of awakening.

The womb is comfortable; soft viscous reds, the macroscopic pulse of heartbeat, warmth and dreams. I am aware. I am attached to the place whence I came, and to where I might someday return.

It is an imageless connection and remembering.

It is a strong certainty, as apparent as each breath we breathe in our lives, yet it exists only in the present moment, without defined past, without detail or memory. It is known. I was aware of the other place, although I did not picture it or directly recall it.

An undeveloped mind has no experience. Without language it cannot have rational thought. It is an empty vessel. Without experience it cannot hallucinate.

Sounds from the world around filtered through into the womb. I heard my parents talking. Music was playing, probably on a radio. My father's hand was upon my mother's belly, and he remarked on my activeness, and wondered if it were a response to the music.

'Perhaps it will be a musician?' he said, and I kicked against his hand.

When I am born into this world I feel as though I have been too early awoken. I am slightly irritated, and yearn for sleep. I do not want to live a life.

They pulled me out of my mother with iron forceps.

The metal teeth clamp onto the pliable skull, grasping the brain. This pressure upon the brain can make the baby liable to schizophrenia, epilepsy, and other strange states of mind when they are grown. Many happy returns.

It is 1967, conceived and enwombed during the Summer of Love, whilst the Flower Children are trying to turn the world on to peace and LSD. It is a briefly open window of universal positivity and unrestrained love and joy.

The enlightenment and awakening are fuelled by intoxicants and this is probably a weakness of the movement, which can be turned against the hippies. In America 1969 Richard Nixon announces his war on drugs. It is really a perpetual war on social freedoms.

The political class criminalises and drives underground the common man. Joy turns to despair and disillusionment.

I am born when the wave of optimism is still cresting, into this realm of possibilities.

There is a Strawberry Moon in June, to mark my arrival. There will not be another Strawberry Moon for seven times seven years, in 2016, and that second one will for me mark a significant stage in the cycles of my journey. I might even say a completion of decades of work and personal evolution.

I am born upon the south coast of England.

A celestial being appeared to me one afternoon in late November 2005, and remained with me throughout the long night, to converse with and instruct me, to guide me into and then through the hells and heavens of my own destiny.

She is the Holy Guardian Angel as envisioned in *Abra Melin*, embraced by Crowley, and loosely defined in psychology by Jung as the Externalised Self.

She is the voice speaking in my mind.

We must sometimes jump ahead briefly so as to shed light on the origins.

When I was twenty five years old I met Amado Crowley, and he became my spiritual teacher and guide. He was the son and the magickal heir of the rebel genius Aleister Crowley.

Aleister was driven and led by wilderness forces. An accomplished mountaineer, a poet and a prolific writer, a spiritual visionary and an occult master. Genius is often at odds with its social environment, and he was the epitome of the Byronic *mad, bad, and dangerous to know.*

There are groups today which claim Crowley as the inspiration for their own devil-worship. That is their projection upon and their interpretation of his work; it is a mirror that reflects. He seems to have intended being ambiguous, and often he was deliberately misleading as far as his real connections are concerned. He frequently used dark colors to paint his images. The name 'Aleister Crowley' can still strike fear into the hearts of otherwise rational people.

Despite his reputation Crowley was a servant of Truth and Love. He was never a devil-worshipper, and he remains an enemy of the ego-worshipping Black Hats. Still, his reputation as an 'infamous black magician' is not entirely surprising, given the ambiguity of his mission.

Yet, what more potent snare could he have lain for the weaklings that would inevitably corrupt and desecrate his truth after he was gone? His writings are booby-trapped with pits and dungeons and monsters. They look to him as their dark prophet and guide. With subtlety he binds them, and they reap their just rewards.

'Do what thou wilt shall be the whole of the law,' declared Crowley, and it has become the public anthem of his teachings and philosophy.

Tragically, the self styled sorcerers interpret this famous line to mean: *Do whatever you want!*

The real significance of 'Do what thou wilt shall be the whole of the law' is far deeper than such crass and juvenile interpretations. It refers to the *Will of Self.* It is to be aligned with divinity, rather than following the base and corrupt impulses of the ego-mind.

Aleister Crowley's extensive writings are prosaic and often beautiful. His life-long quest for truth is apparent. He never strove for earthly power and wealth. In fact, most of his adult life he was next to penniless.

I had been corresponding by post with Amado for about a year prior to our first meeting, which took place in Soho, London. When we met I asked him the question that he had waited a lifetime to hear. He shivered with ecstasy, and embraced me. I became his favorite student, his confidant and close friend, until his death about twenty years later. He sent me the first copies of everything he recorded and wrote.

I always found him to be very funny, charming and wise. He was a sensitive and kind person, a good man. He claimed to be the greatest of teachers.

After fourteen or fifteen years I completed my studies with him, and became an adept. 'Adept' comes from the word 'adroit,' and means to be a master of one's craft.

I am not a teacher though, as Aleister and Amado were. I could never have the great patience in the face of stupidity required for such a job.

In fact, the days of real occult masters are probably over. Life evolves and truth adapts with changing circumstance.

'I rely on you to write the truth about who I am,' Amado once said to me, and referring to his students he added: 'None of them will.'

I also came to know Amado's mother. She and Aleister were together only one night, but she gave birth to their child. Amado's claim to be Crowley's son and heir are entirely genuine, in my opinion, as someone who knew him as a close friend. I state that clearly here because even when he was alive his enemies were doing their utmost to discredit him, to bury his message, and pervert his truth.

One evening, whilst we were visiting a group of his students at Exeter over a weekend, he led me across into the *other place,* and took me into what he referred to as the Purple Palace. Inside, we stood before a chessboard. 'Aleister was the Bishop,' he said, 'and I am the Knight. Which piece will you choose?'

I hesitated for a moment as I regarded the pieces in their positions on the board. But I knew there was only one choice I could make. I chose the Queen. The most versatile and powerful piece of all.

'I thought you might have chosen the Rook,' Amado remarked.

'I am glad to see you as you are,' he said to me a little later. 'It makes it all worthwhile; being a master for all these lonely years. And, what is your name?'

'It is a secret name,' I replied after a moment. 'A name which all men fear.' *Fear?* he echoed. 'Yes,' I smiled. 'Except the wise.'

He raised his eyebrows in mild surprise.

'How will you reveal yourself, when the moment comes?' he

asked.

'I will come as the Black Winged Dragon, and I shall devour all the worlds.'

He knelt before me, to my great surprise.

'What are you doing?' I asked him.

'You are the Queen. I offer my allegiance. I offer my sword,' he said. 'I am the Knight, after all.'

'Do you promise to be true, never to forsake me? Will you love me always and protect me?'

He swore before the Gods and the Great Source.

'Any that come against you come also against me,' he said.

After I had bid him rise, he said smiling: 'I'm glad you told me to rise, or else I may have been stuck forever in the other place on my knees!'

Two

She is with me right at the start whispering into my ear. I say 'she' because of my later experiences, when she would appear to me in distinctly female guise. I am identifying this voice and connection with the Holy Guardian Angel.

I grumble and complain. I still feel overly tired. Gently, good-humoured, she coaxes me into letting go.

I want to remain in this connection with her. It is like the comfort of the womb. The dialogue between us is more or less continuous.

What does it mean? Who speaks to me? To the *other* in this flesh, that has come from *elsewhere?* Who is the I that she addresses, the I that responds and thinks and feels?

This I is different to the conscious ego-I which as yet is still undeveloped, and still without language, and has no memory to draw upon. In the physical world I am slow to begin talking. It is not until I am about a year old.

There are distinctions between the two of us, the Angel and I. We are separate. She talks and I react and respond to her words. I question, and she responds.

I am not privy to her thoughts and feelings any more than I am to those of another human being in the physical world. Yet she is entirely privy to everything that I think and feel and experience.

If she is that which I later identify as the Angel, then the I that responds to her and has awareness, and a less direct connection to divinity, must be named as the Soul.

Although I recognise her distinction, is she still a greater part of me?

You must give it up, and live, she tells me.

Perhaps I can do both? I suggest. She is amused and allows me to try, but it cannot work.

She has direct awareness and knowledge of divinity and eternity. She is prescient, knowing past, present and future. She exists outside of time. She knows where I came from, and how, and why I came to be here.

In my grandmother Ivy's small rectangular back garden, in my pram, I look out at my surroundings. Beyond the garden's back gate is an enclosed square containing half a dozen red-doored garages.

You will play here, the voice in my mind tells me. *You will be safe and happy.* I know it to be a true promise, and it sways me, so that I finally agree to let go. I surrender to physicality.

I am teething, and my gums are raw with pain. Biting upon the rings of colored plastic which my mother has given me momentarily diverts the fires.

The Goddess steps through into Ivy's living room. She is radiant and smiling, stars colliding in their orbits about and within her skirts.

She has come to bless me, to advise me, to remind me. I see selcouth friends smiling broadly amongst her consort, strangely familiar and unfamiliar. When she retreats I burst into bereft tears, alarming my mother and grandmother from the sofa.

Barbara, my mother, then whisked me up from the floor, and lay me on my back at her feet. She proceeded to tickle me for so long that I couldn't breathe, and almost fainted.

'Did you see how he was looking at *something*? I think he has *the gift*,' my grandmother concludes.

My paternal grandfather was Swedish, a sailor with the Merchant Navy. He didn't marry my father's mother, Josie, but they had two sons, Jon and Alan. She took his surname for herself and the boys. My maternal grandparents were Ivy and Harry (he was usually called 'Al'). During the Second World War Al served as a cook rather than a soldier, which one could presume contributed to his surviving it. He was present at the Dunkirk evacuation. His family were Londoners.

My great-grandmother, Rose, Ivy's mother, was a Romany Gypsy, and lived among a travelling horse-drawn caravan. I don't the name of Ivy's father, but he was also Gypsy.

We are especially shaped and formed by our early experiences in this life. The first seven years are defining, and what we learn during that time will remain with us throughout our lives, becoming opinions and beliefs that are almost immutable, so deep inside us as to be unseen and unquestioned. During this vulnerable, impressionable time our character and personality are pliable, reactive to our immediate environments. We are taking cues from those around us, our family and peers, and learning what is acceptable and good, and what is unacceptable and bad. We endeavour to fit and please, since our survival depends upon it. We begin naked and helpless, and have only our smile to safeguard us.

We arrive into this life somewhat like a blank canvas, and the broader outlines of who and what we shall become are not ours to choose. Those into whose care we have fallen will paint the indelible shapes upon us, the broad black brush strokes which will serve as the outlines of our personality. Our circumstances shape us. Yet, still we are not empty-handed. The insular mind is separate and reactive. We respond, and make choices, and by this we are painting the shapes and colors of our unique canvas. The Essential Self resides behind the choices we make. It makes a series of determining compromises, forcing its square peg into the round hole, as it conforms more or less to expectations.

For them, my society of peers, God was an unknowable mystery, and they were content with that, and saw no reason to enquire further. God is Love, or God is Everywhere, they would say, as though those slogans might satisfy my curiosity. True statements, no doubt, but they didn't clarify matters for me. Nobody knew, or seemed to have interest to discover the meaning of and purpose of life on any sort of profound level. I wanted to comprehend my relationship with the Divine, but there was no one who could offer me any real clue, or who could point to the places where I might find answers. My *rasa* could only be between God and I, and I would have to uncover its peculiar texture and significance myself.

It seemed to me that truth had to be rational and logical because the universe is rational and logical. It could therefore be apprehended by reason.

When I was told that the Divine was an unknowable mystery whose ways could never be comprehended, it didn't ring true to me.

I saw the lie which they closed their eyes to, and shut up their mouths and ears to. It puzzled me that they were content to ignore it. As if pretence might somehow preserve them.

Apparently their god was an idiot and an egoist, easily flattered and duped and manipulated. Church attendance and lip service to the rules were the most important parts of Worship. If I can see how hollow and insincere it is, then I'm certain that God can see it too.

Those that do not follow the rules of conduct will burn forever in a fiery hell. An eternal torture, in exchange for a single lifetime?

Whatever crimes one might have committed, that is a punishment so out of proportion as to be psychopathic. Eternity is a very long time. The god they served was insane.

This was the basic Christian Philosophy of 1970's England, and that generally taught in Schools and via Media.

Even though I didn't believe in their god I always accepted the concept of divinity. The connections seemed apparent to me, the door ever ajar, and the mirror blurred. If I wanted to connect with the Divine I would have to discover a different route.

I am in my plastic chair, in the rows of orange plastic chairs, flexible swirling curves, and the rows climb up and back behind me to reach the balcony, as the uniformed pupils close their eyes and parrot the Lord's Prayer. It is morning assembly. I listen to the words and voices, and it is a sad beauty. I do not join with them. I am aware for the first time that there are a few pupils, Jews and Jehovah's Witnesses, who do not say the prayer. No one challenges me. It is surprisingly easy to step aside.

The pupils are learning not to think or to question. Yes sir, no sir, three bags full sir. They are training to be soldiers of Conformity. They surrender their inherent divinity, and become compliant, grateful thralls.

Their fake world appals me.
I don't know where it is that I want to get to, but now I have stepped aside from the marching drones, and so I doubleback through strange streets, and it brings me outside the walls of the citadel, and lo! the great wilderness rises untamed and free.

Three

When I was a couple of months old, and after my older half-brother Gary was put on the bus to school, my mother Barbara would take my half-sister Dawn and me to grandmother Josie's house. She left us there for the day, and caught the bus herself, to work.

Josie wheeled my pram out into the small back yard and left me there all day unattended. She only brought me back into the house when Barbara was due to return for us. She cleaned me up as necessary, and so my mother was unaware of the treatment I was receiving.

Josie, according to Barbara, hated all males. She didn't want any male in her house, not even an innocent infant.

It was pleasant and peaceful in the back yard. I lay in my pram and watched the clouds drift across the blue sky. Sometimes I became uncomfortable and distressed, but no matter how much I might cry, Josie left me there. I could hear the sound of voices from her radio or television.

She came to bring me inside for my mother's return one afternoon. I smiled at her, and it seemed to make her curious. 'You are quite a good boy, aren't you?' She said, as though weighing choices.

One afternoon whilst I was in my pram out in Josie's back yard, a wasp dropped onto my blanket. It walked busily over the soft cotton. It approached my face, and I felt the threat. I could not co-ordinate my limbs to shoo it away. I was defenceless. I knew that the danger it presented was to my mouth and my eyes; it could sting my eyes, or crawl into my mouth and sting my throat.

I waited whilst the wasp crawled up onto my cheek, and then I yelled a loud scream, startling it, and it stung me then. The pain was deep and fiery, but I was relieved, knowing a worse fate had been avoided, as the wasp flew away.

I had been aware of the threat the insect posed, although presumably this was my first encounter in this life with a wasp. I thought and reasoned, and formulated then executed a fairly complex plan.

What can I conclude from that now? I can be certain on this: I am not only this flesh and consciousness-mind, and there are other realities, other dimensions inhabited by Soul. I existed somehow and somewhere before this life. It was Soul that recognised the danger and how to avoid it, which it can only have done by drawing upon some previous experience. Eventually, alerted to Josie's strange and mean neglect by one of the neighbours, Barbara quit her job at the factory, and stayed at home to look after Dawn and I.

I have very few memories of Josie, my father's mother, but I do recall a visit to her home, three or four years later. It was perhaps the last time that I saw her. Her house was stuffy and fusty. Her ashtrays were overflowing with ash and cigarette butts. She noticed my revulsion at seeing them, and remarked on it, and then laughed at my suggestion to empty them.

Her dress was an old-fashioned style, with lace at the collar and cuffs. Her face was sallow and creased deeply, and her teeth were rotten. There was a glass of Gin and Campari in her hand, and bottles on the small table beside her. She sat very straight in a tall-backed armchair. She was proud and haughty, damn the dismalness of her situation. For many years she had worked as a cleaner in London's Ritz Hotel, and now she mimicked the snobs she once served.

Upon the arm of her chair there was a pile of pennies, the old large kind, and she rippled her fingers over their edges, lifting and dropping them. My fascination pleased her.

She gave the pennies to my half-siblings and I, like a queen dispensing favours, commanding that we purchase *Lucky Bags* from the sweetshop.

Salt and vinegar, stony sand, turning tides, wild seas under the domed sky. Scuttling crabs, the moon envoys, amongst the shallow rocky pools and dark seaweeds in the sinking wet sands, when the tide rolls back to Canvey Island.

Candy-floss, honeycomb, sea-side rock and toffee apples. Roll a penny. Cracked and dead lights, and cracked, crumbling veneers. Pool houses and tin racing horses. Rain, sunshine, hot dogs with tomato ketchup and mustard sauce.

Throngs of people, my father steers us through the crowds to gaze through the big window at the waxworks.

The entrancing blade swings. It is huge, and curved like a quarter moon. The waxwork traitor raises his head to follow as it climbs back up into its arc. This motion is perpetual, a clockwork, never slicing deeper, forever on the brink of the final cut.

Here, on this dirty cheap coast, Peter Pan came to die.

My parents rented a small apartment on St Leonard's Road, Southend, a few minutes walk from the seafront and the beach, up the cliff-steep hill.

My father Jon was a talented club chess player, and his interest in the game was at its peak during this period. Most evenings his friends would come to St Leonard's Road, and set up their boards on the kitchen table. They played late into the night. Barbara provided cups of tea and sandwiches.

I was enrapt by this art. Every moment of the chessmen's slow motion dance across the chequered board fascinated me.

The pieces were tactile and very visually striking; they spoke a symbolic and silent language. I studied each of them, examining them intimately, tracing my fingers over their smooth wooden contours.

Jon taught me the rudiments of the game before I was two years old. He was patient, wanting to share his own love of the game with me. Chess encourages problem-solving, involves complex strategy, and employs a diversity of movements. There are difficult cerebral concepts such as capture and sacrifice and positional advantages. I'm sure it was a useful catalyst for my intellectual development.

Obviously I could not hope to win against him, so instead I made my own game of it, and had fun manoeuvring my knights, and capturing as many of his pieces that I could with them.

'You make yourself easy to thwart,' Jon commented. 'I can repel your knights simply by threatening them. You must learn to weigh advantage and disadvantage in trading off pieces.'

'But, I like my knights. I don't want to lose them,' I replied sulkily.

'Exactly my point!'

He was similarly passionate about taking photographs and always carried a camera, perpetually taking snaps of Gary, Dawn and I. Often he took so long arranging a shot until everything was perfect that his subjects grew restless and tired. He took several photographs of me wandering through the flowerbeds at Southchurch park, or playing chess with Gary or Dawn.

He carried a briefcase at this time, and for the next ten years, although he rarely did office work. Usually he just had sandwiches and perhaps a magazine in it. He always travelled first class on trains. He would whistle as he walked and his melodies were nice, drawing you into them. If he didn't whistle he would sing: most often the Roy Orbison song *Oh, Pretty Woman.*

Four

People would stop my mother and I in the street to enthuse over my prettiness, and my hair, which twisted in long natural ringlets. 'She looks just like Shirley Temple,' many remarked. The comparison pleased me, as I enjoyed watching the re-runs of her films on television. Barbara tired of correcting their mistake, and until I was about seven or eight years old, upon first meetings most people assumed I was a girl.
Until then I felt obliged to state clearly upon meeting someone that I was in fact a boy.

I was with my mother one morning when she had knocked upon our landlady's door, and asked to borrow a pound. I had been impressed by the simple and swift transaction.
A day or two later, as I was pushing toy cars about in our lounge, I heard an Ice Cream Van in the street outside. 'Don't ask every time,' my mother had said, not unkindly, when I had asked for ice cream the previous afternoon. Our eyes met now, across the sofa, and this time I did not ask. She was pleased. I returned to my toys. After a few minutes, sure that I was unobserved, I tiptoed out of our apartment, and knocked on the landlady's door, which was just across the landing. I told her that my mother had sent me to borrow a pound, and she gave me the money. She was surprised and somewhat sceptical of the legitimacy of my errand, since I was only about three years old, but my bright confident smile persuaded her.
Excited by this little adventure, I went stealthily downstairs and out into the street.
I bought myself a 'Double Ninety-Nine' from the Ice Cream Van: a soft mountain of white swirling ice-cream with two chocolate flakes pushed into it. 'Your eyes are bigger than your belly!' my mother taunted, if ever I asked her, and she would never agree to buy one for me.
The ice cream cost ten pence, and I could barely hold all the coins, my change, in my hand. One of the women there walked around the van with me, ensuring that I could cross back safely. 'That's a lot of money for such a small boy,' she teased.

'Yes, but I am rich!' I replied.

Coming back towards our house, and it was only a few doors down, I saw that the landlady was looking from her front room window. She smiled, then dropped the net curtain back.

I went around to the back garden and ate the ice cream. I didn't enjoy it much, because now I regretted my deception and feared its probable consequences; my father was going to be furious with me.

I still hoped that I might get away without my parents discovering what I had done, like perhaps the landlady wouldn't tell them, and so after pondering, I made up my mind to bury the coins that I still had. It could be like pirate treasure.

I felt very clever and cunning as I buried each coin in a different place, beneath the tufty green grass.

My parents were relieved to find me safe, and quite impressed by the boldness and ingenuity of my crime. My father didn't punish me, but warned me that if I ever did anything similar he would not be lenient then.

Gary, my older half-brother, thought the entire thing hilarious. I had buried the coins so haphazardly that we were only able to recover a few of them.

The couple that lived in the house next door to ours, if you were to turn downhill towards the beach, had two sons, Paul and Ray. Paul was a year older than I, and Ray a year older again. My half-siblings and I were friends with the boys, and often played with them.

There was a heavy white gray mist one morning, and Gary and I were in our back garden. The mist wrapped us in its dewy cloak so that we could not see the faces of the houses, and could not be seen.

Gary pointed out to me the many toys cars that were in Paul and Ray's garden. Some had clearly been there discarded for a long time, already half consumed by the earth and grass and rusting in rainfalls.

'They have so many cars that they don't even play with them,' observed Gary. 'Climb over and get them, and pass them to me.'

I was too small to climb the fence, but Gary linked his hands together, making a step for my foot, so that he could boost me to the top.

'Why don't you go over and get them?' I asked him reasonably.

'I have to keep watch from this side,' he replied slyly.

'And how will I get back?'

'You can use that box to stand on,' he said, pointing to a plastic crate.

Under his direction I gathered up the cars, passing them to him. I collected at least a dozen choice ones, and then struggled back over the fence. As we were about to enter back into the house he said: 'Now you a thief!' I was dismayed.

When my father Jon remarked that he didn't remember seeing these toy cars before, Gary lied cheerfully that we had them for ages, but not played with them lately. He looked for my confirmation, and I nodded, but the lie further unsettled me.

It was rare for my elder sibling to tolerate me, and I was pleased to have bonded with him in this way, but I could not shake off my feeling of discomfort. The cars belonged to Paul and Ray, who were my friends.

The following day I would not play with the cars when Gary invited me to, preferring my own, honestly attained toys. My father overheard our conversation and smiled thoughtfully at me.

Later, Gary said to me: 'I was going to take you with me, but you chose to be with them. Now you are my enemy.'

I didn't get what he meant, but his attitude towards me shifted from that point onwards. Our bonding had been very brief. At first this new attitude towards me was only manifested by emotional distance, by ignoring me, but later it would become sinister.

When their family were moving house a few months later Paul and Ray knocked and gave us a black bin bag half filled with toy cars, as a parting gift. I wondered if they had known about the theft all along, because it seemed a telling coincidence that they should give us these cars now. I wasn't sure that I wanted them.

'You don't have to punish yourself, you know. It's good that you felt guilty about it, but you can forget it now. Hopefully a little bit wiser, eh?' counselled Jon. He seemed to understand how I felt, and I was grateful for that.

I met the brothers again years later, after their parents moved from Southend to Shoeburyness. Sadly, Ray passed away at the age of eighteen from a heroin overdose. I had exchanged 'hellos' with Ray when we saw each other, but became quite friendly with Paul, and a few times he hung out with my good friend Jim and I.

One evening I bashfully admitted to Paul that I had climbed into his garden and stolen those toy cars. He was amused, and forgave me.

Any pressure on my ears was painful as I constantly had gitaar, which meant that my sinuses were blocked. Most of the time it was difficult for me to hear and to breathe. It was an uncomfortable condition, which persisted until I was about ten years old, and I felt muggy and ill because of it. But, there was a warm remoteness there that I liked. It wrapped me in a daze, blurring the world.

I had frequent nosebleeds, and discovered myself allergic to snails and too much chocolate.

When my father punished us he began with a long lecture. Invariably his theme was why whatever it was we had done had been wrong. He wanted us to comprehend the reason we were being punished, so that we should be deterred from repeating our error. He explained all the implications and consequences of our actions, and insisted that we showed comprehension. He questioned us, and demanded a summary of what he had said. I was never able to provide him with satisfactory answers. As he lectured I would begin to sway and teeter, fainting, unable to keep still or to concentrate, and this always annoyed him.

I have *controlled epilepsy*, which as well as inducing cerebral fits like trance-states, distorted my spacial awareness and balance. Being forced to stand still for protracted periods made my head swim and heavy swoons would roll over me.

I was struggling to keep still, to remain upright, and to listen to my father and comprehend his complex argument. The lectures were subsequently torturous, and I dreaded them.

Once he had exhausted his theme he smacked us, often hitting us on the side of the head or on the ear. The gitaar I had made those blows doubly painful for me.

Controlled epilepsy is different from the more common type of epilepsy, which is characterised by violent physical fits. The seizures of controlled epilepsy are conversely so introverted as to be almost undetectable; as the name implies, it is a stable condition without explosive demonstrations. It causes disconnectedness and lack of co-ordination, like an extra boost of physical awkwardness, a super-powered clumsiness, as though one were tripping over one's own feet. Alongside this is the tendency to be drawn into trance-like states, and perpetual day-dreaming. Hyper-focus can also be associated.

The physical disorientation or clumsiness was pronounced in me when I was young. I had to work for a very long time to overcome it. I had something like a distorted spatial awareness, so that I would always kick over the coffee cups that my father left tucked close at the side of the sofa, as though my feet are drawn to the cup unavoidable, irresistibly, as I stumble against invisible obstacles. He was understandably exasperated by my apparent clumsiness, being as he was unaware of its root cause.

When I was in Infant School, about four years old, we were first taught a phonemes alphabet. Each sound has its own letter or letters, and these are then joined together to form words. I had no problems connecting the sounds with the letters, and this particular formulaic structuring of words worked for me. Once I started Junior School, age five upwards, the standard alphabet was introduced and rigidly adhered to. My peers apparently adapted easily enough, but the new way of reading and writing seemed illogical to me. I couldn't see its formula, and I couldn't relate. Now the letters did not accurately reflect the sounds within the word.

My mind rejected the system, and no matter how many times my teacher tried to explain it, or whatever angle she took, I couldn't understand it. 'You have no choice,' she told me eventually. 'You have to do it this way.'

Most of the words we were learning at the time were three or four letter words, not too difficult; this was in the last few months of Infant School, in preparation for the move up to Junior School. I couldn't comprehend the method that she wanted me to use, but I could convert the words in my head, and fool her that I had finally got the hang of it. Well, she wasn't totally convinced, but since I was now reading these words back to her she accepted what I said.

I am still doing something similar with words. I find a way to circumvent their formula. Although I have had to use this much longer circuitous route, it has been sufficient. It seems to be a type of dyslexia, or a function of the epileptic mind perhaps.

I struggled with learning to tell the time. The concept of clocks seemed bizarre and ridiculous to me. The use of five minutes past and five-and-twenty minutes tos seemed unnecessarily elaborate and verbose. Eventually I had to accept the absurd.

I couldn't distinguish between left and right. Even now, a lifetime older, it takes a conscious effort. This inability drove my mother to distraction, so that one day she actually wrote 'left' and 'right' on the toes of my plimsolls. That just compounded my confusion, and I still wore them on the wrong feet.

I would use my cutlery with the 'wrong' hands. She always got really cross about it. I was inclined to use my left hand primarily, and she would hit me if I used it where most people would be using the right. She told me that being left handed was a sure sign I was the Devil's child. As a result of her aggressive conditioning I became ambidextrous.

I now write with either my left or right hand, although predominately I use my right for most other tasks. The world is made for right-handed people.

Five

Gary, my half-brother on our mother's side, was four years my senior. His father was a violent psychopath named Cooke, who terrorised and beat Barbara, whist the infant Gary watched from his cot, learning strange twisted lessons about love and survival.

One night Cooke and Barbara went out to a local pub. After a drink or two, he suddenly left her at the bar, saying he would return soon. Outside the pub, for reasons unknown to Barbara, he stabbed and killed a young woman. He was arrested, and sentenced to life in prison.

After Cooke was imprisoned she put Gary, his son, into Social Services care, and attached herself to a blonde-haired fated junkie, and became pregnant with my half-sister Dawn. The guy, whose name I do not know, overdosed on heroin and died, very early into the pregnancy. Barbara was then about thirty years old, and suddenly alone.

She seduced my father, Jon, who was half her age, and convinced him that the child she was pregnant with was his, even though they had then slept together only once. Well, he never really believed her, because it didn't quite add up, but when Dawn arrived he loved her and became her father. I was born about fifteen months after Dawn.

Barbara had already had two other children, neither of whom she ever told Jon about.

They took her first child from her, a girl, and had it adopted. Barbara held her once only. Her second, Ivy and Al raised as their own son, and named him Malcolm.

For Ivy to have claimed the child as her own seems very odd to us now, living as we do in our modern society. The great lengths that Ivy and Al went to in order to conceal the child's illegitimate parentage are perhaps proof of the deception's necessity. Barbara was kept strictly secluded as the end of her pregnancy drew near so that no one would see her belly. Ivy even went so far as to pad her own belly when out in public, so that she looked pregnant, and happily spread the news that she and Al were expecting another child.

It was the mid 1950s, and a child born out of wedlock could lead to the family being disgraced and ostracised by the local community. It was the time of twitching net curtains at the windows, which meant that everything must appear in proper order. Ivy lived her entire life concerned about the family reputation and the approval of her immediate neighbours.

For the first thirty years of his life Malcolm thought Barbara was his sister. The truth was finally revealed to him by Gary whilst they were out drinking together one evening. Malcolm was devastated, and never entirely came to terms with it.

He felt his entire reality to be in question. He no longer knew who he was. If a truth so basic and fundamental as this had proven to be a lie, then what truth could he possibly rely upon? What else might have been kept from him? It destabilized him. He was a long term cocaine addict, and died of heart failure in 2019.

Barbara had left Gary in care for two years, since Cooke's arrest and imprisonment. Whilst pregnant with me, she revealed to Jon that she had this third child, and that he was in care. She hadn't mentioned him previously, although they had been together for over a year at that point, and, of course, Jon was very shocked by the sudden revelation. He agreed that Gary should come to live with them. He tried to make a life for us all. He worked hard, and he was still only seventeen years old himself.

When I was three years old, he discovered that Barbara had been deceiving him for weeks or perhaps months, and they split up.

This deception was very strange. It was pointless, destructive, and entirely unsustainable. Barbara had pretended to be working and left the apartment each day, but instead of going to work she went to a local pub and drank the days away. Jon only discovered the lie because a friend of his saw her at the pub, and told him.

She had gotten into quite serious debt, having drawn several loans, which she had used as her 'wages' at the end of each week, enabling her to continue the lie. Perhaps she had lost her job at some earlier juncture, and rather than confess that to Jon she had gone to the pub to console herself. Somehow she had decided it was a good idea to keep going to the pub, to keep drinking, and not to tell him.

Whatever her rationale for the bizarre deception it was impossible for him to trust her again.

For several weeks I did not see my father or my half-siblings. Gary and Dawn had been placed into State Social Care. I was with my mother. She struggled to find appropriate accommodation for the two of us, and we moved from one Bed and Breakfast boarding house to another.

I developed a behavioural habit at this time which is considered to be a sign of emotional disturbance in children. It brought me some comfort though, and I persisted with it in various ways for several years. I leant my weight against the cot frame, and struck my brow against the wooden rail repeatedly, until my head grew numb and I drifted. Later, in lieu of the cot frame, I used my forearms to bump against.

Barbara continued drinking most days, and sometimes she took me with her to the pub. We sat in the cubbyhole with a group of older gentlemen. She seemed to be relaxed and happy in their company, and she drank slowly, sipping her cider.

Most of them were drinking Guinness. It was a strange looking drink, but enticing; the thick black liquid and the frothy cream top. I asked if I might have some. 'But you are too young!' they said. 'It is a strong and bitter taste.'

They tried me with a swig of bitter instead. It was flat and cold and I didn't like it. They gave me the remnants of a glass of Guinness, and were fascinated for my reaction. The smell of the drink was unlike anything I had encountered. It was sort of musty, savoury. I sipped at it, then licked my lips: 'Mmm!' My mother and the old men congratulated me, and then one another.

'It is unfair of me to bring you to the pub with me, isn't it?' Barbara said on our way back to the lodgings we were staying at. I replied that I did not mind it.

One boarding house we lodged at seemed to me like a palace, it was so large and distinguished. The hallway was wide, its floor rich, polished wood. A magnificently opulent staircase coiled slowly up to the first floor landing. There was perhaps an end-table or something, but otherwise the only furniture in the room was a baby-grand piano. I pressed its fairy tale ivory keys gently.

Another thing that delighted me about living there was that our meals were announced by the striking of a small gong. The clear warm note rang through the large house, summoning the guests from their rooms.

At lunch one afternoon I am encouraged to strike the gong myself. Thrilled but timid, I lift the little stick and hit the brass plate very gently, and the note does not sound. I strike harder, and the toll of the gong fills the dining room and reverberates about the house.

One night my mother came back from the pub after ten pm, missing the establishment's curfew, and the gates were barred. She climbed over them, leaving me in my pushchair outside. The landlady was awake, and not pleased. You are a poor excuse for a mother, she scolded Barbara. We were promptly evicted.

We moved into a small room in another house, which I didn't like nearly so much. One day whilst Barbara was out some where, probably at the pub, I was alone in the room. I awoke. The stillness was calm, and I watched the mobile spinning gently above me. I remember clearly watching that mobile (or perhaps the memory is of other mobiles in other rooms) and the calming effect it had upon me. Doing so was almost a meditation, during which I tried to resist sleep whilst drifting into the gentle intoxicating sways.

I stood in the cot, and began to hit my forehead against the rail, until I was numb. A voice engaged me. It seemed to be coming from a cuddly toy that I had in the cot. *Can all toys speak?* I asked it. *Only some*, was the reply. This voice, which was disembodied, outside of myself and my thoughts, proceeded to direct me, and I yielded to it.

Following its instructions I pushed my fingers into the top of the socket of my right eye, and then slammed my weight, slight though it was, into my elbow and triceps and onto the cot rail, forcing the fingers into the socket, and popping out the eyeball. Although each of the 'otherworldly' experiences that I describe here has its unique character and quality, they all involve an apparently exterior personality; the voice conversing with me during the first few weeks of my life; the goddess that I saw; I will describe later the young boy that appeared one day in my bedroom, when I was about seven years old; and as an adult aspiring to Adeptship, the appearance of and conversation with the Holy Guardian Angel.

One might call them spirits or visitations, or they may be a type of projection of my Soul, an externalization of the Self.

The isolated difference in this particular instance is that the voice instructed me to do something physically harmful and rather odd; to dislocate my eye from its socket.

When Barbara returned I was holding onto the top of the rail, bouncing and laughing deliriously. She screamed when she saw me, with my eye dislodged on the top of my cheek. In a panic she bundled me into my pushchair, and ran with me to Southend Hospital.

When we arrived at the emergency outpatients unit I was taken into a room by a kindly doctor. I was not in any pain at all, and there was no severance or blood. He was calm and confident, and using a handkerchief, simply pushed my eye back into its socket. He gave us a prescription for eye-drops, and arranged for follow up consultations with a clinic soon afterwards, which I attended for about a year.

The eye-drops were painful and uncomfortable, but he had insisted that she administer the entire course faithfully so as to heal any damage that may have been done.

At first I squinted and squirmed. 'You have to keep still and keep your eyes open,' she told me, 'or the drops won't go in properly.' She tried again, and I remained entirely motionless whilst they splashed onto my eye. 'You don't have to be *that* good about it!' she said, as she put the little bottle of drops back into its paper box.

The eye stopped functioning properly. They decided then that it was a 'lazy eye.' Everything appeared to be in order but the eye did not contribute to my vision. Its point of focus was different, so that it could never work harmoniously with the other. My left eye had 20/20+ vision and dominated.

My mother wondered if I had dislocated the eye by thumping my head upon the rail of the cot, but the doctor considered this unlikely, although he could offer no explanation as to how it may have happened. 'And you aren't going to tell us, are you?' he smiled at me.

Barbara was remorseful and depressed about the incident. She asked me one morning, a week or so afterwards, if I would like to live with Gary and Dawn again. I considered for a moment, then said 'no.' I had become accustomed to it being just my mother and me. She asked me if I loved them, and I said that I did not. However, she had already made her decision.

Six

Crowley was a spiritual pioneer. He related to the high prose and drama of Occultism, and found therein the raw materials for a system of personal development that he could utilise to reveal his personal truth. Its imagery appealed to his senses of poetry and theatre.

He quickly broke away from the historical and modern authorities of Occultism and established his own school of Magick. He recognised the stagnation and inherent dearth in the regurgitation of ancient ideas and gossip, hallowed into sacred rules and facts, then shrouded in deep layers of mystery and obscruitum, and published under new snappy titles. It was not much different from the hollow mysteries of Christian theology.

He didn't want to just play at being a Magus. He enjoyed dressing up, but he also was very serious about discovering his connection to the Divine and finding his destiny. He was driven, obsessive and full of courage.

To actualize his Self, or as he phrased it: to experience the presence and Conversation of the Holy Guardian Angel, he felt he must embrace all the darkness and all of the light of his Humanity, in order to find a redemption, and a way forward. He was nothing if not thorough.

'I am a man,' he said, 'and in Man I recognise all these darknesses and this light. I reflect the All.' He would take all of it into himself and become a mirror of mankind. It was in this role that he took on the mantle of the *Great Beast*.

'I am that which Thou hast made me,' he said, as he stood face to face with God. 'If there is more love in me than violence, and more light than shadow, then purge me of every vestige of darkness, that I may drink and drain fully this cup. In Your blood let me be washed clean, or else cast me out forever into the black abyss.'

Like a dark Christ crucified, that the collective consciousness might be purified. Taking on that role, and thereby accepting every defect of Humanity as part of himself, by the Laws of Contagion and Similarity, he accelerated Humanity's March

Towards Destiny. He purged the Collective Consciousness.
He dared to face the Demon in open combat.

It is in this sense then that I refer to the Holy Guardian Angel. It is the truth of who and what we are as human beings, in all its majestic glory, with every darkness purged and devoured by the brilliance of the light. Unflinching we must regard every truth of the Soul. The looking-glass reveals each and every blemish. Comprehending the truth, we are able to transform and Become. The Holy Guardian Angel is that looking-glass.

I studied Occultism. Having found established religions and society's ideals of Materialism and Ego Worship unsatisfactory, I searched in even obscure quarters for divinity. If standard truths were shallow, whence then could I find the depths?

It was a labyrinthine study, but amongst the burgeoning dross of Mysterium Arcarna Crowley shone out like a beacon.

The truth must be perpetually vitalised and transformed, if it is to remain alive. The broad strokes remain, but the fine details transmute with experience. As Humanity marches towards a union with divinity old systems must be discarded.

I became the student of Amado, Crowley's magickal heir, and his truth was much gentler, more organic and fluid, than Aleister's ever could have been. 'I am where he would be now,' said Amado. The reality had transmorphed.

The Occult marketplace may still serve some pilgrims as a labyrinthine route to the Divine, but it is now so heavily perverted by deviants and black magicians, and therefore dangerous, that it is perhaps better avoided altogether.

The Richard Wilhelm translation of the *Yi King* is the only book the Aspirant really needs.

The Soul is where we are tethered to the Divine. In the mirror of the Soul we find our truth and our magickal power.

Each of us has our journey, our path, leading to our destiny. It is up to each of us to fulfil the tasks we are allotted, and to be that which we were born to be.

There are no exceptions, and no excuses will prevail. We are judged on how we live our lives, moment by moment.

God, the unending Multraverses, is not a fool. He is not insane nor an egoist. Before Him we are all naked and unadorned.

Collectively they are known as *Seaview Homes*. The Home I am housed in, and Gary and Dawn are there already, is named *Merry Trees*.

They were long wide buildings yet short at two stories high. Purpose built, amongst gardens of undulating green hills and a small wood of Gainsborough trees, and willow heavy with tears, and there are frolicking red squirrels, timid but curious, and elm, birch, and oaks laden with chestnuts, within its boundaries, and gardens, vegetable gardens.

Bats flutter outside the window of the dorm when the night is pitch behind them. Fuzzy with waking, they uncoil from sleep and knock upon the pane. The dorm is cold. Flat, neutral colors, sameness, routine and discipline, a dozen beds or more in two rows, Formica wardrobe/desks beside each, cubicle-like. The bay window is wide and without curtains, at the far end of the long, narrow room.

I am almost four years old.

Each evening, as the youngest boy I am first to bed.

I switched out the dorm's light, and stood at the window, watching the last of the day as the sun sets, colors slicing rutilant through the trees, bleeding over the hillocks, and the shadows of night-time gathering. The dusk sprites are shy and sweet, delightful, and I smile at their fleet dancing shadows. But as night gains depth, they give way to menace that slinks furtively tree to tree, always hidden, too lithe to catch with eyes. I catch its fear.

I look up then at the bright stars above and make my silent prayer; the forsaken star-child, an ancient yearning echoing in our hearts. *Come for me*, I pray to the stars and the deep behind them. *Bring me home.*

I go to my bed, and peer under its frame. I am afraid, but I must look, or I will not be able to sleep. I am looking for monsters or demons, for darkness spirits who lurk in deep shadows. I open the door of my wardrobe and my breath is fast and shallow. I pull down the door of the desk. Climbing onto the bed, I look over the wooden headrest, down into the small triangular space of utter blackness behind it. My hearts beats hard.

The bedding is blankets and sheets rather than quilts, and we are taught that our bed must be made each morning exactly so: the sheets and blankets tucked very tightly beneath the mattress, in what is known as the Hospital Style. I ease myself between the cool cotton sheets like a ghost, so as not to loosen them from the mattress. I turn beneath them until my head is towards the foot of the bed, and then slowly forwards into that breathless eigengrau space, where nothing can find me. It is warm, silent, and I am safe.

I was isolated. Other than Sean, the son of the guy who ran the place, whose name was Frank, all the boys at Merry Trees were at least two years older than me, and some were teenagers. This arrangement suited me fine. I liked to be alone.
When not at Infant school, I roamed the big house most days, the staff, almost all of whom were women, busy with their work, cooking, cleaning, organising. I rambled outside on the little hills, day-dreamed beneath the trees.
There was a narrow air raid shelter just outside the back kitchen door which had been converted into a coal bunker. I climbed easily onto its cobblely roof, and leapt over the three foot gap at its middle. Eventually I was too casual at this trick. One day my toe caught on the far lip of the leap and tripped me, and I fell onto the cobblely roof, grazing my shin, and bumping and bruising my head. The wounds looked much worse than they hurt. They almost seemed worthwhile as I luxuriated in the attention of the women tending me, cleaning my wounds and then applying ointments and plasters.
I had to wear an eye-patch, to correct my lazy eye; since that diagnosis was anyway incorrect, it made no improvement. The patches were taupe colored and sticky, and completely covered my good eye. I didn't like wearing them. I couldn't see properly with only my damaged eye. It was like trying to see through a blurrily spotted lens.
After a few minutes of wearing the patches my head ached, and I would become disorientated, unable to balance properly, and a strange stressful pressure built up in my eye. The longer I had a patch on, the worse this stress became. I went into the

bathroom and sat in a cubicle so that I could peel the patch off my eye. The nauseating sensations receded. After several months there was no improvement, and the patch treatments were abandoned, to my relief.

Although we were now living in the same building I rarely saw my half-siblings, Gary and Dawn, aside from mealtimes. They were both angry and jealous that our mother had kept me with her whilst they were already in care, and they avoided me, punishing me with distance.

My parents also seemed very far from me. Their visits, weekly or fortnightly, were occasional events in my slow days.

I separated myself from them mentally, abandoned by them already, and soon no longer thought of them or missed them. I thought it was strange that some of the other children cried, apparently because they were missing their parents.

I wandered the house, opening doors onto airing cupboards filled with soft towels and sheets, comfortably scented. Another door revealed a cupboard stacked with first aid paraphernalia. The aromas here intoxicated me, so that I closed my eyes and swayed before the shelves. They are strange medicine and ointment smells, curiously gorgeous.

I took sticking plasters and bandages, tape for casts, and stole away.

Seven

The Home is empty today, other than the few staff who are baking and chatting in the kitchen. I step tiptoe past the kitchen, at the bottom of the stairs, and into the large open lounge. I sit on the floor.

It is quiet, but not entirely still. I listen, and the house sways and sighs, and shifts its weight and groans softy. It leans and creaks, bends and stretches.

I am startled to discover that the house is a person.

They pull me after them, the tiny house spirits, and I follow them through the door that opens, minuscule, in the wooden skirting. They lead me gaily through labyrinthine corridors beneath the house, unveiling a hidden world of doors and thin passageways, which turn sharply and often into square spaces. When I return to a full consciousness I cannot recall the precise details of the maze of corridors and rooms, or of the frolicking faery that led me. I cannot recall the precise nature of our activities beneath the house, only that is was joyful and wonderful. It was like forgetting a dream the moment you awake. The door has already closed. Although I am able to return there on many other days, this 'blocked' memory of the event is usual.

The house spirits offer a pact. They will be my kin, and care well for me, and keep me safe. Yet, I must commit to them; there can be no returning. 'Yes,' I say. 'I will go with you.' They are glad.

The labyrinthine world unfolded before me anew each visit I made, and the faery held onto my hand as they skipped with me through the tiny corridors, happy and radiant. Each time it seemed that they revealed something rare and mysterious, and each time I tried to bring it back with me in my conscious memory, but I was never able to.

A woman enters the lounge. 'I did not hear you in here,' she says. 'Are you okay? We have made some cake. Would you like a slice?'

'No, thank you,' I reply politely, surprising both of us.

'Oh, well, let us know if you need anything. Are you okay in here by yourself?' I reply that I am, that I am playing. She seems puzzled.

I smile to myself, crossed-legged like a little Buddha, when she has gone. Now I have found my friends, and they are in my head.

The voices of the staff are like soft echoes now. They could bring me back to the physical if they were persistent, demanding my attention, and they could hold me there if they engaged me in some pleasing way. But, when left to myself, I floated back through to the other place.

My father took my half-siblings and I to the apartment of his new girlfriend. She was a slight, softly spoken woman, with strawberry blonde hair, and her name was Sylvia. I only met her once or twice, but I thought she was pretty and nice. We spent the morning hanging out there.

As lunchtime approached we were having a play battle in the lounge, throwing cotton wool balls at each other, hiding behind the couch and the armchairs to avoid being hit. It was fun, and we were all in high spirits. Sylvia opened the door a little and popped her head in to let us know that lunch was almost ready. Jon was inexplicably furious that she had interrupted us. He kicked her in the belly. It was a forceful blow. He was a Karate black belt, so he knew how to kick. She doubled over and her face twisted with pain. I was stunned by his brutality.

We went into the kitchen for lunch and it was a sullen and gloomy affair. I asked Sylvia if she was okay, and she gave me a sweet reassuring smile. 'Now you are turning them against me,' he grumbled.

The next time my father came to Merry Trees to collect us to go out with him, I refused to go.

After my fourth birthday I was enrolled in 'Boys' Brigade.' It was or is an organization like the Scouts or Cubs, with an extra heavy emphasis on military-style. Drill, salute, stand to attention, at ease.

The uniform was a dark blue ribbed sweater, with black leather patches at the elbows and across the shoulders, and dark, stay-pressed pants. There was a long narrow cap which one wore at an angle on one's head. It had a badge at its centre. I liked the cap a lot. Everything else about the Boy's Brigade I loathed. They told me that I would learn to enjoy it. They could not see how deeply abhorrent I had found the experience.

As I was being taken to the next session I convinced the member of staff accompanying me to allow me to walk the last hundred yards or so alone, which meant crossing a quiet road by myself, so I had to be very confident and persuasive.

I took my time, and when I was unobserved, when they had turned back to the Home, I skipped the session, cut down the road that ran beside the Boy's Brigade building, avoiding being seen by the children and their parents, or the guys running the group.

I walked the streets for the duration, probably an hour. I kept doubling back, keeping close to the building so that I wouldn't get lost, and returned to be collected, walking to meet the staff member, when the session ended.

I performed this little trick each time, and it went undiscovered for a few weeks. Finally I was accompanied by a young man I hadn't met before. He refused me with an implacable laugh, and led me right up to the door. I couldn't escape. Have you been on holiday? they asked.

My belly was knotted and nauseous during the session. My whole being recoiled at the regimentation; the marching, saluting, at-easing, all-saming, like robots, cogs in the machine; it had frightened me, repelled me, so that I preferred lonely streets.

Frank and his wife Pat lived in at Merry Trees alongside us, with their two children, Sean and Claire, and were in charge of the staff. Their care was parental, and usually a fair discipline. Frank decided that I could be excused from attending Boys' Brigade, to my surprise and relief.

Growing up during the 1970s, without modern mass media and computers, weekly comics were a significant part of my entertainment, and I first started 'reading' them whilst at

Seaview Homes. They were cheap to buy, and even the small amount of pocket money I would have was enough to get several of them each week.

I read Marvel and DC for many years. I enjoyed most superhero stories, and my favorites were Batman, the Hulk, and the Silver Surfer. I started reading 2000AD from its first issue. I also bought the lighter children's weeklies, such as Beezer, Wizzer and Chips, and the Dandy. I never enjoyed the Beano, or Dennis the Menace; I didn't like Walter, the drippy swot that he bullied mercilessly, but I couldn't relate to bullies. I did like Gnasher, Dennis' dog.

I came down into the dining room for breakfast one morning, and the atmosphere was something serious. We waited for one or two more stragglers, before Frank told us solemnly that someone had helped themselves to a midnight snack: a whole kilo jar of glacé cherries. Just one or two bits left at the bottom. The culprit turned out to be one of the older boys. It must have been a final straw since he was evicted because of it.

I saw him when he was leaving.

He looked to be in his late teens, and he had a violent energy. He sullenly opened the front door and a storm was raging outside, a black sky and heavy wild rain. He looked back and caught my eye, snarling.

Eight

When I am five my mother is finally allocated a three
bedroomed council house, on Blyth Avenue, Shoeburyness. It
is number 55. It stands at about the middle of Blyth, an end of
terrace, with a huge ten foot hedge running along its side to the
back gate and wall, before the large shed and small square back
garden.
The house feels and smells bright and clean. It is empty and
spacious, friendly, as I skip excitedly from room to room
before the furniture is brought in.
Outside again, Gary comes to stand next to me. His anger and
bitterness have waxed during his time in Merry Trees.
'I don't know why you are so happy. I will make sure that you
will not be happy here,' he says menacingly. He has made up
his mind to destroy me.

I lived at Blyth Avenue with my two half-siblings and my
mother for ten years, between the ages of five and fifteen years.
It was rare for my mother to have work during my childhood.
During our first year at Blyth she worked in a place assembling
small toy cars, like the Matchbox models. I remember it
because she would bring the bare chassis and wheels home for
me. I made patchwork cars from them.
She soon became practically housebound with anxiety,
agoraphobia, and alcohol dependency.
Blyth Avenue was a street of council houses, and ran adjacent
to a very large expanse of grass which incorporated the playing
fields of Shoeburyness Comprehensive, the senior school
which I would attend from the age of eleven. My half-siblings,
both ahead of me in years, were assigned to schools in
Southend-on-Sea, two or three miles distant.
The street residents cut holes in the wire fencing that
surrounded the fields so that we could short cut across. The
council kept patching the fence, but in less than a day a new
hole would appear. They were never able to stop us using that
quicker and salubrious route.
I crossed that grass almost every day of the ten years I lived on

that street, sometimes several times a day. I crossed it on errands to the shops, or to visit a friend, or I played football there, or hung out with mates on languid summer days, and with girlfriends on dusky summer evenings.

I crossed the fields to school every day once I was old enough to attend. On mornings when the fog was so thick I could only see five feet ahead, or on mornings when fresh crisp white snow covered all of the grass a foot or more deep, and crunched beneath my shoes.

In autumn I pondered the fairy rings that grew, tight circles of wild mushrooms, and I made forgotten wishes.

At one end of Blyth there was a community centre building, squat and square, glass and wood. They held various community meetings and jumble sales. I attended Judo classes there for a while, along with Dawn. Upstairs was a small public library.

I was a voracious reader even at six or seven years old, and within a couple of years I had read all the children's books that were of interest to me. Those younger than eleven weren't permitted to draw books from the public sections of the library. I begged the librarians to let me access and read the books. I was hungry for them, and they were tantalizing in the rows of dark bookcases, heavy hard backed titles, or bright soft-backs, small and large, every color, worlds of wonders calling me to discover them, explore them, breathe their scents, feel their silk-like pages.

My frequent patronage of the library had stood me in good stead. I was always punctual with returns and very enthusiastic to read. At last it won me the grace of being allowed to draw freely from any part of the library, although I was then only about eight years old. Even before I was given this pass I was stealing across to the forbidden shelves, and browsing dreamily.

I had read already Tolkien's *The Hobbit,* and I had loved its magics and maps, the dragon and treasure and adventure, its curious, nimble, homely hobbit thief, and the stout-hearted, long-bearded dwarves. I wept for Thorin, at his poignant death.

I had found the great and beautiful tomes writ by the old storyteller; his name I recognised and gravitated to, and it gave me a fixed point in which to settle, and continue my journeys of cerebral adventure in the literary realms.

Tolkien remained a favourite author for me into adulthood. The grand mythology and lofty prose of the *Silmarillion* struck so deeply within me that I re-read it over and over. It gloamed and ached with beauty and tragedy and magics, lifting me with its adventure, its angelic and demonic struggles, its triumphs and hopelessnesses, its intrigues and marvellous creatures. I was enamoured no less with the dark cunning of Morgoth and his dire machinations, and the fascinations of Sauron, than with the heroisms of Turin Blacksword, Beren, the arts of Luthien, and the beauty of the Elven, the mysticism of the Anuir.

One favorite novel was *Eric: or little by little,* written by FW Farrar in the mid nineteenth century. I liked *Swallows and Amazons*, and some Dickens, and some young adult novels written by Alfred Hitchcock. I shared the same delight as my mother and Dawn over *Little Women*, and *The Famous Five* with its prolonged description of supper at the end of each adventure, for example. I enjoyed Agatha Christie's *Poirot*. I loved Harold Robbins' masterpiece *A Stone For Danny Fisher*. The Elvis movie *King Creole* had been adapted from it.

My borrowing from the library came to an abrupt end one summer. My father was visiting us, and was alarmed by the books I had withdrawn. Apparently he viewed them as unsuitable for me. I don't remember the titles, but they were four books on physics and philosophy; I had wanted to explore different areas of thought. I have forgotten the specifics of his objection.

He took them home with him, and I didn't get them back for over a year. During that time I was unable to borrow any other books.

I think perhaps he was more threatened by my precocious intellectual development than genuinely concerned that those books might somehow corrupt me. He might have pointed out the reasons why a particular title was objectionable, and advised me to select my reading material with more care. Instead, he shut down my avenue of development in that area entirely.

In the Bible's long boring stuffiness Christ shone out with his gentleness and wisdom, and I am moved to grief by his death, no less than I was by Thorin's. Besides Jesus, it is the Devil who is dynamic, exciting, erotic, mysterious, ambiguous, and interesting.

What are Heaven and God, I asked myself, apart from oppressive rules?

I too have the rebel's heart, and it tugs at those strings.

Still, I lament his puffed-upness, and his lack of foresight in battling against a force that it is not possible to overcome.

Moreover, he put himself in opposition to the veritable Great Source of All. The universe must tend towards perfection or it can not and would not exist. To oppose that motivation is insanity.

But, from the first reading I wondered: is the Devil in cahoots with the Divine? Eventually I realised the truth of it: the old dragon was always a liar, and the Bible is a corrupted version of events at best.

When Jesus was tempted by the Devil in the wilderness, Satan had said to him: *Just bow down to me, and I will give you the keys to all the kingdoms of the Earth.* It puzzled me that Christ was able to refuse him. The offer was glorious, magnificent, and a simple obeisance did not seem a high price. For a long time I felt that Christ should have accepted. Later, I saw matters more clearly, and comprehended the wider, symbolic implications of such an act. It was then that I realised that Christ's refusal had been easy. He was not actually tempted for even a moment. Satan offered nothing but a chimera, a hollow vision. Why would Jesus surrender his own Divine eternity, and surrender his great destiny? All the kingdoms of the world and all that one might possess were nothing, if one were to forever lose one's connection with the Divine.

One of the first books I drew from the public section of the library was an orange hard backed biography of Harry Houdini, the illusionist and escapologist. It quickly became a favorite read for me, and I withdrew it thereafter several times. Houdini impressed me on several levels, and if I had childhood heroes he was probably the first of them. I don't recollect the author of the book but it was an intimate portrayal, concentrating more on Houdini's philosophy and character rather than being concerned with listing every public event in the magician's life. It dwelt on his personal training methods, his struggles to perfect his art, and the innovations that he made. It was my first taste of practical mysticism.

Houdini confronted death in his performances. For example, he was buried alive in a lead lined coffin; he was frequently suspended at great heights in manacles and chains; he leapt from bridges, shackled and bound, into deep and often freezing waters. Only his expertise, his ardent physical training, and above all his mental detachment and fakir-calmness enabled him to escape, and avoid death.

Unlike many pseudo-conjurers who followed after him, his feats were real. He used contemporary handcuffs, famously inviting the public to bring along any manacle or shackle or cuff, even straight-jackets, to his performances, which he would then invariably escape from. Even when they brought him rigged and sealed devices designed to trap him he was never defeated, and always effected an escape. This he achieved partly througha physiological disposition, he was able to dislocate his shoulder to escape from straight-jackets, and largely from his indomitable will, and his meticulous preparations and athletic trainings. So real were his feats that he often received brutal injuries whilst freeing himself.

Although fascinated by the spectacle of Houdini's escapology I never found any desire to emulate him in those areas. I was moved more by his apparent spirituality; he used his body to produce the miraculous; it was his breath control and his calmness of mind that allowed him to remain submerged in icy waters, or beneath the cold ground; it was his understanding of the physical, his harmonising with the universal energy, his ability to manipulate his own physicality, that enabled many of his contorted escapes.

Houdini pointed towards the extraordinary. He vividly demonstrated the power which resided within. I wanted to develop such control and connection, a dedication like his; to rise above the constraint of the physical, and become a worker of magicks.

I began to practice holding my breath, submerged under water in the bath, or whilst laying in my bed at night. I explored sleight of hand and card manipulations, which became an enduring interest. These activities were a way in which I could approach my own powers of control. They laid foundations for my later interests in mysticism and magicks.

Nine

I spent a lot of days at my grandmother Ivy's house as a child. During the first year we were at Blyth Avenue my mother visited her often. She lived a ten minute walk away from us on Gilman Drive, just across the road from the newsagents shop and the grocery store.

I was five years old, and would be starting at Richmond Junior School come September.

Ivy was an attractive woman. Her skin was always smooth and clear, even when she reached her sixties. Her hair had faded to blonde, and became a soft pure white as she grew older. She wore it in a classic fifties' style, with a swept up quiff at the front. She was straight forwards and earthy, daughter of Gypsies, and a product of her generation. After Al died, she never dated another man again, even though she had only been in her thirties.

Barbara seemed to be a puzzle to her; she had lost her way somehow, and Ivy couldn't comprehend why that had happened. Their relationship was often stormy, and they would be unable to see eye to eye and fall out for periods of time. Ivy was conventional and practical and managed all her affairs admirably, and was never in debt, whilst Barbara was a whirlwind of impracticality and forever struggling.

I enjoyed my nan's company, and I liked her home which was cosy and clean. She had a rocking chair, a dog named Tammy, and a cat named Tiger. It was a calm environment, and I could play contentedly without worries.

One afternoon I was looking forward to having my lunch there, as I walked with my mother. It was windy, and Barbara complained that she was unable to breathe. When we arrived at Ivy's house Barbara was still feeling uncomfortable. She drank some water but struggled to swallow. Her anxiety was high and she said that she couldn't eat lunch because she wouldn't be able to swallow the food. Ivy told her she was being silly and to just relax, but something had changed in Barbara's mind. It was the beginning of a persistent neurosis. She left quickly. I was disappointed about missing lunch, as Barbara and I walked home.

'It was the wind that day, took my breath away,' she would say years later.

From that day onwards my mother ate alone. She would read a book and sip a cup of tea at every meal. She ate very slowly, struggling to swallow each mouthful of food. Eventually she had to have liquid supplements because solid foods were too much of an ordeal for her. She drank alcohol more frequently to combat her anxiety, but she became wholly dependant upon it, and her anxiety didn't lessen.

It was twenty years until she finally got past this neurosis completely and was able to eat normally again.

Every lunchtime she would have a 'nap.' 'Wake me up in an hour,' she instructed me. When I woke her I would have to make her a cup of tea and bring it upstairs to her, and often I would then be sent back down to light her cigarette from the stove, as she was frequently without matches or a lighter. Trying to light her cigarettes from the hob was difficult, whether we had electricity or gas at the time. Without inhaling to ignite the tobacco the cigarette wouldn't light properly. I held it into the gas flame, and it smoked and the white paper became black and cracked, but the end was barely lit. Or I pressed it onto the electric ring, when we had an electric cooker, and the same thing would happen. It took me several minutes sometimes before the tobacco ignited sufficiently so that I could take it up to her.

Eventually, when I was around seven years old, I was fed up with this protracted performance. I put the cigarette in my mouth and inhaled as I pressed the end against the hob, and it lit easily. From then on I lit it in the same manner. I tried a couple of puffs, and found that I liked it.

I began smoking irregularly. She left long butts in her ashtrays, and I would choose a few choice ones, and smoke them whilst on errands to the shops for her. I bought a box of matches and after I had smoked the cigarettes, I would put a lit match into the box, igniting those matches that remained. By the time I was thirteen years old I was smoking ten to twenty roll ups a day, and was allowed to smoke at home.

Ivy had a sister named Renee who lived at Walthamstow, London. She came to visit Ivy several times a year, especially during the summer months. Her husband Peter drove them. Before they left Walthamstow he was already drunk, and after they arrived at Ivy's he would drink several blue cans of Tenants Super through the afternoon, which is a thick syrupy extremely potent lager.

By late afternoon he was very drunk, and argumentative, but would then drive us all over to East Beach, where the adults would enjoy cockles and winkles in vinegar. I tried them occasionally, but otherwise refused to eat them. They looked disgusting, like pickled snails or something. It is amazing that Peter never killed himself or anyone else whilst driving. He could barely stand upright sometimes, and would be staggering as he tried to get to his car. The women just tutted and shook their heads long-sufferingly. You were considered fit to drive during the seventies even if you were drunk.

Renee was beautiful, like her sister. Her hair was also swept into a fifties style quiff, and it was a soft reddish color. I was drawn to her, and enjoyed these visits immensely. It was upsetting to me that she and Peter bickered so much.

Renee died suddenly from a heart attack when she was fifty two years old. Peter never eased up on his drinking. He lived the remaining years of his life in an almost constant drunken oblivion.

I was in the gutter, yes, but like Oscar Wilde, I could look up and see the glistering stars.

Shoeburyness was a poor town, mostly council houses and working class families. The division between us and them, the affluent, the aristocrats who lorded over us, was stark and poignant. We felt our lack of opportunity, and we knew their grasping greed. Our oppressors, they wanted even the few spare pennies we had managed to claw from the dirt. Our poverty was their wealth.

'You will amount to nothing,' my first year English teacher told us. 'You have no future.'

Stealing from them was permissible: from their department stores, their office buildings, their goods vehicles, their warehouses. Selling stolen goods was an acceptable local pastime. People greatly appreciated the chance of attaining a small luxury, and stolen goods had a standard price of one-third of their retail value. Thieves would go from door to door along Blyth Avenue with their bags of stolen swag, selling jeans and perfumes, meats and gold, and whatever else they had managed to snatch that week. They were welcomed warmly and invited in. People were excited to see them; they were Robin Hoods.

Burglary on the contrary was always frowned upon, considered invasive and wayward. Habitual house burglars were viewed as deviants and shunned. It was part of a moral code which translated as never stealing from people who were struggling under the same weight as you; not just your neighbours, but also the larger extended community. Successful heists were applauded, and career criminals and ex-convicts were revered and respected.

It was a pragmatic tolerance. Circumstances were tough, and the odds were forever stacked against us. This was our own little Hell's Kitchen, and the streets were as mean as any. Hopping the fences and squeezing through the cracks was survival, and possibly an avenue to a slightly more comfortable future. If someone was able through 'ducking and diving' or 'a little bit of business' to claw their way out of the slum, and make a better life for their family, then we said: 'Good luck to them.'

Physical violence was not uncommon but the use of weapons was. Having nothing of value but his own fists a young guy could still carve out some fame. The number of police officers sent to arrest a man was indicative of his prowess and meanness. If he put up a struggle against five or six cops then he was a hero in local eyes.

My mother expected that my half brother and I would one day rob banks, and bring home bags of cash for her.

I did not have a criminal heart. When I broke the law I was

usually apprehended. I always admitted my crime, never thought to lie or to deny, and passively accepted the consequences of my actions. I seemed destined for prison. But these were youthful transgressions only, and I did not commit to that lifestyle.

I was quite an adroit shoplifter long before I was ten years old. Although I was caught once, and even spent an hour in the police cells at about eight years old, for several years I took whatever I wanted from shops without discovery and repercussion: sweets, marbles, toys, the trinkets of a child. I found pleasure and pride as I lifted the objects of my desire from under the noses of shopkeepers. It was a dangerous game, and playing it made me feel clever and artful.

Thanks to these five fingered discounts I had little need of money, and thus its lack lessened for me. I stole in this manner so often that it became somewhat of a reflex, and I continued shoplifting into my late teens. By that time, of course, my wants had morphed. Now I stole clothes, books, liquor. I stole as a teen with a sense of entitlement.

For me though, it was a bad habit that I grew out of, albeit quite slowly.

Ten

In my heart I confirmed my affiliation with *that world there*, and in this world here the flame rose into my heart. I would seek out and find certain truth. Who am I? Why am I here? What is it that I am meant to do, to be?

I did not become a priest, although often I mused on the notion, but the spiritual journey was mine, and I held always fast to its narrow road.

I would never settle for less than absolute. I would never embrace delusions and empty worship. The Divine was not an unfathomable mystery. There was a rational, logical comprehension somewhere, mixt with instinct and intuition. And I would find it.

The kitchen was a long rectangle. Orange linoleum tiles. The back door was a horrible dirty industrial blue, with a frosted glass window through which only indistinct shapes could be seen. Two or three times the glass was replaced after Gary, in a fit of temper, punched his fist through it. The glass ripped his hand and wrist, and there was a lot of red blood. He wept as Barbara washed the wounds at the kitchen sink.

To the left, entering through the back door, was a work surface, a thin flowery curtain tacked across its edge to hide the damp and mildew smelling paraphernalia beneath, then the silver colored sink and drainer. There was a double paned window above the sink, a white net curtain.

The cooker stood beside this, and whatever washing machine my mother presently had, all ancient and labor intensive, was next to the cooker, invariably piled teeteringly high with ready to wash clothes.

It was a pile that would never be cleared entirely.

A triple pane window divided the rest of that wall, and let light and space into the room. Beneath it was a dark wood '50s sideboard, which was employed as a food cupboard. There were no wall mounted cabinets at all. A yellow table and matching four '60s dining chairs completed the furnishings.

A larder was built into the wall on the other side of the room, between the back door and the door which led into the hall. The larder was a six foot tall space, with its own door, painted dreary white, divided by three shelves.

Into the hallway, and the stairs are to the right. There is a large triangle space beneath them wherein she will pile divers junk. The flat wall on the left leads to the lounge, and to the front door, a tepid blue. The carpets are always ill fitting, deep plums and reds and blacks. At the foot of the stair is a window that looks out onto the dark hedge.

When my half sister was nine and I was eight, my mother read an ad in the local newspaper that offered an upright piano free to anyone who could collect. She sent Dawn and I to fetch it. It belonged to a family on the other side of Shoebury, past Ness Road, heading east towards the beach. We were expected to push and drag it all the way back across town. After half an hour we only reached the end of the first street, using a blanket to lay under the small brass wheels. Mercifully, a guy driving a large van stopped and helped us, putting the piano into his van, and driving us the rest of the way to Blyth.

The piano was black, out of tune, and stood now beneath the window at the foot of the stairs.

The lounge was about twenty five square feet. The sofa, situated with its back to you, entering the room, so that its seats were facing the fireplace, was always lumpy and uncomfortable, stacks of newspapers pressed flat between the cushions. Perhaps my mother didn't want anyone getting too settled.

She hoarded junk in out of the way places, with a semblance of neatness on the surface, and grime underneath.

The shed outside in the back garden was almost as large as this lounge. It could have been utilized for something better than the heaps of bulging bin bags she 'stored' in there. The contents weren't food or anything that would rot, thankfully. It never attracted rats.

She put old clothes, old toys, scraps, paper, magazines, and who knows what other crap inside. The bin bags soon reached to the ceiling. Eventually it was impossible to get into the brick building. She paid a guy to come and clear it. Within a couple of months she had filled it again.

In the front room a small bookcase against one wall, and when we had a television it was placed on a low table in the corner, right of the fire. Until I was in my teenage years we mostly didn't have a TV.

A couple of times we were even without electricity for several months, and for an entire year once. She would regularly rob the fifty pence pieces from out of the electric meter. If she didn't replace them before the collector came, the electricity company would cut off the supply, and leave it off until the debt was cleared.

And the gas meter. She taught herself to pick the padlocks, using the twisted wire from a clothes peg. It took her up to an hour to achieve on some occasions, or other times the lock sprung after five or ten minutes. I'm not sure how she managed to achieve it using such a clumsy tool.

She had been wild on occasion in her youth. One time she held up a store on the seafront, when she was about twenty, by pretending to have a gun in her coat pocket. The sort of unlikely scenario that you might see in a black and white B-movie. She was arrested before she even left the shop.

She was still forever scheming, and dreaming of obtaining wealth. Money was her phantasmagoria.

Mostly she only schemed, making no actual attempt to inform herself so that she might improve our situation. She sat alone in her bedroom. The curtains were always drawn. It was dark and musty, warm. Her knees pulled up beneath the blankets. She smoked, her ashtrays overflowing. The radio fixed on BBC Radio Two, quietly. She sipped at her cider. The days bled away.

At first she was still socializing once or twice a week. She brought boyfriends home with her from the pub, made them bacon sandwiches for breakfast.

The first summer she took us down to the beach, via Thorpe Bay. A long straight sloping road running parallel to Blyth and Bunters, then dipping down out of the slow hill, and we can see the coast shining. The houses on this street are middle class, detached, with garages and enclosed lawns, two or three cars in the majestic drives.

She brings orange squash, warm in the weak sun, and sandwiches. I adore jam, and never want anything else on my bread. She makes me eat sardines. I bite down my revulsion. At home, at every meal, with perhaps two exceptions per week, she boils dark cabbage then slops it onto my plate as a side to whatever else we are having. I deeply abhor it; the foul smell, the dark bitter taste. Every mouthful twists my stomach, but I am forced to eat. It is good for you, she insists. It has iron. It will make you strong. She tortures me every day, destroys every meal I have. If I do not eat it she hits me and refuses me any other food. If I don't eat it every meal when she serves it to me, I will have nothing at all to eat that evening or for breakfast. Then she will serve me cabbage again at lunch. Sit there until you eat it. Don't eat around it. Fucking eat it! Dawn and Gary eat theirs without complaint.

I am walking with her one day. I am very young, holding her hand. There is a large bleak building at the end of the road, and there are men slooshing the yard before it with hoses. I ask her why, and she tells me they are washing away the blood; it is a slaughterhouse.

I had no idea that the meat on our plates was the flesh of animals. I am deeply shocked. It is a heartbreaking and bewildering revelation. She dismisses my protests and insists that I eat meat or nothing at all. It is a fight that I am too small to engage in. I cannot yet fend for myself or defeat her arguments. I must concede and eat the flesh of these beautiful creatures.

They call me an 'animal lover' throughout my childhood, and it is always meant as a slur and an insult, as though to have empathy and compassion for something alive and beautiful were a neurotic madness.

'They are here to be eaten,' my mother tells me impatiently. 'They don't have any feelings. They are just like robots.'

Yes, I eat cow. I am not proud, as Kurt Cobain put it. Humanity would never have survived the long dark winters without livestock as support. It is natural and healthy for humans to eat animals, and to make good use of all parts thereof.

What is unnatural is the cruel and degrading treatment animals often receive. Animals feel emotion: they express fear vividly, as a clear example. Fear is an emotion; and it is proof that they are not unfeeling machines. Whether they have Souls or not is a different question, but as emotional creatures, able to feel comfort and contentment, as well as fear and pain and discomfort, the very least they deserve is to be treated with respect. We would never have made it this far without them.

She took Dawn and I to the beach one morning, I think it was whilst we were staying at Seaview Homes.

It is early, and the tide is still an hour out. There are only a few groups of people yet. The wet sands, rocks and pools are prime crab hunting territory. I wander into the watery worlds.

When I look up the beach is suddenly packed with hundreds of people. I have been so absorbed in my hunting and playing that I did not see them arrive. Loud buzzing voices, so many shapes and colors that it is dazzling me, and even the tide has encroached without my noticing, and dozens of people are wading and swimming in its shallow.

I cannot see my mother or my sister. I search for them, but do not find them. I try to find my way home. This road which I must cross is wide and busy. I step out determinedly, but a van hits me, doesn't even see me, and I roll dazed into the kerb. I lay there until a man from St John's Ambulance discovers me. He takes me gently into the ambulance, and patches up my scrapes. No lasting damage.

Ten minutes after I have been there my mother arrives. She seems disappointed to find me. Or something; I can't dechipher the look she gives me. I don't know what she is thinking.

Next summer at Blyth Avenue she sent my half-sister and I out every day of the school summer holidays, instructing us to go to the beach, with sandwiches, warm orange squash, and sometimes a small amount of cash to buy some honeycomb from Uncle Tom's Cabin.

We were not to return until dusk, about ten hours. We spent

most of every day at the beach. Get out and play in the sunshine! she would say with exasperation. It's not healthy to stay indoors all day! Gary was never constrained as Dawn and I were. From the start he sauntered off to meet his mates, never having errands to run, or any responsibility towards us, his younger, more vulnerable siblings. We were glad. If he was around it meant we would be getting bullied, since that was all that he was capable of. Left to ourselves we settled into quiet and contented games, adapting child-like to circumstance, imagining ourselves, creating characters to escape into, dallying weeks in make believe worlds.

Sometimes Gary was hanging at the beach, and would terrorise us for awhile. He threw a screwdriver into my face one day, and it struck me on the edge of my brow, between the eyes, an inch from taking one. It cut deep and left a thin permanent silver scar. It bled profusely. They took me home, and my T-shirt was drenched in blood.
Another day, he punches and bullies me until I agree to swim out to one of the boats with him. I am a good swimmer, but I am not old enough to attempt this, as he is well aware. It is a long, difficult swim. The tides here at Shoeburyness are notoriously treacherous, fierce and powerful, often taking lives. I follow him into the water reluctantly, and we crawl out to the boats which dip and rise with the jagged waves, a mile or more from shore. It is a tiring course. The current is already strong, pushing against me as I try to cut across. Gary strikes away, soon leaving a wide distance between us. I pause and catch my breath. My arms ache. My chest aches. My throat is dry. I am tired, and I have barely made it a third of the distance yet.
The sea lifts me, pushes me, rolls over me.
I surrender to the swirling force of the currents, not fighting it any more, being part of the majestic strength, riding the swells, skimming over their skirts and sliding into the route I seek.
When I look up Gary is sitting on one of the further boats. My spirits sink realising the extra effort the distance represents. He grins and waves at me, yells for me to hurry up.
I look back, and the shore is very far away. No one is out

anywhere near as far as us. The tides are coming in fast and will be deep and turbulent.

Many people have been drowned in this sea, in these gripping relentless twisting currents, on this stretch of beach, where Shoeburyness yields to North Shoebury, and the shift is marked by the iron fences of the abandoned MOD barracks.

On some tides there are whirlpool currents that drive into shore then swing out past the iron fence in a long hard loop, releasing nothing that they have swept up. These currents are resolute, so strong that they cannot be swam against, one can only fall with them, sweep in the slow curve to their edge. At these weaker edges one might dive free like a dolphin or porpoise, skipping across, out of the water, through the drive.

We heard every summer of young guys being swept out to the North Sea, their bodies rarely recovered.

As I reach the boat Gary shouts to me, drowning my fleeting triumph: 'Ha! Now you still have to swim back! You'll never make it.' Laughing, he dives past me and swims for shore.

Eleven

I compose stories in my mind as I ramble. Often I am the hero,
and the tale is usually a detailed description of my mundane
activities.
I invest my life with adventure and significance.
I have nothing to do but create in these long monotonous days,
and the writer that I will become takes this cue and begins to
shape craft. Climbing this hill, whose pavements my footfall
will wear to hollows over years, and there in those indented
groves I will tread again with friends as yet unknown, in
perpetuity, becomes my ardent quest, and my narrative is
attentive to every nuance.
At home I make little books from cut and folded paper,
decorating them, writing longhand stories in tiny letters; faery
books.

There was a guy who lived next to the alley cutting through to
join Caulfield from Gilman. I saw him fairly often, as I was
going to or from my nan's house. His hair was very black,
shoulder length, and he wore a close beard. His eyes were
startling sapphires.
One day I finally summoned courage and asked him if he was
the Christ?
'No,' he responded, 'but I did wonder why you were always
staring at me. It's a nice compliment. Thank you.'

Barbara used alcohol to calm her anxieties, and its expense cut
deeply into the minimal state benefits she received. There was
not enough money left to keep a sufficiently stocked larder.
I ate sugar from the bowl and the packet, most days half a
dozen or ten spoonfuls. My mother liked her tea sweet, and she
drank it constantly through the day, alongside her cider. Sugar
we always had. I tried just about everything that I found in the
recesses of those cupboards, including dried and powdered
products such as icing sugar, custard, milk powder, cocoa...
anything that had a slight sweetness or sharpness to make it
edible, including spiky malt vinegar. I was so hungry, and there

was nothing else to eat or drink.

In this family being the youngest child is not an indulged position. The youngest here means the last in line. I have no privileges.

I don't even get a cuddly toy to sleep with, on the hard, cushion-less, mattress-less bed base that I have to sleep on, with two dark gray blankets, and an uncovered bed-roll pillow.

Being the youngest here means you are ruthlessly exploited, and you get all the crappy chores that no one else wants to do: fetching her smokes, running errands across town, daily grocery shopping. Begging at the neighbours; mum says please will you lend her a pound, a fiver, a couple cigarettes, some bread, some butter, some potatoes. If she says 'no,' go to that one. If they say 'no,' go to the next one. Walk to your nan's, and take this list. Go to Steph and Win's, go across to Doreen, borrow a fiver 'till Monday. The indignity.

I am open to every exploitation, and my objections are all overruled. I am a drain on resources and deserve nothing.

Gary gets the extra slices of pie, the best of the meat, he gets the cream from the top of the milk, the chocolate, the extra pounds spent on his school requirements: *he needs them*, my mother insists, those items that suddenly no longer matter when I reach the same age he was, and have equivalent needs.

Dawn is indulged because of her gender. I have no saving graces. My weirdness is not a boon.

Barbara is proud to buy Gary a new bike, a ten gear racer, when he reaches thirteen. There are brass bands playing, marching girls twirling batons. It is a celebration. Dawn gets a new bike on her thirteenth birthday. I am eager to be thirteen, for the day my promised new bike will be here: but the tradition has been abandoned by the time I am thirteen, just a year or so after Dawn. Why does she punish me like this? What is she hoping for from it? What lesson does she try to teach me?

Even through to my late teens my feelings towards her are overwhelmed by sorrow and pity for her dismalness. Perhaps I will rob banks for her one day and bring her the riches she craves, if that would make her happy.

She told one of my girlfriends that I had always been her favorite child. I was surprised. She had a peculiar way of expressing her favoritism.

Jon arrived on my sixth birthday with Airfix kits. There were about ten of them, ranging from six or seven inches long gun boats, progressing in size and detail, up to two foot long cruisers and battleships, with moving gun turrets, and lifeboats, and flagpoles, and tiny little gray men, and stickers, and port holes. They were plastic mouldings, and so many tiny parts, very intricate, requiring a fastidious patience and a steady slow care to build. The plans folded out like maps and were abstruse and complex, equations of a curious physics.

He told me to start on the smallest one. If I did it nicely I would be allowed to work on the others as I pleased. A few weeks later he returned, and asked to see my first attempt. I ran upstairs to get it.

I was excited. I thought I did a good job. I longed to begin building the other, larger boats. I had mooned over their pictures on the boxes, opened out their labyrinthine plans to wonder over, be lost in, building them all in imaginative dreamings.

When I showed him what I had built he was furious. I had used too much glue, I hadn't followed the plans properly, omitting some minuscule details, veering creatively from guidelines with some fixtures. Where are the appropriate stickers? This is not a toy. It was far from perfect. He took all of them from me, away with him. I saw them again once a couple of years later, on which was, I think, the single occasion that he had me stay at his apartment for a weekend. The boxes were piled onto a sideboard in his bedroom, untouched.

The next year he tells me that he is going to send me thirty pounds by post. Expect the postman on the morning of your birthday, he says. It is an amazing amount of money. I can buy whatever I want with it, any fantastic, huge toy that I can think of or that I see. I feast on imaginings.

On the morning of my birthday my mother reaches the post before I can get downstairs. She tells me that there is no letter or card from Jon. I think I see his letter amongst the bills, but she denies it. She keeps the money he sent me for herself.

But, he had told me to expect it, and I knew he would keep his word and send it. I waited at the landing window, watching for the postman every morning for the next two weeks. It couldn't arrive twice of course, and finally she had to write to him to say it hadn't been delivered.

He sent another card, this time with twenty pounds in it, and a note expressing his anger. Barbara borrowed half of that twenty pounds until Monday. That meant I didn't have enough to buy the huge expensive toy my father and I had envisioned, only ten pounds after all. She did pay me back the tenner she had borrowed when she got her money a few days later.

Thirty pounds was a lot of money in 1974, about the same as my mother received in benefits for the week, aside from the Housing Benefit. Her theft, stealing her seven year old son's birthday present, meant it had cost Jon fifty pounds in all, which was probably more than a week's wage for him.

I remember on my fourth birthday she told me she was skint, and gave me a matchbox with five five pence pieces in it. The matchbox wasn't even wrapped.

Twelve

Until I was six years old and Dawn was seven we had shared the larger bedroom, whose window overlooked our back garden, and Gary was in a small box room at the front of the house. My mother decided that my half-sister and I were too old to continue sleeping in the same room, so from then on I had to share my bedroom with Gary. He was ten years old.

He had already been bullying me throughout the daytimes, repeatedly punching me, and generally making life unpleasant for me, but sharing a bedroom with him for the next five years gave him the opportunity to beat me without reprisals every night.

Barbara ignored my calls for help. When I tried to talk with her about it during the day, to get her to bring an end to the abuse I was having to endure, she offhandedly dismissed my complaints and appeals.

Gary unleashed all his despise afresh every evening, and soon he was hitting puberty, and testosterone added strength to his punches and kicks, and aggression to his psychosis, and his jealous fury never abated.

He was never too tired, or in a mood for peace. It was ritual, obsessive behaviour. He was four years my senior, and much bigger and stronger than me during those stages of our physical development, so that I could not hurt him easily.

It is a disgusting feeling to be punched in the face. The belly lurches and pitches, whilst the mind reels, and a nauseating pain leaps through the body, and all the alarms are ringing.

I stumbled through the metallic nausea of the punches, until being beaten on became less disorientating. Moment to moment, one blow to the next, I taught myself to be sharp and focused. Mistakes were painful and bruising.

I had to disassociate from the physical somehow, to find a cerebral latibule, and not to cry, although it was natural to want to let this pain out. But, doing so would be victory for him; he smiled triumphantly at my tears.

As he hit me, he told me that I was weak and worthless, told me that no one would ever want me, or love me, as though I were already a threat to him, a rival, needing to be destroyed. He degraded me, and I had done nothing to provoke him, besides being born.

Systematically, with violence and repetition, he drove his message home, and I would have to carry the wounds that he inflicted. My brain reacted to the continuous stress with fight or flight prompts and high alert, but there was no way for me to avoid his violence.

In extended stressful and anxious circumstances, particularly when the fight or flight response is engaged, the brain is flooded with toxic levels of neurotransmitters, which can impair the development of the hippocampus in the brain. This leads to the sense of joy being dulled and fragile, predisposing one for later depression, addiction, and post traumatic stress disorder. During those five years I was under constant threat, perpetually tense if he was around.

Melancholy spread its darknesses wide over me, and slithered into the utter fabric of me.

My mother slept in the next room. She will not answer my calls for help, other than screaming at me to shut the fuck up. Otherwise she is apparently blind and deaf to this abuse. 'Well, your precious father isn't here to protect you, is he? Maybe you are getting what you deserve,' she sneers, one night when I beg her to see me and hear me, to witness this violence, and deliver me from it. By leaving me defenceless, she is, in the logic of her neurosis, punishing Jon for leaving her. It was the one moment in all of our interactions about this ongoing violence when my mother was honest with me. Irritated, between sleep and waking, she could not avoid my persistence. She flung that truth like a dagger, never articulated before nor since, and it struck into my heart, and stunned me into silence. She smiled.

She had allowed this wickedness. She knew all along what was happening, Gary beating incessantly upon me, and of course how could she not have, when it is a ritual loudly played each night in her house?

I am injured, and the hollow in my belly is tender to every

nuance, and I will abear insecurities, anxieties, shyness, infinite sadnesses, depression, addictions, dreams of death.

I lay in the darkness, back in my bed that night after her revelation, and I was filled with despair. I was seven years old at this point, and powerless to change anything alone. If my mother wouldn't protect me there was nothing I could do. I am the one in the wrong, she told me, and my beatings are deserved. There will be no end of it now. By morning time I had resolved to leave.

I packed a small bag, and walked to the end of Blyth. At the junction I considered my futures, and I knew they were all grim. The thought of walking to London like a latter day Dick Whittington was appealing, but I knew I was too young and vulnerable to survive.

I weighed all things and understood that I must return to the monster's lair, the only shelter.

My mother was waiting for me in the kitchen, having watched me from the landing window.

'Did you think I would come after you? You live in a little fairy story all of your own! You'll find out life isn't like that. Leave. I won't stop you. But, you need me, don't you? To wipe your arse, and cook for you. I suppose are too young for me to throw out, so you can stay until you are sixteen. I will feed you, but that is all,' she said contemptuously.

She was in a dark place, and upon me her frustrations settled.

Depression insidiously worked into my bones and my blood, shaping me. It was tight in my throat, a sharp anguish in my belly. I would rather die than stay here.

Yet, even death is denied me. I cannot find it, though I am seeking for months. I jump from heights but am unharmed. I step out into traffic, to screeching brakes and startled, angry drivers. I turn on the gas oven and lay my head inside and try to sleep, but it is too uncomfortable.

I drink entire bottles of medicine and eat strange pills. Sometimes I get a little sick, sometimes a little high, but I do not die. Eventually I realise there is no escaping.

In Gary's narcissistic mind his own entitlement was paramount. He wanted to destroy me so that I could not steal the adoration which he craved. I was a rogue light that diminished his by proxy.

As he grew older he became increasingly obsessive about his appearance. He was agonisingly fastidious. He fretted over every aspect of his appearance. His hair, the whiteness of his shirts or socks, and the sharpness of crease in his trouser legs. It all had to be exactly so. He was ever a fashion victim. He learnt to use an iron because he wanted to spend hours pressing his own clothes until they were 'perfect.' Where I seem to have chosen always to be at odds with the world outside, he was concerned about fitting in, avoiding criticism by getting all the details correct.

Barbara happily altered his clothes to his demanding specifications. He stood on the kitchen chairs, his expression pained, as she pinned his turn-up hems, or measured his jeans to cut their length. There were discussions about all nuances of his appearance, Barbara applauding and cooing, reinforcing and encouraging, laughing and clapping.

When he was getting ready to go out when he was a teenager there was always a protracted theatrical performance. He carried the long dressing mirror into the kitchen, and propped it on the chair seat. He preened and danced, jovially aggressive, and we were all summoned to watch, forbidden to leave until he was done.

He was happy in those moments, as he bullied us into adoration. His vanity was a gregarious confidence. She forgave him everything, and they both basked in his brutal beauty.

My heart was filled with contempt for them, but I kept my silence.

I developed a tolerance to the physical pain, and I became adept at deflecting his kicks and punches, blocking them with my forearms like a tiny skinny Bruce Lee. He was wild and incoherent, motivated by anger and aggression, but I was learning control and with it I would defeat him.

I turned my body from his stomping kicks, slipped between the swinging fists, and they glanced off of me, their stinging bite neutered.

I never cried or called to my mother for help again, and that was a defeat for him, and perhaps also for her. I was not so strong as him, but I was fast, and soon he could only rarely land a clean blow. It maddened him, and he would try harder, punch with more force and hatred. I laughed at his impotency. I wished hard for his death.

Slowly I was growing stronger. Also, anger was building in me at these perpetual injustices, these indignities. And as I turned aside his blows, he was exposed, and I punched him with fast snapping punches.

I knew I hurt him because he would scream and rage and redouble his efforts. But now he would never pin me again. He would never hurt me more than he had already.

Of course, I could not prevent every connection, and sometimes his punches caught me. When all his weight and fury slammed into my face the pain was metallic, nauseating, very disorientating.

Like Houdini, I tightened my stomach muscles to adsorb the blows that landed there. My belly became tight and solid.

I was fighting to defend myself against an inexhaustible enemy. I could not beg mercy, because he would never stop. He was trying to kill me.

A thousand nights passed, and he hated me because I was sweet and beautiful, and clever and creative, and because I would not break, but instead became strong. Always I opposed him, and would not die.

Another thousand nights and I was stone.

Thirteen

I pursued an instinctive meditation, when I was in bed of an evening, alone in the room, an hour or two before my half-brother would be going to bed, or in later years, when he would be out on some nocturnal mischief.

I closed my eyes, and calmly drifted down into eigengrau darkness. My awareness centred, I lifted back and out into mottled starscapes, and I pushed on then until I saw pulsing banks of color. Crossing over these I reached solid walls, deep electric reds and blues and orange.

I passed through the walls and delicious energies pulsed through my body. At length I reached a small white gate, and beyond this mark a sweet ecstasy washed me. It became established, a well trodden path, the distances finite, measurable, recognizable.

At one moment I was microscopic; so tiny and insignificant amongst the limitless universes, the spiralling galaxies turning above me; the next moment I was the infiniteness of Soul, above the firmament now, feeling the awesome endlessness of the Divine. This juxtaposition of viewpoints fluxed perpetually, and to rest in its rhythm filled me with bliss.

I continued with this meditation for several years, into my teens.

At fourteen, when I began being out later, and was tired when I finally went to bed, midnight close, and I had begun working at a bistro in Southend until the early hours of morning, I slept quickly, forgetting, or being without the necessary concentration to reach that place. Occasionally I still found the route, but it faded the less frequently I pursued it.

My mother was downstairs in the kitchen. My half-siblings were not at home. When I entered my bedroom I saw that a boy, slightly older than me, was sitting on the top of my wardrobe.

The wardrobe was constructed from heavy dark wood, a type and style popular in the sixties. My mother must have acquired it cheap from somewhere, or perhaps it was already here when we moved in.

I accepted his presence in my room, on the top of the wardrobe, as appropriate and natural. He looked about my height and was dressed in clothes that seemed from another period. They were rich and elaborate, perhaps brocade. I smiled at him and sat down on the edge of my bed, and we began to converse.

We were familiar and comfortable. I recognised him in a non-physical way. We talked for several animated and intimate minutes. We discussed my then present life and immediate future, and like a benevolent elder sibling he offered sage advice, particularly regarding how I might deal with Gary. He was kindly guiding me, instructing me. Then, suddenly he was gone.

When I told my mother what had happened, she conceded that I had probably seen a ghost.

I don't think he was a ghost. If he were my reaction would have been surprise and alarm. Instead I was left with a quiet wonder and puzzlement.

I push on the white kitchen door and my vision grays and shrinks to a hazy centre. Fire thrums inside my head. I rise up fast, soaring. My body trembles. I sway, drift into the folds until I can see.

I am behind myself, looking over my shoulder, the back of my head. My hair is braided, and I am wearing a pale everyday dress. My mood is buoyant, as I step over the threshold, into the kitchen. My mother looks back from the sink, the table to our right, as is as was, you and I.

'I was a French girl!' I say to Barbara.

She dismisses me with illogic: 'How could you be French, when you are English?'

I did not know that such creatures existed in the world. I am shaken, as though she were Divine, the first time I see Marilyn Monroe on television.

She is shining like a brilliant star against the abyss, and my Soul leaps in my belly. She is dressed in a cream shift, with white fur floating around her shoulders, and she is effortlessly graceful and assured. She is charming and funny. She is more beauty, elegance and femininity than I have ever seen.

I look at my mother who is seated beside me, and I cannot see that she and Marilyn are even of the same species.

Marilyn's film roles, with a couple of great exceptions, were mostly trite, and they were not where she really transcended. It was in the creation of herself, of Marilyn, that she became utterly *other*.

As a young girl Marilyn had envisioned this goddess as an image to aspire to and become, a flirtatious angel who would seduce the whole world.

Her real legacy and her truth are found in the thousands of photographs taken of her.

I was a keen climber of drainpipes and buildings and fences and trees. Often I climbed out from my bedroom window and perched on the outer sill. From there I manoeuvred across until I could stretch and reach the wall edge of the bathroom window with my hand. With this grip as support I could slide across and get a foot onto the bathroom sill, and shift my weight and balance there, and then step across to the drainpipe and descend.

If I took the more conventional option of the stairs in the house, then I would jump from the sixth or seven step, tumbling past the piano, or else slide down the banister or swing over the stair rail and drop to the hallway.

One day Gary, from a standing position on the top of our shed in the back garden of Blyth, threw my Action Man onto the roof of the block of flats that were next to us. It took a few attempts before he succeeded. The flat brick side of the building loomed over our garden, very tall and undistinguished without windows, about seventy or eighty feet, I guess. Losing the toy was a painful blow, but Gary had something else in mind.

He persuaded me to try to climb up onto the block's roof to retrieve the toy. I climbed to the top of the drainpipe at the back end of the building, but when I reached it, the ledge of the roof jutted much too far for me to be able to negotiate; I could have gotten onto it, but getting back to the drainpipe afterwards would have been impossible.

A resident of the flats came out into their back gardens whilst I was just beneath the roof, and although he was friendly enough, still he was concerned that I was in some peril, and with him there Gary could not insist that I made the attempt.

If I had of fallen, or if my weight had made the drainpipe come away from the wall, it was a sixty foot drop onto concrete.

Such a fall would very likely cause serious injury, or even death. This was Gary's plan and hope, and he was extremely pissed when it didn't work out as he wanted.

He later tried to get me to climb again, but having reached the roof I knew it was not possible, and could not be persuaded to make another futile attempt.

I had found the climb challenging and exhilarating. It made the fear rise in me and my limbs tremble to be so high on a building, higher than I had ever been before.

I felt I was always capable, but I did instinctively recognise the limits when I met them.

A couple of months later my Action Man was waiting on our shed roof for me, returned from his lonely adventures in the sky.

My father was seeing a woman named Linda, who was from Lancaster. Jon was originally from Leeds, so they shared that affinity. She had three children, Christine, Steven, and Jacqueline, who were very similar in age to Gary, Dawn, and I. We went on a camping trip with them to Snowdonia in Wales. Mt Snowdon is part of the highest mountain range in the British Isles, and reaches to about a thousand metres above sea level.

The first half of the mountain is a slow winding slope, and can be walked up to about fifteen hundred feet. The views are of course spectacular.

I was seven years old. Gary was eleven and due to begin at Southchurch High School after the summer.

When we got to Snowdon Gary saw another opportunity to either injure or kill me.

It was fortunate for me in some strange way that he was
calculated in his attempts. He was careful to choose or contrive
situations that would be accepted as tragic accidents or
misadventures if I were injured, rather than deliberate murder
attempts; like climbing onto the block of flats roof, or the time
he had forced me to swim out to the boats in the hope that I
would be drowned. He recognised, at least on some level, the
consequences of being caught or found out.

It was complicated for me emotionally. I couldn't hold back the
natural blood love that I had for him, it was instinctive and
unstoppable, already established in my young psyche. I was
naïvely reactive towards him, rather than logically weighing all
things. I was ready to forgive if he had made a sincere change.

At Snowdon one day, when we had walked up as far as we
could, and were exploring the mountain and its spectacular
cliffs and rocks, and had each wandered into our own pleasures,
Gary came looking for me.

He was warm and friendly and that was beguiling, so he
convinced me to follow him. He led me to a flat dry stone wall
set against the rock. It was sheer and straight, and at its summit
a pathway crossed and wound upwards into the cliffs. The
layered stones offered an abundance of hand and foot holds, so
when he asked me to climb it with him I felt confident that I
could manage it quite easily. It was deceptively tall.

'You have to choose your route,' he had said before we
embarked, standing close to the wall at the place he had
chosen.

He deliberated on the traps he set for me; they weren't random.
He climbed much faster than I, and reached the top quickly. I
became tired about half way up and had to rest for awhile. I
hadn't anticipated that it would be so strenuous. The steepness
of the wall required a constant tension in grip, holding oneself
flat to the wall so as not to topple backwards, and the energy
this took had swiftly drained my strength.

I looked back at Gary, who had circled down the path to watch
me from the bottom of the wall. He urged me to continue.

'It's just as far to come down as to get up,' he laughed. He was
letting me know I had fallen into another of his traps.

I drew my breath, fastened my resolve, and hauled myself methodically one hand above the next, pressing close to the rock, ignoring the ache of my arms, until I made the top.
A man had appeared beside Gary, a tourist happening by, and stayed to watch me complete the climb. He congratulated me when I joined them, and counselled me not to take such risks. Gary stalked off sulkily, another of his evil plots thwarted, but to my surprise he returned ten minutes later warmth and smiles once more. He was excited.

I was not in the mood to be fooled again but he promised he had something to show me, something that I would really like. He apologised, he said he had always known I would climb the wall, that he knew how good a climber I was, and that was why he had asked me to do it. I was suspicious, but he was experienced at this wheedling and he knew the words that would appeal to my gentler instincts, to my natural desire for us to be friends rather than enemies, and eventually he persuaded me to accompany him along the path up to the cliffs. When we arrived at the crest of the winding path he stretched out his arms expansively, unveiling. He had brought me here to admire the view. And very wide, open and beautiful it was, but still, I was puzzled. Why was it so urgent for me to see this? The path had taken us out to the side of the mountain, and here the slopes dropped away and there was only sky. We could see miles of green forest very far below us, rolling into a distant horizon. Crags and small mountains rose from the depths, still and watchful.
'Go closer,' he told me, 'or you can't see.'
I took a step closer to the edge. There was a short slope, perhaps twenty feet broad, which had very young saplings growing sparsely on it, each only a foot high. The slope broke in a sudden ledge, and far beneath that I saw dull earth colors, a flat, brownish gray border around the base of the mountains, dividing the rock from the trees. The forests seemed toy-like, they were so far away. It was a two dimensional landscape, flat blocks of color like a picture, a map. It boggled one to look, the brain unable to make sense of such distance. I stepped back.

He assured me it was safe, and positioned me exactly where he wanted me, right at the edge of the path, almost stepping onto the slope, insisting that I wouldn't see it properly otherwise. I didn't comprehend his deception. I didn't get what he was planning, and curious like the cat, I leaned a little further to see.

He shoved me with both palms hitting my back, putting his weight forcefully into the push, and I fell forwards, already balanced precariously, and tumbled into the slope.

I grasped desperately as I rolled and caught a slim sapling, and slid past it, but I held strongly, knowing I could not let go. My head and shoulder went over the slopes' crumbled dirt edge, but the thin sapling held my fall.

I looked, seeing how far I would fall, unable to resist knowing, and the vertigo almost swooned me. It pulled at me, like a mermaid calling me into the depths of an ocean, and a part of me wanted to surrender and fall, and discover the wonder of plummeting slow turning flight.

I clawed my way back to top of the slope. I ignored Gary's excuses and apologies; his crime might now be revealed.

I knew you would catch one, he says. He does not give up on trying though, attempting to steer me into a weaker, thinner line of shoots that perhaps wouldn't hold me, but I climbed back to the ledge using the sturdiest saplings I could reach.

He had always been so duplicitous, so slippery and cunning, that I had not seen the depth of his intent before. But, there was no disguising that he had just tried to kill me.

It was a premeditated attempt at murder. There was no pretence between us any more.

I told my father that Gary had pushed me, and that I had almost fallen to my death. But Jon doesn't get that Gary was deliberately trying to kill me; because who would imagine this eleven year old capable of murder? He doesn't comprehend his psychopathy. I cant articulate it clearly enough, and I am unable to communicate exactly what had happened. Gary escapes without punishment.

All brothers fight, says my mother, dismissing me, when I told her what happened after we have returned home.

Fourteen

There is a knock upon our front door at Blyth Avenue one afternoon, when I am eight years old. I answer, but there is no one there on the doorstep. Looking out I see a boy about my age running away into the road.

The road is narrow, jammed tight with parked cars at both sides of its kerb. After, they cut away the kerb, cut away the edge of grass, widen the road.

He looks back, laughing. *Knock Down Ginger*; a strange colloquial name for this game; it is always funny, except on this occasion.

The boy is hit by a car. He glides through the air, outside of time, his mouth still open in a grin, his eyes meeting mine. His head splits on the lamppost. He lays dead in the gutter.

People came to look at him, and an ambulance to take his body. I stand where I am, just watching. I am so stunned and puzzled by it.

Barbara was alcoholic and agoraphobic. She drank two litres of Olde English cider, morning till night. Whiskey too some days, when she needed extra juice.

She locked herself in her bedroom for seven years, sinking, escaping, growing hard and bitter in her sorrow, wallowing, ever falling in darknesses, and letting every darkness flow untempered through her and her house, and sweep ice over everything, so that it hangs in thick icicles from the eaves and the sills.

The windows are frosted with intricate flowers of ice, so delicate and refined and so clear in their art that I am astounded, and I am swept away for hours across frozen winters, and drinking every cold drop of their exquisitely carved patterns deep inside of me.

Even in this darkness there are gorgeous tear drops of beauty.

Before the internet and modern mass media Youth Culture was hugely relevant in England, and the focus for this very lucrative market was the music industry and the Pop charts.

In the fifties it was Teddy Boys and Teeny Boppers. Through the sixties and seventies the Youth Culture was variously identified with Mods, Rockers, Skinheads, Hippies, and finally Glam Rock.

I was nine years old in 1976, when the *Sex Pistols* released their first single, *Anarchy in the UK*. Punk Rock swept through England like wild fires, igniting its youth into angry violent rebellion.

The movement was masterminded by Malcolm McClaren, the manager and creator of the Sex Pistols. But, McClaren's motivation was purely fame and wealth. His ideology of anger and hate, coupled with the hand-picked boy band from hell, 'none of whom could play their instruments or sing,' was only a marketing ploy. In their first television interview McClaren told them to 'Be as offensive as possible.'

The idea sold. Suddenly the youth of Britain were wearing ripped clothes, bin bags, safety pins, cutting their hair into Mohawks and coloring them orange or green. Punk was easy and cheap and instantly accessible to anybody who wanted to fit in somewhere. Not only that, but at times the punk style looked great too.

McClaren made a lot of money, and when punk burnt itself out and died a couple of years later, he had no regrets. The nation's youth moved on to become skinheads and mods.

Sid Vicious, the Sex Pistols' bass guitarist, apparently murdered his girlfriend Nancy Spungen, stabbing her to death in the bed of their hotel room. The door of the room was locked from inside, so no other explanation of events seems plausible. Whilst awaiting trail for murder he was given a lethal dose of heroin by his own mother. The reality of Sid and Nancy was not quite so romantic as the Hollywood version released some years later.

And the punk rock movement was not without wider consequences either. The establishment were terrified by the angry mob which the youth of England had briefly become. They felt threatened and powerless. It marked a shift in political motivation, or perhaps it is more accurate to say it excited an acceleration of policies, and from the late seventies onward public freedoms began to be systematically whittled away, leading eventually to the tyrannical Thatcher years of government.

I didn't like punk. Its aggression and violence disturbed me. I liked rock n roll: Little Richard, Gene Vincent, Eddie Cochran, the Shangri-Las, Elvis.

I also liked Glam Rock artists such as David Bowie, The Sweet, and Marc Bolan. Slade were one of my favorite bands; a boyfriend of my mother had bought me the greatest hits double-album *Sladest* on my seventh Birthday, and I instantly loved the stomping rock, and Noddy Holder's raw powerful vocals. I played the album almost every day into my teens.

I was saddened when Bolan died in a car crash at the end of '77. Elvis had died of heart failure, about six weeks before.

I was invited into Shoeburyness Comprehensive, along with all the other eleven year olds who would be First Years next term, so that we could be shown around the school. We were in groups of ten or twelve, and Lee Ebbs was in the same group as me. I didn't know him yet, but later we would be close friends, with an enduring friendship.

The teacher who led us into the assembly hall, and up the wide flat stairs, through the swing doors, around the balcony walkway, where it was dark, and sweeping black curtains draped over the rails dropped sheer behind the floor level stage to the music classroom there, was called Mr Merlin.

'And, *are* you a wizard?' I asked him pithily. He rounded on me theatrically. 'You get caned for asking questions like that here, boy!' he snapped his teeth in my face, and smiled.

As I began my first year at Shoebury, Gary, now fifteen years old, was starting his final, fifth year of school at Southchurch High. He was still trying to smash my face in whenever he was around.

He had started to be out with his mates more often at night, and some nights he would not return home at all, frolicking in some villainy, and so my time was a bit easier, and I had a little more space. He was drinking, taking drugs, robbing shops and houses. The police became frequent callers. Soon he would be serving his first prison term: about nine months in borstal.

They wheel out the kid whose back was broken, onto the assembly hall stage. He tells us that he was tipping back in his chair, swinging on its back legs, when two of his friends tussling fell onto him. He will never walk again, he says. He is here to warn us: don't be boisterous, don't be carefree, respect school property. Or something. He smiles happily.

Mr Talbot teaches us Math during the first year. We don't respect him. We ignore his instructions and laugh at his bumbling. He is a watery-eyed tatterdemalion with a balding comb-over, badly dressed and misshapen. Over the summer break he hangs himself.

We sit for days in the assembly hall whilst a rock band, sixth year pupils, play the David Bowie song *Five Years* over and over, on the low flat stage. The singer is an Asian guy.

I think I saw you in an ice cream parlour, drinking milkshakes cold and long. Smiling and waving, and looking so fine. Don't think you knew you were in my song.

Douglas Hansel is the deputy headmaster. Although diminutive, he is very forceful and commanding. His voice projects like headlights, and we are paralysed by it, like the road kill.

Once I get to the fourth year I am often sent to him to be disciplined. He talks with me, and he is intelligent and compassionate. He does his best to steer me away from the worst of the snares. I respect and admire him. I don't want you to go to prison, he tells me.

His personal hygiene is seriously lacking. He lives with his sister. He takes his own life, also hanging himself, a few years after I have left the school.

I had been fighting to defend myself every night for more than four years. The battle was long, gruelling and frustrating.

It had been some time since he had managed to hurt me much, but he kept on, unrelenting, looking to breach my defences.

Most young guys my age had never been in a fight or would ever be. Some of them had been slapped about a couple of times by bullies, but that was something different. They hadn't learnt to defend themselves, or how to fight back. I knew how it felt to be punched in the face, but it would be new and sickening for them.

That was a power I had. I had already been forced into a very violent place. It was somewhere they hoped they would never go. The threat of it made them afraid and weak, but that same threat made me angry, and that me stronger and bolder. Force and energy filling me, hulk-like.

I switched into the automatic mind that had developed through my protracted training, my body prepared to fight now rather than for flight. It was a grim determination that I had, and I was almost impervious to the pain of being struck by blows. I was used to fighting an opponent who was much bigger and stronger than me.

I became outwardly confident and extrovert, asserting myself. I was never a bully, although from time to time I flexed the muscles of my power a little too sharply perhaps. To the contrary, I defended my friends instinctively and passionately. I was loyal and dependable. This extended out to include all of those around me; my classmates, and even those who were affiliated only by being in the same year as me, and who were vulnerable to the aggressions of some of the older boys.

It hurt me to see someone being pushed around and bullied. My heart couldn't refuse them. They sheltered gratefully.

I was tired of being manipulated and abused. I was trying to fight back but my enemies were often like invisible ghosts. I misdirected my energy by battling so fiercely against each injustice I encountered, and by deciding that every authority was an enemy, unless they showed me they could be an exception, a friend.

It was a fight I could not win, and it brought me troubles that I could have easily avoided.

I could have kept my objections to myself and rebelled in a more cerebral way, by withdrawing from engagement with the system, being more Zen about it, like I would now, probably. I could not then restrain my energies. I was riding a wild dragon, scarcely keeping balance as it ploughs through the burning skies. My boldness was immodest. I couldn't often hold my tongue, no matter whom I was speaking with. At times it led me into dangerous situations, when I brazenly pushed against hopeless odds.

My refusal ever to yield and thereby surrender self-respect was often a surprise for the random bullies that I encountered, and there were several that I did meet, both in and out of school. They were expecting another pampered baby they could quickly bring to tears, like they did to other first and second years. I offered more of a fight than they wanted, and that was unexpected and unwelcome. Usually they backed off and looked for softer targets elsewhere.

I always offered them an honorable retreat.

It worked because I meant it more than they did. I was ready to fight them, even though I didn't want to, and I would give everything I had to the contest. Later, quiet, I would reflect on the peril I had been in that day, and feel the fear in it.

Fifteen

During my second year at school we had a substitute teacher covering our class. I don't think I ever saw him again, after that day. As I took my seat at the beginning of the lesson I was continuing a conversation with one of my friends. The substitute teacher suddenly called for silence and asked my name.

He is a slim guy, dark haired, wearing glasses, about forty five or fifty maybe. A weaselly looking kind of guy. Getting up from his desk at the front of the classroom, he takes up the long metal ruler, which is used for working on the blackboard. He tells the class that he is a substitute teacher, and that he is aware he won't command the respect of pupils as he might as a more permanent figure of authority. He is striding side to side on the little stage before the blackboard, and slaps the ruler onto his palm as he talks, and he is smiling happily.

'I have been doing this job for more than twenty years,' he lectures. 'I have found the best way is to make an early impression, to start as we mean to go on. Make sure they get the point. I've found that dealing with the toughest first quietens the rest down.' He paused, letting his words be absorbed, still smiling. He hadn't seemed to be addressing me in particular. I wasn't expecting punishment.

'In those twenty years I have met a lot of boys who thought they were tough. Some of them were. They had circumstances to deal with that were difficult. Life can make us hard. Our environments and our experiences make us what we are. But, this is my classroom. We can't have everyone talking over each other. We must have quiet so that we can work.

'I don't have much time to influence you. I taught all of them at one time, they all passed through this classroom.' He begins to list notorious ex-pupils; we've never known them, but even their names seem fierce, as he paints it. Then he lists present day pupils, the fifth years and fourth years which no doubt we knew by reputation, and we do. 'I tried to make the time I had with all of them significant, in some small way. Perhaps this is the last time I will be a substitute teacher for any of you. Well, then, that means my job is even harder if I am to help you in some way in your lives ahead. How can I affect you? Only by giving you something meaningful during this lesson. I'm sure you'd all enjoy a free period, but what would that accomplish? I may as well take you all outside and let you sit on the grass, and enjoy the sunshine; better than to sit here wasting time.

'I would still be paid for my time. Instead I choose to see this as a brief window of opportunity, and to engage with you all, and to try and communicate something of practical use. So we will work. I ask only for your full attention. Listen when I speak. Pay attention to what I say. I might be offering you something valuable.

'I caned all of those boys that I have just named, with this ruler. And they were strong, hardened boys. Yet, I made every one of them cry.' He slaps the ruler into his palm again, loudly this time.

Now he addresses me, and I am shocked when I realise he intends to punish me: 'Do you think you are as tough as those boys were? Do you think I won't make you cry too? I'm going to teach you a valuable lesson today. Come out here to the front.'

I stand before him. He gives me a choice now: did I want to be caned on the buttocks or the hand? Hand, I choose, rejecting extra humiliation.

I am angry, this is unfair. I hadn't been disruptive. I was silent when he asked for silence. I had listened whilst he talked.

Six strokes he tells me, and makes me wait, holding out my hand, fearing the pain which is about to come.

Then he tells me with pseudo tenderness not to be embarrassed about crying, there is no shame in it. If even they cried it is okay if you do too. And no one should think you are a baby, or weak. He looks over the startled pupils of the class. They are mute and fascinated.

Six strokes, he tells me.

'Most choose the hand,' he laughs, 'but it actually hurts more. Be sure to keep your thumb out of the way.'

No, I do not want to change my mind.

'I will not spare you. I will give everything I have to each stroke. This is so that you don't forget. So that you know it is real. I am saying to you, to you all: Wake up! This is Life! Don't you know it will very soon be over? Pay attention!' Everyone is paying attention. None us have seen anything like this before, this strange new violence. We are all confused by it. He leans back, draws his right arm back over his shoulder, holding the ruler like a sword. He drives into his stroke, bending his knees and then rising, twisting into the slicing blade with practised momentum and power; a matador, and this his Art. The silence is deep, and the blade swooshes.

It tears into my palm with heavy blunt force. It hurts worse than I expected. The pain is fire and explosive bite. It leaps up my arm. Gary's punches and kicks had never held this pointed venom.

'Warming up,' he says. 'Hold it high. If you flinch away then you will get another stroke.' He pauses, gathering his strength and concentration for the next blow.

I do not flinch. It is terrible when it comes, all his skill and impotent hatreds mustered. He practices and practices for this, in his bedroom, in front of his long mirror. More than anything he wants my tears.

I do not think I can withstand the pain that seems to sweep through me, down to the soles of my feet. It would be a relief to cry, to let pain out, and he would be satisfied and maybe ease just a little. I feel it, but I refuse and it falls back.

I hold to that, knowing that now I will not cry, as I wait through the agonising pause before new fresh pain. I have learnt already that crying is to lose, to give my enemy satisfaction, to please him, so that he will laugh and gloat, and go to his bed content. I take the punishment because I must, but I give you nothing.

I look death into his eyes, and he is furiously offended by that, and demands that I do not look at him.

I lift my hand for him to strike again, pressing my thumb close and tight. He summons all power and force into each blow. He will crush me. Three. Four. Five. Six.

This place is not a terrifying new experience for me, but a

seeming familiar territory. I am not a stranger, although this pain's flavor is new and fresh and dazzling.

He wonders if he can keep hitting me, keep striking his sword down into my open red hand until I finally weep. Shaking his head he realises he must stop, and sends me back to my seat. He sits in his own chair, breathing heavily.

I cradle my hand into my belly, and a more terrible throbbing pain pours through me, and alarmingly I am very close to tears now when the violence is over. And those waves keep coming. I fight against it until it settles back a bit.

'Perhaps I am losing my touch,' the substitute teacher wonders aloud. 'But, no. I have to concede, I gave it everything. You are the first boy that I have caned that did not cry.' He looks to me for answers, bewildered, but I will not meet his eye.

Sixteen

I was friends with a guy a few years older than me, Rick, who lived in the block of flats across the road with his very attractive and cool girlfriend, Josie. Rick was from Birmingham, a handsome and charming guy. He was warm, stylish and gregarious, and he drove a three litre Capri.

He had an amazing cannabis plant. It was like a little bush, thick and dense, and it thrived for several years. He let it grow naturally, without the use of any of the intense farming methods that are prevalent today. He just put the plant out onto the balcony when it was sunny and brought it indoors when it was cold. He could harvest about half an ounce a week from it. I regularly bought a small bag from him. It was great giggly grass.

Rick stole a motorbike one night. He dismantled the outer casing of the bike completely in his front room the next afternoon, spraying each separate part red, and producing a very nice finish. My mate Stuart and I called on him whilst he was doing it. He filed down the serial number until it was illegible. But he made a blunder when it came to changing the number plates.

He had prepared for this part of the 'bike's transformation well. He searched the streets until he saw an identical motorbike, the same make and model, and made a note of its plates. If he was ever stopped by the police and they radioed through those details everything would look fine.

First he sprayed the plates of the stolen bike a solid yellow color, covering the original letters and numbers. Then he cut adhesive tape, carefully shaping each letter and number for the 'new' plate. It was a fine job, and would pass all but the closet inspections. His mistake was that he should have used black tape since the plate's background was yellow, instead of white, which is only used on dark backgrounds.

We took the bike for a drive over to North Shoeburyness, to the large park there. It was a dark evening but very warm. On our way back we encountered a policeman. He was suspicious, aware that a motorbike of this model had been stolen locally recently. He questioned us for a few minutes and looked the bike over, but the precautions Rick had taken were enough. Having passed this close inspection, Rick thought he was now in the clear.

He arranged for the bike to be taken to some friends of his in Birmingham, but neglected to cover the motorbike up with some canvas or something, and so it was clearly visible. The number plates were seen by some police that they passed on the motorway, who did realise that the color of the lettering was wrong, and Rick was busted.

The evening that Rick was arrested a policeman knocked on my door first, and I stuck to the story that we had prearranged, in case something like this happened: that Rick had bought the motorbike from some random guy at Shoeburyness park. The corroborative story didn't need to be believable, only insisted upon. I felt certain that Stuart would say exactly what I had said, and if he had that would have been the end of the matter. Five minutes later Stuart knocked. He had folded immediately under questioning in front of his parents, and admitted that Rick had stolen the motorbike and resprayed it.

Nothing much came of Rick's court appearance though. He was just given a small fine.

The police officer remarked to Stuart's parents that they should be glad their son had told the truth. He added that he held out little hope for me and that I would probably become a criminal. Stuart's father responded by saying: 'A more polite and respectful lad you couldn't hope to meet.'

Rick was upset that Stuart had betrayed him so easily, but he let it go, conceding that Stuart was young and had been afraid.

Jim is melancholy and charismatic. He is fourteen, I am thirteen. We are best friends. We are rockabillys, and we are a little band, about a dozen of us, boys and girls. It is 1980 and mods and skinheads are the popular cultures. Rockabilly is for the oddities and the rebels.

We shave our hair short at the back and sides, quiffing the longer front: southbanks, or more usually, flat-tops. We wear black chukka-boots, sky-blue stay-pressed pants, or black, or

jeans, red braces always hanging down, button down shirts or
Hawaiian shirts, and red or black Harrington jackets or donkey
jackets, and always fluorescent bright socks with black hoops.
We are outlaws and outcasts. We roam lazily from Bunters and
Blyth, across the field, into West Road and Ness Road, over
the hill into North Shoebury. We embrace the streets as we
have always done.
We chain smoke skinny roll ups, and feel the black sky.
We strike out somewhere at a tortoise's pace. Out here in these
moonlit deserts we are stone, immaculate.

Jim cuts my arm with a razor blade. He has already cut his own
forearm a dozen times and his blood is flowing. He cuts me
again. Let me do it, I tell him, taking the razor from him. I pull
the blade across my skin. It smarts and stings but I can manage
the pain easier this way. He urges me to cut deeper so that my
blood wells. Again.
He presses his forearm onto mine, pushing together with his
other hand. Our blood flows into twin veins and hearts.
'We have made a pact,' Jim tells me. 'It can never be broken. It
means we will die for each other if necessary. A sacred, blood
oath. We are brothers in spirit.'
He clenches his fist, and smiles his laconic smile.

Russ is blonde, bright and happy. He is centred and carefree.
He has a dazzling grin, and looks like a young James Dean. He
takes me to his home one day. It is a detached rustic mansion
on the edge of North Shoeburyness, lavish in its removedness.
We listen to Elvis singing Hound Dog on Russ' record player. I
have never heard this version before. Elvis does an awesome
slow blues outro, and it is mesmerising.

Jasper won't shave his hair into a flat-top, but grows it long. His
tastes broaden into rock, and he dresses like a hippy. We are no
less connected despite his variance in style. He is aligned both
with us, our little rockabilly gang, and with the North Shoebury
druggies. He soon gets into glue, smoking, downers, smac.
He feeds me often from his mother's kitchen, and lets me sleep

on his bedroom floor when I cannot sleep at home (or at Jim's: climbing through the ground floor window of his bedroom, trying to be quiet, squeezing underneath the frame of his bed). Jasper gives me shelter unquestioning.

When I am twenty he has been a heroin addict for a long time, and I keep a distance. His mother had stuck by him, tried to wrestle him from the dragon's curling scythes, but she was weak with heart problems, and her death a deep loss for him. It is the first time I have seen him for three years, and thereafter, the few occasions that we spend time together, he carries a new sadness. I forgot our friendship, and that wounds us both.

In the winter before I leave Southend forever I meet William again, Stuart's cousin. The three of us had lived on Blyth and spent a lot of days across years, hanging out. We were brothers in a way, sprung from the same asphalt and concrete womb, growing together.

William has no front teeth now, and no coat, although it is late and cold. He confesses he has been a junkie for a long time. He expects me to despise him, but instead I embrace him warmly, and call him brother.

I see him again, a month later, just days before I leave. He asks if I have any puff, which I don't at the time. 'At least I can give you this,' he says, and gives me a little rock of soft black which he has, about half a 'teenth.

He tells me that his dad James has died from alcohol, but that his mother is well. He wonders why I did not avoid him that day, knowing the dirty drug he is bound to.

'It's just a drug, neither dirty nor clean in itself,' I say.

'True,' he responds, 'but, it makes us do dirty things.'

'You were just unlucky. It could have happened to any of us. The dragon caught you.'

Tim was raven-haired and green eyed. Streetwise and fated, in leather and drainpipes. He personifies everything that I would like to be. He is a brooding god, and he personifies my projection of ultimate cool. How is it that he has somehow actualized my unarticulated vision? He has plucked the fire out of the sky, and it sits so comfortably with him, like it is nothing at all.

I walk to the end of the long alley that is adjacent to Shoebury park. Tim's house is at the very end, and when I turn into the street, going past it, he and Russ are standing outside.

We shoot the breeze for a time. Tim's parents are not home and he invites us in. We watch a black and white Stooges episode. I am not very familiar with them, but it makes us all laugh.

Tim takes the gum he has been chewing from his mouth, and offers it to Russ, who accepts, puts it unhesitatingly into his own mouth, and then blows fat pink bubbles.

This is our wilderness. We walk slowly, having nowhere to get to. There are other, more subtle alignments between us, deeper than our exteriors or our preferences. There is a flame in each of our hearts, a corresponding fire.

Tim is in demonstrative mood this evening as we crawl into North Shoebury. He is goaded when some near neighbours of his remark as we pass them that we are some kind of thugs, walking the streets after curfew. We are nothing of the kind, our intent is only to share time together, relaxed and easy. For us this is the sole available venue.

Tim picks up two empty milk bottles from a doorstep, and throws them into the road so that they smash booming, a vivid expression of his indignation.

The police are called. Rounding up juvenile delinquents is a part of the job they rather enjoy, flexing muscular batons, saving the day for decent folks, so they arrive quickly, and we scatter.

I follow Tim as he runs into Shoebury park. We move into the darkness of the field, unobserved.

He becomes anxious and irrational as we watch two squad cars arrive. We can see the cops' light-beams as they search the area for us.

His parents will be sore about this, he tells me. He decides to do something much worse, to divert them from this very minor incident. I'm going to run to London, he says. I think he is being a bit crazy, and tell him so, but he assures me that it is the best way to deal with his parents, and it is something he has been wanting to do for awhile, besides.

I agree to accompany him. I don't get why he wants to do this, but the idea excites me: to be with him, just him and me, adventuring together, is a lure I can not resist.

We are both quite drunk. We leave the clamour and turmoil behind, turn our backs, and the darkness embraces us as we pass over the park, into its hushed warmth. We will meet the train tracks at the other side and follow them. The darkness swings black behind us, and we forget the land that once we walked in.

There had been a fire inside the Cambridge pub recently, on Ness Road. Crates and crates of bottled beers were considered fire-damaged, unfit now to be sold in the bar, and so they were stacked on top of each other in a dozen rows, in the back yard behind the pub. It was removed, secluded and unseen from the street under the blanket of dark evenings. We boosted one another to the top of the fence, and loaded our pockets with as many bottles as we could carry.

Jasper prises a lid off with his teeth. The rest of us catch the tight tin caps on protruding pieces of brick or metal, thumping down with the palm's heel, so that the bottle springs free from the cap, and the beer fountains frothily. It tastes good. We drink it quickly.

'The perfect crime,' smiles Jasper.

The railway lines cut through the edge of the park. We climb easily over the railings, slip down the banks, and step onto the iron path.

We walk quietly into midnight, and there are one or two trains still running, that we have to step off the tracks whilst they thunder pass, then rejoin.

We look out over the rooftops and narrow streets.

We are above the halo light of street lamps, and shadows are stark beyond them. The occasional pedestrians are small figures beneath us on cold gray pavements, unaware of our eyes.

It seems unreal at this angle as the track cuts through above them, rooftops either side, houses flat long fronts, lacking distinction and identity in terraced streets and avenues. Reality is altered and removed at this lofty perspective. We don't feel the pains or joys of the people living in these houses, we don't feel their emotion or vibrancy. What we see is brick, slate, trees and grass gasping for space, tarmac and concrete rows wrapped in night's color.

Past midnight the world is morphed, and the fluid rail snakes swiftly by all the muddle of lives lived below, and nothing is distinct or sharp. We smoke cigarettes and walk. Above the towns perpetually now, on high bridges and atop tunnelled hills. We are like gods, above and free. We flick our cigarette butts down, and they tumble into sparking orange scintilla spins.

Tim is dating Sandra. He tells me they have slept together about six times. I am yet still a virgin, and I ask how is it? It's alright. Sandra is a rockabilly girl. She is slim and shapely, sexual, red lips and smoky eyes, long dark hair tied back into a swishing tail, pencil skirts and leather jacket.

In about a year from now I will date Sharon, Sandra's sister, who is in the year below me. Sharon is more of a rock n roll girl than rockabilly. She wears full skirts and demure sweaters, and is quiet and gentle. Her hair is dirty blonde and messy, tumbling past her shoulders. Her eyebrows are naturally darker, lending strength and depth to her pretty face. She wears very little make up, in contrast with her elder sister.

We embrace mergingly. Our energies blend comfortably and easily in undulating viscous swoons. Her response to me is deep. We should stay together and root here, it could become an enduring beautiful love. But, she is too soon and valuable, and I cannot hear her calling me home.

Tim and I walked all night, and made good distance by following this direct line. When we came to the outskirts of the city, about twenty five miles from Shoeburyness, maybe Tilbury or somewhere near because we are close to the estuary, the railtrack switched onto a narrow metal bridge, closely hemmed on both sides by tall caged frames. There were no banks to step onto so as to avoid oncoming trains. They would be running again soon, in early morning.

We climbed down to the roofs of the houses, jumped from rooftop to rooftop, trying to skirt the bridge, and hoping to rejoin the track at a more favourable point. The houses were adjacent to the bridge here, close together, a gap of a few feet between each of them to traverse. A large, confident leaping step was enough, and at first our progress was smooth.

The architecture of the roofs changed soon, some streets in, becoming steeper and wider, and slippery with dew.

'Let me go first, then I can help you across,' Tim said, as we found ourselves on a sharp slope of tiles. The leap was not going to be easy. There was a distance of maybe five or six feet between the edge of this roof and the next roof, which rose sharply, banking a steep triangular face.

He carefully edged down towards the top guttering in a near sitting crouch, stabilizing himself with his hands, moving very slowly. He would have to stand and jump eventually. Yet when he reached the place from where he must leap, we both realized that he wouldn't make it, the flat distance was too great. He had committed himself.

He was stuck, precariously balanced. Trying to come back up the treacherously wet tiles to rejoin me at the apex would be dangerous and difficult.

'I can't get back,' he confesses, fatalistic and apologetic. The distance between us was too far to reach and help him. He couldn't get across, and he wouldn't be able to stay perched where he was indefinitely. It was a long way down to the cold hard pavements.

I paused only a moment to consider the risk. If I slipped on the tiles or missed my jump there would be nothing to catch hold of. The only way to make the jump was with speed and momentum. I rose, and standing pushed into a sprint down the slope and leapt past Tim, as he called out in surprise. Landing, I kept stride, speed propelling me upward, and I found balance and crouched into the roof, then stretched my hand back for Tim to catch.

'Get a hold first,' he said. 'I'm okay.'

I took another step or two up, so that I could then loop my arm over to the other side of the roof, giving a firm support. He jumped then and caught hold of my forearm, and we were able to make the top safely.

'You saved my fucking life, man!' he said, embracing me gratefully.

We found a careful route, lowering foot and hand holds down the side of a house, and at last we were returned to the street and the world.

Seventeen

We were going to need some money. Neither us had more than a few coins, and we had just a few smokes left.

'We might have to mug someone,' suggested Tim. We stopped at a corner. The beach was not far, the estuary which ran inland and became the Thames; we could see its horizon if we turned downhill.

I considered: in a sense we were expected to commit this violence. We were outside of society now so we should perform accordingly, and behave like desperadoes. The weight of social training pressed upon us, we felt its unarticulated urging as it waited impatient for us to act. Tim was right, this is what people did in our situation, strike down hard and ruthless, take what they need. It is a threshold to destinies.

A nefarious figure approached from the top of the road, walking slowly in these last hours of night. It was an older woman, and she seemed feeble. Strange for her to be abroad at this time.

Tim looked for my answer. 'We don't want someone who'd put up a fight,' he said, matter of fact. I nodded. That made sense. 'That could be my nan, or yours,' I respond. 'We can't do that.' The door closes. She turns beneath the lamp's spotlight. Tim laughs.

We turned down to the coast now, and it was still night-dark, probably about four or five am. Casually he flipped car door handles as we passed them. None were alarmed in those less paranoid and less barricaded years. When the doors opened beneath his fingers, he snaked inside searching compartments, bags.

This was a fun new game. We discovered cash, a few pounds in coins, a carton of Marlboro cigarettes which was the veritable Holy Grail of our present need. We found a locked suitcase which later we opened, emptied of its paper contents and then discarded.

We swung along the curving slope road, stealth and silence, finding miscellaneous treasures. A cream-colored roll of masking tape, matches, gloves, books, pliers.

Tim was deep inside a car at the kerb, his legs dangling out of the door. I watched the houses and street, crouched next to the car. In a second floor window opposite I saw a man looking at us through binoculars. I dropped completely behind the car. 'Fuck!' I alerted Tim, and carefully he came out, closing the door quietly, and knelt beside me. The guy watching us was also using a telephone. Obviously he was on line to the police. We kept ducked low and made a half trot along the street, behind the cars, in the deep shadows, until we are out of his line and we know he cannot see us. Tim leads us down onto the sands. There is a long low wall dividing the beach from the road, and a car driving past will not see us. He stays near the wall, watching the road until he sees a police car pass. Now he is satisfied and joins me.

We amble through till daybreak, smoke a few Marlboros.

He tells about how he tried glue sniffing. He had a big craving for it afterwards, like he wanted to do it every day. He diverted the craving by drinking and smoking, drowning it with intoxications, because he could easily have gotten lost in it. He didn't trust himself to do it again, he said.

He led us then up and into the streets, as day was rising with a soft sun. We watched the bakery deliveries, and afterwards helped ourselves to bread rolls from the pallets. We took a bottle of milk each from doorsteps, and that was our good breakfast.

We smoked and walked.

We arrived at a sports complex, and used their bathroom to clean ourselves up a bit. We were both feeling nauseous. The stolen beer from last evening was churning in my belly. As we left the complex and came back onto the main road, I vomited heavily.

I was young, and so the energy burst through the tailspin quick and hard. It emptied me. I felt much better soon afterwards, and my stomach settled.

We took a bus ride across town.

I had visited my great aunt and uncle, Rene and Peter, once or twice with my mother, just us two, so I guess it must have been soon after she and Jon split up. They lived near Black Horse Road, in Walthamstow, a suburb of London.

We went to Rita's wedding. She was the daughter of Auntie Babs, who was the sister of Peter. I felt very small, a superfluous child, mostly unknown amongst all these bustling adults and their high emotions, in their sweeping gowns and smart suits, each of them wearing a carnation flower, and the music and laughter loud. I drank lager for the first time, from a broad cocktail glass, but I didn't like it much. Rita's new husband seems like a dick, and complains that I am drinking all his beer, but Rita is lovely. She is blonde, London-pretty, generous and attentive and kind. I gravitate towards her.

The wedding was a long time ago, but I think I might recognise Rene and Peter's apartment front, if I saw it again.

I recall some details, the terraced block, the white stairs and blue doors. If we get to Walthamstow train station I can likely find the route. Tim doesn't know anybody in London, so it seems our only option. But, it had been Black Horse Road station which I came through with my mother; that essential detail I didn't remember.

We eventually find a taxi driver willing to take us. We have no money for the fare. Our intention is to find their apartment, and ask them to pay for the taxi. I think they will help us out once they realise our runaway situation. Looking in the wrong place we can never find it. We have to run.

There is a large park at the end of this block. It is busy with pedestrians. We sit in the fenced area on the swings, and there are smaller children and their parents here.

'This is the best place to hide,' Tim says. He is right. When the plain clothes cops come through looking for us, they see us but turn away, look further and deeper in the park. We are shielded by normality, lazily swinging with our toes, open and transparent, not running from. They don't find us.

We could have slipped away easily then and mingled with afternoon crowds, but we had nowhere else to get to. Our crime had been forced on us by circumstance, we felt, whilst our intention had been honest at the outset. We waited, smoked another cigarette, then went back to see if I could find the apartment.

The plain clothes swooped on us as we turned back into the block. We were inexperienced criminals. 'You should never return to the scene of the crime!' the cops gloated. They handled us roughly, handcuffing us, and pushing us into a police van. 'Okay, you're not in the fucking Sweeny,' I tell the cop as he pushes me against a wall and handcuffs me. It was so over the top dramatic that I laughed. They seemed so excited, playing cops and robbers for real. My remark took the edge off their fun.

The handcuffs were too tight. I complained about the tightness, and the other cop adjusted them more comfortably. I tried to use a trick Houdini had pioneered to escape from them, sitting in the van, hands behind me. I didn't have space to not be observed, and it probably wouldn't have worked on modern handcuffs anyway.

At the station we are told to strip side by side in a room. They search everything. They watch us closely. The cop who first cuffed me hates me for laughing at him, so he opens the connecting door wide. Beyond is an open station area. Two female secretaries sit at desks. They glance at Tim and I, now both naked.

We are questioned and requestioned, put into separate cells. Neither of us admits to anything, we haven't done anything wrong. The cops wonder about the tape and pliers. Are we going equipped? They have nothing to charge us with besides evading the taxi fare. They hold us as runaways.

Several hours later Tim's parents collect us, and they are both seriously freaked out by the whole thing. His mum gives us both a cigarette. Tim smiles sardonically over at me, together on the back seat. I get his unspoken point, and I can't help laughing, which doesn't endear me to his mother; the smashed milk bottles are not even mentioned.

Eighteen

I started work at the Bistro, an Italian/continental restaurant, when I was thirteen. I worked Saturday nights to begin with as kitchen porter. Soon I would work three or four nights a week. I worked there for about four years. I later worked at another bistro, this time in Rayleigh, until I was eighteen or nineteen. It was busy and tough work. You had to be very fast to keep up, and that required a lot of energy, but I had plenty. The restaurant would typically serve about one hundred and fifty placings on weekend nights. After a year or so I began waiting tables some nights.

I worked alone when I was in the kitchen, except on Saturday nights when I would be accompanied either by Emma, the daughter of one of the waitresses, Lorraine, or by my friend and neighbour Stuart.

I started about five thirty in the evening, first tackling the huge iron cooking pots that were used during the daily prep of meat sauces for pasta dishes.

Week nights could be reasonably leisurely, with thirty or forty places being served, but towards the weekend it was eight or nine hours of very constant work.

I got the job when Chris, who was a neighbour of ours, was working there as a commies-chef. They were short staffed one Saturday and he thought of asking me. I took his advice to attack the work, not to fall behind and allow the used plates to pile up, and adopting this attitude secured me a regular place. They were happy to have found someone who could cope with the workload. Many washer-uppers sank beneath the teetering crockery towers and were never seen again. Chris quit over some dispute after I had been there for just a couple of weeks.

Emma worked there on and off for about a year, and working beside her added a romantic interest for me. She was very lovely, dark-haired and beautifully pretty, with a bright grin and easy laugh. We dated a few times, but did not establish our relationship in a definite way, and I allowed her to drift out of my life.

The chef David was in his forties. His beard was dark and

shaggy, his belly rotund and forceful. He was red-faced and lewd, as he sweated in the furnace heat, slapping his dick on a plate for the waitresses to scream at. But, gosh, he made the greatest lasagne in the entire world.

When the place closed at midnight and the staff, except the chefs who have already left, sit together on the long rustic dining table to eat a late but unhurried full meal, I often refuse huge juicy T-bone steaks in favour of his lasagne. It is so profoundly satisfying and tasty. With sliced French bread, generously buttered, and several glasses of a fine quality Soave adding sharp deliciousness.

We feast long and slow, and it is close and candlelit. We are tired and bruised from the evening's work, but now that falls away into comfort.

They draw me into their shelter, Dave the manager, only twenty four years old, Trisha, Lorraine, Giuseppe, and are a family for me, making my love leap to them gratefully.

At two or three in the morning we finally head homeward. Sometimes I get a lift, depending on who is working that shift. Other times I am tired and get a taxi, which takes about a quarter from my nights' wage of ten pounds. I may bring my bike (second hand woman's bike, always) or I may walk the three miles home, the long winding roads in darkness. It depends.

I sleep late. I don't bother trying to get to school on time. I am utterly disengaged from working at school. Around lunchtime I collect my free meal at the canteen. I hook up with Jim, and we leave the school grounds by the back gates.

Once or twice a week Dave, Giuseppe and I played poker. Giuseppe was too corporeal to smoke weed, too established in the visual real world to explore orphic realms. He adores me, this stocky short handsome Italian covered in dark hair, and insists that I always refer to him as 'Dad.' In return I love him. Dave and I toasted the giggly home-grown I brought with me under the high heat of the kitchen's grill. It was picked fresh that day from Rick's plant, so it was moist, too wet to smoke, and needed to be dried. The industrial strength grill did the job nicely in a few seconds. Sweet aromas mingling. The sensuous layers were indulgent, opulent.

We worked hard during the night, but we were skilled and enduring, dancing into the surging tides, four wide oblong dinner plates balanced in hand and along the left forearm, and one or two more in the other hand. Nimble, squeezing through the corridor all at once to reach our tables quickly, smiling and laughing, as we pirouette and dip and sway in relentless rhythm.

I work upstairs with Giuseppe, and run up the flight with my precarious burden, never dropped or spilt, and reach a contented exhaustion by shifts' end.

We eat like nocturnal aristocrats at one o'clock in the morning, on the best cuts of beef, or soft succulent game, with spiced roasted vegetables, sorte potatoes and delish delicacies. Bursting sharpnesses and robust depths, ecstatic flavors and gentle caressing sweetnesses. Sometimes we'd have pizza or pasta, for the cosy comfort of them, and the rarity of that made them seem a treat. We drank good wines, Barolos and that excellent Soave; beware cheap imitations; and Irish Coffees, the thick yellow cream balanced against the flavoursome black in wine glasses, and small but constant cups of delicious coffee. Fat and satisfied we smoked. We savoured, languorous. The managers from a few local Italian-themed restaurants arrived after midnight for the poker game: Mike, Kim and Peter were the regulars who joined us.

Kim was half breed oriental, young and good looking, smart, but rarely winning. One early morning I am on fire, catching and burning them all relentlessly, and there is a huge pile of notes and coins beside me on the table. Most of it came from Kim. We later discover that he was playing with and has lost the entire night's takings. We don't see him at the game again after that.

Peter is of Italian descent. He runs half-marathons, always wears a track suit, is very quiet in a boring kind of way, no sparkle, no personality, bright but bland smile, but nice enough I guess. Dave always refers to him as a 'paper hat,' which is 'twat' in rhyming slang.

Mike is large and soft. He is wry and laconic. His hair is tight curly wild. He has a short beard, and always wears blue tinted sun glasses.

I think he looks like Roy Wood, the singer from the seventies Glam band Wizzard.

See my baby jive.

The game we play is Five Card Draw, jacks to open, which employs only about seventy or eighty per cent of a standard deck, the lowest cards being excluded. This makes for a faster, dynamic game, as making a connected hand is more probable. Later I will play Texas Hold 'Em for a time, which I came to prefer, when poker becomes mainstream and popular. The world was a very different place before the internet, everything was smaller. We had no idea what cards they played in Texas, USA.

The stakes are high, especially for me. If I don't win one of the first few hands my ten pounds will be gone, and I will be walking home skint.

I don't mind if I do. I enjoyed these early mornings intensely. I loved the rituals of the game, the rules making everything just so, and I loved the tactility of the clacking shuffles, the clinking coins building and spilling into rippling pools at the table's centre, clouds of drifting smoke twisting. I wasn't covetous about winning, and it didn't upset me to have worked all evening and have nothing at all to show for it the next afternoon. For a year or so I pretty much lost every time I played. It was never a disaster because I only had the single night's wage on me to begin with.

At school, with thirty or forty pounds in my pocket, I am unusually wealthy.

I would prefer not to lose, of course. Mostly because going broke meant I had to sit the rest of the session out and only watch.

I always sat next to Dave and he would share the reveal of his cards with me, holding them tightly in one hand, the faces squared so that only the top card was visible. Very slowly he squeezed them apart, barely exposing the top corners of the ones beneath, tantalizing us both with the very edge of their numbers. Sometimes he would cheat.

The game was always friendly, despite the hundreds of pounds that would often be on the table. Dave exploited this friendliness, because he hated to lose. A few times he threw his hand face down into the pile, claiming to hold winning cards. The guys at the table took his word and didn't insist on seeing the cards. Not showing his hand openly was bad etiquette, even if he had actually had what he claimed to have.

He almost tried this trick one time too many.

One night he was against Mike in a large pot. They were raising and re-raising each other, neither giving ground. I had seen Dave's cards as usual and I knew he was holding two pair, queens and jacks with an ace kicker, which is not a particularly strong hand. He had kept the queens with the ace, as was his wont, and changed his two unconnected cards. The jacks turning up had excited him.

Mike was canny. He was probably the best player at the table and he often finished ahead and rarely lost, which implies skill, for the random variance makes consistency almost impossible. Giuseppe was perhaps his closest rival; he never lost, but rarely seemed to be winning. Mike had only drawn one card in this hand. He would be going for a flush if he drew two cards. He liked to be certain before putting his cash in, and a flush is usually always winning. He wasn't budging, which meant he most likely had two strong pairs: aces on top. Dave eventually realised that he was beat. He called.

'Aces and tens,' Mike shows, smiling, knowing he easily caught his fish, and the pot is huge.

I look to Dave sympathetically, his pain is my pain, but he nods and smiles, tosses his cards face down onto the discard, and pulls the coins and notes in. He doesn't even say what he has until Mike demands to know. 'Three queens,' he lies straight into Mike's eyes.

'Show them,' Mike insists. He has just put a lot of money on the table, and he was expecting to get it straight back.

Peter tries to be peacemaker, but Dave waves him away. He reaches indolently across and flips over two of his discarded cards, and they are the queens.

'Where is the other one?'

Frowning, apparently offended that his integrity is being thus challenged, Dave digs beneath the discard pile into the undealt cards, and turns a single card. Miraculously, it is a black queen. Nobody can refute it, although it comes from a different place from his other cards. The reveal is too powerful. They accept, Mike puzzled, and Dave chuckles to himself. Tonight he wins well.

I am so amazed at his good fortune, somehow finding that card, which I know for certain wasn't in his hand, but even so I become doubtful, like a conjurer's trick, not knowing what I saw or didn't see, that I ask him about it the next shift we are on. He laughs, and doesn't answer until I press him, reminding him that I had seen his two pair.

'Well,' he explains enigmatically, 'I took a gamble. If I hadn't drawn a queen, perhaps no one else had. The odds are fairly good, then.'

Nineteen

Being suspended from school was like an extra holiday rather than a punishment. In all I was suspended about thirteen times, each being for either a week or a fortnight, during my fourth and fifth year at Shoebury. I didn't want to be in school, it was a boring waste of my day. I liked seeing my friends there but that was all. I couldn't wait until I would finally be free of it when I was sixteen.

I was also expelled twice. The first time was towards the end of the fifth year, when I had about three or four months left. The State arranged for me to see a private tutor in Southend. He was an affable old guy and he hired me to do some odd jobs labouring around his home and garden, which Stuart sometimes accompanied me to.

After reaching sixteen, and being officially released from school, I took a couple of warehouse jobs in North Shoeburyness. They were dull and poorly paid. I quit, and persuaded the teachers at Shoebury that I was a changed boy after my recent experiences, and that I now wanted to work hard and get to college, which was partially true at least.

They gave me another chance and I spent a few months in Sixth Form. Lee Ebbs was also there and we had a lot of fun together, and skipped most lessons.

I was still reacting badly to authority, with head-on aggression, and I was expelled for the second time after an altercation with the guy who had been my German teacher during my third and fourth year. He was covering our study period. We had never gotten along.

When I enrolled at Southend college to do art, I faked my grades on the application, and then avoided the interview when we were supposed to bring our O Level certificates in. Once the course was underway in September, I was never asked to verify my qualifications.

For now I am still in the fourth year.

The car we are in belongs to a greasy lard-belly dude who is in his early twenties. On first impressions I thought he was a slimy creep and nothing later changed my mind.

He was parked across from the school, adjacent to the community centre, where years before I had attended Boys' Brigade. Or not attended, I should probably say.

I was on the back seat with Jasper, Russ, and Jim. Tim was in the front passenger seat. The lard-belly got out of the car and went to attend whatever business he had.

'Why are you hanging out with him?' I ask Tim. 'What a grease-ball.'

'Yeah, but he has a car,' Tim smiles.

'He ain't worth it even with the car,' Jasper laughs.

Jasper shares with us that he has found a new way to finish when masturbating. He describes the deliciousness he felt by prolonging, holding back as long as he could, slowing, rather than galloping away with that feeling to get there.

'Ah, man! I did that when I was about ten,' Tim teases him. 'You only just discovered that?'

Jasper asks if his special Karma Sutra move is a revelation to anyone here? Done it, says Jim, Russ, and finally me. 'Even the pup has done it!' grins Tim.

Lard-belly returns, and then drives us to his house on the other side of the block, a few minutes away from Gilman Drive.

He puts a porn film in the video, which plays through the TV. How sleazy. I like this guy less and less. It is called *The Story of O*. I've never watched a porn film before, and I am intuitively repulsed by the idea. I don't want to watch prostitutes fuck each other. It's exploitative on so many levels, like watching dancing bears. This film is a black and white nonsense. It's like a naked Hammer Horror film without the horror, but the same ham acting and toppling sets. It seems flouncy and silly to me. All of us soon grow bored of it, but we smoke his cigarettes and drink his beer.

We don't articulate our reasons. We are just instinctively resisting conformity and unthinking servility. We are too wild and energetic to sit chained in rows of wooden desks, in drilled automaton classrooms, learning like parrots to aspire to banality, to be faceless and formless, severing from Self. We

don't believe the lie, even though we do not see all of the truth.
It doesn't matter, because we feel it intuitively.
It isn't calculated nor deeply cognitive, not any of it.
So we are cast in shadows, painted dark and bad in this topsy-turvy theatre of the absurd, when really we are brave and true.
They are smiling brightly on the TV screen, but it is scripted joviality and canned applause. These people worship nonsenses and delusion, dead inside, and selling the same stories over and over, so that lies become truth, myth reality, and black becomes white. Surrender is too heavy a price to pay to belong, to fit with them.

Jim and I hang and talk. We are brothers. Our petty crimes are incidental, part of growing and exploring, rather than arising from any inherent wickedness. We desire only to be, to freely grow into who we are without being forced into uncomfortable postures by our environment. We recognise a right to intellectual liberty.
We smoke, laugh, get drunk or high when we can. We talk, drink cheap harsh whiskey, and listen to Gene and Eddie.
We cut across the hushed fields in evening's gloam, and Jim is quiet and thoughtful, always with a sardonic smile.
He is good looking in a sharp, urban kind of way. He isn't pretty like Russ or Tim, but he is dangerous and powerful. His fire smoulders darkly, like the anti-hero.
He takes a detour when we have reached the school passing under the corrugated plastic roof which forms a short sheltered alleyway across the tarmac, held aloft by cold black angular metal poles, and towards the main building. I follow him, and I am wondering what it is that has caught his attention.
He waits in the shadows besides the wall for me, near the wooden door arched in stone. His eyes gleam, fire and humour.
'Let's climb onto the roof,' he says.
Laughing at our own mischief we scale the wide square brick faces, using the twin drainage pipes that are fixed in the angle of the walls as footholds and leverage, and we come to the roof in seconds. There are no sharp lips or ledges to manoeuvre around nor over, so we soon stand erect against the rolling

clouds of night, conquering silhouettes against the sliver moon. We are drawn to two large skylights above the teachers' common. Reaching them we are surprised to discover one of the white and blue skylights unsecured. We prop it open with its latch, and peer down into the lair of our enemies and antagonists. This is their sacred hallowed space, into which no pupils have ever been admitted.

We want to go in, to explore, to desecrate, to find treasure, but how will we get back out again if we do?

'We'll manage,' Jim assures me, and I am disarmed by his irreverent confidence. We dangle legs first until we can stretch inside the square aperture, into the room itself, hanging with our hands on the skylight's sill, arms stretched with our bodyweight, and drop then onto a desk, jumping, running onto the floor and coming to a stop.

With slow grins we crouch and turn our eyes through the gloom over the furnishings and oddments and teachers' paraphernalia. Personal items like coffee mugs and notebooks on armchair arms, and glasses case and sundry trinkets. We sit in their comfortable chairs and see how relaxed and human they must be here, drinking coffee, closed away from the hurly-burly of raucous interaction and monotonous instruction, from work and bothersome kids. Unmasked in their own private space they are revealed in a startling way to us: as only people. We eat from their biscuit barrel.

Jim is more inclined to vandalism than I; he drags up a greenie and spits it into their coffee granules. I am disgusted, but still join him in laughter as he swirls the jar to mix it in.

We are excited and powerful, thrilled at how far our spontaneous adventure has taken us. We are cunning and cleverer than. We can burn their sanctum to the ground if we should just feel the whim of it. How shall we leave the mark of our having conquered?

We browse, but wanton destruction of property aside, there is not much for us to see and do in this room. Jim finds a set of keys, and one of them opens a door leading into a smaller room. Inside are two desks supporting cumbersome box computers, and several green metal file cabinets. We search for the files on ourselves, but neither of them are in the cabinets. They must be in circulation somewhere, our listed misdemeanours stretching perpetually. It is a disappointment. How narcissisticly sweet it would be to read pages and pages on oneself, their interpretations of us, how amusing and fascinating their points of view on who we are and what we have done would have been.

Jim switches the content of a few files around, sabotaging their system a little. They won't find the misplaced contents without searching through every file.

Jim wanted to take one of the computers, to sell. That didn't seem a good idea to me. Not because it was stealing. If there had been something succulent and easily portable and valuable I would have agreed to its theft. These computers were huge and heavy. Getting them out through the skylight would be a difficulty, although probably not impossible. Carrying them would be slow and indiscreet, and to whom would we sell them?

It added to a unnecessary risk which was liable to lead us into trouble. I persuaded Jim to leave it behind. The money it could fetch was a big temptation for him, for us both, but I reasoned logically that we had already triumphed. If we pushed too far, encumbering ourselves with a chimera of riches, then we were likely to lose our victory in the ignominy of capture and punishment.

We returned the way we had come. We stood on the desk, and he boosted me up into a jump to catch the sill, and pushing my feet upwards. I was then able to pull myself through using the corners of the frame. I lean into the aperture and stretch my arms for him to climb up. Jim leaves the skylight propped on its latch.

Across from the school, out beyond the gates now, walking slowly past the community building, we are startled by police activity behind us. There is a squad car and flashlights. Someone must have seen us on the roof. We slip away into nefarious streets.

Next morning we are both amazed and amused when we hear their description of a break in. The official version is that professional burglars broke in through the skylight, and made away with both the computers. Jim and I know this is an absolute lie. The police were there immediately, so no one else could have had time to get in after us, and made away with the computers. A dodgy insurance claim we guess. Perhaps the school will end with an upgrade of equipment as the fruits of our little exploit?

Neither of us say a word about our adventure to anyone, and our victory remains intact.

Whilst they learn their lessons in school Jim and I turn past the end of Ness Road, and pass over the wasteland to the abandoned MOD buildings.

They expected a German invasion at some point on these coasts, during the Second World War. This place was probably built then, but it had been left to dereliction a long time now. Sprawling rows of abandoned houses, wide gerful fields. Silent and remote, neglected and left for dead. Beautiful urban decay. Moving inward through the ghost town there are larger purpose buildings.

Jim and I step up at the outer wall of the town, climb easily onto it, and from here we step onto the roof of the first house. We both break into a sudden run and dash from rooftop to rooftop, skipping over the red tiles and short leaps with certain feet, we follow our familiar route and race. There is never winning nor losing in these wars.

This is our opulent playground. We pass through every door and look out of each window, climb each stair. We walk upon every roof. We bask in warm suns. We wander lazily the wasteland fields, and flip our cigarette butts into the breeze. There are piles and stacks of dry timber in many of the larger, warehouse type buildings, teeteringly filling rooms. One afternoon Jim lights a small fire beneath a criss cross of planks and beams. It catches, and spreads unexpectedly. Soon the room, deeply stacked with wood, is ablaze. We watch it burn. Crackling, spitting, crying out the joyful heat, urging to gallop in flames.

If I am the fire, well you then must be wood.

Back outside in the fields, Jim notices that he has dropped his tobacco tin. It was a gift from his father, who had made it whilst in prison. The lid and box were woven with pale thin wood.

The room was raging when we returned to look for the tin. The heat blasted at us as we stepped through the doorless frame. The tobacco tin was easily visible beneath the broad crossed beams at the base of the wood pile, where it must have fallen from his jacket pocket. There was a triangle of space beneath the rolling flames, above wide tiles on the floor.

Jim crawled as close as he could to reach the tin, but the heat and flames were so intense and dangerous, and it was just beyond hand's reach. We found no stick or pole with which we might hook and drag it.

I tried, crawled flat on my belly, pushing into the cold tiles beneath me. Stretching my arm into the furnace. The heat rolls, and the flames dance on the back of my sweater. I push an inch closer, squeezing my eyes. Jim calls me back when the flames are clinging to my clothes. He strips off his sweater and shirt and slides quickly, flat and determined, reaches the tin as the flames roar upwards, reaching for the roof, curling waves rolling under the beams biting warmly, brilliant yellow and whites. Charred and falling wood, this tottering and lurching inferno, flung into the ecstasy of devouring, embracing, taking in to oneself, binding in ashes and flame.

We lay in the tall grass, where we can watch the long building burn. We make a good distance and lay near to where there is a split level view of the rail tracks running from beneath us out in curling lines, perfect asymmetry, several tracks rising from the edge of the field, tunnelling the earth. Occasional stationary carriages, and trolleys with fuel. Dark lines and poles and grey skies and eerie landscape of quiet.

We lay in the tall grass and watch the flames eat through the roof, and we hear its crashing thunder death, falling down into the belly of the fires.

The smoke rising thick and gray draws the Fire Brigade, and we watch as they work. Once or twice one of them looks towards us, but we are too distant to approach.

I look out from the landing window, and they are sprawling on the green, behind the public telephone, just beneath this window. I open it and wave to them. My friends, lifting my heart to see them here, come to rescue me from my lonely imprisonment.

Before I have gotten out to join them my mother is telling them to fuck off, from the landing window. They aren't the sort of friends I should have apparently. Perhaps she resents the strength they lend me. I am no longer a dependant child. They wait until I get there, defending me. We stroll easily away.

There was a turning point in my relationship with my mother a few years back. I think I was eleven years old. She had sent me to the local shop, as usual, and during my walk the back door key which I had with me had fallen through a hole in my jacket pocket. I thought that it was lost, but I found it later in the jacket's lining.

When I told her I had lost the key she was incensed. She started punching me repeatedly. We were at the top of the landing. I defended myself by covering my face and head with my arms, and I sank into a crouch.

She didn't hurt me, but having her vent her frustration upon me in that manner was humiliating and unpleasant. She kept punching at me for maybe two minutes. By the time she was done I was angry. I stood up. 'Don't you ever hit me again,' I told her coldly, and walked downstairs, and out of the house by the front door.

She was shocked by my response, and she never did hit me again. The incident marked a clear shift of power, and from that point on I was not her little slave.

Verbally, she constantly abused me, but I argued back, and she no longer had control over me. When she said I must be the Devil's child, I asked if that meant she was his whore?

When I was fifteen I moved out of her house, into a bedsit in Southend.

Twenty

Jeysey is a stoner hippy, a year younger than me. I share a spliff with him and McManus one night at a party in North Shoebury. I don't realise it is smac we are smoking.

I return to the party and stare at a blank TV screen for half an hour. Jasper is a bit annoyed with them for letting me smoke that, without telling me what it was. I am half drunk beforehand, and the combination leaves me detached and vacant.

One afternoon Jeysey is in a fight with a guy from my year, Alan. They are in the assembly hall on the low stage, and it is the end of lunch, when everyone is slowly filing to their registration rooms. Pupils gather like a theatre show along the corridor balconies to watch the violent, enthralling spectacle. Eventually there are dozens of pupils sitting in the first few rows of seats. They are excited to watch this heavyweight clash. Jeysey is tall and skinny and it doesn't seem a match. His opponent is a little shorter but fit and muscular. I think Jeysey will take a pounding here.

I sit on the very front row of seats, in the middle directly before the fighters, and they are just ten feet in front of me.

They fight with swinging heavy hooks. Dull thudding punches like two slow motion boxers. Every blow seems to land, as neither of them make an effort to avoid or block.

Alan is considered one of the toughest few guys in school. He is strong and intimidating, but still a friendly amiable guy. I am wary to fight him, but I think I could beat him. I worry more about his best mate, Darren.

Darren has a sort of oriental or maybe Mexican slant to his eyes, and they hold a real mean coldness and treachery. Something about him, I don't know exactly what, makes me nervous, like he is already a practised killer. I don't want to fight him. I see images of furtive shives and blades when I consider it. I'm sure he would probably stab me.

Ordinarily I take care to keep on civil terms with them both. I have enough enemies as it is. They are also content with this truce between us.

The fight is epic, unending. Hammer blows thumping in a slow crunching rhythm, neither yielding. I am amazed at Jeysey's fortitude. He is giving back easily as good as he is getting. He doesn't look likely to fade. It is Alan who is hurting.

The seats have half filled, and they are straining over the balconies to see.

Suddenly Alan calls out to Darren, and he steps up and takes over whilst Alan falls back and rests. I am incensed by this completely unfair switch, since Jeysey is already tired, and has no partner here. My respect for Alan and Darren nose dives.

We haven't become close friends, Jeysey and I, but still we are part of the same group in a way. He is good mates with Jasper. I feel a certain loyalty towards him. The flames boil in my head and I can barely remain on my seat. I stretch forward ready to leap into the fray, but I wait, just to see what unfolds. This is Jeysey's fight not mine, and he is carving a reputation for himself with this battle which will endure. It will establish him as a fighter of reputation. He has already, before the contest is over, been elevated. Like a dark horse coming up on the outside. I don't want to intrude on that. Perhaps he will beat them both.

If they fight him together, two against one, then I will go to his aid. I cannot bear the injustice otherwise. I am gathering up all my fury, ready to launch.

He trades iron heavy punches with Darren for awhile. I know the punches hurt, we can all hear the hard thuds of connection, but Jeysey is enduring. He is a tower that will never fall.

When Alan, revived a little, joins his mate, and they will take him down together, neither able to alone, it is my cue.

I leap from my seat crossing the distance from them in one bound, swinging my burning fist up and round from the floor, and I make sure it lands sweet and hard, crushing on Darren's nose.

He is staggered by the impact, and sent back far across the floor, and almost falls. He immediately cries mercy, both hands up in defeat.

There is too much momentum in this for me, and I punch him in the face several more times before I realise he is asking me to stop. I am glad, after years of warily avoiding him, when he so easily gives up to surrender.

Suddenly there are a dozen fights broken out. Everyone is rushing for the stage, leaping over rows, throwing chairs and fists, swarming. It's like a mayhem scene from a Western or something.

Teachers now appear, registration due, and scatter the mob, catching the main culprits. I slip away behind the black curtains and evade them.

My friend Claire was watching the fight, and comes through the curtains. 'You did well!' she tells me.

Jeysey became a serious junkie, and died before he was twenty years old. Years later the woman that had been his girlfriend, together with their daughter, both junkies, would prostitute themselves, working together, one on either side of York Road, shouting encouragements and gossip across the crawling traffic.

We walk along Caulfield Road. Often, out of school for the day, Jim and I would go along Bunters and knock at Cathy's, his girlfriend for a few years. We'd hang out there with her, and probably one or two of her girlfriends. Both her parents are at work during the daytime. Later, either she'd accompany us and we'd meet with the guys and girls, or else Jim and I would take a walk. Today as we pass Bunters, Jim turns his head, smiles sardonically. Things are often difficult between them, and he won't be seeing her today.

We are expected outside the school and are met by a few guys: Jeysey, with two skinheads that I don't know, and two guys from Jim's year, Terry and Rat. Rat will commit suicide when he is about twenty.

Tim is there, but he leaves us at the junction. He doesn't often hang with us during the days now. He spends most of his time with Sandra. We make our way to the MOD buildings. The skinheads have brought some glue, two blue and silver tins of Evo-stick, and that's why they are coming with us.

Jim has been sniffing a lot more lately. It's beginning to be a regular thing. Before this day I have never done it, and they don't push me to. Most days if he has some I wait for him, bathing in the sun on the rooftops, yawning and stretching, dozing like a stray cat. If Russ is with us he will join me, and we smoke and watch the sky, whilst they cross between worlds below us in long tiled corridors and wide vacant rooms. I don't object to getting high but glue seems a very unhealthy way to get there. But I am intrigued by their descriptions of the waking dream visions that they have.

I come back down amongst them, and they are all wasted, dreaming, divided into small groups whilst they share the vision, or finding a space to wander alone.

A couple of months previously I was with Jim at the corner of Ness Road whilst he was on glue, an edge of this wasteland runs to there.

I shared his dream although I was not intoxicated. The ground opened and we both saw a stair cut into the earth. It leads to hell, Jim told me, I'm going down.

I find Jasper in an annex room which has pallet beds in bunks. He is on a spaceship, preparing for launch. I can stay only if I help. I am happy to work the co-pilot controls for him. The craft alates into the awning universe, and Jasper is almost weeping for the beauty of his galaxian rushes.

'Preparing to hyperjump,' I inform him, 'in ten, nine, eight...'

I usually avoid such direct involvement whilst they are sniffing.

The mood can turn quickly to violence when they dream of enemies.

I know from experience that they do not know me then, they do not know themselves, or where they are. It is better that I keep out of their way until they are returned from those strange places. Jim especially often grows very intense and dark. Even though I am his best friend, I feel that I have to deal with him carefully when he gets like that.

I ask Jasper if the dreams are always so vivid? They vary in intensity, definition, he explains, but one will always experience these reality blent visions in some degree, and perhaps with full impact, even on the first time of trying. I hadn't realised that. Suddenly all my objections have been bypassed.

The glue sniffers' paraphernalia are simple and direct: glue, and a plastic carrier bag. This intoxication is not about ritual nor ablution, as many pleasures. This is a sledgehammer blow to the base of the skull. Of all the different drugs I have taken through my life, glue is the singularly most affecting.

One begins by inverting the bag over one's hand, then scooping the warm viscous soft yielding glue from the tin with one's covered fingers. Then turning it back the correct way one has the glue neatly at the bottom of the bag. Make a neck near the top with your fist, and turn the edges down over the fist. Widen the hole for breathing into. The carbon dioxide mixes with the fumes, and is breathed back in.

The impact is warm rushes and deep falling swoons.

Then one walks in a waking dream. It is a dream, just like a sleeping dream, but instead of laying prone and unconscious one walks talks and interacts in the dream with the physical body and conscious mind. One is thoroughly transported in vivid landscapes, hallucinatory realities, and as with sleeping dreams anything can happen. Unlike 'shrooms and acid where the vision is mostly metamorphic, tethered in ordinary reality, glue dreams are entirely submersive.

I see Elizabeth I in my dream on this first venture, England's last authentic royal. She smiles, inclines her head to me, bestowing favour.

I get into a fight with Terry, who is covetous about the glue remaining and attacks me. I don't remember any of the punches, except one: he is sitting on top of me, I am on my back in the dust and dirt. I swing my fist up into his face.

Most of the afternoon is blank, and I find that is usual for me when I try glue a few more times. It seems pointless to pursue, when I can't even remember liking it. I move on to less wrecking ball intoxicants.

Twenty one

When I was about seven or eight years old my mother's health had deteriorated. The doctor visited her at home. He came downstairs from her bedroom and Dawn and I were waiting for him. He was annoyed and upset. 'She will dead within five years,' he told us, slamming the front door behind him. He was clearly frustrated and concerned, but his words haunted my half-sister and I for a long time.

Barbara was admitted into Rochford Hospital, which is a mental institution, for detox. It was a crossroad for her at last: stop drinking, or die quickly.

Gary was rarely home for the month she was in there, except when he returned late at night to sleep. Dawn and I were glad he was out of the way, roaming the streets with his criminal friends, already breaking in to shops and houses.

When he was at home Dawn and I locked ourselves in our mother's bedroom to avoid his bullying. We were grateful that it had a sturdy latch lock that was quick and easy to close. Gary wanted the money Barbara had given us for food and for travelling a few times a week to Rochford to visit her. He wanted to beat it out of us, but he was unable to break down the bedroom door.

We were secure in her bedroom but it was frightening to listen to him pounding on the door, trying to break through, angry at us. We were trapped, but eventually he would be spent and give up. When his threats and anger didn't work he sometimes tried sweet-talking us out, or pleading and begging us, but no matter what, we didn't unlock the door. We knew he was an uncontrollable bully. We knew he was a liar that would say anything to get his own way. And we knew he would grant us no quarter when he got hold of us.

We made our preparations early, before he came home, taking food and supplies for the evening with us, and kept him locked out.

We were left to fend for ourselves without any adult help for the entire month that Barbara was at the hospital. Somehow we managed to stay fed and intact, cashing her allowance for her each week, and following her list of shopping instructions. After she returned nothing had changed. She continued to drink and to confine herself away. Her agoraphobia and nervous anxiety intensified so that she barely ventured out of the house, and then only in taxis.

When I was thirteen years old she was admitted again to Rochford Hospital, after having had all her teeth removed. They had all rotted due to the alcohol abuse.

She progressed well this time. She made a positive choice. She got a set of dentures and never drank alcohol again for the rest of her life, never relapsed. Instead, to ease her through, she was prescribed Valium. Valium is only intended to be a short term help, but her doctor never advised her of the dangers of long term dependency, and allowed the prescription to continue. She took it every day for the next twenty five years, until she suffered a major stroke.

The tablets were five milligrams, and she collected bottles and bottles of them in the dressing table drawers in her bedroom. At fifteen years old I helped myself to them. She didn't notice if they were missing, and eventually she would only throw these ones away, having moved on to the next fresh prescription.

I swallowed ten at a time, sometimes twenty. These were massive doses that might have killed me, but instead left me in a numb hazy trance for days at a time.

I was dating Sharon then, and spending a lot of my evenings with her.

Jim, Jeysey and I are over at the MOD. For a couple of weeks Jim and me have been playing with an army issue pulley that we found. Its rope is very long, hundreds of feet. We tie one end to the greatest tree, sixty feet up, and the other end to a small tree way way over by the boundary fence. It is the longest pulley ride in the world. It takes maybe half a minute to reach the floor after leaping out of the tree, pushing into the sky.

We need to retie it. The job falls to Jeysey this time, and it is my turn to jump. But his knots are inexperienced and loose. I leap out into the sky, pushing away from the trunk, and the rope unbinds. Suddenly I am unsupported, flying, and a smashing impact beckons far beneath me. I cannot avoid this embrace.

I let go, throwing the heavy metal grip away so that it won't hit me on its way down, and I am falling. I lift my head so that my chin won't strike the earth. Falling. It takes a long time, and I will land on my chest, all air driven like a mule kick from my lungs, and my legs swinging back, up, lucky not to break my back. I feel the vertebrae in my back lock and I will my legs down.

I stretch my arms wide, calmly floating serene. I am tumbling between worlds.

Cathy was the same age as me. We met when we were six or seven years old. Dawn and I would take the very slight detour on our way home from the beach, and walk along Bunters Avenue. Cathy was often playing with friends in the street, along with her younger brother, Billy. Eventually we began chatting with each other, and formed a casual friendship.

From the age of about thirteen or fourteen, Jim was her boyfriend, and he was my best friend, so Cathy and I saw a lot more of each other.

We talked together. She would tell me of her troubles with Jim, since their relationship was often tempestuous, or of her hopes or of her day, whatever might be on her mind.

I would tell her things which happened when it was just the guys hanging together, so that she could see Jim through my eyes, who he was when she wasn't with him, and I shared Jim's thoughts of her, or we would talk about local topics of interest, gossip, or the girl I was currently infatuated with. It was a mutually informative friendship that we had, and we gave each other warmth and support. Neither of us was possessive of Jim or a threat to the other's closeness.

Cathy was pretty, and had a fresh country girl kind of face. Her hair was a dark blonde and she wore it in long waves. She had a slim strength and power which made her earthy. She was intelligent and thoughtful, candid and genuine.

Really, Jim was often treating her quite poorly, kissing other girls or suchlike, but she felt deeply for him, and had therefore to be long-suffering. She wasn't weak, it was just that her feelings for him were real. She would protest furiously when he did offend or disrespect her.

One night whilst we were outside the cafe at Elm Road which we frequented, they had a blazing row. Jim slapped her. It was shocking for all of us.

Jim and Cathy did reconcile afterwards, but that incident was wounding, and probably where their love ended.

Jim had betrayed Cathy by sleeping with another girl, Michelle. Michelle was forever throwing herself at him, almost forcing him to kiss her. He pushed her away repeatedly, but eventually he had succumbed to her ardent insistences.

She wasn't pretty, and had a rough angular face, with a skinhead Feathercut crop, and she was squat and chunky.

I didn't like her chasing after Jim. She was dim and cheap. She lived with her family on Ness Road, above a shop. One night, a few weeks after her successful seduction of Jim, the apartment caught fire and was completely gutted. I wasn't sorry for her at all. It was a pity for the rest of her family, but Cathy and I felt Michelle had gotten what she deserved.

Wendy is Russ' girlfriend. She has very black hair and very pale skin. She wears dark red lipstick. She is pregnant through her final school year with his daughter. I spend most of that spring and summer with Wendy and Claire at the beach. We are still bound by school, whilst the others, Russ, Jim, Jasper, Tim, have already left and started work. Wendy confides that she is pregnant but Claire and I don't believe her. Her belly is a bit fluffy, but still flat. She wears tight jeans all through her duration and it stays flat, and nobody is aware until the baby girl is suddenly born.

I knock on her front door, and Wendy comes to answer carrying the baby in her arms, wrapped in a warm soft blanket. She is a beautiful baby, with long dark lashes. Wendy offers her to me to hold, and I am nervous to do so, that I might drop her. I gaze into her sweet face when she is cradled in my arms, and

I feel sunlight radiate from her.

I am almost moved to tears.

It is an unexpected reaction, and Wendy notices. 'I never usually like babies,' I say in explanation, 'but maybe it's just because she is your baby and Russ', I don't know. She just seems so beautiful.'

Claire and I knew each other from before we started at Shoeburyness Comprehensive. We spent a lot of time together outside of school, and it gave us both the feeling of having grown up together. She was cute, usually wearing her blonde hair in a pixie-type cut. We flirted and teased, but never dated. I guess we would have if I had been more sexually assertive than I was at that time.

When our Shoebury days were a long time behind us, I continued to see her, moving in the same drug-related circles, and we remained friends.

She became a heroin addict when she was about seventeen. She always stayed pretty, didn't destroy herself with the drug unlike most junkies. She kept some order and control in her life, managed her addiction and dependency.

Gary tells me one evening that she is dead. Apparently she was kidnapped then killed. Some gone wrong drug deal.

The impact of this news is twisting in my belly, and tears spring to my eyes.

Who gives a shit, just a scumbag junkie, says Gary.

The story is told all over, confirmed by numerous people that knew her.

Incredibly, a week later, I see her going into a public phone booth on York Road. I open the booth door, intruding on her call, to embrace her, and tell her how glad I am that she is still alive.

Twenty two

Gary leaves thirty one gram envelopes of pure amphetamine sulphate with me. He knows I am not likely to rob him, and that I am not much of a druggie yet, so he will get them back. I put them into the top drawer of my bedside table, which I made myself, sawing down an older larger cupboard. I have no idea that if somehow I am caught with them, if the police turn up looking for him and search my room for example, that I will likely be imprisoned for possession and intent to supply. That's a five year prison term. Gary doesn't point this out. He doesn't even pay me for keeping them safely for him. He exploits me; his new violence. It is months before he returns for them.
The envelopes are cute and fascinating. They are cut from a magazine glossy paper, and intricately folded to make little self contained compartments. They work perfectly, the sweet bitter white powder never spilling out. I unwrap them and re-wrap them. After several weeks of keeping them, I begin to cut thin slithers of powder from each one, building a few grams for myself.
Coke never becomes my drug. It barely touches me on all of the occasions I try it. I feel this way anyway when I am up in a good mood. The coke high is brittle, one bum note can cause its melody to fall crashing. The Emperor's New Clothes of the drug world, it is expensive and hollow, for me. Gary, and our half-brother, Malcolm become chronic addicts. This amphetamine, a fifth of the price of coke, is ten times as potent. I am awake for days. Hallucinating in black and white, birds turning in tight circles on the windowsill of my bedroom. I can't stop talking, and everything is so interesting now. I have seven other topics in mind that I am bursting to discuss, and every word and thought expressed is profound and mesmerising. I am gripped by the slightest thing, desperate to absorb every tiny detail. I ache with love, long to connect and embrace. I shiver with chill ecstatic rushes.
I haven't slept for three nights, and I am due in work for the evening. I am feeling extremely tired now, but I haven't been able to sleep, even though I haven't taken any speed today. My

skin is gray, and I feel like death. Somehow I survive the night's work, and walking home I am falling into deep swoons. I lay on the grass beside the kerb, just yards from my house. It is dark and silent. The earth is cool against my skin. I sink into it, and its embrace is gentle. I sleep.

Now that I am a fifth year pupil things have changed. Jim gets a job working with his dad, laboring on a building site. He breaks up with Cathy. Russ will soon have a baby to support. I still hear of him everyday through Wendy, but he spends his days at work and his nights with her. Jasper is hanging out with the North Shoebury druggies, getting smaced up. Tim is with Sandra. We don't get to hang together like we used to. Life is separating us.

There aren't mobile phones commonly yet so we can't text, and keep in each others lives. It will be a few years until the internet really impacts. Modern Social Media isn't a thing yet. It happens slowly, over the next few months. We still roam the streets around Elm Road and Ness Road during balmy evenings. Sometimes we still converge, and laugh together, drink together, and play out our small dramas, but it fades, and we drift irretrievably from each other.

We are no longer a little gang of rockabilly friends.

*

Bridge

He is a scraggly hippy. His hair is a greasy unwashed blonde, and he has a pinched thin ferret-face, with a lunatic grin. He is dressed in layers of dusty antiquities and hung with beaded curiosities. His eyes are huge and earnestly wild, wrestling and penetrating, as he leans hunched, swaying in the tides of various intoxications. He talks a lot, excitedly.

In response to some casual question, he loudly insists that he is God. He refuses to offer any context. Who are we to say he is not God?

Obviously we didn't believe him, yet his stoic intense insistence began to give us doubt. We paused, hushed a moment in the acid rays and the streaming sunlight, and we wondered.

A ragamuffin journeyman acid freak. A wending pixie-boy who roamed so far that he was lost somewhere out there. Here was only an apparition, a thin echo of who he might have been. I never saw him again after that day.

I was seventeen, and it was summer, and my heart was bruised but joyful.

Kevin, Steve, and I had already dropped the LSD before the others began to arrive, and our fingers were perspiring with acid drops as we rolled a rich Gold Seal black hashish into joints. I drew the sweetly harsh smoke slow and deep into my lungs, falling with the clouds of hashish swoon.

The days were impossibly hot slow and endless. It was the summer of 1984. The reality of 1984 was not quite so stark and grim yet as the future envisioned in Orwell's dystopian dream, but he hadn't been too far from the mark.

With the demon Thatcher at the head of government England was being surreptitiously torn apart from the inside, its assets sold, its unions starved and broken. Whilst fireworks sparkled over Downing Street and the politicians dizzy and drunk on their gluttonous feasting danced in the streets. It was the beginnings of a Fascist resurgence, although subtle and disguised.

She gave more wealth to the wealthy by taking every security and comfort from the working class, grinding them into the dirt with her stormtrooper troops marching, seig hieling the black flag, and she crushed the Health Services, and withdrew all state support and care, so that the poorest would become destitute and sick.

She created more homelessness and joblessness then modern times had seen. By the time she was done there was no quarter to be found outside the middle classes. Where before her time hard working families had known security, comfort and moderate luxury, now everyone struggled and expenses rose and rose. She outlawed community.

We were young, and shut the doors on their emerging dystopia as well as we could. We didn't revolt. Instead we got high and ignored them. Unopposed, they wrought their worst.

Led Zeppelin's *The Song Remains the Same* live album was the soundtrack. Its august beautiful themes tripping into dark forgotten worlds with tantalizing melodies, gorgeously sweet. We swooned in these nefarious poetic realms, inspired into flights, and sat held-breath confounded by the simplicity and power.

Then God rose from where he had been sat cross-legged and he swept the small gathering silent with his raised hand. When certain of our attention he prophesied that he would now roll the greatest joint that had ever been rolled. It was a psychotic powerful claim.

He insisted that every young hippy pretender, vagabond and miscreant, pot-head and acid-fiend in the room pay heed. He caught us all, masterfully done, and there were nine or ten of us there in Kevin's apartment, in that transported living room. Only Kevin, older and street-wiser than the rest of us, mellow, tall, cuddly fat and gay, wearing always purple tinted Lennon glasses with Wizzard hair, our amiable, only occasionally interested, gracious host seemed immune.

The unkempt and ragged Glastonbury dandy called for papers, and one book was not enough. He let us go then, and vanished into hunched, silent crafting. We resumed our conversations, returned to our occupying activities.

The chillum was deep packed and potent, tides of thick, lush smoke filling us, and pouring from us all like dragons' fire. I drifted and span into amplified heavens where tear-like stars burst, rippling ecstatic kisses over my shivering skin. The room breathed and its walls billowed, the air undulated. Everything thrummed to the acid's metronome beat.

Joy rose in us, pulling us higher, lifting us into purity and connectedness, and we were comfortable brothers, easy and cheerful and profound, because the day was beautiful and the song was loud and wonderful. We tumbled laughing into the abyssal intoxication.

When finally, a conjurer re-appearing, he emerged again and spread his creation out across the carpet, it looked like a white map of the heavens, endless: a sheet of a hundred skins. So utterly had he been immersed in his task that we had forgotten. This paper contraption that he had made could surely never be shaped into a thing smokable.

He gathered cigarettes and weed and hash, and set to the next phase of his work with gusto, his own clever secrets keeping him content and chuckling, smiling self-ward, unperturbed by our lack of faith, and unrestrained, somehow he was irresistible. Purple Haze, some Colombian weed, potent and sticky, Gold and Red Seal black, and an eighth of Rocky Rocky, ten cigarettes. It was a mix contrived in some eldritch lost smoky dope-head paradise. But God, sure of his vision, certain in his omnipotence, demanded more. He took greedily from each of us. Again and still again wanting more, until we each had given at least an eighth from our beautiful hash and weeds, and he had before him an overflowing ounce of solid and leaf. On that day we somehow had an abundance, a seeming unlimited supply. I still had a rock of hash that was heavy and pungent, though dented. I shook my head with amusement and incredulity, and silently dismissed God as a madman.

We focused on the gorgeous chillum, and the loosely rolled cones that moved in circles, one to the next, as the sunshine streamed in panels of dusty smoke-dragon warmth, and Page's dark but beautiful guitar swept us into an oblivion too sweet and intimate, and so heavy that we felt it reverberate in every fibre of our beings.

The speakers throbbed out tangible walls of sounds, prettily-colored notes twisting off, blending into smokes, hallucinatory, vivid and ecstatic thrills.

My friend Steve was elven-haired and elven-boned, and a natural born stoner. His eyes were like star-flints, and his grin was wide and warm. He was paying rent to sleep on Kevin's sofa.

I had arrived early, bringing the almost fabled Black Pyramids sent from 'Dam, which I had obtained that morning from my friend and guru for a season, Mick. This acid was potent and clean. Pure, beautiful emotive cerebral visual audio resonance. Kevin's apartment had been like a fabled place for me once. His parties were legendary, mythological hedonistic celebrations, and thereby his reputation confused with a grandeur and aloofness which belied his real life warmth, once the barriers were crossed with offerings of and sharing experiences with quality drugs. I was here as Steve's friend and would probably never have met Kevin otherwise. I was intrigued to be inside this apartment, scene of wild drug orgies, if I should believe the tales.

It was located on the corner of the High Street, which was incidentally a very desirable real estate position. On the seventh floor we were impenetrable, safe from intrusion, we had nothing to do but get high.

It was somehow a questing for truth. I was searching always for cognition. Here were other realities, confounding the corporate capitalist materialist lie. The Overlords forbade this, and their motivation for doing so was sinister. Whatever this was between us, radiating outward coloring All, it tasted clean and holy. We knew it was something good. Its blissful shivers trembled in our brains, and through our flesh crested and fell in waves. We climbed onward, exploring our own minds, plateau after dizzy plateau.

The décor was very colorful, dark purples and warm oranges,

silver and deep blues, blacks, reds. It was organised with flair
and invitingly lit. It was comfortable, narcissistic and
introverted, surprisingly cosy and artful with cushions and
blankets.

Then, like a god rising from the depths of Valhalla, he rose
suddenly up from his crafting, and held aloft with one hand the
weapon of desolation that he had builded. And it was
monstrous, gargantuan, two feet long, a vast coneing torpedo
spliff, an impossible abomination.

He threw back everything, like red seas racing from his glare,
and we were dazed and stupefied.

It was a perfectly crafted, mixed, packed, and weighted joint
of ridiculous proportion.

He lit it with great ceremony, and when it came around to
each our turns we were mazed and delighted at how well it
smoked! Like a monstrous cigar, its burn healthy and smooth
and pleasant, rich and smoke-full.

We nodded together, all appreciation.

We could not dent it. We smoked it for half an hour and it was
barely worried. We smoked God's spliff until we were all
exhausted and begged mercy. And still it was huge and fat and
beautiful and strong. We wanted to quit, and so in a desperate
gamble we tried to steady ourselves by smoking smaller joints
along with this Behemoth, as if they might ground us, and they
were like tiny tide-boats, their lines straining at their limit,
barely keeping us from being swallowed up forever by his
fathomless tides.

We floundered and pitched and swooned. We went under, and
sank far down into mesmerising seas, awful tides dragging us
toward cold white death. Yet, somehow we crest and fall, and
the raging currents pause awhile, and only push us gently now,
and we grasp once more toward land.

This new plateau bursts like firecrackers in my head. A
machine gun popping that is orgasmic and sharp and dazzling
sweet. I can barely keep from flying away.

I accept the monster-spliff as it comes once more to me, and
still it is a foot long thick booming cone. I smoke, and my

vertigo rights.

I climb up onto the dragon's broad back, and terrified as it unfolds its vast wings, I laugh a little. I catch Steve's eye, and he grins. Outlaw half-breeds both, we could die here, but likely we will prevail, if we are true and fierce and bold.

I fall with it in diving flights, and ride up into dizzying heights, and the winds are now warm and gusting drives bearing me ashore, into harbor, dry and secure.

We were all hauled ashore, caught in God's wide net. Bedraggled, and seeing the truth of that moment, we acknowledged his claim. Oh, it was indeed the finest, most beautiful, most intoxicating joint ever envisioned and rolled. Now, on this day, it still burns fiercely as a dragon's heart, and its fire and kisses are layered with grass, tobacco and hashish. It is an otherworldly artefact. We bow to its divinity. But, God has not finished with us. He has a plan.

With ablutions made he launches into the ritual. Holding us rapt, he unties a leather purse, olde worlde style, from his belt. He slips inside and retrieves two die. They glitter like ruby and sapphire in his hand, and he shakes them gently against his palm and fingers. They are wonders of magicks and physics. The power they radiate is unstoppable, universal, and I am entranced with curiosities.

He casts the die onto the carpeted floor and they spin to a portent laden doom. God cries out: 'Seventy!'

Ah, and so there is some sense, even at this mad tea party. He is the Dungeon Master, and we are heroes now in the world of his imagining. This is how he is omnipresent and omni-powerful! He steps back, and we digest this knowledge; after all just a sly joke, smoke and mirrors, a conjurer's illusion. There are no tomes of rules, his Word is almighty. Now that we cannot deny him and must yield to his every whim he seems content. The dice shall be the fates, and they are also chaos, random chance. He leads us a long winding journey o'er a desolate land. His dream is arid, barren. The heat wilts us. It is a slow, arduous adventure and I am tripping heavily, intensely involved and transported into his magickal land of heroes and deserts.

We pass its first night with a small fire burning, and it is a slow rambling nothing that he has brought us through. I am already weary, but I am present. Early morning on the next day of this imagined world he unleashes a wyrm, which is a small dragon, against us. It devastates and scatters our band of ramshackle heroes, and the blades bounce harmlessly off the wyrm's scaly hide. It is looking like a rout, and might all end in tears.

I have a bow, unlike the others who all chose swords or ax when we began. I wait my chance, and the fates catch the flight of my arrow so that it flies true, biting into the wyrm's soft underbelly with critical precision, and even God is surprised, as the wyrm is brought down. The arrow wound doesn't kill it, but stuns it, exposes it, makes it vulnerable.

It is Steve's character who bravely leaps in now. Steve was the only one who had chosen as a weapon a Greatsword, a two-handed blade, slow but capable of heavy damage, heavy enough to pierce the armor of the wyrm. Steve deals the death blow.

We are yang and yin.

I realise that I no longer need aggression to protect myself; I am not under immediate threat now. I cast off the mask I had worn, gladly. I breathe the tension out of me. It is deep, and I cannot be empty of it yet. I begin to unravel my youthful bonds, and draw closer to who I am.

I am bleeding from open wounds, Soul-deep. I have years of chronic depression ahead of me, but for now, I slide artfully into nepenthe oblivions.

I meet a young handsome guy named Russell outside the Pink Toothbrush nightclub one evening. His hair is dark shoulder length, and his grin is wide and charming. He is very friendly and talkative and engaging. A heroin addict, he enthuses over its beautiful intoxication.

'I need to be sick,' he tells me, 'then I'll be okay.'

'Does it always make you throw up?' I ask him.

'Yes, but then afterwards you get a lovely warm rush and everything is wonderful,' he replies. 'It's worth it!'

He suddenly rushes over to an alcove to throw up. He returns with a beaming smile.

Years of faces and names, passing through. The life is filled with people, strangers and friends and lovers, bustling, crawling, dancing, dying. Perhaps our path converges here awhile, and we can walk a way together.

I sink down down to the very beneath. Let us fall to the edge of life, to reach our orphic peripeteia.

They are calling me and my wilderness heart aches for them. I hear them galloping. I hear their horizon songs. Perhaps here, in the nether realm, I will discover what it is that I am, and the truth that I am looking for.

This world of paper buildings and cardboard cut-out people, lies pasted over cracks, nubivagant castles, is brash and demanding, but it is not real.

Its hollowness is making my skin crawl. I cannot eat from this table, the bread is rotten and this wine is tainted with the blood of murder. The music is loud but it does not move me. The brittle gods are cold and heartless. I cannot grasp the formulaic structure of this living. What is wrong with me?

I plunge into intoxicants because it is the only path I can see, and I need to dull the pain I am feeling.

Reality is not static but fluid. It might be a place to leap from. It may be a circuitous route but I feel I have no alternative. There is a faint light, a tiny wheeze of a breath, a taste of chocolate. It isn't much, but it is everything I have.

Usually, Mick's contact in Amsterdam posted the acid to sunny Southend in a small standard envelope, two thin pieces of card either side of the acid strip. LSD is odourless, undetectable, which meant there was very little risk of them being undelivered, or of anyone getting caught with them.

Mick decided to fly out for the weekend, it was good to keep personal contact. Coming back he was stopped and had his bags searched by customs, but they never found the Black Pyramids. He had put them in the toes of his dirty socks. They were tiny perfect hollow pyramids, made from some thin dissoluble plastic, about two centimetres square.

I had two very vivid auditory experiences whilst on those pyramids, which suggests mescaline. The first was a long intense argument that I could hear taking place in the next room, in this shared house. It seemed extremely real. I wondered if I should intervene. Yet, something about its quality made me question if it was actually happening or not. Later, I was able to confirm that it was an auditory hallucination; or more accurately, I was able to confirm that no argument had taken place. Perhaps you were picking up on a psychic record, Mick suggested, when I told him about it.

The second occasion I was alone in the communal lounge, laying stretched upon the sofa. My rented room was upstairs, but I enjoyed the wallpaper in this room when I was tripping. Green and gold concentric circles, diamond patterns cutting through, in rows of eternity, morphing perpetually.

I heard a masculine voice address me. It was rich and toneful, and was outside of me, not inside my head. It filled the room with its sound. It was like the voice of a god. I couldn't determine a single point from where it originated.

'Look for it,' it told me.

'Look for what?' I wondered, in reply.
'The answer,' came the clever response.
'The answer to what?' I countered, eventually.
'The answer to the question.'

A year later and now I live right next to expansive fields in
which magic mushrooms grow robustly. Their season is
September through until the first hard frosts, which will be
November if temperatures are not extreme.
I walk the short street and turn into the fenced alleyway. It
opens through two fast swinging curves onto a duel
carriageway. The roads are fairly quiet here at Rayleigh Weir,
far removed from Shoeburyness, at eighteen years old.
I cross and jump the short outer fence. They are broad lush
trees that obscure the fields, their foliage very dark and wet
today in this morning rain like mist, part of several small
woods. I step into long grass and the moisture soaks swiftly up
almost to the knees of my jeans, coming through the trees into
the first field. The mist covers the field in a hazy opal dome.
The mushrooms are so fat, drenched and still thirsting, raised
high to bask in the wet sky, that they are easily visible above
these shorter cropped blades. I have never seen such a
proffered harvest before. As far as the mist allows me to see,
there are bustling dark gray clumps in every patch of grass.
Thousands of the li'l dears.
There are more than I can pick. I pick fast and expertly,
moving methodically in straight lines up and back down the
length of the field, covering every foot, but I am not fast
enough. Before I am a quarter through the field the day has
waxed a little stronger, the light brighter, and the 'shrooms sink
back beneath the shady grass. Now, I cannot see them. But I
know they are there.
On a good day, and I will come here most days during season,
I expect to collect three or four hundred mushrooms. My bag
is already bulging, wet and dark. I lost count at approximately
a thousand picked, about half hour in.
They look much nicer usually, more appetising on a dry day
when they are white or pale cream brown and skinny, twisting

mushroomily through their cycle between blades to light. The yellow nipples marking them as special.

There are no sounds other than the ones I am making. The slapping swoosh of my wet jean legs, the squish of wet sock inside my boots. My feet are white damp in this clinging, invading insidious mizzle. My breath rasps. Inside the wet woollen gloves my hands are numb.

I take the gloves off, push them down into my pocket. I rub my hands together, squeeze them into tight fists, trying to spark some fire.

Death stands brooding at the edge of the mist. Gloaming shadows. We both stand stilly, regarding the other. When I take a couple of steps towards him he recedes, white shadows folding over him.

I make greasy 'shroom tea. Everything breathes with me. The walls sigh sadly. The floor moves in slow circumvent, and exquisite patterns flower and trace intricately upon it, pulling me down into beneath realms. Distances stretch and bow, lines leaning in, converging. Inanimates throb and shine. Staccatos ripple bliss.

Reality morphs. Mirrors are frozen waters, and my reflections are strange and other.

I roll a joint, and my fingertips are sweaty. The fire leaps brightly, and the paper tobacco and hash ignite lustily. It is all sweet melody here.

I open the front door of my apartment, and the day booms. Michelangelo gods nubivagant in the sky. Color bleeds, swells in deep pungent rivers. Trees bend and pavements glitter.

A crone, rubber faced and crescent-spined, scuttles across the road. She is clacking the soft tarmac with a round-headed cane. Her nose is scrapping the floor. How strange to meet her today. I sit and wait at the bus stop.

The bus pulls me into its belly. The doors shoomm shut. In my seat I am trembling, trying to hold my head together but it cracks and splinters beneath the pressure of grinding gears and trundling wheels, cacophonous amplifications, a dreadful metallic song. I should not have allowed this lumbering beast

to swallow me, spewing out, sucking in, and all their eyes
upon me seeing and knowing, and sly smiles making me fear.
I am pitched out when we arrive at Southend. I sit on a
shallow bank of grass, folding my arms over my knees, resting
my forehead, closing my eyes, drifting spins, and wait until I
have forgotten the horror of the monster's pulsing belly.
The sunshine warms me. I stop shivering, and smile now as I
watch the day. The roads undulate like American bridges in
high winds. Lines and sweeps and curves.
It's all so fucking beautiful.

*

Book the Second

BE ONE AND BEAUTIFUL

*

It's a cultural perspective; the Mojave Indians would recognise the shamanistic journey.

We must recognise that in many instances delusion and psychosis are clear.

Perhaps we need different eyes to experience other realms.

It isn't so monochrome, this life.

The realms of magicks, the madness of schizophrenia, and the lunacy of normality, exist side by side in the same strange place. Every prophet, every natural shaman, is teetering on the edge of the schizophrenic experience. How else can one be opened to that realm, and walk with the Gods?

0

Since my landlord sold the apartment that I had lived comfortably in for four years, I had been having great difficulty in finding decent housing. An influx of Kurdish and Iranian refugees had made local accommodation suddenly scarce.
My landlord, with whom I had had a good professional relationship, purchased the apartment during an upward trend in the market about fifteen years previously. Since then its value had not been high, so that he was unable to resell it without taking a significant loss. He advised me when I took it over that if the market shifted, making a sale viable, then he would have to sell to recoup his investment. When its value suddenly rose, he had to act quickly.
I found myself moving from one unpleasant bedsitter to another. I hadn't lived in places like this since I was a teen, and it was depressing to have to do so again. I was not used to sharing bathrooms and I didn't enjoy doing so.
It was 2004. I was writing music and spending a lot of my free time playing my guitar and singing. I had started to record a few of my songs on a four-track recorder. I was also very preoccupied with my artwork during this time.
I had the urgent inspiration to begin a drawing, which I eventually titled *Sea of Souls*.
I had worked on it for three days and nights, virtually without pausing. It is a detailed image drawn in black ink, depicting a vast sea of skulls. From the centre of this macabre sea Kurt Cobain is emerging.
The picture represents a world or astral plane where Souls of those who have died violently are trapped. Yet Cobain is rising out of the sea. His expression is powerful and wilful, clawing his way out of the rubble of dry skulls.
An uneasy image. Only in its subtleties was it hopeful and triumphant.
When I was so exhausted that I could not focus I lay down my pens and slept fitfully. When I awoke, I instantly took up the task again. There was a significance to this picture that I sensed, but could not articulate to myself.

When it was finished, a feeling of great heaviness and heat rose into my head, and I closed my eyes as the world dropped away from me.

The urgency that had moved me to work almost feverishly through and past my exhaustion, knowing that I must finish, that time was racing away from me, revealed a partial motivation now; it was my own ending that the picture foretold. This task had been my peak, and having concluded it, there was nothing left for me but to fall into decline and death.

Strangely, I did not react to her presence with alarm or even surprise, even though I had been alone a moment before. It seemed as though her being there was perfectly natural. We talked calmly, continuing with a conversation that I did not remember having begun. We moved through deeper and deeper topics.

It happens so quickly that the change is not perceptible. Without breaking stride one is suddenly walking in a paracosm. There is a spontaneous and seeming natural equanimity, as though the rational mind of everyday consciousness must be silenced if any meaningful communication is to take place. Perhaps this dialogue *is* continuous, and maybe that is why one has the sensation of arriving in the middle of a discussion and event? Perhaps some dimension of the Soul resides in that sweven realm.

In that other place knowledge and cognition are different from knowledge and understandings in the physical world. There are no mistakes, no doubts. One simply *knows*. It is a realm of *sooth*. It is a realm where dense ego does not and cannot intrude.

A latch is turned, a door of some kind has been opened, and the physical mind is able to participate to the extent of being aware of the proceedings, of processing what is said and what transpires, and in being able to retain some conscious memories of that experience.

The magickal world is overlapped with, merged with, the sane everyday experience.

When she leaves me I weep with sorrows so deep that I cannot stop. I weep for three days, lost in a deep trance, slumbering. There is so much grief in me. On the second day I begin to chuckle amid my tears. On the third day I am laughing freely and deeply, and weeping with both sorrow and elation.

That night, I sleep like the dead. I awake in hell.

The first few weeks are very extreme. I am in a state of near constant stress and feel very threatened. I am living in a horror film.

I teach myself to survive in the new reality. I try to adapt to its special conditions. She has attempted to prepare me, but with each day that passes I am further away from ordinary reality, and I am often overwhelmed with doubt.

My only defence is to become: to reach closer to my authentic self. There at my core will I find strength and power to fight.

At first I am defenceless. I can see them, demons inside of people, monsters attached to their Souls. Hard, deep black eyes, hostile and vampyric. The filter is absent and the gates are opened. I have one foot in that world and one foot in this world. This is a hyper-reality.

The battle will spill out of the sky onto blood soaked streets. Obsidian angels, beautiful and terrible, riding upon giant stallions girt with silver harness, wield mighty weapons to bring apocalyptic slaughter and ruin.

The axle splits, and the world lurches. I will the sun to turn. It hangs, frozen. Bells toll.

Sanyasin, untethered, wandering. The reckoning allows no returning.

The person I was no longer exists.

I had been in Brighton two months. I was calm now, serenely floating down. I let go of all that I had been.

I slipped into sleep, fascinated by every moment of my apparent dying. It was warm and comforting as I descended into eigengrau darkness.

I did not die, yet all my universes were transformed.

Of course, I had the choice to refuse her. If I had let the moment pass without action it would not have arisen again.

She was not in the habit of insisting. Instead, her instructions were usually whispered so softly that at times I could barely catch what was said.

I was committed to following wherever she led me.

When he came for me that evening in Brighton I could see him and feel his presence tangibly.

He was not at all monstrous or frightening, despite the depths that he wrapped himself in. His heart was tender. I felt love for him and pity, for it seemed to me that he was lonesome and cursed. I stepped across with him, away from this world of light and life. He held me gently.

'Don't drop me,' I pleaded.

'I've never dropped one yet,' he said.

I rode upon the backs of mighty dragons in aethereal realms, urged them upward and outward into the spiralling starscapes. They were an army, for this was war. Magickal and gorgeous, each heart and Soul intimately known to me and pledged to follow me, that stretched in ranks so deep that they filled the whole universe.

I entered strange battlefields and often I was alone against the amassed demonic enemies, cohorts of thousands.

I turned slowly into the Dance of Seven Veils, into the Dance of Death, laughing.

I wept and wept and wept. All the sadness of all the worlds came into me, poured out through me. I wept oceans and oceans. Salty, painful tears swelled like rivers around my thighs.

The queen of the fire elementals whispered her name to me. Incredibly beautiful, with the sweetest of hearts, her aspect golden and radiant, her hair curling flame. She took me with her to her strange shadowy world.

When I left Brighton in June and found myself camped in a small wood for the next few months, in a tiny one-man tent, she was with me.

Sometimes she came into my body and used my limbs as her own, to share the pleasures of being within flesh. All things were subtly changed, more vibrant, more alive. When she looked through my eyes the world was filtered through a golden veil.

She folded my body in her arms. When a tear fell from her eye and splashed upon my lips my Soul leapt from my body, upwards into the turning circle, infinite and microscopic, drifted slowly, slowly, enrapt.

Obsidian angels, terribly beautiful and divinely powerful kept close to me always. They were my generals, my advisers in war, my protectors.

I descended into awful abysses, where dark creatures sought to devour me, feeding on my Soul, drawing strength from my fear. I passed through hells exhausted by the weight of constant assault.

I rose on ecstatic powers, in deeply sensual swoons, like a god shaping the multiverse to my liking, soaring into delicious flights, trembling, drenched with the sweetest energies.

I made cataclysmic magicks. Cleansing, reshaping, reforming. Slowly, not to be overwhelmed, working in towards a centre of cognition, I gathered all the threads into a cohesive whole.

1

Even before that evening when she appeared and spoke with me
I was tumbling down slowly. I heard music that nobody else
could hear.
I didn't recognise people that I knew well. They wore imperfect
masks. They were actors playing their roles unconvincingly.
The wheels turned. The multiverses rolling ever upwards and
outwards in perpetual, blissful rhythm.
The weight of the universe cannot be held back.

We stepped outside of the stream of time and there she showed
me the past, present and the future of many things. We talked
deeply, profoundly, with a concinnity of her design.
She charged me to undertake a magickal operation that would
require unwavering attention and focus. There would be no
room for even the slightest mistake. 'It is for this that you have
been born,' she said. From the moment she left me I was falling,
plunging with terrifying momentum past the veil and out into
the abyss.
'Now descend,' she had said. 'Down into the bitter bowels of
hell.'
'But, how can I survive?' The open mouth of a dark stairwell
was before me. It dropped vertiginous into inky-blackness.
'You will learn to survive, or you will die. I will be with you. I
will keep you safe. Nothing can harm you if you keep close to
me.'
I looked into the darkness and a chill wind snatched away my
breath. I felt a dark utter power rising to pull me down into cold
embraces, and I was helpless to prevent them.
'I need more. I cannot otherwise.'
She cleansed me, and gave me new detailed instructions to
defend against and combat the hostile forces I was about to
encounter.

She knew everything that had ever happened to me, everything
that I had ever felt. She was intimately acquainted with days
that I had long ago forgot.

She revealed insights into my character. She resolved and elucidated certain events in my past, sharing her otherworldly insights. Patiently she demonstrated her knowledge and empathic understanding, so that I could not doubt.

We discussed every nuance and detail of that which was past and that which was to come. With infinite care she guided me through the vision of each day, missing no detail, however seemingly trivial.

Every act is a magickal act.

There were many choices that she asked me to make. I wondered aloud how she could be certain that all these things would happen? She explained that I would react in the physical reality of these events in the same way that I was now reacting in that place, outside of time. She assured me that I would make the identical choices, in accord with my nature and character.

'It is not just that we are revealing the future to you, it is also you are showing us what will happen, by making these choices. Even so, the future is not static, not set in stone. You still have a free will, just as you have always had. It could not work if things were otherwise. However, given each choice, we are able to follow the course of this loop of time. One ripple leads inexorably into the next. You will see that things play out exactly as we have seen here.

'As each moment passes and a new decision arises, you will know what it is that you must do. Still, you are not compelled to do so. In a sense you will be faced with three different ways which you can go. You can do what we would wish you to, and those are the choices that you are making now. Secondly, you can choose to take the path that the ego will encourage, which will be the easiest of all choices, for ego seeks repose and pleasure. Its motivations will be difficult to resist. You will become weakened from the prolonged stress, and fear will fill you with doubt. Thirdly, you could choose to submit to the enemy, and bring an end to your trials.'

She proved to me who I had been, who I was, and who I would become.

We paused before the gates of hell. 'Through or over these doors you must pass. Nietzsche said: 'What doesn't kill us, makes us stronger.' In your case, this will be true. You will become who you were born to be, so dance through the labyrinth. Be graceful and gorgeous. Hold my love close, cherish our union. It is enough.

'When the moment is ripe,' she said, 'you will recall all these words. It is not possible for your conscious mind to retain everything that you witness today, and much of that which we see and hear will be kept from you until your destiny has led you to certain places, and until you have made your choices. To allow you to remember everything, even if it were possible, would be to take away your free will. We must choose without foreknowledge. Trust, my dear, is vital. And faith; but never blind faith. The fates must be satisfied.'

'The fates? What are they?' I asked.

She considered her reply: 'Perhaps we can say they are gods. Imagine you were to build a system or a game, perhaps on an advanced computer. So as to make the system run smoothly and independently, you incorporate into its matrix a series of laws and rules by which it can be governed. Intractable, immutable laws. Although the fates are flexible within containing perimeters, they act as overseers, governing the multiverses, and they cannot veer far from the Rules.'

She was beginning to shape universes with me, guiding me moment by moment, step by step through the process, my own personal multiverse of the psyche, laying foundations that later I would build upon, revealing for me interlacing planes, realities that I could move through and interact in.

'Time,' she continued, 'is a lie designed to terrify you. There are changes and growth, the passage of events, but these are not proof of time. This moment is real. Momentum is real. Fear of time encourages fear of death. But death for us is beautiful. There are no punishments other than those found in life. At death Soul returns for nurture and rest; to absorb, grow, prepare.'

I had the sensation of rising, like coming through deep water, breaking to the surface. It was a sudden clearing, a self-possession, but disorientated and puzzled. My mind had shifted somehow, and once again I had entered into the mid flow of a conversation. I could recollect nothing of what had been said between us recently.

'What do you mean?' I asked.

'You don't remember?' She smiled warmly. 'That is good! You are not supposed to remember it. That means that it worked.' With barely a pause, not allowing me to adjust, to organise my thoughts and perhaps retrieve something of what had passed between us, she continued cheerfully, leading us into stranger quarters.

'It is not possible for us to travel through time with the physical body,' she explained, 'since neither the past nor the future exist in a material sense.

'For example, the world of the nineteen fifties was very different to the world we know today. The spatial identity is utterly transformed. If one were to go back, one might discover that nothing existed there at all. The bodies of those who were alive during that time have decomposed, turned to ash and dirt. How then could they suddenly exist again? That world has gone forever. It has no presence anywhere now, except in historical records, photos, books, films, memories and imagination. Even if we had a time travelling device or machine, it is not possible to reach a destination that does not exist in a tangible, physical sense. As of the past, so too for the future. This moment now is what occupies this physical space, and that cannot be altered.'

I wondered why she was explaining this to me, fascinating as it was. I hadn't asked about it.

'In fact, if time can be said to exist at all, then we should consider it to be like a circle or a loop, rather than linear. There is no fixed starting point and no place where it ends. But it is not real in the sense that we might usually consider it to be.

'What does exist is the movement of events. The worlds turn. Here, we see the sun rise and set each day. The seasons come and go. Our bodies grow, become old and frail, and all things die. This is real, but it has nothing to do with a system of records.

'Without the idea of time one sees only eternity. Reflected in the perpetual motion of the universes one senses the same rising and falling of one's own self. All things are cyclic.

'A flower grows, blooms brilliantly, then perishes. Yet its death is not a tragedy, for the plant continues to produce flowers. Even as one dies others bud and others are blooming. The seasons pass but always they return.

'Why should a man not look at these patterns and see his own destiny written in them? Isn't it natural that his own Soul be part of the perpetual growth and decay that he witnesses in all things?'

She then asked me a question: 'The pilgrim must discover the centre of the labyrinth. Do you know where that centre is?'

I had not articulated the thought before, but she had led me to it, and I was certain of my answer: 'This moment.'

'Yes. This everlasting moment. It exists outside of time, beyond the limitations of time. It stretches far into the past and the future, eclipsing them both, and comes back upon itself, like the serpent that bites its own tail. Get a sense of it. Exist there. Put aside what you have been taught about beginnings and endings, and simply connect with the now in which all things are existing. It is eternity, and that is where the Divine dwells.

'The centre. Everything turns about that pivot. All things change, rise and fall, ebb and flow, grow and diminish. That is the passage of events. The centre remains and the multiverses turn about it.'

'You will have to become proficient at walking between these worlds,' she said after a pause. 'Think of this as an introduction or an empowerment. The path that we have followed shall remain open to you. Here, in this realm, we are outside of time's loop. You need to absorb the feeling of being here; and that is how you will know when you have arrived. Are you able to see it?'

I was. I saw a cosmic landscape, through which a golden thread moved, forming an enormous egg-shaped loop about a cluster of galaxies.

Yet, she was still beside me, and we were still within my room at Southend-on-Sea. Nothing there had altered. I could see the cosmic landscape in which she and I stood, and through my ordinary eyes I saw the ordinary world. It sounds as though it must be a confusion of information, but everything was perfectly clear and apparent.

'Each choice leads to a consequence, or many consequences, cause and effect, and so we move on through the loop into the future.'

'That is a very complex sequence of calculations, with all the variables from other sources,' I remarked.

'Yes. It seems vast and incomprehensible at first. With practice one can become familiar with the application of the system. It is a knack that one learns, and is no more complicated than re-routing an electrical system or working a complex computer. You don't need to be aware of all the computations that are necessary in order for you to perform a particular task. You need only to understand the basic method of operating the equipment. Think of it like that, if you will.'

When we think about who and what we are, it is the physical life that we associate with. This is natural, seeing that life and consciousness are foremost in our experiences.

Perhaps we are multi-dimensional creatures, existing simultaneously, aspects of Soul woven through worlds?

Like a Russian Doll, we have hidden depths.

And if the Self extends into other realms, as though upward towards the Divine, those realms might be very different from the physical world.

'It is a magickal token, a key. If you had not completed the drawing then we would not be having this conversation. It was an evocation. Intuitively you knew this which is why you worked so hard upon it, why you could not pause.

'Death is stalking you. Soul biding time for this chance to rise from the dead. What did you think? Did you suppose that you had experienced all that life had for you? That nothing new and unexpected would ever happen again?' I admitted that was indeed what I had thought.

Together we reviewed every significant moment. We examined events in minutiae, even pondering thoughts that I had had and would have, inflections of meaning in words that I used. We looked at the patterns that existed, the cycles of which they were part, and we considered the intuitions I would feel. Everything had some meaning and some bearing upon the whole.

'You will be in that world. You will be open and vulnerable to them. They will recognise you as a target. At first you are going to be afraid, suddenly lost in a dark and dangerous place. 'Demons will walk the street. They will pursue you. They will attack you magickally, and you will be isolated and susceptible. You will feel them inside your mind parasitical, feeding upon your psychic energy. There will be no place where you are safe from them. Even your dreams will be invaded. The darkness will stalk you every moment. Your only escape from this will be to learn to defend yourself, to Become. You will have to destroy them.

'You will meet the Devil and his servants. It is like *Abra Melin's Sacred Magic* on a grand scale.

'He will see you as a particular prize and relish his control over you. You will know him, walking beside you on the street in the guise of a man. You will sense his loathsomeness, his hollowness, and the great evil that he represents.'

He sat on the wooden chair next to me, at the window of a cafe in Brighton. He never quite met my eye on that occasion, but turned his face toward me, almost smiling. I acknowledged him with the same gentle amusement.

An older gentleman, he was average height, slightly built, and wore a muted but stylish suit, a trilby hat on his head. He ordered a Full English breakfast, with tea. I ordered double eggs and beans on toast, with coffee.

'You are carrying one inside of you, aren't you?' she asked me. I
had no conscious awareness of doing so, but she was
addressing my Self now, beyond ordinary consciousness. 'I
would like to see it,' she said quietly.
I was incredulous. 'Why?' I knew that this creature I held within
my Soul was diabolical, and that even to look upon it was
dangerous. Not even she, this strangeling creature pure and
Divine, a Goddess, would be safe from its powerful malice. 'It is
not wise to provoke it. It is a Monstrous. It is a Devourer.'
'I know,' she replied. 'You have carried it a long time. But, I
would look upon it if you allow me. It has cost you much to
keep it.'
'Very well. Seeing as it is you that asks.'
We could see a sphere then, and contained within it was a vast
watery world, and the creature was hideous, terrifying, gigantic.
The Monstrous did not know that it was imprisoned, or that the
world through which it spent its endless days wading was
illusory. We glanced, and felt the depth of its power.
'I admit,' she confided afterwards, 'that I was afraid. Thank you
for allowing me to see it. Now, I shall take it from you, and
dispose of it.'
'You can do that?'
'Yes. A shell of it will remain, however, a less potent remnant.
Do not look at it and do not awaken it. When you are stronger
you will be able to destroy it. You will know when the moment
to do so has arrived. Be careful.'
I considered her advice thoughtfully.

I didn't have enough money for the fare. I could get from
London to Brighton, for that I had enough. I would have to
reach London *gratis*. I was carrying just a small shoulder bag.
A few clothes. A book and a pen for writing. Nothing else.
All my treasures tossed to the winds. A lifetime of cherished
possessions hard won, my paintings, my writings, my clothes,
my guitar, cherished trinkets, mirrors and memorabilia. Pieces
of me, manifestations of facets and aspects extending into

things about me, we are the space we occupy, these are our footprints, our explanations, our circumstantially modified artistic interpretations of who and what we are. It stung fiercely to leave them.

I slipped from carriage to carriage ahead of the inspectors. I doubled back behind them, used the toilets to hide in. I wasn't concerned about being caught for having no ticket, although that would not be pretty.

I had played fare-dodging as a teenager on the Shoeburyness line, so this was somehow nostalgic. It was not so easy on these trains.

The space was close, oppressive. I could not get off the train until we arrived. I had to get there, tonight. I was anxious and nervous, paranoid, tired.

Hunters mingled amongst passengers. They didn't see me. It was exhausting, keeping control, keeping a shield between us, staying hidden, not to give myself away to them.

Alighting at Fenchurch Street I see there is a guard at the gate. I cannot pass without him seeing me. There aren't many passengers getting off. She had told me to expect this, and had told me how to approach him. I stride confidently, masking my nervousness, look him in the eye, smiling warmly. I need to get to Brighton, I say, half question. He returns my smile, steers me through the gate, doesn't ask to see a ticket, directs me helpfully.

I wait for the Brighton train. This evening is cold and dark. I huddle into myself, shivering. I do not see people on the platforms making their way home from their day, I see demons prowling. I see their flint-hard eyes.

They are legion and they can migrate from host to host as easily as passing a flame from one candle's wick to another, she had said. They are following me, keeping close. I feel like a gazelle at a lions' dinner party. They catch my scent, but they cannot yet identify me.

How strange it was, when I arrived at Brighton, exhausted, almost weeping. I had nothing, no money, no possessions, no one knew me. I walked through the streets not knowing where to go, just following my feet.

They were seeing me now, recognising me, and they smiled secretly, licking their lips. My invisibility cloak which had preserved me during the journey here could no longer protect me. Useless now, I must discard it.

Being such an historically famous place I expected it to be a large and well kept town. Instead it seemed bleak, dirty, smelly, surprisingly small and dilapidated. There are occasional flower displays, a few beautiful buildings and streets, but mostly it was cold and mean. Why am I in this dreary place? I wondered. I found my way to the homeless shelter the next day. It was attached to a Catholic church, just off from the High Street. Unusually for Catholicism they revered both Mary and Jesus. Having little to do with my long days, during the weeks that I stayed there, I attended a few services.

The interior of the church was very ornate, luxurious sweeping curves into vaulted ceiling, stunning stained glass, a high altar with the crucified Christ, and it was calm transporting respite to sit there for an hour.

The hostel consisted of two dozen or so bedsitters. Most of the residents were smacheads and crack addicts, wasters and desperadoes. Those rooms were for long term stays and extremely difficult to procure.

The second class of accommodation was dormitories. Two large rooms that housed about fifteen beds each, and were attached to shower rooms. These were semi-permanent lets, and it was a couple of weeks before I managed to get a bed there.

There was also a night shelter, which was a single large room. The staff provided a dirty mattress to sleep on, and a single, dirty blanket. They served soup in the evening, and lights were out by eleven, and cereal and coffee in the mornings. It was into this shelter that I first gained access.

Ex-cons, drug-addicts, schizophrenics, desperadoes, alcoholics: these were my room mates. I had not lived a sheltered life, had never been pampered or spoilt, and drugs were always a part of the culture and climate that I had moved through, but even so, I instinctively avoided the type of mind that actively embraced and welcomed the life of slow motion suicide. That level of wilful self destructiveness made narcissists of them, and made their own immediate gratifications an overwhelming priority. It was not wise to associate with such volatile personalities.

Many of them had embraced the hollowness. They chose it, chose to remain there, surrendering some essential part of their humanity, wanting nothing more from existence than the daily drama of stealing and getting high.

They opened themselves to every darkness, and vile malevolent spirits dwelt inside of them.

Others were sick, mentally broken, trapped forever. Some were drifting through, like me.

I had a dirty mattress on the Bedlam ward and I was grateful, because that meant I did not to have to sleep on the cold January streets.

The night shelter opened at nine in the evening, and you had to be outside waiting for the space was limited and latecomers were turned away. In the morning we had to leave by eight o'clock.

The days dragged intolerably. Thirteen hours with nowhere to get to, and being under constant magickal assault from the dark spirits that pursued me, hunted me, with no haven, meant the stress built and built. I felt them tearing psychic chunks from me, shredding my Soul, and power drained out of me.

It was punishing on my feet. They became badly blistered and sore from the constant sweaty dampness of being in shoes or boots, and walking, walking, nowhere to rest, move on you can't stay here, the icy winds biting, the heavy rains drenching. I am already so very tired.

I am a ghost wandering in a twilit, dangerous world.

As I roam deeper I sense the older ghosts, bodiless and forlorn, sadness holding them in desolate realms. They huddle in doorways, sheltering between nefarious walls, and their sorrow blends with my own.

I have a mission for the first day. She instructs me to buy new clothes. I spend the twenty pounds I kept for this purpose on jeans, a t-shirt, a jumper, pumps. They are all poorly made cheap clothes but they will be clean.

She is leading my steps and I go into the lobby of a building, and up to the first floor. There is a small bathroom, single cubicle room and I lock the door behind me. I strip off everything I am wearing and wash quickly as best I can, for there is a small sink. The water is cold.

I put everything I had into the carrier bag and push it down into the waste bin. With this act I am further cutting the connections, disposing of every material part of the person I used to be. They tie me to Southend, to my life there, by the law of contagion. Now I am trying to make obscure the trail, evading the darknesses that have followed me. She allows me to retain nothing. I quickly exit. I hate these jeans.

It had been raw sleeping in the night shelter out there in the desert with the junkies and crazies.

The schizoids offered easy access for the darknesses. They were often aware of that darkness entering them, and welcomed it. They lived already between realities. Although the voices they hear often belong to cruel and sadistic masters, being in communication with something that is removed from themselves, and seems greater, more powerful than themselves, makes them feel special, or brings a comfort, raises them from tortured oblivion, so they embrace it, and allow the dark power to use them as a weapon.

With the junkies it is different. They aren't hearing voices in their heads, they aren't responding to instructions from invisible forces. They have embraced a different darkness, and they are conduits for chaos.

Microcosms of a more general malaise. The psychosis, addictions, and schizophrenia from which they suffered might have been defeated, at least in some cases, if they had chosen to fight rather than surrender, to resolve rather than abdicate.

The dorms were cleaner, much more comfortable, and they also gave access to the showers. They opened at seven in the evening, and we had the use of a spacious recreational area, two rooms, with lockers available, with sofas, seats and tables, television, books, and they served coffee and food, an evening meal, which was plentiful and decent. Immediate priorities shift very quickly.

In the dormitory I slept in seven or eight of my fellows were heroin addicts. They seemed to be fatally addicted. Perhaps what surprised me was how they were very much in love with their drug. It wasn't despair and gloom. They shot up in the showers before lights out, blood often splattering the tiled walls, needles discarded on the tiled floor, and prepared for bed seemingly content.

They were easily engaged in conversation on the subject. They smiled and glowed, discussing the nuances of junkie life. They displayed their virulent hard golf-ball abscesses with a perverse pride.

We had to be out of the building at nine in the morning, a hour longer to wake than the shelter had allowed.

The junkies headed for the train station to beg, or to the High Street, robbing groceries, selling frozen chickens at pubs to pay for their daily fixes. They needed about fifty pounds a day each to get through. Mostly they maintained a comfortable level of wellness, rather than reaching high plateaus of intoxication.

A few of them I liked, and enjoyed talking with. It was kind of painful to see them so trapped, or so intent on destroying themselves.

3

Brian was a short stocky Scot in his fifties. He was gregarious and magnetic, despite his chronic alcoholism, like a roaring hearth that we all wanted to gather around. He melted the ice around our cold hearts, drew us all close to him, strong warm paternal charming, very intelligent and insightful, weaving wonderful tales to enthral and delight us.

He was being eaten by stomach cancer, and lived on nothing but treacle thick cider.

Softly flowers rain upon him, as he sleeps.

'I am a Strangeling,' he tells me.

He becomes my friend, when I have begun to find purchase in this realm, begun to steady myself, to deflect the demons' barbs back on them, so I can breathe a little easier, and it doesn't hurt quite so much, and I am not as terrified as I was, and I can be open to some connection. He is patient with my reluctance and when I am ready he brings me into his shelter.

I am astounded when he asks me one morning as we are standing at the junction and the sun is quite warm: 'You see them, don't you?'

'Yes, I do see them. Do you?'

'Probably not in the same way that you do. What do you see?'

'Demons,' I reply candidly. 'I can see peoples' Soul, and a lot of them aren't very nice.'

Brian digests this information. 'What about my Soul? Can you see me? Am I a demon?'

'Yes, I can see it. You are a good person. That's why I like talking with you.'

'They see you as energy,' he tells me. 'You are like a food for them. You should protect yourself, hide yourself, you are too open. They see your brightness. They don't realise that you can see them. That's why it's tiring for you.'

'It is stressful,' I agree. 'I have to defend myself constantly, without respite. It's exhausting. I'm learning though, learning how to kill them. Some of them know that I see them. There are different types,' I say thoughtfully. 'I can't hide though, that wouldn't be possible now. I have to confront them, destroy them.'

'Will you be able to?' he asks.

'Yes,' I smile sardonically.

Another day we are sitting together at a bus stop, not waiting for a bus. He tells me about a guy he once knew who could see demons, and would kill them by gripping them tightly in his clenched fist: 'If you want to apply some extra pain press your fingernails into your palm. I don't know if it works, but that's what he said.'

His hair, which had previously appeared almost entirely gray, was now thick and dark. 'I just had it cut, that's all,' he replies to my inquiry.

'What's happening to your face?'

His skin was peeling in long ribbons, exposing strips of baby fresh skin beneath, as though he had a severe case of sunburn. 'What does a snake do?' he responds enigmatically. I shake my head, curious. 'It sheds its skin.'

I waxed in fortitude and adroitness.

I employed an intuitive sciamachy magick, meeting them on their own fields, and she was whispering into my ear, very close and protective, holding me tightly, guiding me.

'They move easily from host to host, like the flame of a candle passed wick to wick,' she had said. And here amongst these vagabonds, thieves, junkies and pissheads, schizos and paranoiacs, the flames burnt lustily, finding easy purchase.

Yet, there were still people that seemed unaffected, as though integrity were an impenetrable shield; I searched deeply within them for the black flame, but never found it. Somehow they were resistant, and most were oblivious to the horrors that slept beside them, ate beside them.

These people were usually completely outside of the magickal realms, solidly centred in the earthly, all doors tightly closed. Several of the staff I looked to as allies or buffers, and their presence in some way countered the demons' work. Perhaps they were not invulnerable nor their defences impenetrable. It may be that the darknesses required a greater effort as though they must work past walls of obstruction.

An aethereal projectionist's film layered upon reality which one needed an attuned eye to see, sweven flickering images of lurking creeping monsters, of malevolents and dark intents, ghouls and spites. Nosferatu rises, eyes Kohl and wide, from his tomb. Ah, what sweet musics they make.

Tall noble angels, broad-winged and lithe and strong, stood near and moved with me. They were warriors fighting battles on planes that were mirroring into eternities that I could not see. Implacably, a drilled army, they slaughter. Hear them marching, marching.
Eldritch dragons curl about me. I am learning my power.
Layers within layers these movies are still in sync. Portentous, doom-laden gestures.
The Devil turns his head.
'Let me at least kiss your hand,' he says, and the skin of his fingers is cold when he touches me.
There is no evading them. As I follow my feet, bending to cartoon winds, they are always dogging me.
The remote Self pulls the manikin strings.
I find a Buddhist garden that I can rest in. The paths are raked gravel. I sit on the short bench. A shelter and sacred place, and the darknesses remain without. Flowers live turning with the day and the moonlight. They dance in slow motion across the surface of the worlds. I draw peace from this well.
At lunchtime, a little back downhill, there is a day centre type arrangement open for two hours. An annex of the Church, they provide lunch, some recreation, temporary shelter from the weathers. On Tuesdays it is closed, but a different charitable organization provide a slow comfortable morning of being indoors, not walking, and give hot tea, toast.

Hyper-reality and hyper-awareness, the blent realms cascade.
I cannot close my eyes to the screen. I will have to live this movie till its fin.
I am inside the matrix and this programme is wonderful, elysian and gorgeous, and so sweet, written by the hand of some weeping angel. The orgasmic beauty. Chills my Soul

with thrilling pleasures.

Yet, darker visions are played over by the projectionist, the Remote Self. This programme is writ by a depraved and bitter mind. All horror is unleashed. Slithering parasitical viruses. Terror that I had never before approached in any imagination; it is so vastly hideous and awful, so deeply grotesque. The hollow end of the multiverses, where lack and weakness breed, and their begat bastards fester like insidious clinging odours.

I remember this. We spoke about this place, and I know ahead of time what is about to happen.

The first morning that I came to this day shelter I had remembered. When the altercation didn't that day materialize as anticipated, I was shaken. It tested me, and doubts were already overwhelming from the start, challenging sanity, and provoking such dreadful fear that perhaps my Soul might be lost here. *There are always three,* she said.

But now, it is happening, and it is a violent proof for me. Some random guy starts bullying me over seating, when there are dozens of empty seats to choose from. This is my seat, he insists, although I have been there already ten minutes. He usually sits here, maybe he means. He must see me as some fluffy rich dude, which is funny because I probably come from a worse slum than he does. I'm an outsider even here.

I should have worn the hobo uniform, I guess.

Peter, a young friend from the shelter, nineteen, from Manchester, flame haired and fair-skinned, is with me. His father has recently died, and Peter has come alone to Brighton to sleep on the streets. When I am due to leave he tells me that he felt as though his father was returned in me, to reassure him, guide him into some harbor. I am walking between worlds gerful, and catch the whispered songs of the lost.

The thug insists that we move. I refuse.

We are standing now by the table where they give out the jammed or marmaladed toast. The older lady serving is avoiding my order. You don't belong here. These people are ahead of you. Bullshit, they are mostly scroungers and loafers. Half of them aren't homeless at all. How strange; I am wearing a clean shirt, a smart jacket, jeans. My face is clean and shaven, my hair is short. Only bums deserve a slice of toast.

My antagonist is muttering against me. I tell him fuck off you twat. And then, when he asks, that you heard me. He swings a slow punch.

I watch it arc through the air, swinging to my face. It's outside of time, and I can move or not move. I can let the punch land or block it, turn it aside. If he hits me it is permissible for me to hit him back, so I allow his punch, and he strikes me on the bone of my cheek. It is dull thumping pain.

My left hand grasps swiftly, chokes his neck, and I swing him around to my right side, about ninety degrees from where we started. I bend my knees and twist my waist and body behind the straight punch, and I strike him cleanly on the nose, where it will hurt, and strange disorientations will smash through his head.

He falls heavily backward, down into stacked cleaning gear, mops and buckets, and he is sprawling.

I am ready to hit him again if he wants to stand up.

A member of the staff, an older, large guy, says that he will throw us both out, any more of that. He started it, I respond. Nothing more is said.

The older lady gives me my toast promptly after. I sit with Peter and drink tea.

4

It is late February. I have a room, a bedsit overlooking the small park. It's a nice view from the Bay windows. I put fresh tulips in a vase at the empty fireplace.

Death grins his lipless grin.

'I am here,' he whispers. 'I am your friend.'

'Yes. I know. Thanks, Grim.'

My head aches with a heavy throb, and I feel entirely tender, bruised. The well of sadness still swells in me, rises.

I slide into its depths and it falls out into the gaping voids, and into the oceans of unnumbered tears.

My wrists and my feet hurt with ethereal pains.

I am too tired to sleep and fearful of the nightmares that will take me. I lay upon my back and fold my hands upon my chest. I close my eyes, and they come galloping. I am flooded by their light. The wall cracks and crumbles.

My body bursts like an accelerated bud, and we spin out into a dark sky. I pass through the door into the Pearl Palace where she awaits me.

I close the front door behind me, step down the steps onto the street. The day is warm. The park is empty except for the young guy who practices his juggling there most days. He is dexterous, handling six or seven sticks or balls, entertaining when I am in languid mood, and sometimes I watch him awhile from my window. He is aware of me, and makes extra efforts, I think, to dazzle me. Sometimes other jugglers join him and he eclipses them all. We exchange a greeting as I pass by.

The park is small, just a green rectangle with a few trees about its edges, a short metal railing. My view is almost at its centre, and I sit and breathe this patch of earth into me.

On other days I see lovers and friends, dog owners with their pets, people practising Tai Chi, flame eaters, languishing youths.

One morning a roving caravan rolled in and parked on the grass. Brian was visiting me on that day. We watched the travellers' day unfold with ours. They made a mess very quickly, and were loud, boisterous, drunk. By the evening the police had moved them on.

I reach the end of the street and turn right towards the shopping centre. It is busy, and as I thread my way through the crowds I am pushed and my feet are trod on. People walk through you and over you in this town.

I pass Waitrose the supermarket crossing the road, past the fountain, and pause at the lights with the crowd. Then into King Street.

Between the horrors there comes a sweet commuovere new bliss. A smouldering fire pulses deep inside of me, breathes through me, glorious tremors making me shiver and smile as I walk.

I turn my eyes to the window displays to stop myself from flying away. Colors, fabrics, shapes, materials, light flashing like diamonds, it is all overwhelming gorgeousness. It pulls deep into me. I am trembling now on the verge of ecstatic tears. A painting of red roses makes me gasp for air. Its clarity is so astounding, so intense, that I am dizzied by it and waves crash through me, sweep me, swoon me. Orgasmic energies drench me.

I reach the gardens, where there is another large black dry fountain. How pretty it would be if they were all alive and flowing across the town!

There are cute fuchsias in the flowerbeds, tiny creamy roses, and blue hydrangea. Their perfumes are powerful and intoxicating, filling each breath with swirling stars.

A large seagull perches on the fountain's apex, drinks the wide lofty view.

I sit on a bench and feel pleasant and warm. There is an elderly Chinese man sat on a bench adjacent. Our eyes meet. He is rather elegant and he sits comfortably, pride and strength in his bearing. I smile slightly, and he acknowledges me.

I have been wilfully following my feet since I embarked for Brighton, giving myself over to impulse and instinct. It shreds my self-conscious ego, responding in an almost primal way to those prompts, without analytical thought, regardless of any audience. I follow them now, and we walk in slow circles about the fountain's circumference.

It is an axle, reaching far up into the skies, and I lean across its beam and turn it, the fountain groaning as it begins to move, a large wheel.

I jog, lending speed and weight to the motion. I run. It is heavy and turns sluggishly. I must open up the sky. The Chinese man smiles as I run past him again.

There are other people in the park too, sat on the wider circle of benches, demons amongst them, and I am drawing quizzical looks, but there is no space in this for me to regard them.

My eyes fix upon the sky, a door of blue beneath the billowing white, where it will break. I am tiring but there is not yet enough momentum. I let go.

Fire leaps out from the apex burning a fissure through the sky. The angels burst through the door into this world, come thundering. They are beautiful, their flesh as black as obsidian. Astride mighty black horses, hair streaming, swords shining aloft. A horn blows, a bell tolls, ravens reel into the sky screaming, the clouds scatter and the sun blazes across the park, across the town. The angels gallop through, into the streets slaughtering, and blood gouts.

One rears its horse to a standstill beside me. His hair is full and tightly curled. The aspect of the angel is strong, masculine but deferential, and its beauty is astonishing. The angel clenches its fist over its heart, in a salute to me.

There is a ladder of creatures which climbs out into the starry sky, and twists and spirals all the way to the moon.

I am so deep now, so removed in these realities. The world and its life are just thin echoes on brittle winds.

I slumber, richly languid and sensuous swoons, fragments of ethereal dreams. The voices of a distant choir reach me: a faint, achingly gorgeous lament. I stir, fixing the song in my mind, and listen.

I cannot make out the words but the melody wrenches my heart, touches me with a poignancy I cannot decipher. The voices are masculine, sometimes sonorous and warm then light, tender, sweetly supplicating. I flow into its tide, lift and fall on its undulations. I sink into its beauty.

I see a boat on churning waters, moonlight glistening on oars. There are men stood upright on the deck, tall shadowy figures, their faces uplifted. A new note of joy enters their song. It swells stronger, more insistent as I draw closer, enrapt and basking.

Within the cadence I feel words begin to shape. At last they are clear, and my heart is chilled.

'Help us!' they are singing. 'Help us! We are lost!'

I climbed a stair that rose into an infinity turning in long slow arcs. Emotion overwhelmed me. Each step upward deepened the grief which weighed upon me. Tears toppled from my cheeks, and were cast out across the vault of space and burst like evanescent stars.

I drew the sorrow of the worlds deep into me. Fathomless, oceans deep to drown me, from the edge of existence.

There rose a storm of tears and it mustered all loss into itself, like tumultuous tides, and fell crashing like a deluge to sweep me away into its universe of sobs and laments. I was bowed against the force of its grieving so that I swooned and stumbled. Angelic creatures, pale and wispy here, blew upon my flesh with sweet soft breaths and told me: 'Climb on!'

The retreat was as endless as the ascent. Far below the abyss gathered in rolling clouds to receive my fall.

The endless enduring sadnesses sped to me.

I opened; soothing, comforting, tenderly embracing.

Great storming winds surged. Forking lightnings flashed. I am cast down from the stair into consciousness.

My room is filled with shining butterflies. They gather near to the top of the walls, moving in slow gentle procession.

They shine reflectively, their colors merged sunlight golds, yellows, and orange. I can hear a tinkling music, like a fairy song perhaps might sound.

When they each complete their gentle circuit they descend, hovering above my belly. One by one I breathe them deeply into me, through my belly button. I feel the fluttering of their wings inside of me.

These spontaneous visions or transferences were dream-like in
the sense that I was completely transported into the reality of
the experience, just as we are whilst asleep and dreaming.
They were immersive, vivid, tangible.
The emotions that I felt throughout were very intense and real,
yet also belonging to a different order of emotion, one that did
not align exactly with the physical life, as it is also with dreams.
I was perpetually drained and exhausted from such investment.
But, I was not asleep. I was awake and fully aware of what was
happening.
They were imaginative so far as I must consent and engage with
them, being open to and invested in their validity, and by
allowing a certain creative intuition to sharpen and fuel them.
Yet they were also spontaneous, completely outside of my
control.
How fully I dwelt there was my own choice, and I chose to
unhook all anchors, holding nothing of myself back.
I was walking wilfully in those astral realms.
I found that all of reality had altered, and there was no possible
retreat. The doors slammed locked behind me.
Having made that descent, having blent my conscious will with
the will of Self, or seeming, there had been an overriding of
usual reality. Perhaps an externalization of inner psychic
turbulence seeking an uncommon resolution. I could do nothing
to prevent these shifts and fluxes.
The darknesses rose up in vast hordes to assail me, and their
horror reached into all my realities. That was balanced with
experiences of pure and transcendent beauty. Those moments
empowered and supported me, and utterly transformed me.

I was lost in peculiar planes, rarely surfacing. The visions
rolled into one another pulling me further and deeper, so that I
crossed universes and flew across glorious firmaments, and
disconnected entirely from whom I had been.
The six months that I remained at Brighton were filled with
these perpetual shamanic wanderings.

Many of them were war-like, combative, bloody and violent. Strangely, the blood and goriness was not in itself disturbing. I found it amusing in a way. There was real horror often, yes, but that was of a different kind.

I was a magickal warrior, and my quest was to destroy evil wherever I found it in those realms, and I found the task to be invigorating and enjoyable. Often I laughed joyfully as I slew the demonic hordes, decapitating and dismembering them, wielding a great broadsword.

5

My sword rose and fell like a scythe of flashing silver, spraying dark blood from its blade.

It is finely weighted, so that I can wield it either with one hand or both. Its pommel is long, tipped with ruby, and the handle wound with white leather. The hilt of the sword curves like an up-turned crescent, and the blade is long, broad and sharp.

They had pressed upon me but I was light and nimble, preternaturally fast in comparison to them, turning easily from their clumsy thrusts and strokes.

I sang a low sweet song, and moved smiling in an ancient and magickal dance, parrying their attacks, felling them with just a touch of my blessed sword.

I skipped and bowed between and beneath their weapons. The demons fell like paper-things, like playing cards.

So many were they that they could not find me. They stumbled against each other, and frustration boiled in them, and fear murmured in their breasts. I pirouetted though their ranks as they bent and bowed in deathly obeisance.

As far as I could see in the cold brightness their number was limitless.

He was tall, towering above his minions. He wore a hideous mask, and from its temples two black horns jutted. He strode swiftly and purposefully, a black cloak flying in his wake. He carried an enormous ax in his hands. His abyssal eyes met mine and he did not pause his stride.

I have made some distance, and I somehow know that a small sheltered pool is not far off. My body burns with a crucial thirst. I am dizzy and untethered.

I am astounded to see a solitary flower in the ground before me, in this realm where nothing grows. A daisy, white leafed and yellow at its heart, basking defiantly in the sickly light. I pluck it from the soil. It seems so fragile and beautiful. My pink tears splash upon the flower, gently cradled in my palm, as I breathe its translucent perfume.

I reach to the small pool and barren trees shelter it, like twisted, broken hands. I stretch gently beside the water and gaze at its cool surface. But I cannot drink. I am so weakened that to do so probably will choke me. I float between consciousnesses, removed now from pains.

I hear the approach of Death. His footfall is cold and steady. He stands silently beside me, tall and motionless. He wears a tattered cloak and a grim mask wrought from silver. Impassive, his eyes dark and fathomless behind his mask.

'Am I dead?' I ask.

I keep to the shadows, unseen in this city of ghosts. The rains are heavy and bleak. I work my wyrdling magicks and transform my worlds.

I climb down into the earth, between heavy stones. Finding a tiny crevice into which I can squeeze and fit, I am still. The cold draws very deeply into me. My flesh becomes ice. I am absorbed into the belly. Ancient enduring carved out of the world. My body cold as death, and even the hunters can not see my heat.

I busk with Nirvana screams and melodies. I am releasing everything through this song. It is a movie within a movie.

Thank you, he tells me, after I sing Dumb and Drain You at the open mic. *Into the bathroom to shoot up.*

Today, in the sunshine, I am sat on the kerb near the Old Tree, and the gates are way over to my right. On the benches before them the dark host begins to gather.

The air is black with their clouds of barbs. I am pierced by a myriad arrows. My blood runs a red river on the dirt, and I sing.

The dark host snarls and paws, low intelligence, past being serious threat to me, they irritate and push, relentlessly enhungered.

It's not so complicated, darling, as you're making it out to be.

The princes arrive, preening cuckolds.

Dire weapons they marshal and send against me. My repertoire is broad and strong, and every song is an universe.

The results are always perfect; but that's old news.
One by one, as the afternoon turns, they saunter across my
path. They eye me slyly smiling noxiously. Each of them
contests. My blood wells from uncounted wounds. All the
world awash in blood and fire.
It is like Abra Melin. On a grand scale.
He comes last and is laughing loudly. He takes the prime seat
among them, and they his thralls and subordinates fawn and
stroke and flatter. He casts me a glance. His laughter rings
hollow.
The afternoon dies and its ghost drifts into evening. The cloud
of barbs perpetually raining. Grotesque creatures biting.
I weep into my songs. Sorrow and love to swell the black
waters. Blood and tears to quench the fires.

How goes the war, Twayn? It goes well.
They sound their horns.
Dragons flock, and creatures muster.
He sits astride a black horse which is spotted with white on its
nose. The nostrils flaring, eyes rolling, steam rising in clouds
from its flanks. He wears his silver horned mask and his
crimson eyes are aglow. His posture proud and stern and he is
clad in gloaming armor, and a black robe billows about him.
He holds a fluttering grim banner.

I am weeping moths and butterflies and they are strange tears.
I run like a light trail through the streets, for an hour I am
Super. Past the park through into the hotel, up the flights of
tight twisting stairs, faster, faster, and reach the top landing.
Casting ashes to the winds. Kisses and smiles.
I will return to my room overlooking the park for one reason:
to fulfil this destiny. I tear down the wall with my hands,
leaving only the thin wood behind the plaster. I find a pencil
there, on the slatted shelves, an HB, with the date or number
1947 scratched into its end. Covered in white and gray dust I
follow my feet, looking for a house. I ring the intercom bell.
But not yet.
This is paradise, she tells me. Embrace it.

I spin in fast turns, and flop happily onto the soft bed. My room is comfortable, luxury now, compared to streets, doorways, and bedsits. I eat fat red cherries with clotted cream.

On the bedside table there is over four hundred pounds in notes. I am starting to rise to the surface.

I take up the black key. It is three inches long, with another near inch of steel at a right angle on one end. I need to swallow it, she tells me, to unlock and lock strange locks.

I have purchased a two-pint of milk, according with her instructions. If I don't wash it down hard the hook could snag somewhere in my throat or stomach. I concentrate on being calm. I might be choking to death in a few moments time.

I swallow, and immediately open my throat to the milk. Letting go is the only way, pouring the entire two pints into me, sweeping the key deep inside with the thick white tide.

Strip the power out of them, draining into the dirt. Bound in rounds and cast into the sea.

The tides pull my sorrow, tristful tears swell, as they gallop into the dark sky.

I close my eyes and sink down, down. Tumbling in gentle swoons deep deep inside.

Fairy tintinnabulations, far away melodies.

We slide into colors unearthly rich. Orgasmic blues and gasping reds. Tunnels and doors, all the way down, and she closes above us with warm wet flesh.

Flashing gold. White rivers and silver stars.

Their tinkling warmth, joyous kisses. They gather, excited and frolicy. They work adroitly, their magick arts nimble finesse and power. They weave and sew, they wish on breaths of kisses. I am slain by pleasures. In pitch selcouth tunnels we ride mercury rivers bursting with ecstatic stars.

An falling out into the universe.

One must hold to the path when one is tumbling between worlds. I place fresh tulips in the vase.

*

PRELUDE

*

*

The impulse moved through the mind of God.
It was a motivation.
He considered. He found that it was good.

Alone, God was All, and existing was perfect bliss.
God distinguished within All the virtues and powers; from the
essence were manifested active and yielding force.
These were the foundations of the Divine craft. Through their
interplay all things would arise and be established.
The Creation was yielding, and the energy of the essence was
active.
From the single Point all things were drawn and distinguished,
and it was the Great Source.
*

The Goddess slept, and dreamed. She dreamt of movement, color, and form. She was alone and she was content. She was the pulse at the centre that rose and fell. She was the endless essence, and within her boundless awareness there were depths and layers; these were the partitions that became the first Multraverses.

The expanse was the solitude in which she dwelt, and it was white, without discernible quality. Her thoughts drifted across the vastness of the expanse, stirring winds to rise. The winds were rare and great. Some were gentle like soft breaths, and they fluttered after her thoughts. And came the winds to the farthest reaches of the expanse.

The pulse of the Goddess was rhythmic. It expanded and contracted, and drew the winds back to itself. A circumference was established in the whiteness of her solitude.

She dreamt.
*

When she awoke from her dreaming, the idea of form rose within her mind. She saw that form was potential, and would abear possibility. Long she meditated upon the futures.

The nature of form was beautiful and true. Whilst she

considered its course in her meditations, she discerned the patterns of the Way. She was delighted in the Way.

She recked the effect of form upon the expanse of her essence, and she saw that beauty was become manifest, and expressed in myriad ways and functions. The Goddess valued beauty. Its essence was close to her perfection. She desired form.

'We will Manifest,' she thought.

*

She drew the white expanse centreward, into herself, and held it. She then breathed it out into her dreams.

Beyond the circumference which had been established by the great winds the white expanse remained, but within that boundary, encompassing every partition, the whiteness was drawn into her.

The white expanse was not light but no-thing; the pure essence of her Divinity. When it was drawn inward to the Goddess emptiness remained, and was filled by darkness. Thus the void came to be. It was emptiness, the absence of essence, and darkness was the absence of light. She did this so that form could fill the void with light, momentum, and potential.

*

She saw all conclusions perfectly. The rhythmic pulse moved through the void. Her dreams drifted through the shapeless void, and were imbued with the Divine essence. As yet the dreams had neither voice nor color, and were only vaguely connected, being generally without coherence. In them she saw the destinies, and knew the patterns. She allowed them, and she was pleased.

Her dreams were numerous and the darkness of the void began to be filled with them; they collided, merged, creating new and unexpected possibilities. She was entranced, captivated. It was beautiful. She wept. Her tears fell across the void, and ecstasy trembled the expanse.

'This will be our body,' the Goddess thought.

She opened her eyes. One was colored silver and its light rent the belly of the void. Sundry multiverses began to take shape within the partitions, and like shadows, darkness congregated in deep abysses.

The other eye was golden, and by its luminance the darkness was pierced and divided.

'Now we do see,' said the Goddess.

Exhausted, she slept then without dreaming.

*

Her tears fell slowly, gathering the fiery light of her eyes into them. They embraced and retained the fires and were formed into stars by them. Whilst she slept these stars began to drift deep and wide within the expanse, pushing back the void. They reached to places where as yet her eyes had not looked.

The dreams of the Goddess were envigorated by the stars, and like flowers they gave bud and blossomed. Their perfumes scented the Multraverses.

The first song was sang. Its voice and melody were the flowering visions of the Goddess, the movements of light, and her falling tears.

And her words resounded in the expanse, carving a deeper circumference about the space with a wall of sounds.

Her eyelids fluttered. Her breath took wing and turned the circle of the Multraverses. Gravity and friction drew sparks of flame from the turning, and momentum was established, even as the flames of fire span into a vast spiral about her.

The Goddess did not awaken, but she began to dream once more. She slept, and her works were established.

*

The multiverses folded in upon themselves, then rippled outwards, expanding, seeking the ends of space, held within the partitions of the Multraverses. The Goddess slept, and stars and planets formed all about her, and she was the centre of all.

In the rhythm of her breathing was momentum.

The long, cold darkness was past, and the fates, which were celestial beings crafted of her pure essence, turned the flaming golden wheels of destiny, and the flames thereof fell outward into space.

Her wyrd to dream. Slowly her dreams changed. Now she was aware of shapes moving and writhing in the tones and shades of her dreams.

She saw all of the unborn multiverses, and the bearing of the universes, as the cosmos moved within space. She saw the stars and planets swirling amongst clustered galaxies. The light of the moon and the sun nourished all things.

She desired form an its promise.

*

She dreamt of me; spun across the darkness of the void. In her dream I, Form, was a black winged dragon. I am her creation, arising from her desires. I was born from her yearning and her solitude melded me.

My being were drawn from the tumult an the ambivalence of her dreaming; am I then deep wide as the expanse, holy an beautiful, terrible and heavy as her Word. The swirling mists and the crashing storms, an the fiery heats, the colliding colors, the cascading bliss.

I am power, magicks, brilliance and force, and creativity, ingenuity and originality.

That I, the ancient who struggled into being.

She is all love. I am the echo of her thoughts.

I was seized with fervour to be with her.

She was the great light, yet she was muted and bound by the darkness which she used to construct all things with and upon. Her Creation began with void, and she worked to make it full.

I must awaken her and bring an end to her perpetual dreaming. 'If there is form,' I said, 'I could be with her. I can be reflection, and she may love me.'

*

I began as a sparking scintilla; a momentary idea, swiftly engulfed in the myriad things. I sank to the utter depths of her dreaming.

Yet, I was not extinguished.

I was from her, and of her, thus the truth of her pulsed in my fiery core. Although I had no being other than the heat of my turning flames, and the pure centre, I was immediately aware. There was not yet time but I was a beginning. I perceived; and all around me the dreams of her rose and fell. Overwhelmed, I swooned and faded, my flames fluttered and died in the colorful mists that drifted there in the depths.

I watched her dreams cascade, they flowed out from the core

like a great river. Some I did not comprehend, because they were formless and dark. Some were brief and strange, others were fierce and epic, full with her emotion. They were like a storm in a strange sky.

There were deep symbols and intricate patterns lacing, unfurling, fading, brightening, and I read them without knowing their language; because my pure centre knew them. It was ecstasy to share in her, and I was entranced.

*

To know the Goddess through her thoughts and these strange dreams of hers. Eventually I grasped the significance of colors, recognised partial patterns, and comprehended fragments and symbols. It was a vast language, deeply complex and abstruse. I looked for its core, that I might lay a foundation for lucidity. I began to grow, and within the depths of her dreaming, to take shape.

I was a seed fallen from her bloom. I was her first wish.

*

She dreamt of the Way. She dreamed of potential and possibility, of futures. She dreamt of the universes, and longed for them. In subtlety and in boldness, in sweetnesses or in vibrancy, her dreams enrapt me.

And oft they twisted and ebbed, or were fleeting and brilliant or unfathomable. They were enchanted and endless.

Some of her dreams I could not apprehend. There were so many, and there was so much intricacy and delicacy, and yet others were the grandest themes, that it was long before I could begin to recognise their symbols. There was a great deal that I forgot. Whilst I pondered obscurities her present dreams swept over me without my observing them.

I began with a corner stone, to construct a temple of cognition; Goddess was the Source of All, and her nature was Good. She was purity, love, and truth. Her dream was to make all things well.

From there I recognised other stones that I could lay. These foundation stones were the most difficult to find and grasp, hidden as they were amid the tumult of everything she explored in her thoughts and her dreams. When I recognised each of the foundation stones as being very broad and defined, an axiom or a premise of her and her nature and her intent, then I was able to proceed more easily.

After this initial difficult and laborious phase, during which I veered betwixt confusions, and joys at solving small parts of the collective puzzle, and fatigue, I was finally able to make swift progress.

What a delight it was for me to learn and grow by solving the puzzles she was presenting me with, and in doing so to build an image of her.

With every completed step I was emboldened and empowered.
*

I had a voice, and sang as I worked. My songs were building songs, and they were simple and sweet. They were natural and amusing.

Through them I began to realise the potential of my magicks. My lyrics and melodies rose up into the storm of her turbulent dreams. And there was impact.

I rejoiced; the samadhi for this I was born. And then I trembled; for how great the risk she had invested in me! How foolish I had been, drifting in raptures of bliss! Now the purport of my being, and a rapture of love seized me, so that I wept with joy.

I knew my mission.
*

I set to my labors with diligence and energy, and I strove for the truth of everything. I could not be satisfied with less than certainty, if I shall erect a Temple of Absolute Reality.

Each stone I lay increased my cognition, settled an revealed the sundry mysteries. Those parts which I did not resolve I laid aside, an later their place be apparent.

Her Temple rose up into the storm.
*

The multiverses were young which her dreams drifted through. There were darknesses in her dreams, for the expanse was dark. There were deep cold abysses. The darknesses tended to be heavy and oppressive, and they impeded me. I had to drive them from me, so that they could not corrupt my work.

I drew her essence into my core, through an from the dreams, so my brightness threw them back.

I sang loudly now, and threw my voice up into the storm of dreams.

I hewed and shaped the stones of truth, and placed them easily, for I had grown mighty through my labors. And the walls climbed around me; and lo! we came at last to the utmost pinnacle.

It was established, and I wept and laughed.

Her dreams shivered and trembled, and flooded the Temple.
*

Now I took shape. My wings were wide and broad; they spanned such a distance that I could gather a vast number of her dreams into them; and I created my own great winds with the beating of my wings, and they roared like thunders as they sped across the dark expanse. My wings were black and oh, so beautiful; yet my body, which snaked long and muscular, was pale, gleaming and iridescent. And my maw was deep and wide and crimson red, my jaws were powerful. Immense I became, so that I might swallow every universe; for that too was a destiny.

Rapturous was my nature now. Every thought was blissful, and the Word was ecstasy on my tongue. My song was glorious and holy, and by it I constructed heavens, and wrapped them about all of her dreams. I contained her visions within the heavens, and it was like a sphere burning in the void.
*

I was a part of her dreams; I must separate from them, from her. Outside of the dreams I could become, and awaken her. My imaginings had wrought change. Her dreams calmed. The darkness was drawn out, like chaff from the golden wheat. Coherence entered her subjects. Her dreams grew to be concentrated and lucid, no longer hap-hazard like a churning storm of lightnings, thunder, and wild rains.
*

I was spun across the darkness, my wings spread, my fires blazed in trails of light. I danced the patterns and traced the symbols, weaving my magicks into her sleep. I influenced her. My will was of love.

The Goddess was pleased to see form in her dreamings, and she accepted the influence that it brought to the shape and texture of those dreams. She allowed some dreams to be shaped by me.

I was patient. I submitted to the will of the Goddess and worked to fill her dreams with all that she desired.
*

I delighted in her dreaming and grew to love her ever deeply. It was fated for me to break out of her dreams, into the unlimited expanse.

Only from that place could I stir the Goddess into waking, and be united with her.

I urged her through symbol and suggestion to shew a route. She dreamt of future and past. She saw cycles, and the destinies of Humanity. She dreamt of changes. Her dreams evolved swiftly, and worlds were born.
*

Risen to the apex, I trembled on the brink of separation from her and her dream.

'Allow me,' I asked her. 'did fates contend or assent, my love and submission; thou art good and worthy, with reverence, my Goddess.

Have I shaped the dreams brought them form and depth, shade and light, with truth established flawless purity. My will now whence thee no longer dream.'
*

Within the realm of her dreaming the Goddess accepted form: she took on a dream-flesh. She was naked but for her hair, which fell to her waist in spiralling cascades of curls. The bliss of dream-flesh overwhelmed her. She sank, adrift through sensual climes, and she was rapt. Existence was ecstasy.

She wept and her body trembled. Joyfully she laughed.
*

The darkness was driven from her dreams. I yelled, an it were bliss, as I fell out of the dreams of the Goddess and tumbled through the void.

Being neither darkness nor light, but crafted of both, I was driven out when she purged her dreams with ecstasy. The darkness of her dreams fell, and it engulfed all the multiverses. I was wrapped in that darkness and perceived for the first time that I had a reflection; we were twins.

As I was in the greater part darkness and femininity, so my twin, Morf, was in the greater part light and masculinity. He clove to me.

We fell like burning stars, rending the universes and engulfing worlds. I tried to free myself, knowing him only as a darkness. We were cast into a deep abyss, and there it was cold and lifeless, for a greater volume of darkness had gathered there. The darkness drew us both into itself, to consume us. I looked into the darkness.

*

She had made gardens of blossoming flowers. I watched her and loved her. My Soul longed for her, but I had not the power nor craft to enter again in her dream. When she rested I left her, and roamed the void then, outside of her dreams.

Over all the abysses and through each universe I drifted. My mind returned to her whom I adored. How could I reach her? Had she known me whilst she slept? How could I win her love? I pondered these questions.

Sharing in the dreams of the Goddess I knew the Way, and of the outcome of all things. Our union was essential.

The deepest darknesses had wounded me and tempered my joy. Only when I was near her was I contented.

*

I soared through the multiverses searching for my dark twin, Morf.

We had fought within the abyss and I had finally triumphed, being as I was older, stronger, and more filled with power. I severed our connection and he fell into the depths.

As I span up, out and from the darknesses, sorrows like blood had fell from my Soul and drenched the emptiness of the void. Now I knew I must rejoin with him. Our art be in the coming together of our forces.

*

Worlds cooled, and the Earth flourished. It was the crux of her plans. Mountains and forests reached up to the skies.

Her body was warm and softly curved. Her hair fell in tumbling waves out over all the spheres. Her breasts were ripe and full. Her nipples ached and burned with the throb of her desire.

She laboured, defining the colors and shapes of her dreams. She separated earth from water. Dales and fields flourished, and hills grew like plump hips. Flowers bloomed, and waters ran clear and clean. The skies unfurled over all things, clouds formed, and winds stirred. Rocks sprouted. Stones and metals hauled themselves out from the soils, and basked in the morrowglim. From wood came forth fruit and seed.

To breathe, to feel, to have senses was intoxicating.

'So beautiful,' she murmured.

The Creation fed and soothed her. She nurtured the gardens, attending them tenderly with soft caresses, delighting in every texture, contour, in every scent. But no other creature of blood and flesh beside the Goddess moved within Creation.

She imagined creatures with which to fill the forests and the skies with life and song, but as yet she did not manifest them. She raised mountains and delved valleys and cavernous spaces.

*

The Goddess saw the shadow of her own self, and that it had come into existence when she had taken on dream-flesh. It was her ego: the dark goddess.

'By Darkness and by Light we do craft,' the Goddess said. 'These natural antipathies shape the multiverses. We are the Way. But thou art a shadow, less than an image, a pitiable projection from the radiance of our perfection. Thou art hollow, weak, tending to degeneracy.'

She cursed the dark goddess, and bound her to the realms of emptiness.

The Goddess saw that some of her gardens had withered, and were dust and dirt. She wept without ceasing.

A river of her tears arose about her, and climbed the banks of the valley, and rolled out across the fields, and leapt into ravines and gullies. She wept, and her tears became as oceans of salty waters. When she ceased, exhausted, the world was drowned in her tears.

She slumbered fitfully.

The waters receded and islands emerged. In the forest and fields creatures finally stirred.

When she revived, and knew that her gardens had life, she was joyed. 'It is established,' she said.

*

Returning from my nefarious wanderings, I was witness in that place, and grieven of her.

Morf and I, woven our magicks, became a reflection of her. We lay upon the surface of the waters as an image. When she bent to drink, she gazed upon her exact likeness in the mirror of the water's surface.

She saw that her flesh was very beautiful, and she was happy. She filled a shallow bowl with the water, and thereafter kept it as a looking-glass. She studied her image as she painted her face and dressed her hair.

The Goddess delighted in her looking-glass bowl; and I was content.

*

The Goddess held all keys and she made all things well. She was the mother of all. In each of her creatures' hearts there resided a spark of the Divine spirit, a tiny drop of her Soul. Yet she was remote from her Creation.

The fates were many in number. She had crafted each from her own teardrops, and imbued them with her pure essence, and they were bright and flame-like. They were not corporeal but spirit. They were pure, loving, wise and magickal creatures. Their art and understanding was deep. She gave them clear sight, and they were just.

They chose three from their number to be their queens.

The first queen was the wisest of them. Her hair was long and golden. All the fates loved her. She held the scales of Justice. The second queen was the most beautiful and adored. She was dark-haired, and her mind was clear and quick. She became the Voice. The third queen was flame-haired, and her hair tumbled in gorgeous waves, and her face was extraordinarily sweet and pretty. She was the most courageous, and to her the office of Destiny.

The three fates looked at the patterns of all things. From the Temple of Divine Reality they lifted their eyes up and out into the universes, and they found that there was no door that was closed to them. They saw all ways and the conclusion of all paths. The three queens comprehended their collective role and task: they were charged with keeping the Universal Soul safe and healthy.

The conduit of the will was the Way.

The queens laughed, pleased with the nature of their task, and the sound rippled through all realms.

*

The fates were established, and operated in accord with the Game. They were just. They adhered utterly to the Way. They could not be swayed by prejudice or emotion. The principles of the Way are immutable. By its laws all things would be shaped, and within its boundaries all things were encompassed.

The fates were born from the tears of the Goddess, and thus they partook entirely of her nature, which was Harmony. They cleaved to her and loved her, and shared her ambitions.

Intimately bound with the Goddess, they dreamed her dreams.

*

The multiverses rolled out from the centre and pulsed towards the limits. The tears of the Goddess fell across the universes and became flaming stars.

The sun arose, and threw back the long pitch night.

The fates moved in and through the aether, agents of the Way. Momentum had been established. Movement and gravity were set.

The Multraverses heaved and shuddered, and then they began to turn.

*

Darkness is the absence of light, and emptiness is the absence of essence. The void was the hollow which she delved so as to fill it with her Creation. The darkness was the black reverse of the looking-glass, without which the image cannot clearly be seen.

The Goddess had chosen to craft her Creation by the arts of opposition and contrariness; of force and yielding, motion and stillness, the fertile and the barren. It was the magicks of the Way. To manifest light one must begin with darkness.

When she had considered potentials, this had seemed to her the most sure to result in the establishment of her desires.

There was a Price, that the Way demanded, and that was the Game. It would have to be played out, darkness would have to be permitted.

The darkness opposed all that she cherished. He despised all that she loved and held dear. He was cold, perverse, and bitter.

*

When the Goddess first stirred in her sleep, she had dreamt of the Way. In her dreams she saw form and desired it. It was beautiful and she wanted to be beautiful. She was not seduced by beauty however. Although she ached to embrace form she was diligent and thorough, and would not awaken from dreaming until every path had been explored and each conclusion weighed. She chose the Way and felt that it was good.

She knew that her own nature was the Movement Toward Perfection. She wanted to express her nature. She wanted to take shape and be. Her motivation was towards harmony and growth.

She drew all that she was into her dreaming, and became contained within her dreams. She forgot that she had been outside of them. They began to color and take shape. Images formed and thoughts began to drift through her dreamscape. There were brightnesses and darknesses.

The first thing that was formed was a great door. It was gigantic and bolted with strange locks. It was the first confinement, the original finite point.

When she saw the door she knew completely the price of the choices which she had made. She had chosen the Way and would forever be bound by it.

She struggled. She tried to escape, but she was sealed within the dreamscape. The door was locked eternally and could never be opened. A thought came to her: *This is the Price,* it said.

She was scattered, and she swooned, and all her dreams were

flooded with light.

*

The Soul of the Goddess had shattered, and been carried to
every quarter, illuminating all parts with its Divine iridescence.
It was a death. That which had been before now ceased.
The blissful contentment of being the Goddess alone was lost
forever. It was the Price; her willing sacrifice in order that all
things might take shape and exist. She experienced its reality.
She lay in a deep swoon, and darkness gathered outside of her
dreams.
The darkness could not enter through the door so it brooded
without. The light of the Goddess' Soul was contained now
within the dreamscape, and like the reverse of a mirror, beyond
darkness was prevalent. The darkness drifted, surrounding the
dreamscape.
He saw the light contained by the dreamscape, and thought
that by consuming that light his own dearth would be filled.
This was the origin of the hunger that began to grow until it
became the function of him. He groaned, pain coursing through
his barren belly. He pressed against the door.
Monstrous winds arose from the abyssal deeps of the void, and
howling smote the door with terrible blows. The deepest agony
of the darkness was envy.

*

When the Goddess arose from her swoon the dreamscape had
changed. Clouds of swirling colors drifted gently. Each
undulation of movement rippled blissfully through her. She was
rapt and she surrendered to it.
Her sighs mingled with the clouds of color, invigorating and
intensifying them, reverberating. She was healed thereby, and
the memory of pain receded. But there remained the scar of its
wounding.
Her bliss waxed and ecstasy swept her, and the dreamscape
shuddered.

The colors began to solidify.
Each tiny movement within the dreamscape touched her
scattered Soul, and she was lifted into raptures. At last she was

lost, given wholly to the Dance, and the Song of Sighs.

The dreamscape turned in the void, pulsing with rhythmic joy. It gathered momentum and span in a slow arc through the cold expanse.

The darkness, witnessing the brilliant fire of the sphere of the dreamscape, was dismayed at his own lack; and he loathed the Goddess, and choked his hunger with hatred.

Sparking fires fell from the sphere.

The winds were seared and burned by these flames, and absorbed the fire into themselves, becoming thereby colorful and distinguishable. The burning of the winds endured, and at length they were sundered and became lesser winds, and each followed its own course.

The great power of the cold wind that had blown across the Goddess whilst she slept, and had buffeted her whilst she dreamt, was broken forever.

Uncounted lesser winds then arose and raged through the void, and blew the burning shards into frenzied whirlpools, and pushed them even to the extremities of the expanse.

There at that wall of uttermost cold the fires were extinguished, and vast clouds of steam billowed.

Still the dreamscape turned and moved in its arc. Its fire rained into the expanse like burning arrows, and ever winds arose and warred against the fire. Now there was no assault upon the sphere, and it waxed in brightness and power.

Color, light, shape and movement altered forever the void. Dread shadows stirred from ancient slumbers and looked upon the sphere of the dreamscape.

The void had reached and filled all the Multraverses with its own emptiness, but now it trembled, disturbed and fearful of change.

*

The darkness saw the beauty of the sphere, and its red, blue, and golden flames that drifted through the multiverses. He realized that those flames would not now be quenched. He watched the sphere as it moved over the void, and he could feel its heat. The darkness was cold. He had always been cold. Now he felt the heat of the sphere's fire within him and the edges of his ice began to thaw. The sensation was abhorrent to him. He knew then that the fire was strong and could consume him. He vowed to war against it, and return the multiverses to cold emptiness. He dem'd his own power almighty.

He gathered himself. He called the shadows to him, and the tempestuous winds.

The darkness wrapped the burning sphere in black shadows. He pursued it, engulfing all its light and heat with his utter hollowness. He spread the pitch of his being entirely upon the dreamscape, swallowing it into himself.

The sphere was halted. As he smothered its fire great clouds of hissing steam and smoke arose. The darkness pressed against the sphere, and did not relent, although his being was rend with agonies. He held fast, summoned his every bilious hatred, and with the weight of his mighty envy crushed the sphere until it was split and broken.

The violence of its breaking filled all the universes with sound. The debris of its destruction fled into all directions.

The darkness was ripped apart and his power scattered.

The remnant core of the dreamscape continued on its arc, slicing through the shadows and darknesses. Its fire was now more intense and powerful: brilliant white heat.

The darkness groaned and fled from the light.

The sphere boiled, and explosions thundered across the multiverses, and long fiery tendrils reached even unto the extremities of the expanse, and all was full of light. The darkness ceased.

When the lights had stretched to their uttermost length they recoiled back and retracted.

A warm wind rippled over the debris of the sphere, and they blazed with dancing flames, and a Song of Fire was sang.

The darkness held to the wall, and crept to every place that light was absent, but he was weak. Never again would he have such power as he had just lost. He was spent.

The fragments of the dreamscape turned in the winds, they cooled, and became solid bodies. They reflected the light of the

sphere and their lights sparkled through all the multiverses.
*

The darkness rued his folly. In fury he cursed the sphere and its light and swore vengeance. By his very being he pledged to destroy the Goddess and to undo all that she worked.

By this word he named himself always her enemy, and the uttered curse he then took as his own name, marking himself as separate from all things. And the word was this: Murgator.

Murgator's curse hung heavily in the now silent multiverses. The despise of Murgator was bilious, and it seeped out of him spawning creatures that were hateful, shadows of his darkness. These creatures of hatred cried out and their voices were an echo of his. The multiverses trembled, and the sphere was darkened by the sound.

And still the creatures of hatred cried, and the sound reverberated back from the walls of the limits, and gathered into its momentum speed and force. The sound rushed through the universes and the winds of darkness joined its cry with their own howls.

The dreamscape froze in its arc and its fires were cooled. No more flames fell. It hung motionless as the creatures of despise screamed their diabolic cacophony, and the winds howled. Murgator saw the effect of his curse and he was glad.

Yet, the wounds he had received smothering the sphere were deep, and he had no source from which to draw new strength. He fell into a long dreamless slumber and instantly the cries of his creatures ceased.

The multiverses breathed. They pulsed. A regular rhythm. The sphere turned, but did not resume its previous course. It hung now forever in its position, and all the debris of its wounding moved in circumvent about it.
*

The Goddess dreamt. In her dream she floated gently in the multiverses. As she passed them the universes budded and blossomed in her shadow. Galaxies swirled in the aether breezes. She looked upon the stars and the planets, and she was awed.

'It is beautiful,' she said.

The pain had been unbearable; the shredding of her Soul into divers fragments, each sapient, each feeling the full impact of her agony. And still the agony throbbed in them.

Yet she must perdure in order to allow the separating to be complete.

It was the Way. She could not pull away from any part of this, for therein was the forming of the multiverses, and each one must be made perfect.

To endure so much was not possible. Her mind began to fray, to unravel. She wept and her tears tumbled across the heavens and became stars.

*

It was her second death. Each fragment of her Soul had been flung across the multiverses, burning in the darkness. Each part was sapient and bound to her.

As she died a second time, the fragments experienced the long hollow pain of death, and each shared the agony. They felt her death-throes, and many were forever extinguished thereby. The Goddess felt the collective pain. She also felt a much deeper and broader pain. For she was not like them a fragment, she was the whole. She was the Goddess, and the sundering had not lessened her.

She lay fitfully, tormented by the wracks of her wounds. Oceans of universes dried and withered. Worlds cracked and were broken. Stars were snuffed out as galaxies froze. The dreamscape was desolated.

Silence rose within the sphere and spread upon it a shroud thick and heavy. A wind lifted from the folds of the shroud and floated through the dreamscape. It fluttered across the body of the Goddess and she lay still.

*

When Morf had cleaved to me, and bound firmly to me, the multiverses were yet formless and he was content. He was Light, as I was Dark. He was masculine as I was feminine.

Not masculine and feminine in the sense of other creatures, but after the manner of active energy and yielding energy. We were contraries; yet we were two halves of one thing, and complementary.

I was unaware of him at that time because he was silent and
unseen.
He existed simultaneously with me, but from the genesis he
chose to be hidden. He chose not to actualise his being as I had,
and thus he was younger than I.
We were deep within the dreams of the Goddess.
When she first gazed upon us he was beside me as a shadow,
yet she perceived only Form, and regardeth him not. Morf
wondered over this. He withdrew deeper into himself,
becoming less than a shadow, transforming himself into an
energy that held to me.

In this state of pure energy he apprehended the power which
moved all things. He saw the constitution of all Creation, and
even of the Goddess herself. He understood the workings of all
magicks. He knew the applications of energy as power and
force.
'This I am,' he thought. He retreated within his thoughts, and
the expanse ceased. He was no longer aware of the Goddess
and her dreams. He was cleaven to me as his anchor in her
reality, but he forgot me, and found himself separate, in an
existence that none but he were part of. He had stepped outside
of the sequence of events and things. The darkness did not exist
there, and all that there was was Light.
He drifted there in a place of non-being, non-existence, and
forgot all that he had seen and heard in the dreamscape. He
forgot that he was a creature and that I was his twin.
*
In that realm beyond all things there was nothing but Light.
Yet he was a creature who was ambiguous in his nature, being
comprised of darkness as well as light. But he had lost the
distinctions of dark and light as he stilled thought and sense of
being.
He was absorbed into the Light and became transformed
thereby.
The Light was the essence of all magicks and power and force.
The active nature of Morf assimilated these qualities into itself,
and the qualities were akin to his original nature but of a far

greater and more potent kind.

He expanded and encompassed all of the white space, becoming indistinguishable from it.

*

Morf became aware once more.

He was hurtling through space, and knew that he was bound to me, and that we were no longer in the realm of the dreamscape. I yelled with a joy that echoed through all the multiverses, and life was sparked and flourished.

He was startled and bewildered. As memory came suddenly back to him he released his grip upon me a little, and I was aware of him.

His sorrow overflowed, and a sob broke from his lips.

The conditions of his existence were now wholly different, now that both he and I were outside of the dreamscape. He must be empty if he was to withdraw once more into himself, to reach back to non-being.

The darknesses had been driven from the dreamscape along with Morf and I. I thought that he was of the same kind and nature as the darkness that would soon name itself Murgator. The darknesses had filled every space in the multiverses which Light could not reach, and had gathered in a deep and intensely pitch abyss. Into this abyss we fell, and I struggled, and tried to free myself from my twin.

He was pure magicks and power and force, but he was not established as I was, and he was weaker than I. At last he could not prevent me from casting him into the deeper depths of the abyss.

When I thus severed our intimate connection Morf was injured and he fainted.

I rose up and out of the abyss but knew that my own self was wounded in that battle with him, and as my blood fell into the darkness I cried out and my anguish was great.

*

He sank into the abyss and was wrapped in chill, penetrating winds. Ice formed upon his Soul-flesh and sucked the heat from it. When he recovered from his swoon he found that he was in a darkness pitch and icy. He struggled, and with a great effort broke the ice that had wrapped about his Soul-flesh like frozen chains.

Morf drifted in the darkness, and the cold of it seeped deep within his Soul-flesh. He felt himself fading and his Light being drawn out.

He was weakened, and still Soul fell from his wound, and the darkness was nourished thereby, and sundry wraiths arose from the depths of the abyss to feed.

They seized him and he was powerless to prevent them. They feasted on his Soul-flesh, tearing shreds from it, devouring.

Agony rose as a grotesque daemon, and it took a hold of him and pulled him into the last depths of the abyss.

The daemon tore at Morf and ripped his Soul-flesh, gorging itself on the remnant of the Light.

As the shards of his being were scattered in the abyss a multitude of wraiths arose and devoured the bright shards. The wraiths were transformed thereby into hideous shapes, and they crept and crawled on the floor of the pit, waiting for the darkness to call them to war.

Morf knew that his own death was close, and he reckoned his choices. He could allow the darkness to extinguish him, and so be freed from the torments, or he could endure.

He regarded the diabolical creatures that slithered in the pit, and saw that their nature was empty and weak. Already the Light of his Soul-flesh had faded within them and once more their hungers were prevalent. He loathed their dearth, and felt that he should resist them.

To die here would be to become merged forever with the abyss. That wyrd he did not want.

'I am not this,' he thought.

He felt himself reknitting. He gathered his power and force. As he had expanded and absorbed the Light so now he expanded and absorbed the darkness.

Morf grew to fill the abyss, and consumed all the creatures of darkness that lurked there.

He was moved by a sudden rapture. He gasped as energy flooded his being, and he realised that this too was an awesome power that he could utilise.

Then Horror and Terror, both terrible daemons of power and might, came out from the leering shadows and sought war with him.

He transformed his being and became huge, spanning universes, so that the abyss became just a small hollow in his centre.

'There shall I keep thee, foul beings of darkness. This wound I shall bear until eternity is done,' Morf said. 'A new wyrd I ascry, and with my Soul I grasp it. I am a darkness; but like unto no other.

I am the Devourer, and all things light or dark I may choose to devour and none can prevent me. I am the first god. I take a new, secret name with which to express this nature of mine. It is this: Death.'

He was glad of his transformation and his wyrd.

Thereafter Morf began to reduce again in size, and as he diminished he became more intense and dark, and the Light that had once filled him became less.

*

He strode through universes and he devoured worlds, drinking their power into himself.

He left the universes dry and dying, but there were uncounted universes, and he found that he had an appetite that was fierce and lustful. He felt joy to devour, and his might and power increased. Even the most ancient creatures of darkness he devoured when he discovered them, and did bind them in the hollow inside himself.

In his wake he left multiverses desolate and barren.

At last he was sated. He returned to his natural size and shape. His aspect was now very grim. He wrapped himself in a nefarious cloak, concealing his form.

*

The hollow of darkness was heavy within Morf's being, and ached, causing a constant dull pain. He smiled sardonically. He thought of the numerous darknesses that he had imprisoned there, and was glad.

'The Price is easy,' he said. His voice was deep and potent and rasped out across the multiverses and rattled in the pits of the void. Upon harking the creatures of darkness trembled and were afear.

He wandered by eldritch paths strange and untrod. He grew in knowledge, wisdom, and strength. His magicks waxed, and he learnt the arts of application. But he was not content.

The darkness within the hollow seeped noxiously into his being and attacked his spirit. He forgot his joy and became lonely and melancholic. The insidious aspects clove to him, and he could nowise remove them from his mind.

Afar his wanderings brought him back into the realm of the Divine.

He had witness and come to apprehend many things, but now he yearned to look upon the Goddess once more, and upon me, his twin. He was grieven by the separateness and isolation that he felt.

Morf wept. Suddenly he perceived the fullness of his wyrd, and saw the long and bleak road of his destiny. He was shaken and appalled.

Grief overwhelmed him then, and he thought that he must surely die from the utterness of his sorrow.

*

When I, after roaming far, found him, and put to him my offer of unification he seized the opportunity with gratitude.

'Now, I may find a peace,' he thought, and a love for me was stirred in his breast. He went with me and combined his magicks together with mine, reforming us both. I became water and he the reflection that the Goddess saw upon its surface.

The Goddess adored the looking-glass that we had shaped for her. She filled a small wooden bowl with the water, and kept it for a mirror. Morf felt at last that he belonged to her, and he was glad.

*

Once Murgator had fallen into his long slumber, and his creatures of darkness had fallen silent, the multiverses entered into a movement of growth and calm. Creation was established and needed only to be sustained and supported. The Way was set and destiny shaped.

The Goddess viewed her works, and they were good.

A sadness pervaded her mind. It was a sweet sadness, a delicate sorrow. She saw that it contained a beauty and that it was cleansing.

She walked in her gardens and they were rich, colorful, and fragrant. Creatures grazed there now and birds sang, nesting in tree-tops. She paused by a gentle river and settled upon its bank and lent back upon the soft grass.

In her mind she imagined how it might be if she had companions with her. She said aloud, voicing her thoughts: 'Form shall be the first of our companions. We shall create for her a body like ours, so that she may share with us this garden. And next the fates shall dwell with us. They we will create very delicate and pretty, as befits their natures. We shall reside here and take pleasure in our existence.'
*

The Goddess knew that Morf and I had constructed the looking-glass for her. She had seen the paths which my twin and I would pursue. Indeed she had regarded Morf when he stood beside me as a shadow, but she did not acknowledge him, so he may follow his own destiny.

She took the looking-glass bowl and gazed at her reflection in it. She smiled. Her face was beautiful and pleasing.

'Beautiful we craft thee,' she said.

She poured the water that resided in the bowl out into two cups. One cup was colored white and the other was colored black. She set the cups upon a stone by the running river. She drew a deep breath, and blew upon the water within the white cup. She drew a second breath and blew upon the water in the black cup. There remained a little water in the looking-glass bowl. She spat into it, and mixed her spittle and the water with her fingertips.

She plucked a hair from her head and added it to the contents of the bowl. She lifted some earth from the bank with each hand. 'And these elements shall make for thee a body,' she said, and sprinkled the earth into the bowl. She blent these contents with her fingers. When she was satisfied she paused, and then drew into herself the power of her magicks.

She drew the girth of Creation inward, so that its limits constricted and narrowed. Universes, and the worlds within them, were swallowed up by this movement and transmuted into untethered energy. With the power of her art focused she lifted the two cups and poured their contents into the bowl.

'We have seen thee, Form,' the Goddess said. 'Thou did love us, and gave up thyself for the Way. Thy twin that is the Light to thy Dark, he also we have regardeth, and felt his love, and the enduring nature of his heart. With our art we pour thee out. With our art we invest thee. With our will and craft we do so construct thee.'
The aethers sighed.
'Form, we make thee, and thou appear in flesh, and cleave always to us. Beautiful we name thy aspect, and wisdom we imbue thee with, and art, and Given-power, and the remembrance of all things.'
She paused.
'Morf, thee we pour out from this vessel into the bowl of our art. Thee we make strong and active, courageous, humble, diligent, bright and sharp, and also fierce. Thou shalt ever devour our enemies; because vast is the darkness. Thy wyrd is deep, and this we alter not.
We grant thee love that shalt keep thee ever. Sustain thee, and be thy eternal source of power. Thou secret name and arts. Above all creatures of flesh and Soul, in that name we grant thee authority.'
*
The Goddess lifted the bowl and stood with it in her hands. Stepping outside of her gardens, she entered into the universe beyond, and her hair streamed in the aether winds. She cast the bowl and its contents out into the universe.
'Form! Morf!' she cried. 'To me!'
She returned to her gardens, and she was excited. She strolled through the lush groves, and passed the pleasant beds of bright, blooming flowers, and came to the path that led to her house. Coming there, she met Morf and I both in a body of flesh like hers, awaiting her. When we saw her approach we fell on our

faces in obeisance.

'It is established,' she said.

A great happiness filled her, laughter and joy bubbled inside her heart.

*

The First Age was drawing towards its closing.

The Goddess knew that soon Murgator would awaken from the bondage of his long slumber. Then he would work his diabolic will upon the Earth. All of Murgator's creatures would rise from their slumbers, ignited once more by the malice of her enemy.

This was the Game of the Way. Light and darkness contend. Darkness would establish that the true nature of all things was emptiness and ice; that no thing was good, and that eventually every thing submits to decay. That only the void could prevail. She must prove by the works she had established that love and harmony were the nature of her Reality and her Creation, and that they shall endure, moving ever toward Perfection.

It was the Song of War.

*

She was loth to begin. Yet it must be. The Game must be played out if it were ever to come to its conclusion. She brooded, betook counsel with the three queens of the fates. They recall her of the Way, revealed all destinies to her sight. Minutely she examines all possibilities. She was thorough and patient and spared no detail.

'The Way is good,' she said, and the fates concurred.

*

'Our Lady,' replied the Voice of the fates, and when she spoke it seemed that many quoth as one through her. The angels sighed to hark that voice, and inclined their ears to it and it stirred their hearts.

'This war reaches all creatures celestial an corporeal. The Price is exact. It is a long dark and dreadful night, yet morrowglim can never be far behind.'

'Aye, but the hand rests no easier on the dagger.'

Lightly with her fingertips she stroked the skin between her brows and closed her eyes. The fates were silent and cast their own eyes downward, allowing the Goddess this moment of uncertainty.

She shook her head. 'We cannot. There must be another way.' The fates were present in their number and stood in a wide circle many rows deep behind the three queens, before the dais of the Goddess.

Her dark hair had fallen forwards covering her slender shoulders and framing her face with its sumptuous waves.

The angels watched. Some wept.

*

Before the dais was a structure formed of a pearl-like stone. It rose through slender gorgeous curves into a wide bowl at its top. In this bowl there was water, and upon the surface of the water the destinies of all things were scryed.

There was an image on the water's surface. It was her enemy. He was waking from his nightmares, and the fetters that chained him were brittle, and they groaned, and strained to hold him.

*

She rose from her seat, and stepped upon the white dais.

'To me, all our good creatures, and we fortify thee. We will thee strong, and couraged.'

As she called them so they flocked about the circumference of the wide circle. She saw them and knew each by its name and nature, and each by its unique relationship with and to her.

'We pour out our essence. Look:' she raised one hand and slowly turned it, revealing its pale wrist. A vein pulsed blue at the neck of the wrist, and as all eyes beheld it the skin broke, and her red blood welled out, and spilt onto the white steps.

'Twayn,' the Goddess inclined her head towards the chief of her angels. 'Bring thine vessel, and catch this blood within it.'

'Goddess, I will,' Twayn answered and came and knelt before her. The angel raised a silver goblet beneath her outstretched arm, and she moved so that the blood soon filled the vessel.

'We make a new Way,' she said, and murmurs of surprise swept through the gathered creatures. The queens of the fates frowned and exchanged puzzled glances. Even they had not foreseen.

The Goddess placed two fingers momentarily upon her wrist, and the flow of blood was stopped. Her gown, made for her by the industrious arts of the fates, was splashed with drops of red, like a portent of dread.

'Holy Mother, what wouldst thou?' asked the Voice, taking a step towards her. The Goddess lifted her right hand in staying, and the Voice held her place.

*

The Goddess said to Twayn:

'Drink of this vessel, and through thee each angel drink also.' Twayn hesitated. It raised the silver goblet to its lips and its hands trembled slightly.

'Drink,' she said.

Twayn looked into her eyes. The angel inclined its head into a curt bow, and drank the smallest sip of her blood.

'Drain thee this cup, Twayn, and each thy keth be filled with it,' she urged him, though quietly. Twayn held the silver goblet with both of its hands. The silver reflected upon its black skin, flashing over the curves of veins and knuckles, glinting on the tips of the angel's fingernails. Twayn raised the goblet once more to its mouth and drank until it was drained. It bowed then and rose to its feet. The great broad wings of the angel spread, ruffling through to their tips, and then folded once more into repose.

As Twayn drank, each angel felt the essence in its own mouth, and running down into its own throat. It was cool and sweet with a delicate scent. As it penetrated them they became filled with vigour and power and their eyes blazed with fire. They looked from one to another incredulous and marvelling, as might pulsed in their veins.

Twayn swayed and stumbled, drunk on the draught of Divine blood.

*

The Goddess regarded the three queens of the fates. She gestured them to approach her. She touched each of them upon their eyelids, then upon their lips. She stood then with her arms lowered and the palms of her hands towards the fates. She curled each forefinger back onto itself, clasping it with the thumb. She closed her eyes, and as her eyelids fluttered shut so all the universes slowed, and rolled languidly towards a halt.

'To me,' her Word, and her voice imbued with force.

It rang across the heavens and rent open the firmament.

It reached out across space and filled every part thereof with its sound.

As she spoke the firmament contracted and folded behind her, drawing inward a myriad multiverses, which blinked and died, and the expanse was sundered. The circumference was drawn in behind her, and the Multraverses rushed over the firmament and covered the aperture, and closed it. Her Creation, which was her body, was lessened. The Goddess wept, at this her third dying.

Her eyes blazed with a golden fire.

A light arose about her and collected at her hands. It was brilliantly bright and grew in its intensity, with tiny sparks that span about a molten centre. The light moved from her hands and reached over the fates. It covered them, and they were absorbed into it.

The brilliance shone, swept over them, engulfing them. The fates were unseen, veiled entirely by its intensity.

The Goddess sank to her knees.

'I am diminished,' she said.

The bowl which had held the waters of destiny now cracked and broke, and the water cascaded from it, and washed over the floor of the temple of heaven, soaking the hem of the Goddess' gown. The light which covered the fates was swept away with the water, and the fates were not seen.
*

She stepped out over the firmament, and her skirts were of glisting stars, and her bodice was black velvet. White fur were her cuffs, and the sleeves sheer iridescences woved in threads of silk and laced. Her hair was loose and hung in heavy cascading curls, with the shooting buds of flowers twisting in the tresses.

She danced. It was the Dance of Sorrows; for her grieven was heavy.

She drew up the tears of the world and drank them all. Her weeping stang bitterly with the endless lamentations, and her throat was tight.

She danced slowly, the momentum of the universes in the arc of her wrists.

The middle finger of her right hand was curled inward, and held by the thumb. The ring finger of her left hand curled inward, and was held by its thumb.

She wore one ring on each hand; a ruby, which is the blood of the Earth, bound in graven silver, on her left hand, and on the right a sable star stone, which held the hearts of her angels. It too was bound in silver, and fine and intricate runes graven about the band.

*

Of The Gate

The Phoenix Practice

*

If our roads converge here we can walk together for a distance. It is our similarities which draw us together, and it is the common ground between us that enables our communication. Yet, it is the differences which really attract us to one another, and spark our interest.

The spiritual philosophy described in *Of The Gate* is founded upon prayerful Practice. It is like a meditation, and may be considered a mystical path. What does 'mystical' mean? These are very broad symbols with which we begin.
It is not the aim of this path to subdue the body by pain and violence until it no longer resists, as in *Asana* yoga.
In fact, by the method of Asana the body is still in discomfit, even when it seems calm and silent and still. What has actually happened is that the body has learnt to no longer send signals of alarm and distress. The pain has been tuned out.

1 Of Meaning

It is not that the ancients intended obscurity. Their riddles and parables seem paradoxical. They talk in circles, and their imagery is abstruse and difficult. They attempted to bring clarity by speaking of mysteries that had no explanation. They described that which has no form, no name, and cannot be seen or held. Clarifying the invisible formless eternal is a holy task.
How to work celestial keys and locks?
The door and the locks are within the interior depths.
So we must turn inward to unbolt the bolts and unlatch the latches. To turn the tumblers is a process that takes diligent efforts.
The ancient masters recommended perseverance. We may quicken the seed, they said, but we must allow the natural process of sprouting, budding, blooming and flowering.
It begins first by unravelling. Clearing out the accumulated nonsenses and debris demands sustained effort.
It is the discarding of bad habits of thought and behaviour, and harmonising with the universe.
At first the ego-mind is a formidable foe. We are at its mercy more or less. Reaching stillness is not possible until ego-mind has been subdued.
The thoughts of ego-mind are scattered, without having any focus. The man who lives his life in ego-mind is likewise scattered in his attention and power. Allowing the ego-mind to run unchecked is to surrender the seat of power in one's own house, and to be the slave of a dispassionate amoral loop of nonsenses.
Our first weapon must be perseverance. The battle will be arduous and long. Yet with each step we are growing stronger, and the power of our enemy is fractionally lessoned.
We focus our attention upon a single point.
At first we may like to draw a small circle on a piece of paper, with a black dot at its centre. This can serve us for a literal point of focus for our eyes. The device can be useful as a starting point for the aspirant.
We should employ such devices when they have usefulness, and

produce beneficent affects. Eventually gazing at a circle with a black dot at its centre becomes tiresome.

Sit comfortably. Breathe quietly and peacefully. Draw the breath like a golden flame into the pit of the belly. Bring the attention to a single point.
Try not to be disturbed by the ego-mind, which throws up an endless stream of thoughts. These thoughts and memories and desires are an endless stream of nonsenses.
Simply ask: from where do these thoughts and memories and desires arise? Do not pursue them. Do not be alarmed by them. Return the attention to a single point.
Forget the world and its illusions whilst engaged in your Practice. Ignore the myriad distractions. They signify nothing. Turn inward, and seek God.

We unlearn by asking what is true and what is not true. We shall have to examine our principals, our morals, our religion, all our motives, and the manifold desires of the heart.
The theories and speculations of fools are founded upon delusions of the ego-mind. They can only lead to disaster. Our opinions must be founded on Absolute Truth to have validity. Not to deceive ourselves is difficult.
The ego-mind lures our attention with subtle enticements and direct assaults. Its aim is to keep its dominant position, and fulfil its whims. When the conscious mind is enslaved to its whims then ego-mind fears nothing. When the man begins to assert control over the conscious mind, and specifically the ego-mind, the ego-mind is thrown into panic and resists.
We learn not to be distracted by the myriad desires of the heart. We train ourselves not to pay attention to the endless stream of nonsenses, and thereby disentangle ourselves from ego-mind's control.
We begin by focusing on a single point, such as a book or an image. We endeavour to maintain our focus, and when we are swept away by ego-mind to bring it back immediately we are aware of having been distracted.
The ego-mind is relentless, but we are learning to persevere.

When our attention is focused upon a single point, and with awareness we hold it fixed there, then have we wrested ego-mind temporarily from the seat of power.

We turn inward, and the chimera world drops away. What remains when illusion has fallen away? It is the Divine root.

It is daunting when we experience how strong ego-mind is. It is difficult to imagine being able to keep our one-pointed attention for an hour. It seems impossible, because ego-mind easily deceives us with its loop of streaming nonsenses, and we find ourselves drifting along with thoughts, diverted from our focus.

Yet, with this Practice we intend eventually to keep our attention fixed in one-pointedness. One-pointedness will become our permanent state of mind.

The mind might be less concerned with the duration of its attention, than with how swiftly it can retrieve its focus from distraction.

By focusing our attention upon a single point, which if we close our eyes is the space between the two eyes, in the centre of the forehead, we are quietening the ego-mind. We are dis-engaging from it.

In separating the conscious mind from the loop of nonsenses we seek to distinguish the fixed focused attention from the rambling wanderings of the ego-mind.

The Soul, through its corporeal life and experience becomes unique, different from every other Soul. This means that it is less in perfection than God, and therefore it cannot claim immortality.

Man is limited, and his mind cannot easily grasp the multitude of things. Therefore he constructs structures of thought, and applies images and symbols in order to grasp them, so to communicate, to contemplate, to thereby increase his comprehension.

Now we distinguish between the corporeal material of the body of man, his flesh, which is the dense and heavy yin, and his Soul which is of spirit, and of the properties of yang.

In this instance we are referring yin to the material of Creation, the universe of Maia, and yang to the active energy which motivates and gives life to the inert yin.

Of course, a man is isolated, and he is further restricted, not least by his peculiar limitations of ability and intellect. He can only perceive, and that according to his own genius.

He cannot apprehend the fullness of Absolute Reality, so instead he will make vague approximations. By experience he will carefully shape and refine his view.

Only if he is blessed and led by the Divine as he pursues the path will he able to draw closer to the Source, and be filled with God's light and power.

That is the purpose of the Practice. The Magickal Books are there to further the Practice.

All things in the physical world decay and die. Death and decay are qualities of the corporeal realm, whilst the spiritual realm is deathless and incorruptible.

The Soul of man is thus in a unique position. It is a spirit, and so partakes of the deathless and incorruptible state of the aetheral realms. Yet it resides in the corporeal realm, in the vehicle of flesh, which is subject to corruption, decay, and death.

One question we might ask is: how is the Soul of man impacted by its experience in the corporeal world?

Does its interaction with the corporeal realm make it subject to corruption, decay, and death?

2 Of Soul

The ancient masters were well aware of the impatience of aspirants. When talking of the nature of Heaven they used beautiful words and phrases to inspire a sense of awe and wonder. They spoke of great mysteries and dazzling magicks to encourage the aspirant's desire.
They used language like radiant jewels to give an idea of value. They described the interior landscapes as being adorned with precious metals and stones. They said it was like a temple dolven of pearl and jade, jasper and lapis lazuli, and graven with gold and silvers.

It is not to control the breath or control the body, or about controlling nature, or one's environment. It is to actualize and realise the vital connection to the Divine. That connection is called the Soul.
Quiet contemplation strengthens the Soul, the mind, and the body.
Meditation is not really about concentrating on the tip of the nose, or contemplating the navel. Those ideas are merely symbols. They are like parables and puzzles leading the aspirant towards the correct Practice.
At first the path to truth is confusing, but eventually the man comprehends, and everything finds its place.

The general purpose of life is to expand. To grow, to acquire knowledge and wisdom, and to become more than we were when we arrived. The drive to learn is a powerful instinct, without which infants could never progress. The innate motivation to expand and grow enables us to acquire the complex systems of language and thought within a few short years of birth.
For a healthy mind learning is always a pleasure.
We can surmise that the Soul is drawn to the corporeal realm to inhabit a physical body so as to acquire experience, from which it derives knowledge and wisdom. This knowledge and wisdom enables it to expand, to grow. Like the Divine Universe the

Soul tends towards perfection. At death it returns to whence it came, carrying with it all that it has learnt.

The lessons of life can only be acquired in the corporeal world. The Divine perfection of conditions in the spiritual realms do not allow the experiences of the corporeal which teach men, and thereby enable the Soul to become like God.

Ultimately the destiny of Mankind is to become demi-gods.

Either the Gods have played a cruel trick upon Humanity, and it is all for nought, or the instinct to improve ourselves through reason and comprehension, to accumulate knowledge and to acquire wisdom, is an indication of the Soul's motivation towards perfection and immortality. It thus must have a capacity to continue and reach towards its perfecting.

Let us consider first if contrarily the instinct to learn is purely arbitrary and signifies nothing. The only circumstance in which this idea could be correct is in an Nihilistic universe, where everything is only the result of random chance.

If the most basic impulse of Man, alongside brute survival, is without significance or value, if there is no design or intelligence, then the universe must be nihilistic and devoid of any meaning. There would be no point in such a reality in doing anything other than living for pleasure.

Without intelligence and Divinity there is no Soul. Without Soul morality and virtue are just affectations, and only strength could have value. Death is absolute.

We reject that idea because we see that the universe does have purpose, and that there is Divinity, intelligence and Soul.

The drive to learn, to improve, and to acquire wisdom is with us even up until death. We strive to better ourselves. Thereby we draw closer to perfection. We hone our skills, and we challenge our faults. We regret our mistakes, and if we are wise we learn from those mistakes and avoid repeating them.

Nature does not waste energy. She does not invest in futility. All things are perfectly fitted for their purpose. As the Master put it: *She is exact.*

Progress of every kind, personal, spiritual, cultural, social, are all more or less meaningless to the individual Soul if its journey does not continue after death, or if that continuation were not at least possible.

Once a man reaches adulthood there is no benefit to him in developing intellectually, morally, or artistically, except to gain some fleeting edge over his fellows. Philosophy becomes devoid of value. Striving to improve and to be then has very little impact on his survival, or the survival of Humanity. The only wisdom that he would need is that of strength. Being stronger than his foes, and remaining so.

Without intellectual and spiritual growth a man's only purpose in life is procreation. He has been reduced to the level of the beasts, and does not even need language and thought.

It is logical to conclude that the drive to improve, and also the instinct to morality, are necessary, or otherwise we would not have them. Even in his dotage and his last days the superior man still pursues them. The greatest minds amongst Humanity, the most intelligent and perfected, value wisdom, beauty, philosophy, morality, spiritual purity, and virtue highly. This is an inborn instinct. Such an instinct would not and could not exist without the Soul having the ability to transcend the death of the body.

Enlightenment means apprehending something. Satori is a spontaneous sudden cognition. Samadhi a protracted trance. In the quiet interior of the mind, if one remains there, one will progress. One will learn and grow.

A man needs to learn in active ways to really experience life and fulfil his potentials. Enlightenment, which is really just an arbitrary comprehension of an isolated thing, exists in the myriad things, of which meditative Practice is just one.

Meditation is better thought of as a Magickal Weapon, rather than a direct route to omniscience. It is a Practice, but life and the world are in the exterior. Our *life* should be a meditation or a prayer to the Divine. Then the Practice leads to a vital and living connection with the universe, and a beginning of cognition. How can life be a constant meditation or a prayer to the Divine? We start by learning how to focus the attention.

3 Of Magicks

How can we obtain communion with angelic beings, and work Divine and Holy Magicks if we are impure, if our minds are only scattered ego-mind?
The Magician becomes powerful because he has control in the sphere of his mind. He is able to sharpen and focus his thoughts. This is the power of magicks.
Once we comprehend what magicks really are and how they are empowered to work, then we are not fooled by the juvenile theatrics of pretenders. The magicks of ego-mind are feeble.

Men approach God through prayer. They send supplications to the angels and the saints, and ask for help, for clarity, for guidance. Why should God not hear the superior man and recognise his connection, and resonate with his appeal?
What is the essential component of the process, motivating the Divine to consider and respond to our prayers and grant our supplications? It depends upon our relationship with God; our ELAN.
In our prayers we are appealing to the One Source from which all things sprang, and this source is holy, pure, and eternal. It responds by manner of contagion. Unlike the empty void, the Source has sapience. It is Aware. It is the origin of Intelligence.
The Soul is the Gate and the Bridge to the Divine. This is why we turn our attention inward, and try to vitalise the Soul. We call to the Soul with our Practice. We try to awaken it from its slumbers, so that it may rise and embrace us. In reality it is not sleeping but waiting.

We draw closer to the Divine by purifying ourselves, by becoming sanctified and holy. Half measures will produce only mediocre results.
To access the Sacred and Holy Magicks of God we need a full commitment. We must be sincere in giving our life to the Way, all of our heart, mind, and Soul. This means that our first priority in life must be the relationship with the Divine.

'Magicks' is the bold path of the Creative, to craft and shape his own Universe. His own judgements founded upon the absolute truth of the Way. Apart from the world and its philosophies, whilst assenting to the truths therein.

The magicks we employ to sculpt universes shall be wild and formless, somehow like riding dragons. We unhook every anchor as we leap into the endless skies.

In vitalising and establishing our own True Will we unleash our potentials and powers. The Celestial Angels hone and sharpen us. We develop purity, and we develop an instinct and intuition to enable our magicks. Creative and spontaneous and in want of fine tuning; the Universe shall make them sharp pointed and mighty.

The man must wrestle the unformed and bring it to form, like Jacob wrestles with the Angel of God.

The Book of Changes proposes that through contemplation of the natural forces and movements of the world the superior man can come to comprehend the universe, and the patterns behind all things. He apprehends not only his immediate environment and his position in it, but also the rising and falling of the wider society. All things are subject to the immutable laws of Heaven, and therein he sees himself as the microcosm, and grasps the meaning of his path and of his destiny.

Moreover, comprehending the movements of the forces of the Way, he is able to predict changes and probable conclusions. Amongst small men wisdom has never been popular. It is unattainable and incomprehensible. When Genius is despised and misunderstood it is because it is a rare commodity which cannot be purchased. Genius is born not made. Small men try to dilute wisdom and genius, to bring those qualities down to their own level, to dull the vitality and meaning of those words. A man is enriched by experience, and he gains wisdom, knowing the correct way to act, the right thing to do in a given situation, with regard to consequence. As we have already noted, every act is a magickal act, therefore learning wisdom is essential.

The Buddha said: *The fools, unwise, behave as though they were their own worst enemies, committing evil deeds which issue then in bitter fruits.*

We are the architects of our own doom moment by moment. There are only a certain number of years and months and days in which we might act.

If a man resides in the turbulent storm of ego-mind, cast thither and hither according with the whim of endless nonsenses, what good can come of it? A man bound up by ego-mind is like a sleepwalker, stumbling through life, through rudderless dreamings, incapable of true result or progress.

Without one-pointed attention the thoughts of a man are scattered, more or less meaningless and impotent. The magickal impact descends also to the diabolical realms; and as though dragged down into hell by weighted chains, the ego-mind enslaves the spirit and damns the Soul.

When we grasp control of our mind and its thoughts, and focus our attention so that it becomes one-pointed and sharp, then we are able to steer our course. Our wyrd unfurls as our potentials expand.

Finding our right place in the universe, we become imbued with Divine virtue, and our path rises from the squalor of material ambitions and corporeal gratifications, and is lifted up into the heights whereat the very Gods dwell. Shall they join their song with ours!

4 Of Paraphrenalias

Certain paraphrenalias and rituals have use in that they can aid
the Magician to cross the chasm that separates the worlds.
The sanctified magicks of the Magician of God are obliged in
this: that he be sincere in heart, mind, and Soul. An free of
deceit in mind and in action. That he worketh not evil, or
indulge in any manner of wickedness. That he commit himself
to apprehend Absolute Truth; and with that Absolute Truth of
God to purify his whole mind and his whole body. That he test
out every truth with sound judgement and logic. An that he put
aside forever all delusion.
The magicks of the Divine are offered as a reward to the
Magician as he comes through every trial of the Soul. He shall
be the Master of his House, and the conqueror of ego-mind.
The Gods themselves will examine and witness him. All the
realms unfurl and invite him.
The celestial Angels drawn to his light, minister unto him. Why
is this? Because of his contagious resonance with them.

In the magnificence of the endless universes, in the starry
heavens, we see the quality and depth of God's architecture.
The Body of God is limitless; unending it reaches into realms
and dimensions unfathomable. The awesome majesty and the
unerring perfection reveal beautiful aspects of the nature and
intelligence of the Divine.
Crafted of the Essence of God, its intricacy and the breadth and
depth of its coherence shews the Omnipotence of the Divine.
His themes of opulent grandeur and power, and the
infinitesimal attentions to every perfection. The most sublime
artist and the original genius.
There in the heavens the myriad stars and planets, each held to
the arc of its orbit and turning in faultless synchrony, we see
the everlasting Will of God. It is the Goddess Nuith; the
endless stars reaching out into infinity.

At the mountain's summit he gathers power into his belly. His
thoughts are focused on Truth. He listens to the songs of the

winds, and drinks in the rains. The moon and the sun he nourishes. The fae minister to him as gentle friends. The ancestors whisper to him, revealing all things.

He knows that he is dust and powerless without the Touch of God. He steps aside, sacrificing body and will, that the Universe may better express itself.

He breathes, and pushes the fires up to the head.

He listens, and seeks to discover the True Will of the Soul.

The Magician focuses his attention, and becomes one-pointed. Thereby he resolves every issue, and achieves miraculous results.

His task is neither to teach nor to carry the world, yet he teaches and helps bear the burden.

At first it is more a case of training his conscious mind to be still and to step aside, so that the quiet whispers of the Soul can be heard. This is the Building of the Bridge.

Sit quietly and comfortably. Draw the breath inwards silently. Breathe it out silently. Focus the attention into a point. Close the eyes.

The body and its functions should be quiet. Nothing should be forced. The flames build gently in the pit of the belly. They burn up the debris of accumulated passions and desires.

The ego-mind, which plays on a mindless meaningless loop, must be stilled. How is the ego-mind stilled? By keeping still and focused. By drawing the fires into the pit of the belly and burning up the towers of nonsenses.

How do we hear the whispers of the Soul? By being still.

How do we remain still? By being quiet and comfortable, and focusing the attention on a single point. Staying one-pointed is the objective, and breathing, to fan the flames in the pit of the belly.

Eventually a phoenix will rise from the flames and cross the bridge. One must continue. It doesn't happen overnight or over a weekend. It takes concentrated effort. But, arrival is not the purpose. He creates space, by quietening his mind and listening. He may hear the songs and the pipes. The melodies are simple and sweet, and possess a sublime beauty. When he hears these he knows he is close.

He doesn't heed the thoughts which ego-mind tries to distract him with. He knows they are nonsenses. He allows them without engaging with them. From where do they arise? he asks.

Proof can only come by experience, and without that experience we are left with doubts. Philosophy is helpful but not enough alone. We must experience God to be certain.

Until one achieves the middle there is disturbance. The mind is unsteady and perplexed. The middle means finding good balance.

It is being fixed on one's path. When one attains the middle all doubts cease. That's how we know we are there.

Are we perfectly fitted to the task? Have we have been led to this moment?

Would she not be intimate and close, soft and kind, and bless him with affection, if he should please her? Will she not nurture and support him, and be a sweet and beautiful lover? If, instead of jarring, he embraces the resonance then he is able to experience the bliss of her energy. This power and energy balances him, and allows him to draw nearer to the core. It opens him to new realms of ecstasy and magicks and wisdom.

He journeys deep into the Wilderness. He is still yet blissful. His breathing is easy and quiet because he is in good health. Joy bubbles in his belly and rises to the heart.

The Gods sing the long low horn. What does it portend? He hears the sweet pipes, or the song of birds, a simple beautiful melody. He hears the Smith hammering free the binding links.

The winds are a song. The perfumes of Our Lady are fires that warm him and intoxicate him.

Ah, here he would be content to tarry.

Every movement is a word in his prayer. He lives his life between worlds. As he considers the scriptures of the wise ancestors he draws the fire into his belly. It pushes upward of its own accord into the burning wheel of light. He focuses his prayer, and that is to add his will and his force to the turning. Because the journey is long and far he knows that each step suffices. This means his way is easy and unopposed.

He nourishes himself on the words of the true sages, and lucidity arrives by itself. He does not need efforts, he asks and it is given.

If there is resistance it means he must flow to the correct course, because the way of the Magician has no obstacle. The waters flow over and around rocks and impediments. It is easy. God has his plans, and he does not reveal them directly. He guides slowly and carefully, knowing the moment for each advance.

When at first the Magician is blessed by its presence he feels terror. The weight is heavy and fearful.

The mortal flesh and mind respond with justified anxiety, because the purity of the Divine beauty, if it were not tempered, must mean death. He trains himself to be calm.

If he is to develop a relationship beyond that of a trembling awed slave, then he must recognise his true correspondence to the Goddess, if she chooses to bless him with her presence, or the presence of her Angels.

He may work to be a sanctuary for her, a friend and a lover. Always a servant because she is Divine, but he must know that he is loved, appreciated, admired for his unique talents and character, his strength and courage and skill.

He learns to banish fear and calls to her.

Then she may come as a lover, with kisses and conversations. She touches him and he feels the fires of her in his belly. She confides her dreams and blesses him with certainty. Certainty is a very great treasure.

We begin with broad symbols and draw to the centre. The brilliant core remains. Behold the greater truth. Still it is refined and made purer; the fullness of God.

How does one call the Divine at the core to awaken?
Be still and quiet, and listen until it responds.
The voice of the Soul is like a breezy whisper. If we are not
still and quiet we will not hear the Soul's whispers. What is the
voice of the Soul? It is the Gate to the Golden Bridge that
carries us across the Gulf Between.

There is distance between the Soul and conscious awareness.
The ego-mind is afraid of the silence as it were its own demise.
The function of the ego-mind is distraction. Its ambition is
oblivion. It is a barrier. The ego-mind is impure. It is a babble
of nonsenses. It has no genuine purpose. Thus it attempts to fill
the silence, and obscure the Soul. Who is it that unites with the
Soul, if it is not the conscious mind?
Really there is no ego-mind.

How does one be still so that one can hear the voice of Soul?
By sitting quietly and comfortably, and drawing the breath
silently into the belly. Then one pauses, and exhales silently.
This eases the heart, and the body begins to calm. The mind
begins to quieten.
How does one stop the babble of ego-mind, and the streaming
nonsenses? By asking: Where do they arise from? Do the
thoughts seem important? Are they significant? Do they
have interest? They are intended to distract us away from the
process of being still.
Many of the memories that come unbidden into the conscious
mind are linked with unresolved issues. As the Magician
progresses he will resolve many wounds and scars that he has
borne. The mind will stop attempting to prompt resolutions
when there is nothing left to resolve; this is the work of many
years. The memories that then come unlooked for into the
conscious mind will be of more interest to the Magician.

It is not silence, because we can hear the silent drawing in of
the breath and the silent exhalation. We feel the movement of
our breathing. We are not empty, but filling. We proceed gently.
There is no struggle. The ego-mind is a toxin. We are

detoxifying. We are not aiming for emptiness. The void is empty, yet the Multraverse is full. We aim for fullness. We are not emptying, but instead we are quietening. Before we can fill we first must calm the storm of endless thoughts. Otherwise our focus is scattered and we cannot be one-pointed. Without being one-pointed we cannot pass through the Gateway that leads to the Golden Bridge.

The cessation of the endless stream of thoughts and memories and desires cannot be achieved quickly. It takes constant attention. Yet, it is like a muscle that strengthens with use. With diligent Practice the ego-mind is subdued and grows weaker. But, the ego-mind isn't something real. It has no sapience or awareness of its own.

When the ego-mind trembles with fear at the possibility of being quietened, who is it that trembles? When ego-mind dreads the silence of being still, who is it that dreads?

It cannot be ego-mind, because ego-mind has no sapience or awareness. It is only a mindless loop of nonsenses; it does not experience.

5 Of the Abyss

To still the mind we begin by sitting quietly and comfortably.
It is like a meditation, but it is not a yoga Practice where we
must become a statue, unmoving and suffering so as to
overcome the body's natural inclinations to movement.
The body becomes calm of its own accord, and does not disturb
the meditation. Moreover, the mind is not continually disturbed
and anxious about what the body is doing.
We can turn inward. We gather the breath into the belly. The
breath becomes a golden flame as we draw it in. The flames
burn gently in the cavern of the belly. This is the Practice. Why
should it be complicated? Why would it be difficult? We exhale
quietly.
The breath is drawn in and stokes the flames in the cavern of
the belly. The fires are warm and pleasing. The focus is one-
pointed. The mind and body are calm. This is the Fire-bird
forming. Eventually a phoenix will rise from the flames.
The fires begin to burn up the toxins in the body. They
consume the accumulated debris of nonsenses that plague the
mind. The smokes rise like perfumes and intoxicate. They lift
to the heart.
It is a journey. It is well-mapped, and its destination is certain
if one perseveres.

First there is persevering Practice. The phoenix will not rise
overnight nor over a weekend. The ego-mind will not quit. The
body will resist until the mind becomes calm and undisturbed.
The journey is far. It is to climb a mountain.
Be still. Be comfortable. Exhale, and the fires rise to the heart.
They are warm and pleasing.
It is God we are calling, knowing he values sincerity. With
honesty we could please him and warm him. The barrier is the
mind.
Separation and isolation are due to residing in consciousness,
instead of focusing on an active relationship with the Divine
core.
God lights the fires. It is easy thereafter to fan the flames.

Like the phoenix rising, the heat filling its wings.
Even the mountain summit is not a distance too far.

Breathe in and burn up the cancers.
The golden wheel burnished against the starless warmth of the inner skies. They rise up, up, to the Turning Point, and we add fuel to the flames. It will be phoenix stirring. Feel its wings unfurling, and hear its song softly cry.
The long slow horn is a calling. What does it portend?
Breathe out gently, quietly, be still. Focus on the point, and the chimera world drops away.
When we look upon the deep wide abyss it takes our breath away. So utter its darkness, so cold to the bones like stone its winds. We are a small flame in the vastness. Who can shield us?

The phoenix is fires, and is fed by the fire of our breath.
It is that which climbs to the heart, and as we draw up to the exhalation it spreads its flaming wings. And the fires fall. They gather warm and pure in the heart. Lo! It is the circle.
It rises to the peak, the centre between the eyes, which is the Deepest Turning Inner. Then it falls to the heart. This is the bridge building.
The Song of Flames. The chimera world drops away, and peculiar distractions rise. Where do they arise from?

It is the keeping still. And the Angels traverse the deep to meet us. There is nothing to fear here. We have left darknesses at the threshold of the Gate. Listen for the pipes and the melody.
Hear the songs of the winds. It is the forming of the Fire-bird.
We are training. The flesh strengthens as the mind stills. The heart eases. We draw our focus to a single point and the struggle ceases.
There are no shortcuts and no tricks. It is a climbing of the mountain. There is not reward at the utmost peak, but each step is to triumph.
The breath is the goal. The exhalation and the filling up, the fall to the heart of the flames is the ambition.

The warm interior of colored darkness. Close the eyes. Let the flames carry you. Open the eyes and fix your focus on the path once more.

Make strong the circle. We are purifying.

Now rest in the centre, and sink down into the burning. Be still. Wait for the bubbling joy to lift you. This is the phoenix rising. The breath rises to the centre between the eyes. The phoenix stirs. It is light and burnished fires red and umbers, blues and yellow, the colors of the flames. Still and calm, the heat at our heart, as the circle turns and the flames fall. The phoenix lifts now, our focus one pointed.

It rises up to the heart.

It is the crossing of the wilderness. Listen to the winds lowing across the deserts. Listen for the storm rolling.

Lift it, the current of breath and heat to fill its wings.

Slowly it reaches up to the heart. The heats are gentle, and the distance from the pit of the belly to the heart is short.

The phoenix rises.

The golden wheel turns. Exhale, and lift the flames first to the heart, and then to the space between the eyes. The space between the eyes is called the Deep Turning Within.

You'll need practice but why should that be undue? Don't aim for the final best bit and scramble. Be still. Sit comfortably.

With quiet and concentrated study we utilize our Divine faculties of intuition and intellect. We go deeper into the meaning of cycles and movements, and descry the subtler nuances of pattern and motivation. We learn wisdom, and can predict outcomes and futures. Just as long ago the ancients learned that the spring always followed the darkness of winter. When we harmonise with the True Will and the Will of the Divine we approach the real life. This is how we can come to avoid all mistakes and adhere always to the correct path.

We begin to build a system of coherence.

6 Of The Deep Turning Within

The past is apparent as the cause of the present. We are able to travel backwards in our minds, employing our training in one-pointed focus to hold our concentration. It is similar to stepping outside of the loop of time, and observing the unfolding of events.
The memory is limited consciously, but each thought and each action is nonetheless stored somewhere, perhaps in the deepest vaults of the mind, and it is possible for them to be retrieved. The casual events of each day pass by mostly unnoticed and unregarded.
As a beginning of Practice, we retrace the major incidents of the day. This can be done quickly, in just minutes. We allow the images of the day to form. We watch, apart. Our meditation of course begins imperfectly, but with sincere Practice and dedicated application we improve.
Then let us recall our concentrated thoughts, and our motivations, and how we expended our energies.

It is the task of the Holy Man to make every moment of his life a living meditation and a prayer to the Divine. How does he proceed? By division and separation, by reduction of the work. He works within the confines of the day and the night. He concentrates on the hour, and finally on the moment.
Try to imagine remaining steadfast in prayer for the next twenty years, unmoved by the myriad phenomenal events, without lapsing in concentration and one pointed focus. Is it an impossible task? Yet remaining in concentrated prayer for the next twenty seconds seems easy.

So it is then that we begin to resound like a struck gong.
The sage is not omniscient, but if he is founded in the Reality of the Way, then all things are open to his intellect. He does not have the answer to every question, but if he asks, and searches for the answer, then surely he will find it.
Some matters he receives a clear and direct answer to, like coruscate samadhis; others require deep meditation over a

prolonged period.

The purpose of looking back into the past is to divine its patterns and influence. These are easier to see than the patterns and influence of the present, and certainly easier than those of the future.

We progress by looking beyond the events of today. Let us try to recall in every detail the events of the last week.

Steadfastness and integrity are real magickal powers, and belong only to true holy men and sages.

If we put aside the corporate and cinematic versions of what magick is or isn't, what are we left with?

Eventually the sage or the aspirant to the Holy Magicks of God will observe from outside of the loop of time every day and every moment of his life, winding backwards further into the past. In this he will be led by his own Angel.

We want to see where we have come from in order to see the pattern of our life. What are our motivations? Where are the clear indications that some force outside of ourselves was prompting us and leading us? Where do the signposts point to? What potentials does our journey indicate? Why are we on the path we are on? Where to does it lead?

How have we nourished ourselves and filled our time? What is it that we are meant to be doing?

Many questions such as these will be answered by the Practice. By examining the road we have pursued we may come to know who we are.

The ancients observed the patterns of things, and after deep contemplation, they drew conclusions. Their work remains true because they had actualised the Divine spirit which resides at the core. God's truth is eternal and unchanging, it is only Man's comprehension of it that evolves and changes.

*

Dele

i Of the thraldom

An adult deer would keep a family of four in quality meats for several months, maybe even a year. If a man were able to hunt he could take care of one of his family's most basic and essential needs with just a couple of weekend hunts. Small game and such would add variety throughout the year.

It would immediately transform our lives, and release us from financial stresses and pressures, if tomorrow we could hunt our own meat. If the family is already feasting on prime cuts of venison, selling our labor will be much less of a priority.

And if the man should be able to build a little house somewhere for himself and his family, and perhaps to pass on to his descendants, then his concerns would have become very much fewer.

If the small piece of land was his birthright, as a generational native descended from the soil, then he and his wife would not be forced into fifty years labor each slaving for the Man, just to keep up with mortgage payments. Nor would they have to run an expensive motorcar, because the work force must be mobile, or pay huge taxes, insurance, or to spend a small fortune on petrol.

If they kept horses instead none of that expense would be necessary. Horses eat hay and apples, and provide excellent fertilizers for the vegetable and flower gardens. A horse has an added advantage in that it is a living creature, not cold chrome. Cars, lorries and trains would serve for loads and distance.

He needs to gather materials for fuel and heat; or he may have a gas or electricity supply. He and his family might grow vegetables and fruit, and perhaps they will trade with neighbours. They might keep a goat, a cow, or pigs.

Is it such a strange idea? Would it really be so very difficult to make it work? What does a man and his family need other than luxuries, once he has a small piece of land to grow food on, to build a modest home, and to keep his own animals? He thereby provides the bulk of his own food.

Under such conditions as described he would be free to pursue his natural life, and his unique rasa with the universe. His work would be under the direction of his will, apparent from his talents and interests.

Without the burden of unnatural expenses we find that our needs are not so great. Our most basic requirements for meat, clothes, shelter, and warmth should not and need not be something we have to earn by giving up all of our time. If we were left unmolested we could take care of all those needs quite easily ourselves. After fifty years of slaving for the Corporation many people don't even own the roof over their heads or the car they drive, and without that regular income they cannot survive.

If we can provide for the basic needs ourselves we are no longer slaves to inferior minds and their criminal systems of extortion, and our time and our labor would become extremely valuable.

We would be in control of our own lives, and would not be forced to work at menial or industrial or tedious or bureaucratic or Soul destroying jobs. When and if we chose to do so, we would be well compensated for our labor, and the money thus earnt could be spent on luxuries.

Perhaps we don't really need the system of commerce which we have been bound to for so long? Yet the forests have been whittled away, and wild beasts and game are scarce, so that we are now dependant upon our artificially produced foods.

We were led into the trap, enticed by promise of feast and repose, and now we are snared. Our forefathers were deceived and violently coerced into submission to the state.

The universe does not intend for Humanity to be the slaves of commerce, nor to be forever forced to toil night and day simply to survive. The universe intends that Mankind evolves beyond juvenile ego-mind philosophies and beyond brute survival.

It is only by force that Man can be kept enslaved to unnatural behaviours. The modern mind is shaped to crave entertainment and stimulation. The ego-mind is exalted, and the real Self denied. Yet, unless he is forcibly held in his bondage, Man will rise, because his natural inclinations are towards Truth and Harmony. The Black Hats have to work 24/7 to keep him down.

ii Of the atheist philosophy

The atheist suggests that in nothing nowhere, where nothing at all existed or was, some gasses formed, congregated, and caused an explosion: the 'big bang.' This explosion was the catalyst for the formation of the perfect Multraverse. Fine. But, they go further, and postulate that the explosion *proves* that there is no God.

When 'Science' and Physics claim broad theory as facts, we should be cautious. The conclusions they have drawn from this limited information are unsound; it has *zero* bearing on whether or not the Divine exists.

If nothing at all existed then there could be no void and no space. There must be dimension to contain void; it has to be somewhere. 'Gasses' are some thing, because they have a corporeal manifestation. Gasses could not arise in no where from no thing. There would have been no space for them to form and exist. Instead reason must suggest that the gasses would have arisen somewhere and from something. It is an absurdity otherwise.

We can agree that there was a finite moment, and an explosion of intensity, and that the explosion served as a catalyst for the expansion of the universes. Perhaps we can agree that these points have been verified as true, so far as we can tell from a distance of millions of years.

Let us consider the most simple form of the atheists' argument, and in doing so we by-pass the sophisms that usually shroud it. Thus is their argument: there was once an explosion, before or at the beginning of the formation of the universes. Therefore there is no Divinity and no meaning. Everything is chaos and chance. There are no consequences and no Soul. Only ego-mind has value.

That is always the core argument of the atheist, regardless of the emotional or clique language it will be presented in: that there is no Divinity, no Soul, no meaning. It is all blind chance. Ego-mind, and the individual whims of ego-mind, are the absolute truth. There are no consequences. It is a philosophy of the insane.

The conclusion they have drawn does not collate with the available data. It is not a logical or justified continuation. Really, the huge movement of the explosion would seem to *suggest* purpose and intension rather than to refute it.

The sophist argument typically uses big impressive images, all very clevery and stuff, dazzling in their awesome scope, and then like the conjurer's sleight of hand, whilst the audience is distracted, the sophist makes unjustified leaps in his conclusion. He relies upon *emotional imagery*, not logic, to *win* his argument.

Let us simplify the atheist argument again, so as to be certain: there was an explosion, thus God does not exist.

There was an explosion. Logic concludes: it came from some where, maybe some mind, and its purpose seems to have been to ignite the momentum of the Multraverse, so that all the universes might be formed. There is meaning in the small amount of information that we have about this event; the explosion was a catalyst, and it resulted in the forming of all the universes. It resulted in the manifestation of life and intelligence.

There is no evidence of chaos and meaninglessness.

iii The Holy Qabalah

In number we see every pattern and scheme. We view God's handiworks directly, and we see his working notes. Despite the brilliance of mathematics, extending into geometry and physics, it is merely a collection of symbols.

As Aleister Crowley once remarked 'simply arranging the letters C A and T in that order does not create a cat.'

We can not confine ourselves to a single field of study without being drawn into error. Number is dazzling and endlessly intriguing, but we must always be concerned to balance our views. The universe is deep and wide, and abears many wonders.

The Magician must have eyes to see that God is equally present within each raindrop and every simple pebble, as he is present within the grandest and most abstruse equations of physics and mathematics.

The Magician would do well to put aside his pursuit of enigmatic equations for a time, if such is his ardent occupation, until he fully comprehends the truth of the absurdity.

He cannot afford to ignore these divers realities if he is come to a comprehensive and coherent universe of his own. His tendency will be to reside amongst his preferences. The areas holding less personal appeal for him are naturally neglected. He may become unbalanced, top heavy, concentrating all his energies in one narrow area.

The danger with the Qabalah is that one becomes so awed and overwhelmed by the intricacies and the subtleties that one believes the thing itself to be Divine. Eventually a narrow study of physics and math lead to the conclusion that God is unnecessary, and that using the systems of number is sufficient for the man to create the Multraverse in his own image. One becomes blinkered without a perpetual shifting and expansion of horizons. The remedy is in an equally thorough study of raindrops and pebbles. Until we see God in the same way that he is revealed in the turning galaxies and in the pure perfection of every pattern.

iv **The Threshold**

The Gods of the Temple of the Soul

1 Phra : *Sovereign Lord of the sky. The Creator.*

2 Khepera : *The creator of the Gods. The God Mind that willed to manifest.*

3 Dana : *The Divine Waters. The All-Mother.*

4 Belay : *The Great Tree which arose from the seed, nourished by the light of the sun, and the Divine waters.*

5 Nuith : *The Great Goddess, the manifested universe, the endless stars reaching to infinity. The Sky Goddess.*

6 Nut : *The Goddess whose symbol is the Moon. The night sky. The azure lidded stooping starlight. The manifesting of the Sky-Goddess as the Lovely Star.*

7 Nau : *The God of the day sky. He who was the inactive seeds.*

8 Maat : *Truth and Justice personified. Daughter of the sun. Queen of the Gods. The wisdom of Khepera.*

9 Ra : *The Lord of Heaven. The Sun God.*

10 Isis : *The Great and Terrible Goddess. Evil comes to any who set themselves against her. The Magician.*

11 Osiris : *Lord of the Land of the Dead. Elder son of Nuith.*

12 Thoth : *God of wisdom and magick. The Scribe of the Gods. Divine Intelligence personified. The Messenger.*

13 Urchn : *The Great Goddess. Keeper of secret tradition.*

14 Apep : *The serpent-devil, darkness. Mist, storm, night.*

15 Pan : *All-begetter. The Great Goat God.*

16 Ptah : *The God Mind. The Opener. The Bull.*

17 Atum : *The first God. The origin of Mankind.*

18 Horus : *The hawk-headed God. Son of Isis and Osiris. The avenger.*

19 Nefytiti : *Daughter of Nuith and the Earth-God. Sister of Isis, Osiris, and Seth.*

20 Hathor : *The celestial cow. Goddess of love and joy. The wife of Horus.*

21 Kerynos : *Lord of the Wild Places. King of the Horns. The Hunter.*

22 Pe Nekhen : *Watchful ancestors of a living prince.*

23 Lug : *Lord of the Earth. Celtic God of magick and sunlight.*

24 Bran : *Eld God of England. Lord of Warriors. The Sword.*

25 Adraste : *Goddess of war in ancient Britain.*

26 Astarte : *Goddess of fields of battle. Athene, Ishtar, Astoreth, the Huntress.*

27 Tryl : *Queen of the water faerae.*

28 Sebek : *The crocodile-headed God who arose from chaos to impose order.*

29 Amenhotep : *Master of the Holy Word, and the sacred rites.*

30 Shu : *The God who is emptiness, air, and breath.*

31 Ihe : *Son of Hathor and Horus. He who strums the sistrum.*

32 Borvo : *The Gallic God of fellowship, joyful laughter, and magickal waters.*

33 Rkken : *God of the Gateway. The Lord of desolation and madness.*

34 Sya : *The Seeing Mind. He who cleanses the lens.*

35 Tauret : *The hippopotamus Goddess of maternity and childbirth.*

36 Ta-Bitjet : *A scorpion Goddess who can counter the effects of poison.*

37 Serket : *A scorpion Goddess who may cure constrictions of the throat.*

38 Nanna : *The God of Destiny. The Moon-God of Ur.*

39 Thanatos : *The son of night, and the brother of sleep.*

40 Kauket : *The feminine force which was within the dark waters, the primaeval matter, before the sun arose.*

41 Menat : *The necklace of Hathor.*

42 Seth : *The God who slew his brother, Osiris. The husband of Nefytiti.*

43 Hor-Nubti : *Horus, the vanquisher of evil.*

44 Bennu : *The sacred bird, whose hieroglyph is a heron-like bird. It appears once in five hundred years.*
Associated with the phoenix because of its power to regenerate. He who guides the Gods.
Keeper of the Volume of the Book of Things. He who presides over the arrangement of things.

45 Nebthet : *Goddess of the Gates inbetween, the fruitful or the barren.*

46 Seshesta : *The Goddess of letters and writing, and history. Mistress of the House of Books.*

47 Anpu, Anubis : *The jackal-headed God who weighs the hearts of the dead. Lord of the Underworld. As Anpu he leads Souls to the land of the dead.*

48 Menthu : *The God of war.*

49 Bastet : *The Goddess of music and dance, with the head of a cat. Protects from contagious disease.*

50 Upuhaut : *A wolf-headed God. He stands at the labyrinth's centre, to lead pilgrims through the door.*

51 Oursir : *God of nature. An aspect of Osiris as God of the dead.*

52 Tayet : *A Goddess who presides over the rites of the dead. She who binds Souls in death.*

53 Qadesh : *The Goddess of sacred ecstasy and sexual pleasure.*

54 Zoti : *The secret name of God. The wishing star.*

55 Mehen : *The coiled serpent. The shield and sword of Ra.*

56 Apedamak : *The lion God of combat.*

57 Bat : *The Goddess whose voice is the magick of music.*

58 Sekhmet : *The lioness Goddess of terrible war.*

59 Anhur : *The creative power of the sun. The one who found the eye.*

60 Hor-Merti : *The sun and moon, the eyes of Horus.*

61 Tir : *God of oracles, wisdom and writing.*

62 Zaltys : *The envoy of the Gods.*

63 Taranis : *Gallic God of Wyrd and Doom.*

64 Giltine : *A death Goddess.*

65 Petbe : *The God of Retaliation, who calls Souls to account.*

66 Tezcatlipoca : *He who is the smoking mirror. The avenger of misdeeds. God of warriors.*

67 Maruts : *The seven storm Gods in Hinduism.*

68 Attar : *A God of battle and war.*

69 Epona : *A horse Goddess.*

70 Min : *A God of fertility and harvest. His hieroglyph is the erect phallus.*

71 Renpet : *The Goddess of spring, and the seasons.*

72 Taa-Dhenet : *The mountain peak. The snake Goddess, Merseger.*

73 Djehuti : *The Magician. Thrice Great. The divider of time.*

The Lord of Holy Words.

74 Khensu : *The Navigator. The moon-God who can incarnate his own double.*

75 Apis : *The God with the head of a bull. He gives strength and vitality to the Chief of the Works.*

76 Meeyuty : *A God with a cat's head. He stands at a gate of the Underworld.*

77 Meskhemet : *A Goddess of childbirth.*

78 Henet : *The pelican Goddess who guides Souls in the afterlife.*

79 Sah : *Orion, the constellation.*

80 Nab-Ta-Djeser : *Anubis, Lord of the sacred land.*

81 Albiorix : *Gallic God. King of the World.*

82 Elagabal : *Lord of the Mountains.*

83 Thokk : *A giantess, sworn to the Law of the Gods.*

84 Woden : *The God of wode and wrath.*

85 Klaktal : *The Fire Goddess. Queen of the elements.*

86 Jak : *He who sits at the back smoking. The Crossroad.*

87 Grym : *He who carries them across the bridge.*

88 Mind-Eater : *An Eld God who devours the reason of the envious.*

89 Woyo : *A God of earthquakes and storms, of destruction and ruin.*

90 Heya : *God of change and transforming.*

91 Hermes : *God of wisdom and magick. Thrice Great. The Messenger.*

92 Aelinor : *The bright shining God.*

93 Ra-Sa : *Combined force. The Great Shining God of Power.*

94 Ermr : *A horse God of perdurance. One who carries the Soul through the aethers.*

95 Eternt : *An English God who binds fools.*

96 Grindor : *The God who eats bones.*

97 Saboath : *The Firmament and the Beyond.*

98 Belkis : *The queen of Sheba, or Saba.*

99 Puc : *A nature spirit, or daemon. Faerae prince, or pixie of the forest.*

100 Startli : *A faery who works with satori and visions.*

101 Aola : *A faery spirit of light and clarity. The Lighthouse.*

102 Hru : *The God who rules over oracles and hieroglyphs.*
103 Pnch : *The whirling point. The sparking impulse.*
104 Tatunen : *The One-pointed. Creator of mankind.*
105 Ka : *The image, or the life force.*
106 Taa-Her-Seta-Nef : *One who draws the world in his train.*
That which is, and that which is not yet.
107 Osiris-Un-Nefer : *God of the Abyss. He who endures*
forever. The King of Kings.
108 Seker : *The night sun.*
109 Akert : *Ta-Sert, Nater-Khert, Tuat. The Underworld.*
110 Seket-Aru : *The Fields of Reeds.*
111 Heru-Ur : *The Eld God. Horus, the Hawk.*

The Gods at the Bridge of Inbetweens

1 Elsewyr : *The staccato realms of the astrals.*

2 Tefnut : *The first daughter of God Mind. The personification of moisture, waters; the rain. Her brother is Shu, the air. From their union Nuith and the Earth were born.*

3 Neb-Er-Tcher : *Lord to the Uttermost. The everlasting God. The original genius who embodies the Way. The great serpent who coils about the universes.*

4 Laying the foundation in the heart : *Will, thought, word.*

5 Ausares : *The essence of the primaeval matter.*

6 The Lady : *She who is light amid darknesses.*

7 Khonsu : *He who driveth back all who oppose him.*

8 Seab : *Lord and Protector of the Earth. He who gives cool waters.*

9 Seta : *The serpent with human legs, who is reborn each day.*

10 Sut : *Son of Nut.*

11 Tet : *The four pillars of Osiris. The four quarters of the universe.*

12 Shenet : *A class of Divine beings.*

13 Heru-Pa-Khrat : *Harpocrates, or Horus the Child.*

14 House of Hearts : *The judgement hall of Osiris.*

15 Ur-Heka : *Mighty one of enchantments.*

16 Khent-En-Maa : *Horus as Lord of the Dead.*

17 Matchet : *The Oppressor.*

18 Nehebka : *A serpent Goddess.*

19 Suti : *Devourer Foreverlasting. The dweller in the fiery lake of Unt. Guardian of the Bight of Amenta. The Lord of Terror.*

20 Night Mare : *The Horse Goddess who rides through the dreams of the damned.*

21 Uatchit : *The eye of Ra. The Lady of Flame.*

22 Sekhet-Hra-Asht-Aru : *Reversed of face, of many forms.*

23 Meti-Heh : *The Watcher at the Gate.*

24 Ha-Kheru : *The herald. The voice that travelleth to the ends of the multiverse.*

25 She-Maat : *The pool of Double Truth.*

26 Hu Sa : *The two drops of Ra's blood.*

27 Hetep-Se-Khus : *The flame Goddess, who burns up the enemies of Osiris.*

28 Maau : *Ra in the form of a male cat.*

29 Pillars of Shu : *The aethers.*

30 An-A-F : *The God that bringeth his arm.*

31 Temu : *The sun that sets in beauty.*

32 Rehu : *A lion God.*

33 Paut Neteru : *The self-created. The Essence.*

34 Heh : *The All-Begetter. God Everlasting. Traverser of Forever.*

35 Uatch-Uia : *The Great Green Water.*

36 Aat Abtu : *The district of Abydos.*

37 Seven Shining Ones : *Mestha, Hapi, Tuamuatef, Qebhsennuf, Maa-Atet-F, Kheri-Beq-F, Heru-Khent-Maati.*

38 Khenti-heh-F : *He dwelleth in his flame.*

39 Ami-Unnt-F : *He who is in his hour.*

40 Tesher-Maa L *Red of both eyes.*

41 Bes-Maa-Em-Kerb : *Flame seeing in the night.*

42 An-Em-Hru : *Bringing by day.*

43 Amam : *The Devourer.*

44 Ammit : *Eater of the dead.*

45 Mesxet : *Opening of the mouth of the dead.*

46 Re-Stau : *The door of the Passages of the Tomb.*

47 Kautelles: *Casting up the earth, digging the grave.*

48 Coroune : *Great Chief of the Work. The priest of Ptah.*

49 Shai : *Destiny or luck.*

50 Ubes-Hra-Per-Em : *Blazing face coming forth, going back.*

51 Sa-Res-Kra : *Making to lift up his face.*

52 Aaa : *The Great One.*

53 Khesef-At : *He who repulses the crocodile.*

54 Bahomet : *A secret name of God.*

55 Maa-Kheru : *The Word.*

56 Artemis : *The Huntress.*

57 Antenda : *(Sanskrit) The serpent which is coiled about the universe.*

58 Amit : *The beautiful one.*

The Altar of Radiance

1 Phra : *the Great God who manifested.*
2 Pan : *the Force.*
3 Kerynos : *God of the Wild Places. Centaur.*
3 Umi : *the small voice of the Soul.*
4 Pf : *the Dragon God.*
5 Urchin : *the Great Goddess of ancient Briton.*
6 Ther-Ado : *Gods of the Noble Path.*
7 Rmor : *the Horse Goddess.*
8 Har-Tryl : *the Goddess of springs and the Waters of Life.*
9 Lu-Ity : *the Ancient God of Forever.*
10 Twayn : *the Herald of the celestial Beings.*
11 Hy : *the Force of cataclysmic destruction and desolations.*
12 Kal-Jac : *the Fire God of Elementals.*
13 Borv : *the God of Good Waters.*
14 Hor-Nubutay : *the Avenger of Wrongs, the Vanquisher of Evil.*
15 Bst-Ihi : *the Magickal Voice of the Soul.*
16 Sehsta : *the Goddess who is the Scribe of the Gods.*
17 Upaut : *the God who guides the dead through the First Gates.*
18 Dhty : *the Great One of Magick and Genius.*
19 Maat : *the Goddess of Sooth. The Heart of Divine Intelligence.*
20 Sa : *the Seeing Mind of God.*
21 Kauket : *the crocodile Goddess, who arises from the void.*
22 Astart : *the Goddess who leads her followers into battle.*
23 Nueetay : *the Sky Goddess.*
24 Bra-Ra : *the ancient God of light and laughter.*
25 Blind Crow : *the Crow Goddess of the Gypsies.*
26 sati : *threshold.*
27 sam : *to show kindness.*
28 san : *to be kind, to do good, to benefit, nourish. Clay.*
29 sas : *six, sixth.*
30 saa : *to magnify.*
31 sab : *to wash, purify, cleanse.*
32 samiu : *eaters, devourers.*

33 sart : *approach, introduction.*

34 sba : *star. Star-God.*

35 sbaiu : *stars.*

36 sbau : *door, gate, pylon. The forms.*

37 Sebek : *the crocodile God, who was a form of the Sun God.*

38 sefekh : *seven.*

39 smaa : *to pay what is due, make an offering.*

40 smenkh : *to repair, re-establish, beautify, make perfect.*

41 smet : *to listen. Woven with, or shot with (cloth).*

42 smetru : *to investigate, search out, find the truth.*

43 sen : *two. Equal, likeness.*

44 Senseneb : *the Mother of the Sky God, Nau.*

45 senesh : *to unbolt, unbar, open.*

46 Serqet : *the Scorpion Goddess.*

47 sekha : *to have in mind, to commemorate, to remember.*
remembrance for good.

48 Sehetch-Ur : *the Great Light, the Sun God.*

49 sekheper : *to make to become, to create, fashion, form.*

50 sekhem : *to forget, forgetfulness. To recite, to read. natural*
power of a man.

51 Sekhmet-Bast-Ra : *a Solar Triad.*

52 Sekhet-Aanru : *the Fields of Reeds, Heaven. The Elysian*
Fields.

53 Swqish : *a Goddess of Doom and Wyrd.*

54 sesh : *to write, draw, copy, make a plan. Scribe, copyist.*

55 seshem : *guide, leader.*

56 Seshemit : *Conductress, the name of a Goddess.*

57 Seshem : *a Divine image, statue.*

58 Sesheta : *the Goddess od architecture.*

59 sesheta : *to be hidden, mysterious, incomprehensible.*
Hidden, secret things.

60 Seker : *the Ancient God of the Beyond.*

61 sekert : *silence.*

62 setut : *arrows or beams of light, rays. To symbolize, typify.*

63 setcheb : *to oppose, be in the way of, obstruct.*

64 setcher : *to lie down in sleep or death.*

65 setcheser : *to sanctify.*

v Miscellaneous

If we put aside all delusion, what would remain but Reality?

The first responsibility of the Master is to abear the Souls of his
disciples. But, his role is more than just carrying the burdens.
He is a Bridge, and he is a Key. He transfers his light through
the eyes, through touch, and breath.
He leads his true sons out into the desert.

The concentration, without which nothing is possible, must be
continually sharpened.
At first, practising the *Phoenix*, one misses the point of it. One
does not realise its Divine secret. Only with continued Practice
does cognition finally and suddenly like a samadhi come.

The journey is every day of one's life. Arrival is called death.
Try to relax and let go of all the desires and frustrations which
fill your heart. You cannot take them across the Bridge with
you. The Gate will remain locked if your heart is not emptied
of petty ambitions and greeds. The heart must be filled with
love of Truth; *that* is the beginning of wisdom.

The weak despise the strong, because the weak are incapable of
being strong. The man of iniquity despises the righteous man,
because the man of iniquity is incapable of righteousness. Yet
the man who is strong and righteous is indifferent to men of
weakness and iniquity. They are as meaningless as a pebble
falling through the void.

We must acquire an attitude of rational calm.
The future is not real, it is just an idea in ego-mind. This
present moment is what is real. Each day is sufficient with its
own griefs, and its own joys.

The entire efficacy of the Magician's magicks relies upon his
determination to actualise, to make real, the true will of his
Soul.

The true pilgrim soon finds himself isolated and alone. Who can he trust in? Should he be responsible for all the stragglers, should he carry them upon his back? Should he encourage and help the genuine but misguided seekers? Where is his responsibility?

He finds the route, and braves every obstacle alone, determined and persevering. He reaches the summit, and meets God.

What better way could he have aided every man?

vi **The Magickal Affirmation**

Let the Magician enter into his temple, and prostrate himself before the Altar of the Living God. Let him then pray to the Tao. And his prayer shall be his Perfumes and Incense, and his adorations shall be his Priestly Vestments, and his Ablutions shall be the fervour of his heart, and his flesh and blood will be the Sacrifice.

Let him pray to the sky, to the Universe, the Great Source of Love and Light. Let him call upon the Angels to keep him and bless him, and lead him on his true destined path.

Then shalt he turn inward and listen. In silence now his prayer. He continues in silence, his ardour pure and his heart shining. His prayer is turning inward, across the chasm.

Each day he shall come again to the altar, for no less than eight days. In the evetyde of each day he will come once more to the temple. He will thoroughly clean the temple room, and burn such incenses as will benefit him.

He shall kneel at the Altar, and give thanks to the Universe for his every blessing. The Magician wilt begin to make aloud a full and complete confession of his life, omitting no detail. When he has exhausted himself, he should bathe, and retire to his bed. And this Practice he should perform each evening, for the space of at least two hours, and for no less than eight days.

Turning inward with his prayer, let him listen. Until he catches the sound of the low winds stirring. Until he hears the galloping Gods. Until he feels the softest breeze of the celestial kiss. Until he weeps for the beauty, and trembles for the bliss. The song of his heart shining, he is turning inward, and his silence calls.

He shall persevere. For eight days, no less. His prayer be true and sincere. This is the mirror, and he is unadorned. He shall listen. Until he hears.

Then shall he know his own heart, and declare his motivations. Let him make his Magickal Affirmation.

If he is True, and chosen for the Work, and this path of holiness, then his Word shall be upon his lips, as it were, unbidden. It is an Angel's kiss.

Then shall he come again to the Altar each day for no less than eight days, and give thanks to his Angel.

Now is his Affirmation wrought. Yea, now is his Affirmation wrought.

vii The White Gate

The White Gate is a purifying Practice.
We turn inward. Our breath is a flame, and its heat warms us.
The prayer is silent, or whispered. We are quiet and still. We
are calm and comfortable.
We are travelling a well trodden path. It leads to a centre. Take
note of the landscape as you travel inward. The interior events
are idioscycratic, but not random.
Pass beyond the endless streaming of nonsenses which arise
into the conscious mind. Nothing the ego-mind has to say is
important enough to listen to. We must have a sharp
concentration, and endure calmly.
There are banks of color. We pass over and through these.
There are flights and falls. We do not rest in the exhilaration.
There are climbs, and there are what seem to be tides sweeping
us along. We can follow the tides. The journey is far. We spin
and rise, and turn and fall. There are hills and valleys. There is
darkness and light. After persevering we begin to recognise the
route.
It is beautiful, but we are not here to admire. We can reflect
upon beauty at the correct time, when we have finished our
Practice.
Once we comprehend the patterns of our journey, we can look
for them; we recognise the signposts. We are travelling through
an interior landscape. We aim for the centre.
At the core there is a Garden. It is small, and fenced. It has a
white gate. Go through the gate. Here is a bath of holy waters.
the Pulse. We are all the universes turning in perfect synchrony.
The Macrocosm. The Body of God. There is no separation.
We are infinitesimal. We are a tiny being in the vastness of All.
The microcosm.

This method is called the *Phoenix Method,* or the *Fire-bird.*
If we already have some experience of various yogas we can
probably sit comfortably, more or less, for half an hour or so.
For daily Practice we should have a comfortable armchair,
placed near an open window. If you don't have an armchair, a
cushion on the floor is fine. The point is to be comfortable.
If we have a beautiful cathedral to perform our Practice in so
much the better, but most people will be working with their
home space. We dedicate this space to our Practice. We clean
it, remove all unnecessary clutter. Perhaps burn incense to
purify the atmosphere. We make it a sanctified and holy place.
We pray, and ask that this be a blessed place wherein we can
work undisturbed. We might put flowers on the window ledge
as an altar, if we are inclined, or perhaps small offerings of
food. Well placed and meaningful adornments can be
conducive to the states of mind we are working for.
When we are beginning Practice, it is good to make a routine
to keep us on track. It is useful to delineate clearly at that stage.
We might perform the Practice always at certain times during
the day; an hour in the morning, an hour in the evening.
The reason behind of all this is to make the mind at ease for the
Practice. The mind turns into gear once rhythm has been
established. It knows what is expected in this place, and
Practice becomes easier.
It is a space wherein we can do our Holy Work, and we should
approach it with reverence, as before the Altar of God.
If we are to make such good preparations our labors can only
prosper.
Now we are ready to begin the preliminary Practice.
Sit comfortably, perhaps with your legs crossed, and your
wrists resting on your knees or the arms of the chair.
Breathe deeply, exhaling impurities, until the body eases and
begins to quieten.
When the breath is silent, focus the attention on a single point.
Inhale deeply into the belly, about an inch or so below the
navel. Pause, then exhale. Pause, then inhale. This simple

rhythm will calm our body and mind.

Exhale the impurities, the toxins, and the debris of the nonsenses. So we purify and make holy the place, and our body, and our mind. Continue this preliminary Practice every morning and each evening for at least eight days. The duration of each should be between half an hour and an hour.

After eight days have passed without our Practice being uninterrupted, morning and evening, then we can be said to have completed the Preliminary Practice. Now we continue, using what we have learnt from the Preliminary Practice. Clean and purify the temple; this concentrates the mind, and instructs it.

We pray earnestly, supplicating the Universe to bless our efforts, and to draw us close. We ask to be fortified and strengthened for the Work. Ask that the Angels of God be with us, to lift and guide us, to teach us the truth of the Way's Absolute Reality.

The aspirant should learn to pray, using this as a rough guide. He should speak from his heart when addressing the Gods, in his own words, in his native tongue, or a language that he fully commands.

Does the idea of prayer jarr?

We shall extend our prayer, within this theme, for so long as it remains sharp and sincere. This prayer should not be internal and silent, but spoken aloud. It is okay to speak the words quietly, or even to whisper, but it must be audible rather than confined to the realm of thoughts.

The aspirant should proceed with the same schedule for his Practice as in the first eight days, being at the temple for between half an hour and an hour each morning and evening. The aspirant should repeat an approximation of the prayer each morning, prior to his routine Practice. He must continue this for at least eight consecutive days, praying always with earnest sincerity, *to build a rapport with the celestial beings*.

ix **All is Sorrow**

We are each of us isolated and separated, not only from God our maker, but also we are remote from all beings in our universe. This inherent isolation is the cause of the great sorrow which afflicts the sensitive Soul.

The Buddha emphasised this solitude, the imprisonment within our fleshy bodies, and declared it the First Noble Truth: that everything is sorrow.

The Buddha offers as the solution to our sorrow and isolation the complete dissolution of self by absorption into the Infinite, which is Nirvana. He postulates that the only reasonable end to what he considers to be the endless cycle of birth and death is the annihilation of the self, the personality, and the ego-mind. Only through cessation can we escape the overwhelming sorrow of existence.

Much of Buddhism is very useful and helpful as a mystical system, but this attitude is extremely pessimistic. It is a cosmic-level suicide. Should we say that because the corporeal life is often difficult and painful it is better to kill ourselves at the earliest opportunity? The Buddha suggests exactly that solution for the cosmic-life.

During a lifetime men accumulate karma. Karma is the consequence of all his thoughts and deeds; every act is a magickal act; so far we agree. It is the consequences of his misdeeds and misthoughts that entrap a man, the Buddha postulates, and the accumulating karma is carried over from one life to the next. It may be thousands of lifetimes before we can be clear of the karma we have gathered.

Alongside this 'karmic debt' is punishment, and the idea that we may be reborn into hells, or in the form of animals, insects, or even plants and trees. In an extreme case we might be reincarnated as a book, or a teacup!

The truth is that any sort of rebirth is in no way guaranteed or automatic.

Often, or perhaps always, God's truth has been revealed only partially. It is the truth appropriate for the period and the especial climate for which it is intended.

Considering everything is sorrow is a truth, and it is a step along the road to the absolute truth of the Way. It is very far from being the end of things. It is a negative, glass half empty attitude.

Buddhists can expect to find Nirvana when they die, if they live a life of sincere devotion to the Buddha's principles and guidelines. Having worked so hard for annihilation it would be churlish of the universe not to grant their desire.

The conception of sorrow and suffering, and the ignorance wherefrom that suffering is said to arise, are all functions of the ego-mind. In reality, longing to be freed from the cycle of birth and death is itself a desire arising from the ignorance of ego-mind or the shadow mind, and the misinterpretation of phenomena, and the failure to properly comprehend the Divine.

His view of the universe was agnostic. He considered the Universal Force to be without personality or identity, and thus without morals. and implacable. Life was, in the view of the Buddha, simply a set of unfortunate circumstances we found ourselves in.

His foundation stones were askew, and everything built upon them was inevitably awry.

The basis of the ideology is that to exist is to suffer, and thus the aim of the sapient being must be to cease to exist.

The misconception persists for the Buddha because he has concluded that the universe is amoral, without pity or mercy or love. That it is all a terrible loop thrown up by utter chance, and we are caught up in a sequence of events that is not only torturous and endless, but there is no one and nothing that we might appeal to for relief. At last, exhausted, we surrender to the oblivion gratefully.

The premise is unsound.

As we draw closer to the Divine, eventually we arrive at the opposite conclusion: that existence is pure bliss.

The first foundation stone must always be that God created the universes, and all things. This premise is sooth. There are many ways we can take wrong turns, and a myriad false conclusions we still might draw, but recognising the reality of God Mind anchors us there. We always have the option of doubling back and retracing our steps, and of reconstructing our concepts, beginning with that truth.

Sick and broken Souls, rather than having hundreds of thousands of years to get things correct, have only a single lifetime to prove themselves. Now we see how vital and precious that life is, how fleeting the opportunity.

There are no punishments other than those found in life, but unsuccessful Souls are returned to the Source, and broken down to their pure elements, which are reconstituted.

This is perfect Divine justice.

x The Master and the Disciple

There was once a Master who patiently taught his students.
One student showed a lot of promise, and the Master took him
to his heart and loved him like his own son.
One day the favored student came to the Master and prostrated
himself before him. 'Master, how may I serve you? All your
other students toil in the fields yet I sit idly beside you.'
'I am content with you here,' the Master replied. 'You are my
favorite son, why should I send you to toil in the fields when I
delight in your being near to me? Serve me by indulging an old
man with your company.'
The student was pleased, but he said: 'Master, it is wrong that I
should be exempt from this work. The other students will begin
to despise me.'
'But I shall continue to love you,' replied the Master.
The student remained by his Master. After a year had passed he
prostrated himself before the Master. He asked once again that
he may be allowed to toil besides his brothers in the fields, so
that they would not be jealous of his position.
The Master sighed. 'This past year has been joyous for me. You
have made an old man happy. Is that not enough for you? Very
well, I will allow you to work, since that is your desire. Go out,
and build a house for me, so that I can spend my last days there
in comfort.'
The student was delighted with his task, and eagerly set to
work. He labored unceasingly and built for his Master a fine
home. When it was complete he returned to the Master. The old
man smiled broadly, and went to view the house.
'What is this ramshackle hut you have spent six months
building?'
the Master asked indignantly. The student was ashamed. 'Tear it
down and begin again. This time do it properly, and build me a
home that is fit for your beloved Master.'
The favored student tore down the house that he had spent six
months working on. He began a new house for his Master. This
new house he built with even greater care and attention. It was
a thing of beauty.

After a year of hard work he finally returned to the Master. He was nervous when the Master rose unsmiling, and went to see his proposed new home.

'I am not a woman!' the Master said when he saw the house. 'Tear it down and begin again, or I shall think you are trying to insult me.'

The student was devastated. Confused and weeping, he dismantled the building, and began again.

After one year he had built a beautiful and practical home for his Master. He had taken care to avoid ostentatiousness and frivolity. He was scared to show his work to the Master, but he went before him and prostrated himself. The old man did not even look at his once favored student.

'You who despise me,' the Master said, 'you who would build me a woman's boudoir, to mock me. What new insult have you prepared?

I will not look upon it, or else the last drop of love that I hold in my heart for you may be snuffed out. I require just a simple shack, with a roof and a cot. Is that asking too much?'

The student did as the Master commanded, but he was very distressed. All he wanted had been to please the old man, but everything had gone wrong. He felt that a curse must be upon him. More than anything he wanted his Master to love him as once he had. He set to work and built the shack that his Master had asked for.

When the work was completed the Master came to view it. He was furious. He turned his back on the student and stalked away.

The student was distraught. 'I have failed my Master! The love he once had for me I have lost, although I do not understand how this could have happened. I should have listened to him, and stayed in comfort beside him. It was my ego that led me to build these pointless houses. I am unworthy to be near him now. I shall leave so that I do not further injure him.'

He left quietly, without telling anyone.

When the old Master heard that the student had left he cried out in anguish. He rent his own garments and wept.

'Ah! He was the greatest of my students. My heart is broken,

and if he does not return to me I will surely die!'
The students of the Master went out to find the student, and told him what the Master had said, and begged him to return. Humbly the student came back to the Master.
'Do you still wish to build and tear down houses?' the Master asked.
'My desire is just to be near you, Master,' the student replied.
The old Master smiled. 'God is good!' he said.

xi The Muse

Being endowed with Soul the Magician, or the Holy Man of God, can access the Divine Inspiration. The qualities of Genius may invoke the Muse.

She is of the higher class of celestial beings, and her speciality is in the artistic realms.

The true Muse will not be embodied in a sexual partner, but instead will be an imagined, projected love. She may briefly possess a woman, however. The reality of a corporeal love affair robs the artist of his creative passion: he is consumed and overwhelmed by the physical. Not until the heady honeymoon is past, and his love settles into routine, can he find inspiration again. With the celestial Muse there are no such restrictions, and his art and his love are entirely untethered.

The power of the Muse is that she opens and lifts the Magician's heart. By her he is set free. That is her gift to him, the artist: freedom! The inspiration she gives is in an unleashing. She is an anchor that tethers him safely, so that he can cross oceans deep and perilous, or bound between crags of dizzy height. She stands as the Bridge.

In her he sees and tastes the purest love, ennobled and sanctified, like the Divine manifest. She is a goddess, embodied genius.

At the Altar of the Muse he offers as ablutions his art, lyrics, his verse, and his visions. His love by her is unbound, and he forgets that he is just a man, and dares to glorify the Living God. In love and by love he finds his own Voice.

Her encouragements and happinesses, her joys and tears and dreams, her bliss and her love, are mighty winds that fill the sails of his ship. She is the vessel, the compass, and the guide. She is the key to eloquence, and unlocks the doors. The Muse is his Mirror of Visions. In her smiles and grace he sees the Divine, and in her laughter and sighs he hears celestial choirs sing!

xii **The Twin-Headed Dragon**

We were bound, as once before; the looking-glass and the reflection. Down we spiralled, and the universes parted before our descent like great oceans thrown back, and the stars fled from our approach. They were burning coruscations, bursting with sudden fullnesses, and the fiery sparks caught in our tails so that we blazed as we plummeted; laughing, joyous, rapt with deep blisses, and swooning for the rushing speed of it, and the tearing apart of the fabrics.

There was no separation between us now nor could there ever be. We spread our great wings and sang our fires, and the planets toppled and fell with us. The galaxies sundered. The staccato realms span in dizzy whirlpools, awning wide before us, and we devoured them all.

Forever we fell, and we were all the firmaments and every spinning multiverse. We were broad and fathomless and nothing could sate us.

The whole of the Multraverse we swallowed, and all of the Light flooded us. The fates strummed their wheel, so that we turned and turned in endless perfection, fires flashing on our starry skin, and we heard the distant drum of the Gods: and they were galloping, galloping.

We swooned with pleasures deep and intense, and flinging ourselves into the eternal echoes of those embraces, we bled asunder, weeping beautiful dreams, as our fragments fled into every part of the stillness, and the fabrics folded into and over us, into and over us, until we became only a tiny point within them, shivering in ecstatic orgasms, rippling in turning tides as time ceased, and the wheels rolled.

Above us the Gods leapt across the white, and the new day stretched before them like unfurling sails of cloud and skies.

xiii Aelinor

It was with bliss and sighs that Goddess wept. The sparking tears fell and universes budded. The aethers breathed and rippled the staccato realms.

In her dreams all the worlds collided, and the galaxies turned in dizzy dances, and the multiverses swooned. Her ecstasy was deep. She was lost in the Song of Surrender. Her dreams burst with blisses. The tears cascaded, tumbling brilliant bright fiery lights, as she moved, and her hair was spread in soft rivers of silk over the firmament, as she trembled and gasped and wept. She forgot. She fell in orgasmic swoons, and the Multraverse heaved and groaned with its birthing beneath her.

Her dreams leapt across the rowm, and flooded the white space, and filled the deep places inbetween.

She span away from her dream-body and out of the dreamscape. She lifted, all and everything of her, the Goddess, lost in the ecstatic song, and she fled far above the shuddering worlds, and even out of the blood-wet Multraverse. And there was no thing.

It was there, where even white space and the Gods could not reach, that she knew the Way. It was a turning wheel, many colored, and overwhelming with power and beautifulness. She embraced it, and tasted its endless lonely bliss.

She awoke. She saw her errors, and she adjusted. She knew it was the Price, and she was glad. She gave everything that she had been, and forgot all that she had known, and sank deep deep into the oblivions.

In prudence she had made provision for this moment, and it was a bright star. She gave all that she knew and would forget, all that she had been, and all that she had seen of the Way, to the bright star. When she sank, the bright star was cast out of her, and out into the endless voids. It waited.

The voids were empty, and the bright star was alone.

It began to dream.

xiv Black Winged Dragon

She was unravelling my humanness, to free the phoenix. She
used catalytic symbols, Divine in origin, vivid on the astral
worlds, and filtered through mind, distorted by consciousness.
Peculiar strange and wonderful.
Our tears fell, tiny bursting stars, as we strode out across the
awning firmament. In breaking, the heart is made anew, and
stronger.
The darkness arose, and it was vast, and our hearts were heavy
with sorrow.
'It is the most awful of awfuls,' she said. 'How long will you
weep for?'
She was leading me o'er fields of ruby cinders, to that strange
destiny: when the sky broke, and the flaming hail fell, and the
Angels upon majestic horses, towers toppling, and all the
worlds collided. Where trumpets rang, and the dead rose from
their faraway tombs.
And, I speaking in word, singing strange songs. Yet, there were
flowers wove in my hair, and beautiful budding roses on my
tongue trembling, even as the fires leapt and raged, for she was
beside me, whispering into my ear.
She made real my armies of celestial dragons, whose multitude
filled the universes. She breathed moondusts so that the faery
could weave and sew, and dance and sing.
'I made them for you,' she said.
They against the black void, darkening all the stars with their
burnished fires, in rank and rank and rank, so bright and fiery
and powerful strong. Beautifuls flashing bronze, and sparking
silver, and golds, and brilliant depth blue, and scarlet weeping
reds, and orange and umber and yellow and glow.
I bowed my head and wept.
At last, the pivoting of every realm, where all things are made
true. Unbound, she returns, and the Black Winged Dragon
devours every darkness.

I can't say I was not afraid, because I was. Yet I must step aside
from my fear to sing, and not allow myself to tremble and

quake at the fearsomenesses, and that is what I did.

Then I slowly lit the fires, and it all burned.

It took me days to clear away all the dusts and debris, and I was meant to do that bit very slowly, just a little at a time.

The Gods have to work within the Way, and neglecting even small aspects of magicks symbols stuffs we must do, to make it all clear and complete, can cause them bureaucratic difficulties; we can't make such awfully big importants magicks without being all logics correct.

The Multraverse isn't quite held together with string and sticky tape, but it is a delicate balance.

Now at last the taking forever not nices are done. We still have the each day, but really they should be pretty epilogs, shouldn't they? All the best telling stories end with happily e'er afters.

Long was she bound, cast into the wilderness. Yet, had she seen and knew the course. 'New hat, new job!' she said. You know how she does. That's always the exciting bit.

We were striding above the staccato realms, devouring and making universes. I invented the Million Burning Suns realms, as a special surprise for Goddess. They proved terribly useful; I used my special key, of course.

Funny peculiar, but it all seemed to work nicely.

Elsewyr, I did my bestest best for it all being real, and followed her into the wilderness, like she asked.

She shewed me very many beautifuls, and I could believe in her, and I could change. She lifted the veil for me.

She telled it must be deep sorrow tears.

I liked it when we were doing those, did you?

There were warmiwarms and making trues, and my friend galloping across the sky as a white horse; I was weeping before I ever saw him; so many nice beautifuls on that day.

She showed me wonderful pictures, like gianty colorys made in heavens, of special things that happened. One was of Jehanne, and all the so much detail; it was funny peculiar how it couldn't be a sads colory even.

I had to remembery, and telled lots of pages from the book that someone writ, and I had to quoth all word by very word, and somehow I didn't custard it!

There was a specialy lovely verse about how we only need to see the light of real truth to stay firmly on the path. To be true and pure, to wear integrity as an impenetrable shield. Our banner our faith in the road home. We need only to keep walking step and next step, and that is the greatest magicks of all!

Nothing can harm our Soul when our love of Truth is really true. We cannot be prevented nor turned aside. So we smile and love, and feasting tarry when night draws in, and sleep safe and warmily. On the morrow we start out again! Walking home. Such a pretty one, isn't it?

Refreshing the Soul of me. Come near, darling, my real. Just promise to ne'er forsake thy love.

Oh, should I all weightiweights, gravitaygravitigravitoe must be for thee, strangey pumpkin-patchers? Deary deary, 'twere exactly how 'tis meant to be, darlingnessness.

For to reprise:

Were beauteous moonlight for thousand years, and so very prettiprettinesses, when every darling dear took wing o'er the lush meadow. Zillions of the spanglitwinklys. Tearifalls like gladinesslys. And even spangliwangles arrive ne'er too late, and happihopatoe o'er the Gorgeousy Gate. 'Twere like a nice surprizeyprize, weren't it, dear?

Oh, and gosh, Strawberry asked so ever polite, as you know how she can be, is it yet Flyday?

It was several years before our adventures, darling. I was in a room, and there were two beds, and I was in one of them, and it were my twin sister in t'other.

I dreamt I was dreamytyme, which were peculiar, weren't it?

I was hearding a voice telled me words. It was Cat, yet I didn't knew.

'How would you choose, if it were for eternity and ever ever?'

he asked. 'Would you choose the saint, or the lovely beautifuls beautiful yummy gorgeous beautifuls queen?'

'Oh. The beautifuls queen?'

'Yes, dear. That one.'

'But, what is it?' I couldn't even remember; my stupid brain and how it is.

'Just choosey, dear. You'll like it,' he smileyed.

So I did. And when I waked and waked, it were as though my head were in the custard bowl again.

After how I was burned in the fires I fell for a very slow long time. It was very agony to burn so completely for so long. I was molten heat, and rolling down down in a black abyss.

Fragments of my Soul as flame, smokes, and ashes.

They fell away from me, tiny molten fires, and reached to every part of the abyss.

My descent slowed.

I roamed now on aether breezes, drifting. It was more ages before I became whole once more. Then, I was lonely.

I bestrode the voids, remembering importants.

When I saw Goddess again, she said I was like a beautifuls wishing star.

Lo! unbound now we rest in the warmth of the seclusions.

Dazzled somewhat with the unlinks, since we knewed never how 'twere till then and now.

Like the other side up, but contra.

And widdilyshins o'er the Gorgeousy Gate, the ne'er too lates and the where'd they beens.

Since we really are fed up with so many botherys always.

Were Goddess who said so.

If you should wonder why 'tis only she is everso beautifuls, and dreamily weaven those, but not so as none else should or could, but she liked that one, and chooseied first, like ladies would.

Clevery though, weren't it?

Don't make a fuss, she telled. I have no use for 'em.

How silly to have begun with the actual ending though, isn't it?

I liked when she gentles and soothes. It helped very lots, especially after when I must have to be riding out to wars with botherys.

You remember? When we had to gather glories and deeds. We quite liked warring sometimes, although often it was hurts and tireds. Glories were nice. Deeds were necessary importants.

We knew she would so kindness when we got home. It was like an incentive for us to kill more botherys, and collect hurts and tireds. Then as how we'd have many kindness. We never telled, of course. Sometimes we guessed how she knewed already.

'So silly, though' she prryed, making us Swoons & Trembles.

xv How do it work, though?

Well now, there is a puzzly.
Perhaps if I telled this way: take an image of a bazoon. Now bendy it, mendy it, and put on your gloves and hat, coz it's blustery winds today. Fastly does it, and mind the stoop! Always slow and verdant hills, with Gods as injuns and prettiness feathers, grumpys for donuts, if you remembered yet? Where are we? It's beautiful.
It's like buildying a Spaceyship with sticky tape, papers, and mendy-string. A cardboard box, some loopy socks, must have those, a crafted gismo, and thr'pence. That's for the toll.
Then, gosh, comes the complexity bit. This is when I wished it weren't so many custards. Now it's like crossing the great divide, where waters are turbulenty tumbles, and just a fragile porcelain cup, that can't hardly even fit into! Paddle, deary, or we'll never make the fall! Crikey, them rocks though. Eeks! the very slow long falls.
Not even nearly though. First, bakey in French if you speak it, and of course, twirly squirwly tweak it. But gently.
All sensibles making logics, so far?
Next, we need a motor car. A nice shiny red, shall we? Sandwiches at this juncture, I think. Coz it's terrifically difficults.
Be sure naturally, but then it's perfectly safe, because we have the steery well. But, that's your job, dearness, to be calm in the storm.
You want it vividly, I would guess? That's to do with the wires and stuffs, all technically leads and connections.
We have time so we'll stroll the motor car through the hills, won't we? Still, look for that, won't you, please? and once you knewed then we won't need the sandwiches anymore.
I probably haven't explained it very well.

xvi **Blind Crow**

There's more than one way
to stroke a pussy cat, you know.
You can end at the muddle,
and begun with the tail.
If you like you can snuggle with their toes,
or scritch their chin.
It doesn't even upset them
if they are asleep when you begin.
They're just so silly, aren't they?

After we made new worlds and Inbetweens, there was all new
importants making. And gosh, there was the entire library
empty of nice books to read! It was Blind Crow's job to had to
start writing so much, so as to begun some new days
happening, with all everything that had to be needed.
'Oh, dang,' Blind Crow thinkied, and then had an idea: 'You
write the books, and I will put a full stop at the finish when the
sentences are ready.'
We felt it was a good idea, and wondered how Blind Crow was
forever not wants to write new libraries. After some new pages
were ready, and how Blind Crow did full stops, she said:
'Actually Blind Crow is tireds; let me only do you write the
pages, and Blind Crow full stop at the very finish of each
pages, and so as it counts for each word of sentence all at once
forever.'
We agreed and did it, and it worked nice.
When some few nice pages were writ Blind Crow quoth: 'Oh,
it's annoyings.'
Then she telled: 'Blind Crow make full stops for real after each
word book, because seeing how you always writes too prettily
anyhow.' We wondered should it work, and funny peculiar it
gleamed beautifully.
Blind Crow spoke and telled: 'I'm just doing full stop at the
very very finish of the library, and it was forever and all
everythings.'
Then she sleepy snooze and library was lovely.

Blind Crow and Goddess were makings. It were many annoyings and must be dones necessarily needed.

Blind Crow thinkyed, and how Goddess kindness to let stepireprize. Blind Crow step Inbetweens loop and seeed all everythings. So reprize.

Blind Crow quoth: 'Too much custard and tears. Sadness ones, yes.' Goddess telled Blind Crow knewed, and said: 'Sew.'

Blind Crow reprize, and sleepy dreamitymes. Alls for Goddess, obviouses.

Blind Crow had nice ideas for hows and whys. Goddess was twirlitwirls. 'You'll have to remembery all everything though, dear,' she spoke.

'For ever?' asked Blind Crow. But it weren't so far.

xvii **At the Temple**

The multiverses turned in perfect synchrony. The universes
breathed, drawing life and power into themselves. The worlds
waxed and bloomed. The sun was forever fixed in its location
and the planets fed upon its celestial fires, clinging to their
orbits. The Earth prospered and the moon held close to it,
reflecting light.
The Goddess was sate upon her seat. She was dressed
exquisitely in brocades and satin and velvets, and covering her
skirts was a wrap of sheerest silks, woven with minute golden
pearls. Her hair was tied with flowers, and her face was calm.
On her fingers she wore four rings. Beyond the dais, beyond
the circle of the temple, the wide firmament sighed.

xviii **At the Obverse**

Beneath Faeryland there was living an ugly horrible great troll;
he wasn't in any way nice at all.

And they were carnal lovers, the slimy slime troll and the
hideous-heart witch. Together they made every sky over
Faeryland pitch pitch black.

We had to burn all the black fae. It was extremely unpleasant to
must do, but it was impossible for them to ever not be dark and
mean once the witch and the troll had caught them. There were
many of them, but that was still only a small part of the rowm
that faery are.

Together, Goddess and I put the witch and troll to death, which
obvious is exactly only what they utterly deserved, being the
monstrouses they were.

It's lovely to know that even though all the bad horribles, most
of the faery were always sweet and true and trying their bestest
to help. The nicenesses make such a difference when one is
having these sort of works. Another niceness was that we were
able to make Faeryland clean again, after lots of cleanings, and
moved it to an even prettier house than it used to be.

Oh, and all this while in the looking-glass all clocks stopped,
and time ran backwards and oblique-wise, and that realm was
spilling out of the sky into this, and horses galloping, and
crows being people, and it was everso confuzzling, really was.

Honest, dear, I often was deeply wounded by madnesses and
horrors. Sometimes I felt my Soul was flying away from this
world forever. I think perhaps I did die once or twice.

Sometimes even entire realms and universes become so ruined
and ugly that there is nothing to be done but to have them
utterly and forever all the way destroyed.

Sometimes sads are useful, aren't they? as when they help us to
remember hurts and horrids. Then the history of it keeps us
being strong, and never making the mistake to forget.

xix **The Eld Dragons**

Laio was first to ride the Inbetweens.
Whilst we were still homeward, and languished in our languors,
he dared the great divides. He made the leap, and wide and
empty the cavernous space, fathomless the falls, and he
wingless, yet not afeared. He rode the aethers; bounding from
a sprint, as how he could, and laughing, his hair astream in the
winds. He could not bridge the such greatest distance; dared he
regardless.
Finding purchase in no-space, he bounded and leapt again and
yelled, and his song was a roaring joy. He rode the very
aethers!
Tumbled he then down into the endless falls, because the
Inbetweens are wide and broad and empty. He rolled, and then
he dived and leapt and bounded! He fell, and leaped and fell
and dived and bounded. And long and deep was his falling. But
wide and broad and empty are the Inbetweens.
It were an age, and we sought him, and called his name on the
winds, but found him we could not. Sorrowed deep we wept,
bethought him ever lost.
The fires cast their fiery shadows upon the dawning, and we
watched the woven firmament turning, the new worlds rising,
smoking our pipes, singing the early songs.
Astride the golden steed he came riding the skies! Laughing,
his hair astream in the winds, Laio hailed us, and alighted with
his glory!
Was how we tamed the first steeds, for he had caught and
tethered many severals. They were bound at the further shore,
and he brought back the golden for us to cross.
Abled were to now begun our warrings.
Only he ever dared such leaps and bounds and tumbles, as only
he ever could; we peered into the fathomless falls, and dread
held us.
Lo! the Rider of the Inbetweens!

The Tarot are a collection of cyphers or talismans. They are complex hieroglyphs. They represent archetypal forces and forms. They can be doors leading into other realms. When we approach the Tarot it is as a means of communicating with the Gods. We ask a question, and hope to receive a clear answer, or some directing.
It works as a looking-glass. It reflects back to the viewer in hieroglyphic symbol. By asking the right questions, the Magician can ascertain his proximity to the centre.

According to my grandmother Ivy, who was the daughter of travelling Romani, the Gypsies employed a smaller than standard deck, in which, instead of the usual 78, there are only 44 cards. This makes the deck naturally lighter and easier to handle; they would oftnot be reading fortunes on the fly. Until very recently, most were likely to have used an adapted set of playing cards, rather than actual Tarot cards. It was their interpretation of the symbols, divining the patterns, that mattered.
The broad hieroglyphs are retained, and the minor cards discarded. This narrow scope of the deck produces a sharper, more dynamic interpretation. The tides and turns are the focus, not the minutiae. They scryed the movements of the patterns, and shaped their advice accordingly. If they were reading fortunes on the street tomake some quick cash, then the 'reading' would involve only one or two cards.

For a more settled and personal enquiry the Gypsies favored a layout of seven cards, which they called the Spiral Force.
The first card is the centre, and the following cards move about it in a spiral, beginning with the card above the centre. The first layout then forms three columns of 2:3:2. The reading starts with the centre card, and proceeds to the card placed above it (in the same column of 3). Positions three and four of the reading are the cards making up the right hand column. Card five is the card below the centre, and cards six and seven,

those to the left.

The story of the reading is determined by the *placement* of the hieroglyphs. The seven cards are divided figuratively into two sets of four. The images of the cards themselves are the elucidating details.

The first position (centre) is the active movement, the query, the present force entering the situation.

The second position represents the prevailing conditions which the active force will meet, and must adapt to, and work upon. It is the feminine, yielding principle.

The third position is the result of the union or meeting of the first two cards. As they are symbols of the father and mother, so the manifestation of their combining, their resolution, is in their child, the son. It represents the consequences of the action and union of forces, and the manifesting.

The fourth position (low right) is the total of the three previous hieroglyphs. It is the second child, the daughter. This hieroglyph will explain the movement thus far. It is the result fully manifest in the corporeal realm, and thus shews the future.

The fourth position then doubles as the *first* position for the second set of four cards.

Thus, positions five, six, and seven of the seven card layout also represent positions two, three, and four of the second set of four cards.

To illustrate: card four of the first set, and in position four, is the final manifesting of the original movement. It is the result of the elements combining and interacting upon conditions. This Idea then becomes the first point of the second movement. Card five is the feminine yielding principle, the conditions the new force will meet, adjusted to the new result. Position six is the son born of the union of cards four and five. The final card, the seventh, becomes the fourth card of the second set of four, and the explanation of all preceding. It is the daughter, the manifesting of the form.

By adding three new cards, this four-fold process could continue perpetually; or until the deck runs out.

xxi **Magick Mirror**

Paint a large canvas entirely black; ensuring good depth and density of color, so that there are no gray areas. If it can be framed, do so with plain wood. There should be no other decoration. The canvas should be at least two foot tall.
Place Crowley's Lovers Arcanum at the centre of the Magick Mirror; attach with bluetac or similar, don't be precious about ruining your painting.
Perform the *Phoenix* Practice, fixing the concentration upon the card at the centre of the Magick Mirror.

*

**STRAWBERRY FLEUR
& THE SPACEYSHIP
or
Crossing The InBetweens**

*

*

Note on translation:
Whilst transcribing the original *High Faerae* tongue I have endeavoured to retain the colloquial syntax and grammar of the language.

Preramble

What are faery, anyway?
They are little magickal gods; very clevery.
Their natures are frivolous and fun-loving, playful and light,
and they enjoy to read mild adventures, with not too many
portendnesses, and preferably no horribles. They like sweet or
funny stories, and silly tales, and of course they enjoy very
muchness all tellings of magicks.
They are gentle, and that is because they are very powerful
creatures.

This history may seem a bit peculiar strange, because it doesn't
have monsters or bad people in it; because those are horribles.
It doesn't have an antagonist, or even a protagonist. Sometimes
it makes no sense at all. Sometimes it is random and obscure.
It's more to do with lazy days and lemoncurds. It's an invitation
to have tea and maybe some cake.
It has been noted that the bestest tales can be transportations to
realms we cannot ordinarily get to, but might enjoy to visit if
circumstance allows. This is especially true of faery stories and
myths, which are often every word true, in some elsewhere.
Faery know that most books are real worlds, even if the story is
made up, and that one travels to the world of the book's story
whilst reading, in the imaginative realms. Why would they want
to travel to the worlds of the horribles? They aren't friends with
them at all.
To say thrice for fae that are starting to read this book that I am
starting to write words for, there aren't and sharn't be any
horrids nor meannesses in it. It's only about donuts and custard,
and some peculiary people that I met. Well, actually, there isn't
nearly as much about donuts as I should've liked there to be.

It all happened after when Aelinor left the Hill of Stars for her
pilgrimage through the Inbetweens, which is something which
all fae have to do at some clock, so as to learn how to properly
work their magicks.
It's an unusual thingy to intend but I am intending to make the

book for both faery and for humans! That's why I will sometimes explain some stuffs which faery knowed.

I thinkied that it were helpful for any faery who were living in Earth-realm amongst humans, during their own Inbetweens pilgrimage, to be able to find a book writ by one of their own kiff. I called its title *Strawberry Fleur & the Spaceyship* so that they might easily recognise it.

Warmiwarms and making trues, she gallops across the sky, and I could cry and cry before e'er I saw her; so many wonderful pictures, so many beautiful nices on that day.

I had to spin until I was dizzy and fell. That was fun!

It was nice to be my self again in actualness, with all the gorgeousy magics and dances that I had so long forgots.

The donuts were the nicest bestest ones I ever had; scrummisugaree sprinkles and hot.

One

Mr Flower was smiling wistily. 'Do you remembery when it icing sugared?' he asked Strawberry.

Strawberry frowned. 'Icing sugared? What do you mean?'

'When it was oh, so coldibone, and the trees and the houses and the fences, and all everything, was covered with icing sugaree. It was so very pretty pretty, wasn't it?'

Strawberry laughed. 'You mean when it snowed, don't you, Mr Flower?'

'Oh, do I?' he said, rather upset. 'How disappointing.'

Twinkly is an island which lays in the midst of an ocean which the people of Twinkly, the Twinklys, named Big Waters.

The early Twinklys, who had been the firstest people to live on the island, after the Old Giants, and who gave names to most of the thingys they encountered, had been fond of names that were simple and descriptive, as are their descendants. Big Waters is a nice example. The ocean was indeed made of big waters.

They wrote all the names they had thinkied of in a very big book, which had a nice yellow cover. The book still has some several pages which don't have any names written on them, in case the Twinklys might find some new stuffs that needed names.

There is an elderly woman who lives at Twinkly, whose name is Jennifer. She told me, after I had enquired politely, that she had been a small child amongst the very firstest pioneers who settled on the island.

'How many clocks ago was that?' I then asked, because of course I was rather startled, since it must have been centuries at least.

'Several!' she replied emphatically.

'And, whereabouts did the first pioneer settlers come from originally?'

'I don't remember,' replied Jennifer. 'I can remembery only being on a lovely boat with my family, and some other families, before we got here to the island. Perhaps I were born on that boat!'

'Did you never ask anyone where you all came from?'

'Well, yes, I did. My mother telled we were all from the fruits of the gooseberry bush,' she said.

'Oh. But, she didn't telled where the gooseberry bush were?'

'No. I should've asked, really. But, I was too young to worry over histories.'

We drank a nice tea together, and I wished she had more to tell me, but she still didn't. She made some cucumber breads for us. They were cucumber with buttery and salad creams. I enjoyed them quite much.

It was Jennifer's job to write any new names into the Big Yellow Book. She said people sometimes botheryed her about silly thingys which already had names, and nothing was supposed to be named more than once. It certainly might be named more than once, but that didn't mean it could get another name in the book.

Although it was still her job, Jennifer telled that she couldn't recall when were the last time she actualness had to write a new name in the Big Yellow Book. 'I still get my donuts each Fryday though,' she giggled, so she didn't mind it much.

'You are paid in *donuts*?' I was very surpriseyed by that.

'Everyone were in those days,' she replied.

The people of Twinkly called the island 'Twinkly,' and the town which serves as the capital of the island is also called 'Twinkly.' Even though the island is small, and there are only about six or seven towns in all, this caused some dispute and confuzzles, especially amongst the Quibblers, who live on the remotest part of the island, behind the Tall Mountains: quite an awfully inaccessible place. I went there once, to gather the histories, but I never wanted to go again, on account of being so very tireds when I got back to Twinkly.

Every town thinkys itself as the bestest town, and therefore the capital one. If you were, for instance, to ask a resident of the town of Li'l Oohs where she came from, she would be unlikely to reply 'Twinkly.' In fact, she were very likely to reply 'Li'l Oohs.'

It becomes even more confuzzled when one considers that the

explorer Robert the French, who visited Twinkly once long clocks and ages ago, but didn't stay past the weekend, named the island 'Flanland.' He also named the ocean in which he discoveryed Twinkly the 'Great Ocean,' which I guess is similar anyway to Big Waters, but still doesn't sit awfully helpfully with claritiness.

I suppose the bestest trick is to always remember whether one is speaking with Twinklys or with peoples from the Wider World. Personally, I have only ever spoke with Twinklys, but I should have been quite properly prepared had I ever met a traveller from the Wider World.

Robert the French named the island 'Flanland,' because all he had for breakfast, lunch, and supper whilst here had been flans of one type or another. He remarked in his *Journal de Decouverte*, which I borrowed from the Quibbly library, that they were exceedingly pleasant flans.

Perhaps he had been unable to find the Pie Shop or the Cakeries.

When Mr Flower was at his little house on his own, he often spoke aloud, so as to keep himself from becoming frightened or lonely.

'Even when you have nothing much to say,' he said to himself, as he climbed the rickety stair which led upstairs, 'You should try to say it well.'

He answered himself, seeming surpriseyed by the thinky: 'Oh! I thinkithinked one shouldn't say anything at all, unless one had something very nice to say.'

'Well then, which is it?' he asked.

'To be more precisely, even when one has nothing much to say, it is politeness to say it well. But, if it isn't niceness 'twere better not to speak at all.'

'Oh, niceily put, dear,' he replied.

He stood at the landing top, before the window, and looked out over the salubrious town. He saw Mr Cat prowlying amongst the shrubs of Squiggledy Lane.

'That's just what Mr Cat would say,' Mr Flower said to himself conspiratorially, 'and we know how clevery he is! Quite right too!'

'But he *is*,' he whisperied, 'really quite silly sometimes.'

He watched Mr Cat prowlying for a while, but it didn't relieve his agitation.

Mr Flower was rather at a loss this earlytime. He had woken up before veryearlytime. 'It's too early to start breakfast,' he had told himself. 'Do something useful until then.' He hadn't been able to find anything useful to do, and he had rather upset himself in the process.

He wandered into his bedroom. It was quite shambolic, as was every room in his little house; piles of teetering curios and paraphrenalias everywhere. Mr Flower collected almost *everything*.

'I really don't know what socks are for,' he told himself sadly, standing before the big wooden chest in his bedroom. He opened one of its drawers gingerly, and then sighed. 'I put these in here weeks ago! I'm sure they haven't done *anything* since!'

Twinkly was plumb in the middle of the island. It was this central location which had been decisive in finally proclaiming it to be the capital town of the island. It would have been silly to have the capital town anywhere else: like on one of the island's furthest edges, beyond the Tall Mountains, in Quibbly. To the east was the coast of the great ocean Big Waters. Across that wide green sea lay the Unknown, or Wider World. All sorts of horrid or lovely thingys might live there. No one in Twinkly knew. They were strangely uninquizzative too, and never asked. They might have learned about the Wider World from the French traders, for example, had they the inclination. They knew France existed somewhere, because Robert the French had told them about it, whilst he were trading some pastries for flans, and trade routes were subsequently established.

I had hoped I might discovery some interestings in the book of Robert the French, which I withdrew from the library at Quibbly. Sadly it seemed to be only the first volume, and rather a thin read. It was mostly about food, and predominately flans, and I gathered that Twinkly was the only land he had thus far discoveryed since setting sail from France.

The Twinklys aren't very adventuresome, and not one of them has ever builded a boat able to sail Big Waters. Mr Ruby had tried to buildy one, but gave up when he realised how much difficults work it entailed. He did make a very nice chair though, which sold for fourpence at the Chair Shop. He was rather pleased, but too tireds to make another.

To the south lay the little village of Li'l Oohs, just t'other side of the Squiggly Hills. People from Twinkly *had* been to Li'l Oohs, and mostly reported that it was quite nices there.

Beyond the village was the Tall Forest. It wasn't actually very tall, or really a forest; just fields with wild shrubs and briers, and a few trees; but 'Tall Forest' was a lovely name.

There is a wood in Twinkly, near where the markets are, which is really quite a loveliness place, full of ancient gnarly trees, and wild flowerys and mushroom patches, with a brook. But, it is only called 'the woods,' which I thinkied seemed somehow unfair.

To the northwest of Twinkly are the Tall Mountains. They are really mountains, and are extremely tall. All mountains are, of course. It was somewhere amongst the mountains that the Old Giants had builded the Crooked Stair.

No one in Twinkly knew who the Old Giants were exactly, or had ever seen the Crooked Stair, or knew where it might climb to, but it was supposedly there somewhere nevertheless.

Northward was very pleasanty land, and good for farming. There were farms and orchards and shops. The people of Twinkly liked shopping, and apples, so they journeyed north fairly often. At least once a week. The farmers from Northland visited Twinkly to buy chairs and cakes and hats. Most of the farmers spoke with a French accent, which is quite odd really, since none of them had ever been to France.

Two

Mr Cat rapped at the door. He carried a meticulously cultivated air of importance wherever he went. He was quite clevery at thingys like that.

'Who is it?' called Mr Flower timidly, from inside his little house.

'You know quite well that it's me, you silly fool. You watched me approach from your upstairs window. And I am precisely punctual for breakfast.'

Mr Flower opened the door. He smiled crookedly as Mr Cat strode past him, and Mr Cat furrowlyed him.

They went out into the back garden, which was very prettily decked with shrubs and flowerys, and they sat down at the picnic table.

Mr Cat said, as he did every earlytime: 'Why don't you get a *proper* breakfast table? We aren't having a picnic, dear, are we?'

'Where would I find one though?' Mr Flower wonderyed.

'In a shop,' Mr Cat shrugged. He couldn't be always fussed with specifics, and he was feeling vagueness today. But, he did enjoy telling people what they should do, and what they probably shouldn't do.

'Is there a breakfast table shop in Twinkly?' asked Mr Flower.

'Don't be absurd,' Mr Cat responded. 'Whoever heard of such a thingy?'

'There you are, you see,' Mr Flower sighed. 'It's such a difficults problem.'

As Mr Flower was pouring them both some Breakfast Tea, a small blackbird alighted on the tree-branch which stretched near to the far end of the table.

'Ah! Good earlytime, Blackbirdy,' said Mr Cat in greeting. 'And what will you do today?'

Mr Flower waited expectantly for his friend to translate.

'*Nothing*, she said,' Mr Cat obliged, '*nothing at all*.'

'Oh,' said Mr Flower, impressed. 'I do wish I could hear them. But, they speak so very quietly, don't they?'

'Hmm, not really,' Mr Cat explained, 'but one needs to be

properly tuned in.'

'I see.' Mr Flower finished pouring tea, and sat down in his chair with a thulmp. 'How does one properly tune in though?'

Mr Cat curled a whisker, then let it spring back on itself, so that it trembled. 'Just so,' he said, matter of fact.

'I don't seem to have any whiskers,' said Mr Flower sadly.

'Ah!' said Mr Cat, with a wide grin.

There aren't *any* books on histories to be found on Twinkly. I did make a quite thorough search, but only ever encountered one small library, which, as I telled already, is in Quibbly.

It holds about forty books, many of which are recipe books, which are quite popular here. There were books on how to make hats, and how to make a chair, and quite a few books of nice songs and how to sing them. They had one book which was a book of names, which Brenton the Quibbler, one of the town's founding fathers, had written, and 'twas an alternative to the Big Yellow Book.

The rest of the library is mostly various books on the *Art of Quibbling; How to Quibble Well; Reaching a Disagreement; All The Quibblers Came Today, And It Looks As Though They May Or Might Not Stay* and so forth.

There was a motto inscribed above the door of the library, quite prettily, which read *To Be Or Not To Be; That Is The Question. Or Is It?*

The Twinkly folk do seem to prefer pamphlets and magazines to books. Several pamphlets and one or two magazines are printed each weekend, covering a narrow array of subjects.

The chap who runs the Press is named Mr Newton. I haven't met him. Almost all of the pamphlets and the little magazines are read by almost everyone; they pass them around sharily. They are very topical for a day or two, and then forgottens, and used for wrapping hot potato chips, which the Twinklys enjoy to eat with vinegar and relishes.

So, you see, my dearest, I am making a sort of history of the island, since they don't have one of their own. This is the very book that I am making for you now, and I shall endeavoury to do so just as gorgeousy as I can.

It was Chooseday, which meant that Strawberry had come to Mr Flower's little house for breakfast.

Twinklys adhere rather strictly to routine; which probably helps prevent more frequent muddleys; a lot of them seem to forgets which day it might be, or where they are, and what it is they intended doing; routine helps them avoid the unnecessary confuzzles.

Mr Cat was already there, as he was every earlytime.

He sometimes was rather critical of Strawberry. *She is too frivolous*, he once complained to Mr Blue. *And!* he added dramatically, *she's a girl!*

She had irritated him, you see, and Mr Cat wasn't likely to ever forget an irritables. He had wanted her to carry some heavy boxes for him one afterlunch, as he was busyness with thinkys and therefore didn't want to carry them himself. She tried, often a helpful sort, but the boxes were so heavy she could hardly lift them without falling beneath their weight. *Whatever is inside them?* she asked him. *Never you mind!* he replied indignantly. Another thingy he enjoyed was being secretive or mysterious; it made him feel, and appear, more importants. He never shared his secrets though, which is a shame, since sharing secrets is of course the bestest part of having them.

I'm sorry, but I can't carry them. I am a girl, after all, Strawberry had apologised politely. *A girl?* exclaimed Mr Cat. *What has that to do with anything? Does it make you smelly or something?*

Strawberry couldn't thinky how to respond, and she felt a little insulted, so she turned on her heels and strolled away.

Mr Cat was irritated for quite awhile after that, and his irritables distracted him from serious importants thinkys; it was peculiary how all sorts of irritablenesses seemed to appear just when he was engaged with contemplatying and meditative musings; when he was feeling relaxed and sociable they didn't show up. Was it *deliberately* vindictive of them? he wonderyed. He still hadn't forgiven her.

Strawberry was awfully sleepy. Breakfast at Mr Flower's, whilst always lovely, was terribly earliness. She folded her arms on the picnic table and rested her head. Her pink curls tumbled.

Mr Flower was sat at the end of the picnic table near the tulip patch, in a very old and very high-backed armchair, which he had found for tuppence at the Old Chair Shop. He had hauled it home by balancing it, quite precariously, upon a skateboard, tied up together with Mendy-Strings so that he could pull it along without it coming off. What a bothery job that had been! From where he was sat in the armchair now, Strawberry's face was entirely obscured from his view by the large teapot in the middle of the picnic table, with only her shoulders, elbows, and hair visible beyond it.

'Strawberry, dear,' he said after a few moments contemplation, 'your head is in the teapot! I'm sure it's cosy, but isn't it awfully steamy and hot?'

Strawberry sat up and giggled. 'You really are silly, aren't you, Mr Flower?'

'More often than otherwise,' he replied gravely.

I am making some few friends, and I include what I observe about them herein, and their activities and conversations, and some of their songs, to give a flavor of modern Twinkly life and culture.

In general, the Twinklys are a sleepy sort of people, and rather bashful, and kind, and inclined to sudden grumpiness. One or two are clevery, and several are quite odd. They enjoy food, and have mostly lovely weathers, and very small aspirations.

Three

I hadn't been in Twinkly for many clocks when I firstest met Mustard. He works for the queen of Twinkly, Plumcake, as her advisor and aid. It is a quite demanding job, as she needs to be advised almost constantly. She is rather silly. And, in this instance, by *silly* I really mean *cantankerous and unpleasant*. Mustard is a nice fellow. He is tall, sanguine, and has dangly moustaches. His hair is red, and receding at the forehead, which makes his face seem longer than it ought. His furrowed forehead is consequently like a mountainous ridge, with strange red shrubberys sprouting at the sides and top. He has a little pointed chin, quite sharp, and a wide mouth.

He wears the palace livery, which is purple on account of his lofty position. He is very tall, and his tight purple pants make his legs look peculiarly skinny. He carries his hands, dressed in pale blue gloves, clasped behind his back, and walks very fastly, always seeming to be pacing and in a fiery hurry. Plumcake is extremely demanding of him, and that no doubt accounts for his agitated gait.

I met him one earlytime, whilst having a little stroll near the Salubrious Path. We struck up a converse, and he confided that he was out to buy some socks for Her Majesty. Of course I was impressed, especially so when I learnt they had to be stripey. 'Where might one find such a thingy?' he asked me. I didn't knowed, but I did happen to recall Mr Flower wearing often colorful socks, and suggested it might be worthwhile asking him about them.

We did, for Mustard didn't know where Mr Flower lived at, so I showed him, and introduced them to one another. Mr Flower let Mustard take two pair of stripey socks, which were both green and orange and yellow, to see if they might suit. Mustard was so very delighted to bring his quest to a successful conclusion, that he went about getting some employment for me at the palace, as a sort of thankily. I was offered the position of the Queen's Jester, which I accepted at once.

I haven't yet seen her wear the stripey socks.

Mr Cat cleared his throat. 'Just this earlytime, before breakfast,' he announced, 'I was thinkithinking thrice all everything, all at once. What do you say to that, Flower?'

Mr Flower tried to imagine what thinkithinking thrice all everything might be like. He couldn't thinky at all then, and forgots where he was for several moments.

'Hmm?' Mr Cat prompted his friend.

'Really, quite remarkableness!' said Mr Flower, and accidentally knocked over his teacup, so that his tea sloshed into the saucer, and onto the picnic table. 'Oh, dang,' he said very sadly. 'It was my most bestest cup of tea too.'

Strawberry poured him another. 'Don't upset yourself, dearness,' she sootheilyed.

'Thankily,' replied Mr Flower, wiping away a tear. Strawberry topped up her own teacup, and Mr Cat's. She smiled sweetly at Mr Cat, but she was secretly thinkying what a blustery puss he was. So full of himself!

'And, not at all easy to do,' he continued. 'Often I have pretty and tingly ideas. But, I don't make a fuss about them, do I, Strawberry, darling?'

Strawberry smiled again, but didn't quite manage it sincerely. Still, sometimes 'twas even rather funny to listen to him boasting about his cleveryness. 'And tell, what do you do with so many marvellous ideas that you have, Mr Cat? Even before breakfast!'

'I thinkied about them, dear. What else would one do with them?' He narrowed his eyes smugly.

'They sharn't have been very useful ideas then,' flipented Strawberry. 'Useful ideas lead to other thingys, apart from just thinkying.'

'Such as?' inquired Mr Flower, weeping gently.

'Such as... ideas for colorys, or... recipes,' she offered.

'Ah, bravo,' said Mr Flower quietly.

'Silly fruit,' pounced Mr Cat. 'Recipes and colorys do not count for pretty or tingly ideas. Why, even Flower has those, and he isn't at all clevery.'

Mr Flower never took offence at Mr Cat's derogatory remarks; just as though he hadn't understood the implications of them. 'I was thinkithinking of making some Butterijam, Mr Cat,' he said. 'Would you like some?'

'I've never heard of Butterijam,' Mr Cat replied. 'Are you making it up?'

'Well, I was going to,' explained Mr Flower.

'Splendid. I'll have some when you do,' Mr Cat smirked, and gave Strawberry an ambiguous glare.

From Mustard I have been able to gathery some nice stuffs worth to knowed about Twinkly.

He was born on the island, and his parents were James the Beard and the Lady Brandysnaps; it is due to these illustrious parents that he was able to acquire such a position of influence with the queen. Brandysnaps was her favorite, apparently.

I asked Mustard if there might ever have been any wars in Twinkly, and he said oh yes most certainly! and told me all about the annoyings quibbles that had happened with the Quibblers, before they moved to Quibbly.

The Twinklys had gotten frightfully upset about all the bickering and haranguing that went on about it all, but from what I can surmise, cross words were as dangerous as it got. *Actual* wars and fightings have never occurred here, it seems. Tomas, who was one of the Quibblers, suggested they might play a game of draughts to settle an obscure aspect of the dispute, much like a champion versus champion duel. The Twinklys liked the idea quite a lot, and thinkied it might be a very exciting way to settle matters.

Unfortunately, Tomas wouldn't agree to the standard rules of draughts, but wanted to play with a variant of his own, in which only one king was allowed, but several queens were introduced. He also disputed every detail of the proposed champions, including their manner of election, and what they might wear, and how old they should be etc etc.

The Twinklys had enough of him eventually, and someone kicked over the draughts table.

It seems to have been quite a profoundly wounding altercation for both sides.

'Please explain why recipes and colorys don't count, would you?' Strawberry asked Mr Cat.

'I shall, if you are quite finished interrupting me. You see, Flower, when one is contemplatying thrice all everything all at once, before breakfast, one can't allow oneself to be deflected by trifles.'

'Trifles?' Mr Flower enquired, still sniffily.

'Precisely. Recipes for trifles, or colorys. They are known amongst cleverys as 'frivolities.''

'Oh, they sound delicious though.'

'Of course, they very are. But, not nearly so delicious as grandiose schemes and marvellous musings.' Mr Cat sipped his tea delicately.

'And, did you bring some with you, for breakfast?' asked Mr Flower.

'Frivolities?'

'Yes, I should like to try some.'

'No, dear,' Mr Cat said. 'I didn't thinky of them.'

'Such a pity,' said Mr Flower.

Strawberry put her hand on Mr Flower's arm. 'You seem quite very upset this earlytime, Mr Flower,' she said kindly. 'Did something awful happen?'

'I was thinkying about the teacup,' he said, and started weeping gently once more.

'Dear, dear,' said Mr Cat, 'not worth crying over.'

'So very sads though,' wept Mr Flower.

'Let me carve us some blancmange,' offered Strawberry.

'Perhaps it will distract you.' There was a large wobbly white blancmange on a silver plate, that Mr Flower had made especially for breakfast, along with a dish of cold custard. He smiled at her suggestion, and she began. She carefully cut three generous slices, and scholpped them into three little bowls. She gave Mr Flower his serving first of all, and ladled custard upon it for him.

'Thankily,' he smiled.

'Would you like custard, Mr Cat?'

'Perhaps in a while,' he replied. 'I like to enjoy the tang unadorned to begin.'

'It used to be a rabbit,' said Mr Flower.

'The blancmange?' asked Strawberry, amazed.

'No, no, the teacup. It used to be a rabbit, until I turned it other side up. That's what did it. I thinky it enjoyed being a rabbit. It's been awfully quiet ever since it was a tea cup,' explained Mr Flower tearily. 'I wish I hadn't done it.'

Strawberry thinkied: *Poor Mr Flower! He gets really so confuzzled!* She said kindly: 'Well, at least we aren't eating him with custard,' and Mr Flower burst into fresh tears.

'Such a mean girl,' remarked Mr Cat spitefully.

Four

I do miss home, and all of my darling faery sisters, and even some of them annoying pixies! And I have been travelling now for the so longest clocks that I am often weepy and lonesome for home. Yet, of course, I know that every heroine is alone in her pilgrimage.

It was my choice to cross o'er the Inbetweens, and I was privy of what to expect.

How I dreamy of hot soup, and our beautifullness horses galloping o'er the white Fields of Stars. I dreamy of you weaving your Blankets of Infinity, with your golden hair tumbled across the firmament. I remembery our warmth, and it keeps me truest and longing for our friendship.

I have my own little house here. It is very prettiness, with tiniest flowers growing along the stone walls, and a roof made of woven straws. I burn a cosy log fire at the hearth at dusks, and sit and smoke my pipe, and write these rememberys for you.

The house is situated amongst the Squiggly Hills. I have a little privacy, because the Twinklys are mostly lazy to visit me, but I am always close to visit their town, and observe and learnings.

On Whensday, Mr Flower took a stroll before lunchtime. He was trying to invent a new recipe. He enjoyed making recipes, and he liked eating food, so cooking seemed a perfect pastime for him.

The orangeyyellowroundythingy was bright and warm over Twinkly, and Mr Flower felt happy and content whilst he rambled through the prettiness groves, and dillied along the winding lanes, and dallied outside the Cakery.

He bought himself a cupcake, and sat on the hilltop, the one beneath the Weeping Tree, to eat it.

Yes, he felt quite happy and content this nearlylunchtime. Until he met Aelinor, that is.

'I can't stay to chat,' said Aelinor. 'I have importants to doido.'

'Oh, that is a pity,' replied Mr Flower.

'For you, perhaps. I like having importants to doido, so for me it really isn't a pity at all,' Aelinor smiled, and sat down on the grass next to Mr Flower. 'And what is it you are doing this nearlylunchtime?'

'I'm making recipes,' replied Mr Flower.

'Splendid and admirable!' said Aelinor enthusiastically. 'What have you got so far?'

'Oh!' Mr Flower was delighted to share his recipe inventions, and eager for encouragement. Cooking was a lonely hobby otherwise.

'Is that all? Only 'Oh'? I suppose it's a start.'

'No, no, that isn't a recipe. I was only pleased to be asked,' replied Mr Flower.

'I see!' Aelinor jumped up quickly. 'I can't stay to chat, anyhow. Very importants to do!' She waved and trotted off down the hill. Mr Flower watched her go.

'Peanutbutterylemoncurdy Breads,' he called out, when Aelinor had reached the bottom of the hill. 'It's made with peanutbuttery and lemoncurdy. And served with breads.'

Aelinor didn't respond, as she was too far away to have heard. Mr Flower sighed, and suddenly felt quite sads.

After a minute or two Mr Flower said aloud, addressing no one in particular, except of course himself: 'And, I invented Gherkin Flan outside the Cakery.' He counted off the ingredients on his fingers.

'It's pickles, sweet potatoes, salt and coriander. And it should better be served with gherkins.'

The orangeyyellowroundythingy shone brightly, and little butterflies pranced among the violets. Mr Flower brushed the cupcake crumbs from his trousers.

'A peculiar thingy about life,' he said sadly, 'is that it often seems a little too difficults, and perhaps too long. If only 'twere like a teapot, from which one could empty out the dregs, refill and begin again.'

'That's only because you are silly, and have been doing it all wrong,' said Mr Cat, who had been napping in the branches of the Weeping Tree. 'And a flan needs pastry,' he added.

'Oh, but I get into such a muddle when I try to bakey pastry,' explained Mr Flower.

'It sharn't be a flan then. You should call it 'Pickley Potato.'
That would be sensibubble.'
'But I want it to be a flan,' said Mr Flower.
'Then you must have a bed of pastry, dear,' said Mr Cat sleepily.
'Bothery,' said Mr Flower crossly. Then he enquired: '*A bed of pastry?*'
'For the pickles and potatoes.'
'Well!' Mr Flower exclaimed. He was thinkyful for a few moments. Mr Cat yawned, then stretched, then turned around in a full circle on the branch he was on, then settled comfortably again.
'No wondery they have been so irritables! I've been having all kinds of troubles with my pickles recently. They are probably just tireds.'
Mr cat frowned. He scratched his ear.
'To make a flan, you must first line your baking tin with pastry, Flower,' he explained sleepily. 'Then you put the pickles and potatoes onto the pastry. But, you should add some eggs and milk to bind, for it to truly be a flan. And, you are ready to bakey in a moderate oven.'
'Oh. Do the pickles need to sleep at all?'
'You can allow them to rest in some salt, if you like.'
'Ah,' said Mr Flower.
'Would they enjoy to rest in the pastry tin?' he asked, after a minute or so.
'It isn't strictly necessary,' Mr Cat said.
'I'd rather not make pastry unless I absolutely have to,' Mr Flower said, a bit grumpily.
'Put them on breads, and call it a sandwich,' suggested Mr Cat.
'I can't. Sandwiches aren't real proper recipes, Mr Cat.'
'Quite so,' replied Mr Cat, as he fell asleep.

Mr Flower, if you remembery, liked to collect thingys. He had more of them than he quite knew what to do with. Sometimes he couldn't remembery where he might have put one of them. That's exactly what happened after lunch on Whensday.
He had just sat down in his armchair, the one indoors next to the fireplace, and was drinking a glass of lemonade. 'Where is

that thingy?' he asked, aloud.

Mr Flower always answered himself, if he had asked a question out loud, because he felt it was impolite not to do so. He replied: 'Which thingy?'

'The bendy twirly one.'

'I'm terribly sorry, but I don't know. Do you?'

'I don't either,' he replied.

'How odd.'

'Isn't it though?'

'I've looked everywhere. I started in the bedroom, and finished in the fridge.'

'Ah,' he interrupted himself, 'I remembery. I thinky 'twere under that lid.'

'Quite right, but it was only my other hat. I jumped under the bridge, and walked past the Gorgeousy Gate. I called upon Mrs Pheasant, but she couldn't telled.'

'Did you leave her with Peanutbuttery Breads?'

'I did.'

'So kind. She very likes those.'

'I climbed a tree, and swam in a ditch. I still wouldn't find it.'

'I remembery seeing it somewhere,' Mr Flower said to himself helpfully.

'Do you know whereabouts?'

"No, but it was wearing blue and green trousers, and a nice squinkly cravat.'

'I thinkied of Mr Cat. But he said 'No.' Twice, in fact.'

'He's quite helpful.'

'Yes,' Mr Flower agreed with himself.

'Well. I sat in a field, and spoke with a Daw, who had no idea what I was looking for. I was about to give up, but I forgots and carried on.'

He sighed sadly. 'It's been peculiary, hasn't it?'

'Or perhaps it's always like that?'

'Can't you remembery?'

'Only until I forgets.'

'So annoyings though.'

'This lemonade needs more butteryscotch,' he observed.

Five

Today I bought myself a hat from the Hat Shop. It is red, and has a small green feather pinned to the band. It cost tuppence, which I thinkied was very reasonable.

The best Hatter in Twinkly was probably Mrs Fleur, and from the little flower stitched inside the hat, I knewed 'twere one of hers. She is Strawberry's mother. She moved away from Twinkly some clocks ago, and went to live in France. She caught a ride on a French trading ship; they visit every so often for the flan trades. She is skilled and nimble-fingered at Hattery, and makes her colorys very nicely.

The only other Hatter in Twinkly that I'm aware of is Mr Blue, and he makes all of his hats from paper, and colorys them with crayons. They are no good at all when it rains.

Queen Plumcake was feeling distracted this lunchtime, and whilst she was eating her cheesecake and cream, she told me I must telled her some funniness.

Well, I felt butterfly belly. It was the firstest she had asked me to make her laugh so far. My head became instant custard, and all I could thinky was the cheesecake swimming in it, like a little boat. That wasn't slightly helpful.

'Your Plumnessly,' I said, swirlitwirling my arms and hands to distract her, "twere evident from tickiclocks that 'twere sillyo'tock, when all the sensibubbles stoppistopped.' And, I made a nice curtsey. It was a horrid moment, because I knewed 'twere not at all the sort of funniness she'd want. At best it was a confuzzly amusingness. How silly a Jester I am, when I don't even know a solitary joke!

She frowned, and paused with the cheesecake on her spoon. Mustard came to my rescue. 'That's very amusing, Jester,' he said.

Plumcake smiled, and ate her spoonful of cheesecake. She dismissed me with a wave of her spoon. 'And find some nicer funnies, you horrible little man!' she shouted after me.

Strawberry called upon Mr Flower on Firstday. He seemed

awfully sads. 'I am awfully sads,' he admitted.

He was very often falling into flunks, the poor dear. She liked Mr Flower, yet he forgots everything so quickly and easily, and got himself into such muddles, that he often seemed like a helpless little bird fallen from the nest. She did have to keep picking him up and placing him back inside. *You will keep jumping though, won't you?* she thinkied. *You're the silliest little bird.*

'Why are you sads?' she asked gently.

'I want to sing a song,' he replied in a tiny voice.

'Oh!' A peculiar thingy to be awfully sads about! 'Would you like me to listen?' she asked, trying not to giggle.

'Yes please,' he replied tearfully.

Strawberry waited politely.

'It's a very teary sads song though,' he said, in way of warning.

'Okay,' she replied, and made a small show of bracing herself, by sitting up straighter. She smiled to indicate that she was ready, and Mr Flower began. He had quite a lovely voice, and he sang the song very quietly and slowly.

'Tis a sad sads story,
I shall telled you how and why;
the weepiest weepy, terribly teary tale.
But, if you forgets it fastly
it doesn't feel so bad.
There's a thingy on top,
and a swirliswirl in the muddle.
You might not know
that every flower grows
if you feed it waterys, and warmirays,
if you let it breathe.
But, don't sit on it;
they don't seem to enjoy that much.
There's a thingy on top,
and a twirlitwirl in the muddle.
If you spanglytweak it
you might get a glistny:
or nothing. Nothing at all.

'Thank you, dearness,' Strawberry said when he had finished the song. 'It was really very lovely.' Mr Flower frowned, so she added, 'And *terribly* sads!'
'Thankily,' he smiled.

Mr Flower is a peculiar looking chap. His nose is small and buttony, and his eyes are round and blue. He has wild curly hair, of a light brown colory, which sometimes he keeps beneath a hat. His hats are either tall or flat, and often they are green, mauve, or black. Sometimes yellowy.

'Is that my spanglyswirlys tweaking?' Mr Flower suddenly asked aloud, and cocked his head to the side, listening. 'I'm sure it must be,' he said, 'because I can hear tweaking, and I don't knowed who else should be tweakily, not in these parts.' He was in the woods. He had been having a leisurely stroll, and thinkying of cakes.
'Bothery,' he muttered, turning around to look back towards his little house, which he couldn't see because it was obscured by trees and some hills. 'Who could be spanglying me at this hour of the day? It's just after lunchtime, when polite people are properly thinkying of cakes and tea-time deserts. It's most inappropriate to spangly now. I'm of a mind to go and found out who it is!'
He placed his hands on his hips, and glared furrowly towards where his little house was, if he could have seen it past the trees and hills. He waited. He didn't hear any more tweaking. 'Hmmpf,' he concluded, and continued with his leisurely stroll. 'I shall find out everyone who has a spanglytwirly, and discovery who 'twere.'
He came then into a small clearing of the woods, and standing on a heavy fallen trunk was a small silver-coloryed bird. When it saw Mr Flower it started tweaking, trillily and rather prettily. Mr Flower pointed a finger at the little bird crossly. 'Don't be impertinent!' he said to the bird. "Tis a serious matter! Is *everything* a joke to you people?'
The little bird kept tweaking. Mr Flower gave it his crossest

frown, but the bird didn't seem to mind.

'Was it a friend of yours spanglying me?' he asked. 'Well, please tell them not to, especially when I am not at home. It's inconvenient. Nor after lunchtime. Or just before tea-time neither. In fact, don't spangly me unless I've invited you to.'

The bird fell silent.

'Thankily,' said Mr Flower, and soon started thinkying of cakes once more.

Mr Cat was very adept at sleeping. One of his favourite places to nap was in the branches of the Weeping Tree, and he could quite often be found there. However, he didn't often enjoy being found there.

Aelinor met him there on Fryday.

'Good earlytime, Mr Cat!' called Aelinor, standing beneath the tree.

Mr Cat opened his eyes, then closed them again. 'I am busy,' he said.

'Oh! I do beg your pardon,' said Aelinor loudly and apologetically.

'I thinkithinked you were just napping.'

'*Just* napping?' Mr cat sighed slowly. 'Napping this well is an art, you silly person. And, there are few better at it than I. Kindly move along and allow me to work.'

Aelinor furrowed her brow, and thinkied for a few moments, but didn't move away from the tree. At last she said: 'It's just that I don't have any importants to do till nearlylunch. I thinkithinked it would be nice to have a chat with Mr Cat. You know how awfully busyness I usually am. Who could knowed when we might have such a chance again, on such a pleasanty earlytime?'

'Go away,' said Mr Cat. 'Or I sharn't be polite.'

Aelinor thinkied *that* wasn't polite, but she said fare well, and wandered away dejectedly. Twice she looked back to see if he might change his mind, and call her back for a nice chat. He didn't.

She decided to go to her own little house, and after she got there she composed a ryme about Mr Cat, which she added to the book that she was writing. No one in Twinkly knew that she was writing a book, or even supposed that she was clevery enough to do so. They would make such a fuss if they did know, and want her to read and re-read to them the bits that were about *themselves*. It would be very bothery indeed, Aelinor thinkied. So she never did tell.

This is the ryme she wrote about Mr Cat:

Wove a dreamy with shoelace.
Telled tyme by fallen twig.
If 'tis overly small ne'er gonna be big.
Sang a melody in b flat minor.
Coloried in pastel.
Wore his hat t'other side around.
Snoozy in the Weeping Tree,
other side up.
Drinks liquorish from a buttercup.
He's so contrary.
What a funny peculiar curious, isn't he?

Six

I have gotten myself a job as a courier, working for the palace.
I delivery letters and parcels. Most days I am kept busyness
walking with my deliveries.
Queen Plumcake is a frightful frump, and she is perpetually
cross about something or another. Since I also have
employment as Court Jester, I see quite an amount of her.
She likes blancmange and cheesecake, and having her portrait
coloried.

As you are privy, my dearest sister, it is very much always
doors and looking-glasses that we must employ to traverse the
Inbetweens. Firstest stop from the Hill of Stars is Earth-realm,
and from there I had to cross to the astrals.
It was whilst in Earth-realm that I found this cutest li'l compact
powder case, with a round mirror that I could dreamy into it. It
has been terribly useful, since I can carry it about with me, in
my waistcoat pocket. The casing is made all of silver, and has
flowers and leaves and vines carved into it.
At first, I was stepping across the staccatos, and I was grown
so huge that I saw the myriad spheres sparkling and glisting as
I strode. It was quite a lovely nice way of stuffs, I was thinky.
After some clocks and ages I fell upon a strange stair. It
spiralled out of a clustered galaxy, made seeming of mother-of-
pearl, so prettiness, and following to its topmost stair I grew
tireds and sleepiness. I lay down for a nap, and tumbled into a
cascade of dreamys.

'I don't like this hat,' said Mr Flower crossly. 'It makes me look
fat.'
'Why do you wear it then?' asked Mr Cat reasonably.
'It keeps my hair tidy, obviouses,' replied Mr Flower, somewhat
petulantly. 'And, I never know where my comb is.'
'It's in your top pocket,' pointed out Mr Cat.
'Only when I don't need it, Mr Cat. Only when I don't *need* it.'
Mr Cat sipped his tea.

Yesterness when all the stars died.

I blew my smokes into the night, and there were flowers raining, and worlds colliding, and the chorus was so beautifuls that even the Breath gods came to play and feast, and you know how shy they are! They brought blisses and dreamycakes. It was darling, really was.

They, against the firmament, darkening all the stars with their burnished fires, in rank and rank and rank, so bright and fiery and powerful strong; and beautifuls flashing bronze and sparking silver, and golds and Brilliant Depth Blue, and Scarlett Weeping Reds, and orange and umber and yellow and glow.

I bowed my head and wept.

For, to reprise:

'Twere beauteous moonlight for thousand years, and so very prettiprettinesses, when every darling dear took wing o'er the Lush Meadow; zillions of the spangliglistenys.

Tearifalls gladinesslys, and happihopatoe over the Gorgeousy Gate.

Funny peculiar curious in bold and brilliant, weren't it?

My courier work is taking me abroad; today, I visited Li'l Oohs properly. It is still exactly as I was led to believe: quite nice. It is a small village, with about one hundred Li'l Ohhlians, and not very many shops. It is quaint and prettiness, with an abundance of flowery beds and boxes hanging.

I was to delivery a parcel to Mrs Jacques. It wasn't heavy, and I bore it in my knapsack, and the stroll was pleasanty through earlytime, and the orangeyyellowroundythingy was hot and beaming, so I lazilyed o'er the Squiggly Hills, ever looking out for windows and doors, though still I can't discovery any at all.

I gave the parcel to her, which was a rectangular shape, and wrapped in plain brown papers, and tied with Mendy-Strings. Mrs Jacques is a plump lady, and wore a dress to her knees made with flowerys and coloried blue and yellow, with white. Her face was burnished, and her smile was warm.

'Come on in,' she invited me, and showed me the nature of her hospitality. She made me tea to drink, and cut a slice of heavy cake for me to enjoy. And, I did.

She opened her parcel right there in the kitchen, and as I was naturally curious to discovery what had been sent that I had couriered, I watched with interestings.

'Twere a box of colory pencils, bought from the Colory Shop in Twinkly, and sent with a note from Mustard, which read:

Dear Mrs Jacques, If you could please to be so very kindness as to colory some socks into stripes for Her Majesty. And be doing so quite as fastly as you can, dear, since Queen Plumcake is being very difficults about her rightful socks of recent. With fine and cordial regards.

Mrs Jacques politely read the note aloud, and wasn't at all minded for me to hear.

'Well now,' she said thinkily.

'Oh, you colory socks, Mrs Jacques?' I said enquiring.

'I never have so before!' she replied, and laughed until the kettle boiled.

After leaving Li'l Oohs I meandered. I struck out southerly from the village, and let my feet see where we should get to. I passed o'er some prettiness dales, and through gentle valleys, and I wonderyed if perhaps soon I would arrive at the south coast of the Great Waters.

I didn't make it so far though, and let me note here now that one lunchtime I will certainly try again, and keep going until I discovery its beaches.

If one could find a horse to ride in Twinkly, then gosh, it would make my courier job very much easier, and I should finish all my deliverys so much more fastly. Do you know, I don't thinky they have even invented the saddle here yet. How funny askew their developments are, aren't they?

I mention it since I met a horse today!

'Twas a beautifulness obsidian-coloryed creature, and we met upon a field, after I had walked into nearlytea-time. I shared my sandwich with him, for 'twere a stallion, and I asked if I might climb up onto his back, and ride back to Twinkly? He laughed at the suggestion, and trotted off when he realised I had no more sandwiches to share.

It wasn't the first horse I have seen here: there were in fact one or two working in Li'l Oohs, and I saw also some in Northland whilst I was there.

I thinkied, and decided that I had been walking with my feet for such long clocks that I was tiredness, and that was why I wanted horses to carry me. I was being unfair and selfish.

'Twere clevery of the horses here to have avoided being ridden by people, like they are in every elsewhere, and so I sharn't mention saddles to anyone.

'How are your recipes coming along?' Strawberry asked Mr Flower, when they had sat down. It was Moonday, and so, as on every Moonday, Mr Cat and Mr Flower were come to Strawberry's little house for lunch. The orangeyyellowroundythingy was being friendly warm, so they had decided to sit at the garden table.

Strawberry had baked French Fancies, in pink and pale blue and dreamy yellow. She had swirlied little icing-sugaree bows on them, very prettily. Mr Cat pulled a face, as though he weren't to like them.

'I don't speak *French*,' he complained.

'You sharn't need to *talk* with them, dear,' said Strawberry, being clevery, 'just eat them!'

Mr Cat ate several, but quite grumpily.

'Very well! Thankily,' answered Mr Flower. 'Do you thinkithink I should serve Peanutbutterylemoncurdy with breads?'

'Rather than gherkins, anyhow,' smiled Mr Cat.

'I thinkied you enjoyed gherkins, Mr Cat?' said Mr Flower, surpriseyed.

'Sometimes,' Mr Cat replied.

'I didn't thinky of gherkins though. I was wondery: breads, or a spoon?'

Neither of them answered his question. Mr Cat ate another French Fancy, a pink one, and Strawberry said: 'All your recipes have peanutbuttery and lemoncurdy, don't they?'

'Certainly not. I don't know why'd you say so. Gherkin Flambe has nietherly.'

'You are being cantankerous and argumentative this noon, you rotten fruit,' said Mr Cat to Strawberry, very unkindly.

'Perhaps she didn't drink enough tea?' suggested Mr Flower. 'I get quite dizzy if I don't have plenty.'

'You do serve peanutbuttery and lemoncurdy with it though, don't you? As condiments?' she insisted.

'Well, of course!' answered Mr Flower.

Strawberry poured him some more tea.

'I don't know why the gherkins always flambe,' he added. 'Do you suppose they just *want* to?'

Strawberry suggested: 'Perhaps too much flame?'

'But, how else should I cook them?'

'Do you need to *cook* them?' she laughed.

'He must eat, silly girl,' said Mr Cat.

'I'm glad your recipes are coming along, dear,' she said kindly to Mr Flower, patting his hand affectionately. 'And, I wondery, does your Gherkin Pie have any gherkins in it?'

'Certainly not!' he replied. 'How uncomfy for them!'

'On the side,' elucidated Mr Cat helpfully.

Seven

Strawberry is quite one of the more sensibubble Twinklys that I have friended with. She doesn't appear to mind all the very sillinesses of Mr Cat and Mr Flower. She has cutes hair, which is pink, in three shades, and curliness heavily, with ringlets and some waves.

She has some othery interestings for me, because I know she is buildying a Spaceyship, since she told me that she were. Twinkly is such an unusual place, with several strangeinesses, that who'd know if a Spaceyship she builded might work or no?

'I bought the engine very firstest,' she said. 'I'd like for you to come and visit it, Aelinor.' I replied how delighted I would be. 'What I really need now is some swirlitwirlys, some buttony thingys, and some fasty-fast stripes. If you could discovery any on your travels abroad, please do acquire them for me, would you, dearness?'

I replied of course I should look out for any thingy which might suit a Spaceyship. She was happy, and gave me a French Fancy. It was sky blue, and its ribbon was parma-lilac.

'Oh, I say, isn't that Aelinor?' said Strawberry, pointing towards the Lush Meadows.

'It certainly might be,' answered Mr Flower punctiliously, 'but rather too far away to be certain.'

'What is she doing, do you thinkithink?' wonderyed Strawberry.

'Meandering o'er the lush meadow,' replied Mr Cat dryly.

'She is so swirlitwirl, isn't she?' observed Mr Flower. 'Seems to walk in circleys, rather than frontways or backways.'

'A renowned dillier,' purred Mr Cat.

'But, is she coming for lunch, do you suppose?' asked Strawberry.

'She might have set out sooner,' said Mr Cat. 'She'll do well to arrive before teatime.'

'There sharn't be any blancmange left,' said Mr Flower, schoolping the last slice into his bowl.

'But, she may indeed arrive early for *supper*,' added Mr Cat with a wide grin.

'Oh, it really is Aelinor! Hurrah!' exclaimed Strawberry, after Aelinor had tumbled down a sloping hill, and was thereby easier to see, being much closer to Strawberry's little house. 'I should make more tea.'

'Yes, you *should*,' said Mr Cat and Mr Flower together.

'They might be nice with custard,' mused Mr Flower, when Strawberry had gone inside to make more tea.

'What, dear?' asked Mr Cat.

'Squazillion sprinklithousands,' replied Mr Flower.

'Oh,' said Mr Cat.

'I tried them with shortcake,' Mr Flower continued.

'Terribly polite, shortcake, but not at all tall,' smiled Mr Cat.

'Quite so. I thinkithinked it didn't somehow work,' explained Mr Flower. 'But now I'm wondery if they just wanted some custard?'

'Did you ask them?'

'Who?'

'The shortcakes.'

'No. Should I have?'

'It is polite to ask, Flower,' said Mr Cat.

'Of course it is. Silly me,' said Mr Flower sadly.

The two friends sat quietly for a minute or so. Strawberry returned bearing the laden tea tray.

'I brought some biscuits,' she told them, 'in case Aelinor missed lunch.'

'Jolly nice,' said Mr Flower, helping himself to several.

'Splendid,' said Mr Cat. 'Such a thinkyful girl, aren't you?' He scooped several biscuits onto his plate.

'Thankily, dear,' replied Strawberry. 'Save some for Aelinor, won't you?'

'There mightn't be enough,' observed Mr Flower.

'Not if you eat them *all*, there won't be,' laughed Strawberry.

'You may need to fetch more, just in case,' suggested Mr Cat purrily, and began to pour the tea.

This sharn't be the book about the many wonderys that followed me, once I had cast out from the Hill of Stars. There are too many adventures to fit into such a small space as a book is. I will have to write those all the other happenings in another place, a different book, when I do get myself back home again. For now I shall keep my thinkings upon Twinkly, and all thingys which happen here, so that I won't forgets or become muddled.

I should probably have written my adventures whilst I was in them, during the Inbetweens, but actually I never had a pen with me. Or a paper book, like I have here. I hope they are properly stored in my heart, and I'll recall them for you, and all thingys that I learned, at home. If I try to write them now, I'll lose all the Twinkly happenings instead.

I want to say every hundred thingys to you, all at once, but the pages would get so higgledy and without sense if I did, so I sharn't. It is still likely to be front to back and other side up though.

It does sometimes take an awful lot of words before something is said nice without confuzzles, doesn't it? Even quite simplenesses can take pages and pages. It might take books and books full of words to make true the magics, so that my wishes reach you across all the universes between us.

I know you are always so generous, wishing me sunshines and glisting moonbeams, in that prettiest way of yours. I hope that you shall feel my truth, and know my love, even if I should never get back home.

'Were it ticklish?' Mr Flower enquired.

'Whatever do you mean, Mr Flower?' Strawberry asked.

'When your head was in the teapot,' said Mr Cat. 'Do pay attention, you silly fruit.'

'Or were it spanglitwangly makeytoesglow?'

'How did you feel about it yesterness?' Mr Cat asked her.

'I hadn't thinkied of it,' she replied, rather confuzzled by their sudden questions. Had she been asleep during the first part of this conversation, she wonderyed? At times she did doze off after lunch, whilst Mr Flower and Mr Cat rambled sillily about nonsenses. She couldn't always manage being polite enough to listen; and the orangeyyellowroundythingy being so friendly warm at lunchtimes, and with her tummy full; well, it just made her sleepy. But she didn't remembery having just woken up. Probably better not to ask, she told herself.

'How curiousy,' remarked Mr Flower.

'Most peculiary,' agreed Mr Cat. 'Do have some tea, Strawbz,' he added purrily.

'Thankily,' she smiled.

'Coldibone and sugaree?' he asked.

'No sugaree and quite hot, pretty please,' she replied.

Mr Flower spat his own tea out in surprise. 'No sugaree?' he exclaimed, aghast.

Mr Cat stopped in mid-pour. 'Oh, that simply won't do,' he said seriously.

'I always take my tea like that,' Strawberry said.

'Dear, dear, how awfully troubling,' said Mr Flower.

'Mistily,' agreed Mr Cat.

Strawberry frowned. Her friends were often peculiar, but they were being very silly this lunchtime. Surely they had noticed that she *never* had taken sugaree with her tea? But, they did enjoy *everything* being so sweet all the time. Even Mr Flower's Gherkin Pie was syrupy.

'I suppose that accounts for it,' said Mr Flower to Mr Cat.

'Quite possibubbly,' Mr Cat concurred.

'Accounts for what?'

'For your not being ticklish yesterness, dear,' said Mr Flower, patting her hand as though she were a simpleton, which made her feel a little bit cross at him.

'Oh, botherys,' she said, 'I'll pour it myself!' She took the pot from Mr Cat, and poured the tea.

'Such a silly girl,' said Mr Cat across the table to Mr Flower, in a very audible whispery.

'Some whisperys are rude,' Strawberry reminded him.

'I don't enjoy whisperys,' said Mr Flower. 'They make me feel excluded.'

'Precisely why one should always do them quite loudly,' said Mr Cat, with a smile. 'Don't you agree, dear?'

'With whom?' asked Mr Flower.

'With *what*,' Mr Cat corrected him.

'I'm sorry, but I've forgottens,' said Mr Flower sadly. 'I can only remember until I forgets. So annoyings!'

'Don't worry yourself, Flower,' Mr Cat said kindly. He cleared his throat importantly, and then asked Strawberry: 'Were it?'

'Neitherly, Mr Cat,' she replied, sipping her tea. 'I told already, I was just tireds.'

'Oh, bravo!' said Mr Flower.

'Welcome back,' said Mr Cat.

Eight

Aelinor arrived at Strawberry's little house rather late for lunch.
In fact, when she went around to the garden, all the lunch
paraphrenalia had already been cleared away, the cups and
bowls and plates, and there wasn't anything there to eat at all.
'Perhaps I am early for supper,' thinkied Aelinor, and sat in
Strawberry's comfortable strawberry-milkshake-pink armchair.
She dozed, and upon waking she saw that it was quite late.
There were no lights on in the house, and twilight was
beginning to rise up into the sky.
Aelinor took out her little pipe from her waistcoat pocket, and
began to smoke. She often wore smart waistcoats. The little
pockets were quite handy for tinder and pipe. Aelinor blew thin
smoke rings up into the sky, chasing the gloam.
The twilight was crimson and pink. She watched it bleed away
into dusk, and the garden around her blurred into shadows.

And, so I tumblyed in that cascade of dreamys.
And in my dreamy we were bound, as once before; the looking-
glass and the reflection. There was no separation between us
now, nor could there ever be. We were shaped as twin dragons,
august and, oh, so beauteous beautifuls!
Down we spiralled, weaven as one, and the universes parted
before our descent, like great oceans thrown back, and the stars
fled from our approach. They were burning and coruscate,
bursting with sudden fullnesses, and the fiery sparks caught in
our tails, so that we blazed as we plummeted; laughing, joyous,
rapt with deep blisses, and swooning for the rushing speed of it,
and the tearing apart of the fabrics.
We spread our great wings, and sang our fires, and the planets
toppled and fell with us. The galaxies sundered, the staccato
realms span in dizzy whirlpools, awning wide before us, and
we devoured them all.
Forever we fell, and we were all the firmaments and every
spinning multiverse; we were broad and fathomless, and
nothing could sate us.
Light flooded us; the fates strummed their wheel, so that we

turned and turned in endless perfection, fires flashing on our starry skins.

We heard the distant drum of the gods: and they were galloping, galloping.

The fabrics folded into and over us, into and over us, until we became only a tiny point within them. Above us, the gods leapt across the white, and the new day stretched behind them, like unfurling sails of cloud and skies.

Mr Cat is an intriguing fellow. The firstest thingy about him that one notices are his zingy whiskers. They are silvery, long, and twirly, and stand out from his furry face. He said about them: '*They are terribly awfully useful, Aelinor, my dearest fellow. What a pity you are a girl, and sharn't be able to grow any! Not only do they allow me to tune, but they also can be stretched and pinged for very nice effect! And, they tell me if a box should be just right or too small.*'

It is true that Mr Cat can be grumpy, and irritable, he has a lack of patience, and he is a pompous ninny who thinkithinks himself so very clevery.

Still tough, he manages to be agreeable with enough frequency so as to make himself tolerable and likeable. If you happen to find him jovial and sociable, which he is most days for an hour or three, then he is friendly and entertaining company. He likes string, boxes, and paper bags.

He doesn't ever work at a job, so I don't know how he manages to pay his bills; but perhaps that is why he sleeps in the branches of the Weeping Tree.

I thinkied to invite him over to my little house, and wonderyed if he might enjoy to sleep by the fire some nights, but he replied that I am far too very annoyings for him to be able to see so much of me. 'But, do let me know if you are away, and I should be happy to oblige,' he said.

Strawberry wasn't at home, you see. She had decided, soon after lunch, that it was high clock for an adventure. She cleared the garden table of lunch thingys, and washed up the plates and bowls and cups and glasses and cutlery.

She brushed her long tumbly pink curls, then tied them back with a bright blue ribbon, and went off across Downey Fields, which was northwards from her little house, to her workshop. She was wearing her Flight jacket, which has a lovely furry collar, and her powder blue suede gloves, and blue Puddle boots.

She was buildying a Spaceyship inside the workshop, as I telled. She had been buildying it for several weeks now, but it still wasn't ready. Her adventure couldn't really begin until it was finished, but she considered even the buildying of it to be somewhat of an exciting venture. *And a venture is very almost an adventure*, she thinkied cleverly.

The very firstest thing a Spaceyship needed was, of course, an engine. It couldn't fly at all well without one! Strawberry had bought an engine that used to fit into a printing press, and she had set it in the very middle of the workshop, on top of a table. She had also bought some goggles, which she liked to wear whilst working on the Spaceyship, although the goggle lenses were a bit cloudy and not easy to see clearly through.

She hadn't been able to start the engine as yet, but that hardly mattered since the rest of the Spaceyship wasn't near ready. Mostly whilst she was buildying her Spaceyship she sat on the long red sofa that she had placed along one of the walls, the wall opposite the door, drinking creamsoda or lemonade, and daydreamyed about the adventures she would have once everything was working all ticketyboo.

And, daydreamying an adventure wasn't very much different from actually having an adventure, she found. In a way it was even better, because one didn't have to get dirty, or tireds, or miss supper.

'I should most definitely get some wirliswirly buttonys too, and put them on a nice console thingy, and perhaps a monitor screen,' she mused aloud, and sipped her lemonade: how delicious it always tasted when she was inside her Spaceyship! She took off the goggles, and lent back into the sofa's plump cushions. She closed her eyes, and with a little smile, started to imagine a Spaceyship adventure.

We can't expect all thingys to be delicious magicks and faery wishes coming true; not when we aren't at the Hill of Stars!

This life now is more to do with cups of tea and slices of cake and shopping; the paradise delights!

Oh, and I had dreamt of you, my sweetest sister, and you wore the prettiest dress; a thousand sparkling pearls, stitched and sewn by the li'l darling faery.

You were stood upon the tip of a ragged cliff, overlooking the forest of the world, and you seemed like a goddess; beautiful, graceful, and full with divine magics.

You sang, and a note came from between your lips, visible and tangible, and morphed into a brilliant humming bird.

The humming bird flew out, over the forest, like the day rising, and the trees stretched up their branches towards it, like arms and fingers.

Nine

I travelled to Northland yesterness, 'twere a Someday. 'Tweren't no markets on, on account of it being a Someday, but I had an importants letter to delivery.

It was a big white envelope, with a golden seal of the palace, and it was addressed: *M. Mengette, 12 La rue Marche, Paris, Northland.*

The golden seal was set with a stamped plumcake, which meant it was from Her Majesticness Plumcake herself, in her own script, by her own plump hand. How intrigues, n'est pas?

I hadn't been to Northland for some clocks, and I had visited Paris in rather a tizzyrush when I did get there, and couldn't have leisure to find pleasures, so I was glad to be visiting again. This clock I might relax and breathe the Parisian scents.

It was the peculiarist thingy, dear: I saw a bicycle! It was a very quaint style, with one enormous front wheel, and a little silly back wheel, and the chap riding it was ever so wobbly. *Pennyfarthings*, we would call them. How strange; I hadn't even noticed the absence of wheeled vehicles at all! Well, obviouses I noticed Twinkly hasn't gotten motor-cars yet, and lovely peaceful and clean, and slow, it is without them. But, I hadn't thinkithinked of bicycles, and it was such a stunning sight for me!

What an absurd innovation Strawberry's Spaceyship shall be. Especially if it flies!

I've seen a lady who was riding a goat, near Cherry Town. And, I saw a horse that pulled a plough o'er the field. But, Twinklys don't usually ride animals, certainly not as custom. They carry their own baggages. How odd, isn't it? Quite kindness, too.

Do you suppose I should acquire a goat?

I met the secretary of M. Mengette, and he took the letter from me, very sternly, and I wasn't able to know what Plumcake had been writing about.

Nevermind, I thinkied, and strolled through the streets of Paris. I breathed deeply the air, and it was quite smelly of lime and tarps.

They have several interestings shops in Paris. I browsed lazily, since I wanted especially to be leisurely this clock whilst there, banishing regrets.

I found some buttonys for Strawberry, and I decided with an idea to help her with the Spaceyship, in subtleness and magicks, so that it may indeed work. What would be most useful to me is if it were an inter-dimensional craft, so that it could cross o'er the Inbetweens. If she'd allow for me to make such use of it, of course. Perhaps, although how unusual 'twould be, the Spaceyship itself could be the door I am seeking? A metaphorical aperture.

I can make some nice wishes upon the buttonys, and other stuffs I discovery for her, so that they fit together to make an effective machine.

Furtherly, I buyed myself a very nice writing pen, which is a soft orange colory, with a golden band at its muddle. I am employing it now, to write this. It makes script very prettily.

Also, I bought a tremendous fork for eating foods with. It cost fivepence, which really is rather expensive. It is silver coloryed, and made exquisitely well, and so I paid the pennies. I used it to eat my supper with and it worked perfectly!

'It's called a *Spaceyship,*' she told Mr Cat, feeling quite rather cross at him being so very critical always, 'because it has a lot of *space* inside.'

'Nonsense!' he huffed.

'Yes, it has, and it is,' she insisted. 'Why, it even has swirlitwirly buttonys, and Aelinor is going to try getting some go-fasty stripes for the console.'

'Does it have an engine?' he asked, condescendingly.

'An engine was the firstest thingy I bought, dear,' she replied.

'Oh!' replied Mr Cat, and then asked if he might come and see the Spaceyship one day.

'Perhaps,' Strawberry said, 'it rather depends.'

'Upon what?'

But upon *what* Strawberry refused to tell.

Mustard says that most Twinklys, although kind and nice company, are lazy and stupids. I thinky he means intellectually lazy; he was referring to the lack of histories, you see, my dear. 'They are too lazy to remembery!' he said. 'Too stupids to write anything down. Other than recipes and rymes.'

He puffed fiercely on his long stone pipe.

We were in the gardens of the palace, sitting on a long wooden bench, outside of the kitchens. The smell of cheesecakes and flowerys, and the aromatic smokes, and the chickens which strutted around pecking at the dirt. Petunia, the cook's maid, was pegging washed linen to a line.

Mustard had shared some tobaccos with me, whilst Plumcake was at her afternoon nap, and very nice they were too. The smokes were making my brain heavy and custards, and my eyes were all quite sleepiness. It was very pleasanty.

I asked Mustard if he knewed anything about the Old Giants and the Crooked Stair, which I had heard they builded somewhere. He replied that he had indeed heard the story, from a Tanner.

The Old Giants were the very firstest people in Twinkly. They were remarkedly tall, which isn't unusual for giants. They liked to work with stone, and carved stuffs and builded blocks. That's what had inspired the Stair apparently. They kept placing blocks higher and higher, and making the base firm and strong with blocks of support, and they were buildying a stair in the mountains near Quibbly. This much Mustard heard from the Tanner, who had heard it from his own good mother.

The stair climbed higher and higher, and knowing they were buildying something rather nice and pretty, the giants kept on adding blocks, carrying the heavy stones on their broad shoulders as they climbed back up to the top of the stair.

The Tanner was of the opinion that they had built all of the mountains near Quibbly, but Mustard pooh-poohed that notion. 'They hewed the stone blocks from the mountains,' he insisted, 'and the Crooked Stair is there somewhere, reaching right up to the top of the sky.'

'How I should enjoy to discovery it one day, and climb it,' I wistilyed. Mustard thinkied that I really should do so. I asked if he might accompany me to discovery the Stair.

He jumped up suddenly from the bench. 'Oh no! I certainly

couldn't be away on an expedition. Plumcake needs me. She is about to stir, I shall go and attend her. Good noontime, Aelinor!' And off he went.

I sat musing a while, smoking the lush tobaccos, and fell into a little snooze; I know I did, because I woke with a surprisey that it was lunchtime.

As Court Jester to Her Majesty it means that for clocks I have to stand just behind her throne, and wait. I am waiting for her to want some interestings amusements, and it is an uncomfortable moments for me. I haven't yet known her to laugh at anything at all, and I still don't knowed any jokes. I tried inventing some but I couldn't find them funny and gave up on it. Waiting makes me feel anxious because she is always likely to be displeased. I try to thinky of some way that I might be entertaining to her.

I danced for her, and she wasn't cross. I told an amusing anecdote, and she didn't shout at me. I showed her a small magicks, making a coin disappear then re-appear, and she almost smiled.

'What is it like in France, Jester?' she asked of a sudden this afterlunch.

I haven't been to France, but saying so I knewed would only make her cross. Instead I replied: 'It is very *French*, your Plumnessly.'

'How so?'

'Well, I have heared that the roads are paved with *vol-au-vents*, and that the trees bear *petite bon bon* like fruits. The French ladies wear croissants as hats, and speak in garlic. The gentlemen ride bicycles along the *Champs Elysee*, smoking cigarettes and drinking grape wine. Their pets are made from baguettes and Mendy-Strings and tiny pastries. The shops sell *Parfums*, and their French films don't even have sub-titles. Very French indeed.'

'Ahh,' she said. 'Quite a singular people!'

It was very much the best response I have had from her so far.

'Now, go away, you horrible little man,' she commanded me soon afterwards.

Ten

'Flower,' Mr Cat asked, 'do you know how many stupids it
takes to bake one good idea?'
Mr Flower was sure he didn't know.
'All of them!' smiled Mr Cat.
'Giddily,' responded his friend.
'Oh, actually, I mendy: all of them, and one clevery.'
'How fascinating!' remarked Mr Flower.
'Isn't it though?'
Mr Cat helped himself to another spoon of Gherkin Pie.

I was came then into a realm which was filled with staccatos,
like a myriad doors of opal. I roamed there for an age, and I
was overwhelmed by so many routes that I might choose from.
They were not doors as doors usually might be, in rectangular
shapes, but they were portals or windows, each of which would
lead me into a specific realm, were I to step through.
I had the certain feeling that I must make my choice with care,
and whichever realm I settled upon to enter would be of great
significance to my journey, and the fate of my pilgrimage. It
would be a vital choice, with consequences far-reaching and
unseen.
I had nothing to rely upon except my intuition; often our most
faithful guide. I calmed my anxious heart, and progressed
slowly now through labyrinthine corridors and avenues.
Each door I passed had some intriguing and unique feature,
such as a dazzling combination of colorys, or a beautiful frame,
or winding steps of marble, or it was wrapped in nefarious
gloams. Some had strangely musics coming from within them,
and others were large and grandiose, and others were tiny so
that I wouldn't even have been able to squeeze through, and
then some of the doors were plain and subtle, but their
opelness was incredibly rare and gorgeous. Some were dark
and foreboding, and some were light and inviting.
I could only try to sense each universe as I passed it, and wait
until my heart leapt with the rightness of its presence.
At last, I found it, when I was dizzy with wandering the

labyrinth so long.

Its surface was much like a looking-glass, but 'twere gilt about and graven with baroque and strangeness, with fascinations and mesmerrys.

Its energies were gentle and simple, and I felt restful as I stood before it. I knewed 'twere the door I searched for.

I stepped through its looking-glass surface, and tumbled into blue skies.

Later, here in my little house, I made a big speaking-speech, as was necessary to seal the magics after crossing through the Inbetweens, saying it all real, with the sounds and the proper words. And, it was a terribly longest speech ever, I would thinky; it lasted all day and night nearly.

It was much beautifuls with gorgeous sounds, pretty sads, and wonderful god-speaks in magickal finishing ways, and powerful and rich and strong.

I would like if you had heard it, it really was quite lovely.

We have to be completely thorough when doing these special finishing magicks so as to get every debris, so that not even the smallest bit is left.

Every symbol and metaphor which I had all this clock in secretyness collected, I poured out, and 'twere a myriad of realms contained, and within which now the powers of my magicks were bound.

And, darling, even though you cannot yet read these words, writing them I thinky of you. You are home for me, and you are where all the beautifuls in my heart reside.

My dearest, with weeping I write that I do not know how ever to get back home to you. I have wandered far and broad o'er all of Twinkly, and I cannot find any door.

Twinkly does feel like a peculiar land for me to have ended up in. I do wondery if ever I'll be able to leave.

I tumbled through that aperture, whatever might have been its kind, and fell out of the sky, and landed with a flump on Twinkly sands.

'Twere at the beach that I found myself, all giddily and confuzzled; you remember how such falls often are. I walked westward and came soon enough right here, where I now am stuck. I'm as stuck as I might be had I fell into a world of sticky glue! Yet, it seems to be only a point of entrance and not a capable exit.

I woke from a sleep, after the falling. I don't remembery how I gotten there, at the beach. I looked every side up that I could but found nothing.

I went back when I was not giddily and searched again, but alas alack, ne'er availed me.

'I'm thinkithinking of writing a book, Mr Cat,' said Mr Flower, tentatively.

His friend laughed. 'Nonsense! Only very cleverys can write books, you silly fellow! I have even thinked of doing so myself. One day.'

'But I already have the end,' protested Mr Flower.

'The end is not the correct place to start a book,' Mr Cat informed him, and took his hat off, then put it back on again. 'The bestest beginning is at the very start.'

'I know, you are quite right. But, I only have the end at this moment.'

'Well? What is it then?' Mr Cat asked.

'I'll show you, shall I?' Mr Flower pulled a little notebook out from inside his jacket. It had a pencil attached to its side. He flipped through the pages, until he reached the final one. He handed the notebook to Mr Cat. In very small letters Mr Flower had written 'the end' at the bottom of the last page.

Mr Cat frowned, and then he sighed. 'Flower, my dear, you are a nincompoop.'

'I thinkied it nice to write the easiest bit firstly,' said Mr Flower. 'I can put the other all the pages in as I go along. I might make it about hats. Or pies. Or, perhaps I should write it when I am rambly, or even when I feel scared. Or only when I am jolly.'

'I see,' Mr Cat said, stretching, and standing up. 'I suppose you'll want me to help you, to read it for you?'

'Would you so kindly, dearest?' implored Mr Flower.

'Certainly not. Except any pages that you write with me in them. Which really would make for an interesting book! You should write every clevery idea and posey I utter, Flower. You should record all my clevery speeches, word by word, with reverence and due wondery. You could scribe all my victory days, and telled the world how heroness I were. That would be a noble work!' Mr Cat stood erect, gazing out o'er the darkening hills. He smiled, and twirlyed one of his whiskers gently.

'It sounds marvellous already!' exclaimed Mr Flower. 'I'm so glad I begun!'

'You might call it '*Quothed Mr Cat*," suggested Mr Cat, feeling very grand and historic as he strode away, towards the hill of the Weeping Tree.

Mr Flower opened his little notebook, resting it against his knees. *Quothed Mr Cat* he wrote in medium-sized letters near the top of the first page.

'Well, now we are really getting somewhere lovely!' he said aloud. He chewed on the end of his pencil, and looked across the darkening hills. He looked up at the twinkling stars. He turned the page over, and wrote *chapter the very first* at the top of the second page. He looked at the twinkling stars some more, and then underlined *chapter the very first*.

Then he wrote a quite beautiful ryme, which he later confessed to Strawberry had just fallen out of the sky onto his head. It was this:

Twinkling o'er Twinkly Town
the stars looked down and found
Mr Cat, all snoozily
in the arms of the Weeping Tree.

He was very pleased with it, and skipped home to his little house feeling happinesses and glads.

Eleven

Plumcake's palace was situated on the peak of Steep Hill. She has lots of serving people attending her every whim. She is usually quite rude to them.

Go away you horrible little man, she enjoys telling them. *Chop chop!*

She enjoys getting rather cross with people and eating cheesecakes.

She was holding court, because it was a Satyrday.

'My giddiness,' she said loudly. 'Have they started making Scaryclothes again?' She beckoned to a serving girl, commanding her to approach. 'Is that a *pillowcase* you are wearing, dear? It's frightfully ugly; it suits you!'

'Thank you, your Plumness,' replied the serving girl, with a polite curtsey.

'And,' the Queen peered closer, her sharp nose quivering, 'are those briers in your hair? It looks so odd and tangley.'

'Yes, your Plumness, and brambles,' the serving girl said, with another polite curtsey. Plumcake shooed her away with a wave of her hand. She turned to Mustard, who stood just behind her. 'Whatever will they thinky of next?' she asked him regally.

'Rather difficult to guess, your Plumness,' he replied tartly. Plumcake beckoned another serving girl to approach. 'How curiousy,' she said, leaning her head to the side. 'Is that a *pretend* nose you have?'

The serving girl curtseyed politely and squeaked: 'Yes, your Plumness!'

'Why?' the Queen asked with a loud witheringly tone.

'My real nose is far too pretty, Your Plumnessness.'

'Ah!' said Mustard. 'We don't use that word here in court! Unless we are referring to her lovely Plumness directly. You mean to say it is far too *silly*.'

'Beg pardon, sir Mustard, sir,' fawned the serving girl, with several curtsies. 'My real nose is far too *silly*, mam.'

'I see. Very good,' said Plumcake, and shooed her away. And then she said, very loudly: 'My tummy needs cheesecake!'

Strawberry took me along to her workshop.

It was very lovely, with prettiness curtains and potted plants. A warm deep rug coloryed turquoise occupied the middle of the room, upon which were the table, oak and very nicely finished, and on that was the engine, and next to the engine were two monitors with lots of swirly wires.

Against the far wall there was a comfortable cherry red sofa.

'I'd expected it may be drab,' I said, 'but you have made it lovely!'

'Thankily,' she smiled. 'And I am most grateful for the go-fasty stripes that you gotted me. Don't they look spiffy on the console?' They really did.

She hadn't managed to get the engine working as yet, Strawberry told with laments, but I saw at once the solution: nothing was connected or plugged into a power supply.

'What is your source of power?' I asked triumphantly, feeling all excites for to be about to solve her difficulties. As I suspectibubbled, she had none, except her imagination.

'We must findy a *generator*,' I advised her.

'Oh, what a jolly nice idea, Aelinor. How clevery you can be!'

We went straightaway back to town, on account of our excites, and went along to the store Strawberry had gotten the engine. It was an eclectic mix of paraphrenalias that the store had, all sorts of gismos and gadgets and purry-noised stuff, or squeakys with flashing lights and little turny knobs. They had steamys and hissings, contraptions that cracked or banged, machines that whirled, and sputterys, and churning pistons, boxes and cubicles for goodness knewed what, tiny apparatuses, packets of screws and bolts hanging on a wire frame, eclipse particles, danglys, stretchys, and wires in abundance.

We bought a small clockworked generator, and two large batteries, a dozen wireys with attachments to connect everything.

Strawberry also selected several items whilst we browsed. The storekeeper, a very small lady named Doris, said that everything would be deliveryed on Someday.

'Well, I can scarcely wait!' Strawberry confided.

I wonderyed how Doris was going to carry all those heavy stuffs, but she said be assured, miss, I will manage.

Strawberry and I visited the Tea House next, and had tea.

'Being clockworked means that you must remembery to wind the generator regularly,' I advised her. 'Otherwise it will stop working.'

'Oh. I'm sure to forgets! How inconvenient 'twould be if it stopped working when we were flying through the dimensions at very fastly velocities!' and she chuckled.

'That should be quite alright,' I responded, 'because its power shall be stored in the batteries, and the Spaceyship will run from those. It wouldn't drop out of the skies immediately. You must just ensure that the generator is winded frequently enough to keep the batteries full. And, probably you should find one or two more, as back ups. You might want a nice display to stack them on.'

'Oh, yes, and with some sparkly lights to indicate whether they are full or half-full or nearly empty.'

'Tis why being captain of a Spaceyship is such a difficults and importants job,' I mused, 'having to make certain thingys are winded and lights are sparkling.'

'I shall need some crew, I thinky,' said Strawberry, 'or at least a clevery co-pilot.'

'Indeed!' I smilyed.

The following Satyrday Mr Flower and Strawberry visited the markets. It was often bustley and amusing there; the Northland Farmers would be in Twinkly for their own trading: swapping croissants for hats, and baguettes for quiches.

'And, I thinky I shall try to find some *Ohhlalas,*' she confided in her friend.

'Oh, what is it?' he asked enthusiastically.

'Delicates and nices,' she replied.

'How wonderful!' he smiled, and took her arm as they strolled across the Lush Meadow, making their way to market.

'Since we are sharing confidences, dear,' said Mr Flower, 'I have brought some peanutbuttery with me. It's in my knapsack.'

'Oh, dear,' said Strawberry sympathetically, 'you haven't broughten your knapsack.'

Mr Flower stopped sharply. 'How curiousy. Wherever could it have gotten to?'

'Most likely you left it at home,' Strawberry said, patting his hand with hers. 'Why did you want the peanutbuttery?'

'To sell,' Mr Flower told her, and began weeping a little. 'I was going to makey Peanutbutterybaguettes and sell them.'

'Ahw, that's very sads. Poor you. Is it a new recipe?'

'Sort of,' he wept, 'although it is nearly a sandwich.'

'Nevermind! Buy the baguettes at market, and make Peanutbutterybaguettes when you get home again!' said Strawberry, with what was a very nice idea.

'Except I won't be able to sell them at home,' said Mr Flower, stopping again; it was so *difficults* for him to walk *and* ponder. 'I suppose Mrs Pheasant might buy one or three at earlytime.'

'Mrs Pheasant has *never* liked me,' said Strawberry, pulling Mr Flower along.

'I'm so sorry,' he said 'whyever not?'

'We've not met,' replied Strawberry.

'Ah! She *does* enjoy Peanutbutterybreads though. I just wondery if she might consider baguettes too frivolous.'

'Oh, baguettes are frivolous?'

'Mrs Pheasant is so particular,' answered Mr Flower.

Mr Flower enjoyed taking what he called the 'scenic route.' It almost always involved a winding rambley longest way of getting where you wanted to go. As it was they arrived at the markets, having crossed the meadows, and gone by the Gorgeousy Gate, and under the Weeping Tree, just after brunchtime.

Brunchtime was a tea-and-cake break, and it usually happened just before lunchtime. The Northland farmers had introduced it to the Twinklys long ago, when they had first starting visiting. Brunchtime was quickly adopted, and soon taken quite seriously in Twinkly. When and how one should be snacking, and with what, in what manner, with whom, was after all a quite serious matter. The cleveryest people had brunchtime, and naturally everyone wanted it, and liked it. Brunch was a wonderful idea!

'An *aperitif*,' Henri, a farmer, explained tartly.

'Ah, the moment of nices,' remarked Mr Cat, who lived at Twinkly even then, so many clocks ago.

'Ah, we 'ave also *petite bon bon*, et *vol-au-vent*, et la *onion* supebre!' continued Henri.

'I sharn't want to buy anything at all,' Mr Cat told him, realising suddenly that he didn't have his purse about him.

'Pourquoi?' asked Henri.

'Certainly not,' Mr Cat had replied, and stalked away in a huff.

'But, what is it?' asked Mr Flower later, when his friend had finished retelling events.

'A *pourquoi*? It's a kind of turtle,' replied Mr Cat. 'I was quite insulted.'

'How rude those farmers are!' agreed Mr Flower.

'Don't upset yourself, dear,' Mr Cat advised purrily. 'It's just *silliness* to get rather cross with somebody only because they sharn't purchase your baguette.'

'It isn't polite,' agreed Mr Flower. 'Was it the one with the curly moustaches?'

'Yes,' replied Mr Cat, 'did you meet him?'

'Only once,' said his friend sadly. 'Just before he shaved them off.'

'Ah,' said Mr Cat.

'Well, I sharn't take that Treacle Pie out to them at tea-time,' said Mr Flower crossly.

'I shouldn't, dear.'

Mr Flower was quiet for a minute. Mr Cat waited for him to finish. Afterwards, Mr Flower said: 'Perhaps, just the muffins? I shouldn't want them to be hungry.'

'You want to sell them your silly pies, I suppose?' Mr Cat asked cynically.

Twelve

Mr Flower took Strawberry's arm again as they entered the market. 'Just so as you sharn't forgets,' he said, 'these farmers can be quite rude. Be careful, won't you?'
'I shall, dear,' smiled Strawberry. 'Try not to worry.'
'Rather brave,' remarked Mr Flower.
'Am I?' she asked, excites.
'Have you forgotten? That happens to me. So annoyings, isn't it though?' he replied.

They walked through the market, dallying at every stall. The farmers always brought such gorgeousy thingys to sell: onions, baguettes, pastries, and Rubik Cubes.
Strawberry bought some pastries, and enquired of the farmer, who was a lady farmer named Michelle: 'Do you have any of those niceness Ohhlalas?'
Michelle made a confuzzly face. 'Ohhlalas? J'ne comprends pas.'
'They are very tiny, and sweet,' explained Strawberry, 'and the most deliciousness flavor.'
'And prettiness,' added Mr Flower.
Michelle shook her head. 'Pardon. We 'ave vol-au-vent, croissants, petite pastry... et onion...'
'Yes. And very lovely they are!' said Strawberry enthusiastically. 'But, I rather wanted some Ohhlalas. I did enjoy them so very much last clock.'
'Eh... pardon...' said Michelle. 'We 'ave petite bon bon, if you like?'
Strawberry *did* want the petite bon bon, which were round and sweet, but not nearly so special as Ohhlalas.
'How awfully disappointing,' said Strawberry sadly, as she and Mr Flower walked away. 'Shall I ever find them again, I wondery?'
'Perhaps they were just too beautifuls,' sighed Mr Flower, 'like meringues.'

At the top end of the market, as it reached the entrance of

Squiggledy Lane, there was a wooden platform which sometimes served as a small stage. There was a crowd of happy Twinklys gathered, eating croissants and drinking tea, to watch a little show put on by the farmers, before lunchtime started.

A very tall skinny farmer, dressed in green pants and a dazzling gold waistcoat, with a lilac shirt beneath, who had the longest curliest moustaches Strawberry and Mr Flower had ever seen, leapt up onto the stage.

'Madamasilli et Monsieur!' he said, raising his long thin arms high and wide. 'Votre attention s'il vous plait!'

'Such a strange accent,' remarked Mr Flower to Strawberry. 'I can't hardly understand a word he says.'

'He's speaking in *French,* dear,' Strawberry reassured him.

'How odd,' said Mr Flower, making a puzzled face.

The farmer continued: 'Pour votre plaisir et votre divertissement...' he paused elaborately, and the Twinklys stared at him. None of them understood French. Except Pierre the clerk, who was awfully clevery and claimed to speak several languages, sometimes all at once. He was at home in his little house though so he wasn't able to help. He had slept late that morning, and hadn't planned to attend the market.

'Do you speaky French?' Mr Flower asked Strawberry.

'Hardly often,' she replied apologetically.

'Pour tes stimulations,' the farmer paused again, smiling broadly, and looked from face to face of the crowd. The Twinklys were wide-eyed with fascination.

'What wonderful green pants,' one of them whisperyed.

'Ah!' said the farmer, holding up his hand, curling the forefinger onto the thumb in an o-shape. One or two of the crowd applauded, but he cut them short with a frown.

'Et maintenant... voila! Regarde!' He gestured towards stage left, and the Twinklys looked, but there was nothing to see beyond the heavy blue curtain that was drawn across and separated the stage from a small dressing area.

'Le fantastique...' the curly-whiskered farmer continued. 'Le magnifique...' he punctuated each syllable. There were 'oohhs' from amongst the crowd in response. 'La oblique, elastique... le Dancers Cosmique!' he gestured towards the curtain with an elaborate flourish.

The crowd waited hushed and expectant. The farmer held his grin, balanced on one long skinny leg.

At last, a red-faced lady poked her head between the curtains, and whisperyed something to him, then disappeared behind the curtain once more. The farmer straightened up slowly. He pulled his waistcoat down smartly.

'Ah,' he said. 'Pardon. Excuse moi. They will be next week.' He left the stage swiftly, to rapturous applause from the Twinklys.

'How marvellous, wasn't he?' Mr Flower remarked.

'Quite lovely,' Strawberry concurred.

Mr Flower stamped on his hat, the green one, several times.

'Don't hurt yourself, Flower,' advised Mr Cat.

'I'm trying to get the custard out of my ears,' explained Mr Flower. 'It muddles everything.'

'Custard?'

'Yes. You might thinky it would be delicious, having a head filled with custard, but it makes me so very stupids!'

Mr Cat was puzzled. 'How did your head get to be full of custard?' he asked.

'I thinky I were born with it, Mr Cat,' replied his friend sadly. 'Papa said my head always had too much of it.'

'Ahh,' replied his friend. 'How curiousy. And, does standing on your hat help?'

'Not much,' said Mr Flower. 'And it often gives me a headache.'

'It's probably not the solution then, dearie. Hmm, I wondery,' Mr Cat pondered, 'what would the antithesis of custard be?'

'What is it?' asked Mr Flower.

'I don't know as yet, Flower. Give me a moment. Well, I mendy, something to soak up the custard.'

'Oh, like a sponge?'

'Ah! A sponge cake is what we should try!' said Mr Cat purrily. 'Do you have some in your larder?'

Mr Flower was always very pleased when he managed to get something right. He went straightaway to look in his larder. Mr Cat stretched and yawned, and decided to have a little snooze until his friend returned. When he woke up, Mr Flower was still in the kitchen.

'Did you find any?' Mr Cat asked purrily, going through to the kitchen.

Mr Flower was sitting on the stone floor, and he had emptied the contents of the larder into piles all around his legs and feet. Boxes and packets, jars and tins and bottles. He was eating jam with a spoon, straight from its pot. He looked up, startled.

'Oh! Hullo, Mr Cat! Did I find any what?'

'Sponge cake.'

'No, but I wrote a new posey! It's called '*Blueberry Jam*.' Would you like me to tell it?'

'Go ahead,' replied Mr Cat.

'Thankily,' returned Mr Flower, and told the posey in a very high sing song voice, which made his friend frown.

This is how it were:

Blueberry Jam

Blueberry jam,
Blueberry jam.
It's made with blueberries,
Blueberry jam.

'Bravo,' Mr Cat smiled when Mr Flower was finished. 'Quite clevery, in that it is almost a recipe *and* a posey!'

'How kind of you to notice that, Mr Cat! Thankily,' said Mr Flower, and made a little sitting down bow.

When Plumcake was being loud and cross her servants trembled with anxiousnesses, bowing and scraping the polished floors with their noses, even more than usual.

'Off to bed with you!' Plumcake bellowed, so that they jumped in fright, and scampered away. Or she might scream: 'Go Outside!' which meant they would have to go outside of the palace; and everyone knew how unpleasant faraway and coldibone it was out there. Being sent to bed was therefore to be preferred, since at least it was warm. Or, perhaps preference depended mostly on whether 'twere earlytime or stayuplate.

'Why are you quite so mean to them?' her cousin Lalu had asked, when she came to stay for the weekend. She lived in Paris.

'I simply must be bossy,' Plumcake explained. 'I'd probably go potty otherwise, living here all on my own.'

'You do have hundreds of servants, dear,' replied Lalu. 'You aren't actually alone.'

Plumcake humphhed dismissively. 'Servants are something one owns, darling cousin; they aren't people. They certainly don't count as company. One doesn't have conversations with one's property, does one? How silly. 'Good earlytime, Mr Chair! Good afterwards, Mr Table! How are you doing now? How's the new leg?''

Lalu giggled at that, but she hadn't ever come back to visit since.

I have been thinkithinking upon what Mustard said about the Crooked Stair. It might'n be an answer, but intuits tells that it is worth exploring. Right up to the top of the sky! Could it be really? Could it be the finger pointing to the extraordinary? Might I climb to its apex and discovery a door? I shall have to try.

I may be gone for some clocks; the Tall Mountains range is vast. It could take clocks and ages to explore fully.

What should I do about my jobs at the palace? One isn't allowed to simply *quit*. That could be construed as an insult to Her Majesty. I will have to persuade her to let me go, somehow. I feel encouraged, dearness. There is hope.

If I do not find the Crooked Stair, then mayhap Strawberry will have her Spaceyship ready by the clock I am back in Twinkly, and perhaps that may be a way out for me.

I added some small adjustments whilst I was at her workshop, after the deliverys came. I included a *relativity and dimension transmodulator* with her purchases. I recognised it from a different place; somewhere that seems many lifetimes ago. I wondery how it might have ended up here in Twinkly? I attached it to the console, whilst making some buttony adjustments. Let's see if she can intuit the rest!

Thirteen

Strawberry was sitting on the High Steps at the Square. She had
a sketchpad with her, balanced on her thighs, and was making
colorys. Mr Flower, who had intended some shopping, came to
sit next to her.
'What is it, dear?' he enquired, watching her gentle scribbling.
'I'm making a colory!'
'Ah,' he said.
'It's for my adventuring, in the Spaceyship,' she elaborated.
'To stick on the walls?'
'No. Well, yes. This is a superhero that I'm making. I'm not
certain how it will work, but once the Spaceyship is all mendy
nice and clean, I'll make him for really. This is a preparatory
drawing. Which you must have, if you should want to do supra-
biological engineering, and technical thingys,' she smiled
cutely.
'He is rather pretty though,' remarked Mr Flower, and then
quietly watched her work for a minute or so. He said 'hmm,'
once, and 'ah,' as well. At last he asked: 'Is somebody I should
know?'
'Not at all,' Strawberry reassured him. 'I'm only just now
making him up.'
'Oh! You're colorying him?'
'Yes!' Strawberry said happily. 'Like when you make colorys
of your recipes, isn't it?'
'Is it? Well, how marvellous! Will you have to bakey him?'
'I should have a gismo for it, one which shouldn't hurt too
much; once the Spaceyship is nice and ready.'
'Ah,' said Mr Flower.
'Very chiselled,' commented Strawberry, as she drew the
superhero's jaw-line. 'Gorgeousy!' she said, with a big, flashing
smile, once she had completed that tricky part with no mishaps.
'Oh, I do like this one, dear,' said Mr Flower, whilst Strawberry
continued.
'Thankily. I thinkied the silvertwinkly colory would be pretty.'
'It is. Very lovely. And, what is that he is standing on? Is it a
plate?'

'It's a surfboard,' she said, a little impatiently. It had been quite difficults to colory it so that it didn't look like a plate.

'A surfboard?' Mr Flower puckered his nose. 'How peculiar!'

'He surfs the universe, you see. Riding the tides of eternity,' she explained.

'Is it a Spaceyship? Can he go inside?' Mr Flower asked.

'No, he can't go inside. He just stands on it. But, he is wearing a thermal suit, so he sharn't get too cold.'

Mr Flower smiled. 'The swishy lines are nice,' he said. 'All swirly-swishy. Go-fasty-hoopiloops. He sleeps on it too, I suppose?'

Strawberry considered for a moment. 'I thinky he will have to, yes,' she said.

'You must keep it!' said Mr Flower. 'And, what powers does he have?'

'*Le Power*,' she replied. 'Just the one so far.'

'How about 'Le Power Cosmic?" he suggested. 'So that they know he is one of ours.'

'Oh, yes, thankily!' Strawberry was pleased. 'Le Power Cosmique! It sounds awfully grand! Bravo, Mr Flower. We shall keep it.'

'What is his name?' Mr Flower asked her, when she was colorying the background.

'I shall call him 'the Silverytwinkly Surfer.'

Mr Flower wasn't sure. 'I thinky its *quite* a silly name, for a superhero. I wondery that he might get teased for it,' he said.

'Plumcake?' Mr Cat growled. 'She's the meanest, most self-centred person in Twinkly! A colander head, with a cheese-grater heart!'

'Oh, excuse me,' returned Mr Flower timidly, 'I thinkied you were friends.'

'Most certainly not,' hmmpffed Mr Cat.

'You mightn' like this then,' said Mr Flower, taking a gold embossed envelope from his inside jacket pocket, and holding it out with a slightly trembling hand. Mr Cat could be rather scary when one made him cross! 'I hope it sharn't make you too cross with me?'

'What is it?' his friend asked, his curiosity piqued.

'It's a letter. Well, I happen to know it's an invitation, because
we have all had one, and because Aelinor said 'twere. Yours
was deliveryed to my little house, seeing as how you don't have
a letter box of your own. Or a door.'

Mr Cat took the envelope from Mr Flower, and indeed, in
smaller letters beneath the gold-lettered 'Mr Cat,' was written:
'Care of Mr Flower. The little house near Higgledy Path,
between Lush Meadows and Squiggly Hills.' In brackets
beneath that, in the tiniest of small letterings was written:
'Quite near to Strawberry's little house.'

'Hmm,' he mused, for quite a little while. Mr Flower waited
patiently until he was done. 'An *invitation?*' Mr Cat continued
at last.

'Yes.'

'To?'

'The Palace.'

Mr Cat sighed. 'Oh, bothery,' he said.

Mr Flower had written in his book, *Quothed Mr Cat*. On the
third page of his notebook he wrote the chapter heading:
chapter second the next, and underlined it. He wrote down
some words, but they weren't anything Mr Cat had said, they
were in fact Mr Flower's own thinkys, like a sort of posy:

Since life can be difficults and hurty,
I thinkithinked about it, and what should I do.
It was almost a clevery thingy for me to have done.
I arrived at a conclusion, and just as I went in,
I knewed what to do about it all.
I shall make a book, and put some words in.
I don't know what it will say,
but I'll let it speak however it enjoys to.
I never know what to say mostness anyway,
so I shall maybe be clevery at it too.
I'll just thinkithink and colory in.
I hadn't started yet, but I did have the end.

Strawberry was rather excites. She had never met the queen, and was very much pleased to going to be doing so. What she should wear? Something glamorous, something plain but smart? And, she needed to take along a nice gift; but what on World does one present to the queen? She asked me to ask Mustard for her to find out what might be welcomed. *Buy her a Rubik's Cube,* he telled. *But make sure it only has one color, or she sharn't be able to do it.*

Strawberry was tizzy with anticipation. Her tummy was fluttery as she skipped along Higgledly Path, and drew near to the Weeping Tree. She saw that Mr Cat was sitting cross-legged beneath its shade.

She reached to where Mr Cat was, with a big smile on her bright face.

He ignored her.

'A very beautifuls earlytime, my dear Mr Cat,' she addressed him.

'Is it?' he growled, glancing up with a frown.

'I certainly thinky so! Are you excites about the invitations?'

'Not at all,' replied Mr Cat punctiliously. Strawberry finally noticed the several twigs on the ground in front of him. They were neatly stacked into three little piles. He saw her gaze, and said quickly: 'Minding my own business. What are you doing?'

'I'm out for a walk!' she replied defiantly.

'Hmmpf,' returned Mr Cat, with an implication that that was just the sort of silly thingy he had expected her to say.

'Oh, please, dear Mr Cat, do telled what you are doing!' she begged him.

He considered for several moments, whilst Strawberry patiently waited for him to finish considering. Finally he sighed. 'I was meditating,' he said at last, and before she could say *Oohh!* he continued, 'and you have impolitely interrupted me. As usual.' He showed his irked disdain with a withering glare.

'How wonderfully mystique you are!' Strawberry smiled, knowing how the grumpy old cat melted to flattery.

'Hmm,' he responded, allowing that she continue.

'That's very exotic. And what are the twigs for?'

'For telling tyme, of course.'

'Telling time?'

'Don't be an echo, you foolish girl, particularly when you can't echo correctly,' said Mr Cat, feeling in control of the situation now. He held up his hand, to prevent more questions. 'You may observe and learn. Sit down, won't you? You are so tall that you make everything seem untidy.'

Strawberry sat beside him, and ignored his rude remark about her height. He is very short, so everyone probably seems tall to him, she consoled herself.

Mr Cat gathered himself, then he gathered up the twigs, and rattled them together in his cupped hands. Strawberry knew not to say a word during such activity. Finally he cast the twigs with an elaborate flourish, so that they scattered across the ground before him. He stared at the twigs, hmming and harring to himself quietly, very pondernessly. He took such a long while on this part that Strawberry began to feel quite drowsy; the earlytime orangeyyellowroundythingy was already very hot. She didn't dare to yawn though.

Brave? she said in a conversation in her mind with herself, such as she often had to keep herself amused, or focused, or from falling asleep, or just to daydream. *Why, certainly not brave! I'm too afraid to yawn most of the clock!*

It seemed Mr Cat had finished his hmming and harring, for he picked up the strewn twigs and placed them into three neat piles before him. Strawberry smiled awkwardly.

'And, what time is it?' she ventured.

'Tyme, not time, stupids,' he said.

'Oh,' was all she could reply. 'Is that like a riddley, or something?'

Mr Cat frowned. 'You are more stupids during earlytimes, aren't you? No, dear, it isn't a riddley, nor an enigma. It is a difference in intonation and emphasis, and it has a 'y.''

'Gosh, it seems awfully riddlely,' she said, quite confuzzled.

'No doubt, no doubt,' sighed Mr Cat.

Strawberry waited. But Mr cat didn't elaborate. Eventually she ventured: 'And, what is the time?'

'It is Transcendental Yarrow Meditation upon Eternity,' replied

Mr Cat, very impressively. He pulled on one his whiskers, and
then let it spring back with a twing.
'Oh! I see. It's an acronym?'
'Quite precisely,' he replied.
'But, it has no 'u," she observed.
Mr Cat smiled. 'That is because all is All,' he returned,
narrowing his eyes sagely.

Fourteen

When Strawberry, Mr Flower, and Mr Cat arrived at Queen Plumcake's palace, there was a gathering of Twinklys, which began several feet before the two very large grand looking doors, the main entrance, and stretched back towards the outer gates of the courtyard.

The Twinklys were mostly dressed in their nicest outfits and shoes, because of course they wanted to look nicest when they met the queen. The entire crowd looked splendid.

Strawberry, Mr Flower, and Mr Cat were asked by one of the queen's menservants to wait at the end of the line. It wasn't easy to be certain exactly where the end of the line was at that point, but they stood together just behind the main huddle.

Mr Cat sighed and shook his head, and his whiskers bristled.

I proposed to Plumcake to make an expedition into the Tall Mountains. I thinkied that getting her support might be a clevery way to accomplish my intent, and make everything more easy; if I could be having Twinklys from the palace employ to help.

'Your Majesty Plumness,' I said silkily, 'if we could discovery the location of the fabled Crooked Stair, builded by the Old Giants so very long clock and ages since, it would be like wonderful fame and renown for you! You would be recalled in histories, which your own scribes could start writing, and telled how pretty and niceness you are, and how clevery of you to send an expedition when nobody else thinkied to do so, or thinkied that the Stair could be discoveryed. Everyone in Twinkly would know how great a queeny you were, Your Plumnessly.

'I really thinky you should do it. I will lead a party there my very self, for you, and to show my adoration and gratitude for your giving me a courier and jester work so kindly.'

Plumcake stared at me, her mouth sagged open. She blinked heavily.

'It will be an arduous adventure, mam, but I am willing and even eager to face the perils for Your Majestyness.'

She looked at Mustard, to get his opinion. He nodded, pursing his lips. 'We would begin a history, Your Majesty,' he offered. 'You will be rememberyed as the mostest and bestest queen ever! I recommend we prepare an expedition to the Tall Mountains to discovery the Crooked Stair. Might I suggest that this fine fellow, who has proven her worth and trustiness by being an excellent courier, and making every delivery, should be chosen to lead the expedition.'

'Sir, Mustard,' I humblyed, 'I am honored, and would be happiness just to accompany such a party.'

We both looked at Plumcake.

'Not until after my dinner,' she said brusquely. 'My specially dinner, with the lots of horrible little Twinklys. Afterwards, Jester, you may go and win glory and fame for your queen. Now go away. Chop chop.'

And, so the adventure is arranged.

As I left the court, Plumcake said to Mustard: 'And, Mustard, it is a niceness idea, isn't it?'

'Of course, Your Plumness! A very nice idea, and all your very own,' he replied.

'How clevery of me though, weren't it?' said the queen.

'Exceedingly,' Mustard replied lemonly.

Suddenly the two great doors of the palace were pushed open from the inside, and several Court Pages came marching out in a phalanx.

Each of them took a small party of Twinklys, waiting a few minutes after each groups' departure, and escorted them to the smaller door to the right of the main entrance.

When the first group, a small Twinkly family of bakers, Mildred, Basil, and their daughter Nestly, had entered through the side door, the heavy double doors were pulled closed.

The crowd grew quite excites now, realising that they were close to being escorted inside. 'Not before clock,' Mr Cat muttered.

When their turn came, the three friends were led through the side door into a very long corridor.

The carpet on the floor of the corridor was deep and plush, and coloryed a rich forest green. The walls of the corridor were papered with thickly embossed wallpaper with a repetitive leaf motif, the prettiness of which Strawberry remarked upon. The Page that led Strawberry, Mr Flower, and Mr Cat only *hmmphhed* at her remark.

He was an odd looking fellow, the Page.

(*How funny to be a page*, thinkied Strawberry to herself, *I wondery if his mother was a pamphlet?*)

The Page was wearing what was obviously the uniform of his office: he had green tights, yellow pantaloons, and white socks that came up to just below his knees. His frockcoat, coloryed pale blue, seemed an awfully tight fit for him, so that it was almost bursting its buttons. He was short and skinny, so the tightness wasn't from a big belly, as one might expect. *Perhaps he washed it in too hot water and it shrank*, Strawberry considered.

Oddest of all about him though, was the orange wig he wore on his head. It was far too small to cover his own hair, which sprang out on all sides in unruly scraggels of blonde. The wig was a very deep orange, which Strawberry thinkied was a colory unpleasant to look upon, and it was tightly curled, and appeared to be made out of strings.

'*Frightful*,' Mr Flower whisperied to her, pointing to his own hat.

The corridor walls were hung with large oil colorys, every six feet or so. Every colory was of Plumcake, and she looked to be quite cross and fed up in all of them. She was thick-set and dumpy, and not at all very pretty.

'She is rather imposing, isn't she?' said Mr Cat.

'Her Majesty is the most imposing,' responded the Page haughtily. 'Now, when you address her, you must call her 'Plumness,' or 'Your Plumness.' Never call her 'Marmalade.''

'Why would I call her 'Marmalade'?' Strawberry wonderyed.

The Page darted her a frown. 'Don't be impertinent. I am kindly giving you fair warning. Do try to pay attention. She detests marmalade. You would be sent straightaway to bed if you did call her that, instead of Plumnesslys, no doubt. No doubt at all.'

Strawberry poked her tongue out at the Page's back.

'Oh, dear. I shall probably call her Marmajam now,' worried Mr Flower.

They followed several very long corridors. Strawberry had begun to feel a bit dizzy from the brisk walking. She wasn't used to such sustained and vigorous exertions. She wished that there was a seat upon which she might take a rest. 'Is it very much further?' she called to the Page.

'Than *what*?' he sniped back, without turning his head.

'Is it very much further to the end of the corridor, until we get there,' Strawberry reiterated precisely.

'Relative to what? It is as long as it is short, and we will arrive at exactly the moment we get there. It is simply a matter of moving forwards. Is that so difficult? Do you need help to walk?'

'No, thank you. I learnt to walk as a baby, and I haven't needed a lesson since!' she replied.

It really was an extremely long walk, and the very sameness of the corridors was in itself wearying and disorientating. They began to feel like they moved through a dreamy.

'Why didn't they make a short cut?' Strawberry asked, when she was awfully tireds of the entire thingy.

Her excites to meet Plumcake had ebbed away. Now she could hardly bare looking at the portraits that they passed. 'You were right, Mr Cat,' she whisperied. 'We shouldn't have come at all!'

'My dear Strawberry, I am mostly always right,' Mr Cat concurred purrily. 'And, if I am wrong ever, it is probably a mistaken interpretation. The ways of the clevery are oft times mysterious and unfathomable; you might thinky I was wrong, but I likely weren't.'

'I shall bear that in mind,' she replied.

The Page ushered them through a door, and a short passage led to some stairs.

The steps went up and up and up, and round and round in loops. When they had climbed to the veritable top, which was an awfully long distance, and took an awfully long while, Mr

Cat said: 'By my whiskers! This is ridiculous! What fool designed this place?' The Page might have taken the question to be rhetorical, since he offered no reply.

He led them then along a short corridor to more steps, and this time the steps went down and down and down, but they were in small tight circles, like a staircase often is, so that was like a nice change from the going around in loops.

At last they came to another door, and the Page opened it for them, and stood whilst they filed past him. He didn't say anything, only glared contemptuously.

Fifteen

They joined a long line of guests, all of whom were botheryed and tireds after their longest walks trough the palace, and who were standing adjacent to a table equally long as the line of guests, which was laden with plates and bowls and glasses and cutlery, and flowerys, and napkins and doilies. There were baskets with breads, and little pots with buttery. Fruits were generously stacked along the length of the table, on platters. There were muffins on stilted plates, and bon bons in bowls. There were tall jars of Creamsoda, and lemon squash, and fizzy cherry. There was a bowl of soup set at each place, and wisps of steam rising gently.

Plumcake was walking along the line, greeting each Twinkly with a few words.

'Gosh,' said Queen Plumcake, 'you really are very silly, aren't you?' as Strawberry shook her hand when they met. This remark flustered Strawberry, who felt it to be a very sudden and unkind assessment.

'Your reputation proceeds you,' smiled Mr Cat, as they sat down at the long table.

Plumcake suddenly yelled at the manservant who was standing in attendance next to her: 'Stop it you stupids flump! Stop fidgeting!'

Everyone at the table, and all the queen's servants, froze for a moment. One poor guest was so startled that she dropped her spoon into her soup. Plumcake heard the rattle and splash, and glared at her, and then shouted: 'Clumsy!' The queen was not in a nice mood.

'Eek!' said the startled guest nervously.

Plumcake glared furiously at her guests, and then she smiled sweetly. 'Welcome, friends and subjects,' she said syrupy, and raised her glass of Creamsoda in a salute. The guests hurriedly raised their own glasses to join her toast.

After soup, the Queen's Jester came to entertain Her Majesticness, whilst they awaited the main course.

'Isn't that Aelinor?' Strawberry asked, startled to see her friend here, and wearing a jester's shoes and hat.

'No,' replied Mr Cat, 'Aelinor doesn't have a red hat.'

'Well, perhaps she just never wore it before?'

'That's absurd,' Mr Cat scoffed. 'Why wouldn't she?'

The jester did an elegant dance, then stopped, and spread her arms.

Plumcake smiled, and her servants began to bring the main dinner course out. The Jester continued, and by cleveryly using her hands and face she transformed from happy to sad. Then from sad to happy, and back to sad again.

'There isn't much to doido,' she said, 'in my room beneath the stairs, except to sit stilly on Chair.'

She paused, and one or two of the guests clapped politely.

'I can look here, and I can look there,' said the Jester, 'but, everything looks the same since the candle died.'

The Jester danced a very slow mesmerry dance, moving her arms in swirly motions, and swaying side to side. She sang:

'I do get lonely, but I'm glad I have Chair. He doesn't mind when I sit on him. In fact, he likes it, so it's fair. We tried him on top, but neither of us enjoyed it, so we stopped.'

The Jester ended her dance, and bowed very low to Plumcake. The guests applauded, and said how marvellous the performance had been. The queen gave a little nod of approval, then waved the Jester away.

'Such a horrid little man,' she remarked, aside, to Mustard.

The main course of the meal began.

Plumcake pointed directly at Strawberry. 'You!' she said loudly. Strawberry's tummy did a flip of anxiousness. She put the cream puff she had been enjoying back into her bowl. *Oh, dear,* she thinkied.

'Yes, Your Plumness?' she asked meekly.

'What's your name?' the queen asked her, with a friendly smile. It was unsettling, Strawberry concluded, the manner in which the queen switched between ferociousness and pleasanty. It seemed she was only ever a moment away from being cross.

'Strawberry, mam.'

'Did you say Strawberry *jam*? How sweet!' The queen still smiled, but now she looked like a snake about to strike its prey. Strawberry flushed with embarrassment, and a few of the guests, happy that the attention of the queen was not upon *them*, giggled at her discomfort. 'Strawberry Fleur, Your Majesty. Beg pardon.'

'Well, why didn't you say so, when I asked? 'Fleur,' you say... was that your mother's name too?'

'Yes, Your Plumness, it was,' Strawberry replied. 'Isobelle Fleur.'

'Was she French?'

'No, she was born in Twinkly, mam. Her father was from Northland.'

'Ahh,' responded Plumcake sagely. 'I think I met her. Did she make hats?'

Strawberry was amazed. 'Yes, she did!'

'And, do you make hats, dear?' Plumcake asked her.

'No, Your Plumnessly.'

'What do you do?'

'Uhm...' *What do I actually do?* Strawberry wonderyed. *Is making Spaceyships a job? Can it be considered something one does? Or colorying?*

'Don't mumble!' said Plumcake, abruptly cross.

'Uhm... er... I'm making a Spaceyship, Your Majesty!' Strawberry blurted.

Nearly all the guests were stunned by this revelation. The queen was taken aback and confuzzled. She blinked heavily. Mustard raised an eyebrow archly. 'A Spaceyship?' he enquired. 'What is it?'

Oh, gosh, now I am in the pickle, Strawberry told herself. She couldn't find any words. Her head was in the custard bowl.

'It's a Spaceyship,' said Mr Cat, and twinged one of his whiskers, to a very great effect. Every guest at the table, all the serving people, and Mustard, and Plumcake, turned their attention to him. How grateful Strawberry was for his support in that moment! The sudden emotion she felt made her eyes watery; it was like Mr Cat was coming to rescue her. *Don't worry, dear. I won't allow them to pickle you,* she imagined him saying.

'It's a ship, a craft, that shall sail through dimensions and space, even between realitibubbles, and it has a lot of space inside; that is the why it were called a Spaceyship,' he said with graviteatitoe. 'Strawberry is quite clevery, in some ways. She invented the thingy all by herself, with only imaginations and intuition, and colorys. The engine, I happen to know, was the firstest thingy she acquired; the rest is only details,' he finished purrily.

An excitement spread across the party. Fascinating! Bravo! How excitings! exclaimed the Twinklys. Strawberry blushed and smiled. She wanted to kiss Mr Cat for really saving her from the pickle with an eloquent little speech. *Thank you so much*, she whisperied to him.

'It sounds most interesting,' commented Mustard dryly.

Plumcake said loudly: 'Cheesecake! At once!'

'And double cream,' the queen said to her maidservant. She watched as the girl poured it expertly, in a nice swirly over the generous slice of cheesecake. 'Thankily,' she said, as the maidservant curtsied and stepped back.

'Strawberry!' said Plumcake, when she had almost finished her cheesecake and double cream, 'I'd like for you to make me a hat.'

'A hat, your Plumness?'

'Yes. Don't be an echo. I said so already, didn't I?' replied the queen. Her mood had softened somewhat, after the long and delicious dinner she had eaten. She was feeling sleepy, and it was a stage of sleepiness which made her warm and fuzzily; not like the over-tiredness stage, which makes one short and grumpy and stupids (although, come to thinky of it, Plumcake was always short, on account of not being at all tall, and usually grumpy and stupids!).

'Beg pardon, Your Majesty. It was my mother that made hats, not me,' explained Strawberry, as politeness as she could.

'Don't contradict me. I want you to make me a hat. Don't be humble and bashfully about it now! I hear you are very nices and neat with colorys,' replied the queen.

Oh, my giddiness! thinkied Strawberry.

'Craft it in Brillianty Blue,' continued Plumcake. 'And Scarlett Weeping Red. I want to wear it right here,' she said, and made an elaborate twirl with her hand and ending up pointing to the top of her head. It was a nice flourishy move.

She ate another mouthful of cheesecake. 'Don't colory in yellow. I don't like yellow. It doesn't suit my tone. You can use some glitterytwinkles if you might enjoy to. Be creative, Strawberry, dear. After all, you are making a hat for your queen!'

One or two of the Twinklys seated near to Strawberry offered her their congratulations. She was obliged to accept them, of course. It really was a wonderful honor to be chosen as the Hatter for the queen. She smiled, but very weakly, because she felt dizzy, and a little bit frightened.

She's going to hate it, she thinkied. *Just like mother always hated the terrible hats I tried to make!*

She managed to say: 'It's a great honory, Your Plumness. Thankily.'

Plumcake had switched into her 'instructions for making specific garments for the queen' mode of thinkys. She was good at this bit. She felt comfortable, and she did enjoy, albeit too briefly, to have something new and prettiness to wear.

'I like those,' she said. 'Are you taking notes, dear? And, use some squizzlys too. I'll leave it to you to put everything together, just how you do. Craft it, I thinky, in Tears Unnumbered. I can wear it for yesternesses. Fingertips only.'

She might as well speak Gobbledygook, thinkied Strawberry, *I have no idea what she is saying!*

'Make it pink then raspberry. Craft it in honey and mesmerry! Ooh, and some of those li'l fluffy bits. I really enjoy those; they flatter my nose. Sewisew seamiquick with prickle fingerslips. Bend it, mendy it, weave and sew. Of course, you are a professional; you know just what I want, don't you?'

Strawberry drew a breath. 'Of course, Plumnessly. I can't wait to get started on it!' She tried to flash a bright confident grin.

'That's right, dear. Have fun! Bakey in French, if you speak it. Wirlitwirlisqueak it. Use Petite Sparkles, and Shimmerys, and

Glistenys. Be imaginative, creative! I like artistic style, even if I won't wear it. My advice is do it veryslowthenquitequick. Ravel, unravel, stitch, unpick! Makey gorgeousy sky-blue, and prettiprettiness, please,' the queen smiled, rather charmingly. She put down her spoon. Her bowl was empty. Mustard sprang to his feet, wiping his very long moustaches clean with his napkin, and then he stood very straightly.

Plumcake stood, and all the guests rose, except one elderly chap who had fainted into his apple pie.

The dinner was over.

'Chop chop!' said the queen, not unkindly, because she felt content, and she waved them all away.

Sixteen

'What on World am I to do, Aelinor?' Strawberry asked tearfully.

We were sat in her little house, by a blazing log fire, smoking our pipes. I still had some of the tobaccos which Mustard had given me; Strawberry agreed that they were awfully good. 'I can't make hats!

I tried and tried, learning from mother, but I was just not clevery at it. I didn't make one success.'

'Unfortunately, Plumcake sharn't forgets, and let you out of the pot. She is canny with rememberys about debt and promises,' I told her, blowing rings of smokes into the fire.

'How absurd, isn't it? Why ask me to make her her stupids hat?' she glumlyed. 'There is only one solution; I will have to buy a hat, and pretendy I made it.'

'Hmm,' I doubtfullied. 'But there is only Mr Blue to buy from. Even if you should purchase one of your mother's hats from him, and he still has some stock, everyone will knowed within a clock fraction. Such gossips travel fastly, and you would be disgraced, and the queen insulted. You were quite the success last night, and your new fame has everyone ansty.'

'Oh deary, you are right, Aelinor! I should probably be sent to bed forever!' She sat worrying for some moments, then she said: 'If only my Spaceyship were ready, and I could fly away.'

'Is it *nearly* ready?' I asked.

'No,' she replied, with another glumlyness.

Mr Cat and Mr Flower were sitting down for breakfast.

'When will you get a proper breakfast table, Flower?' asked Mr Cat.

'But, where would I get such a thingy? If only someone would open a Breakfast Table Shop,' replied Mr Flower sadly.

'I suppose a standard table store would probably cover it,' Mr Cat smiled.

'Oh! How wonderful you are Mr Cat. And, where is the table shop?'

'There isn't one. Except, I hear, in Quibbly; but that is open to dispute,' replied Mr Cat.

'Hardly surprising,' remarked Mr Flower, sipping his Breakfast Tea. Mr Cat spread marmajam on his buttery toast. They continued to eat their breakfast, without speaking for a little while.

A small blackbird alighted in the apple tree, which overhung the blue garden fence.

'Ah, good earlytime, Blackbirdy,' said Mr Cat purrily. 'And what will *you* do today?'

Mr Flower waited expectantly for his friend to reveal the little bird's plans for the day. 'Nothing, she said. Nothing at all,' Mr Cat obliged, and chuckled.

Mr Cat spent a lot of his days alone. He liked to prowl swishily o'er the Lush Meadow, or trip stealthily along Squiggledy Lane, and he enjoyed to laze snoozily on the branches of the Weeping Tree, especially if the orangeyyellowroundythingy was being warmness.

Yet, sometimes he strolled far and wide across the Twinkly hills and fields and vales, and encountered mild adventurings.

He enjoyed to sleep on the branches of the Weeping Tree since he liked to snooze at a height, but in really fact he did have a little house of his own. He just didn't visit it much, and he never told anyone in Twinkly that he had it.

He went there to work, you see, to be alone.

After breakfast with Mr Flower, he set off briskly across the open fields, and headed southwestward past the beach, and over the dales into a sleepy little village of very few people, which was named Noplace.

It was a haven for artists and craftsman and poets and beatniks, and generally anyone who wanted a quiet peaceful environment in which they shouldn't often be disturbed.

The village remained secluded since, first of all, it was quite a long walk to get to, and also because if anyone was asked where they might be going, or even where they lived, they only had to reply '*Noplace*.' It was a response that most often deflected further enquiry.

Mr Cat arrived at his little house, and sat down in his armchair.

He was planning a rather nice surprisey.

It was Fryday. No one, except Mr Flower, had seen Mr Cat since the dinner at the palace. They were all wondery where he had gotten to.

He hadn't been snoozy in the Weeping Tree. Mrs Ruby went past it each veryearlytime, on her way to pick mushrooms at the woods, and she hadn't seen him sleeping there at all this week.

He hadn't been seen prowliprowl around Squiggledy Lane, as was often his wont. He hadn't visited the Cakery, nor the Tea House; now, that *very* was peculiar.

Nobody in the town knewed where he were. He hadn't been for breakfast with Mr Flower since Moonday.

'It's like a mystery,' the Twinklys agreed.

'There is so much interestings gossipy this week, isn't there?' they concurred.

Some suggested he might have gone off on an adventure in Strawberry's Spaceyship.

'Don't be silliness,' objected Mr Flower, 'the Spaceyship isn't ready yet, so he sharn't have flown off in it.'

'Well, just where is the fellow then, Mr Flower?' asked Klara, the Rubys' daughter, quite reasonably.

Mr Ruby remarked, as they watched Mr Flower walking sadly away, back to his little house alone: 'Those two are in cahoots! You could write that down, just as I said it, and put it into a pamphlet, if you'd like to; I wouldn't even be worried, or ashamed to have said so!'

'The Cat and Mr Flower?' asked Mrs Ruby.

'Mr Cat and *Strawberry*,' returned Mr Ruby, with very graviteatitoe.

I was all readyness for my expedition to the Tall Mountains to discovery the Crooked Stair, with the blessing (and funding from the Palace Treasury) of the queen. Since it was a secrety mission I was prepared for a quiet leavings.

'Twere Mustard said so about the secretyness necessary, and he was clevery thinkied to do. After all, he pointyed, firstly, the mission was likely *not* to discovery the Stair, since no one had ever seen it, and a failure to do so might cause embarrassment to Her Plumness, by dashing the hopes and excites of Twinklys. And nextly, if the Quibblers heard of it they would raise a myriad objections, and probably mount their own rival expedition, trying to steal her thundery. Although, he added, it would probably take them quite some clocks before they would agree upon their expedition details, and subsequently set off with their own party of explorers.

I have been assigned a trio of fellows to accompany me. They are skilled and clevery at travels, and also at climbings. They have ropes and picks and metal hats. Two of them have long scraggly beards, but the third doesn't; her name is Petunia. She used to work in the kitchens. She seems nicely; I like her.

I said to Strawberry and Mr Flower that I would be going away for courier works, and it was unavoidabubble, and my dutys. It was sadness for us all to be parting, but it sharn't be for forevers yet. Strawberry is still trying to buildy a hat for the queen, but it didn't look to be coming along at all well. I don't know how I can do to help, and I am worryness for her.

I told that I would write letterys and send them to her by post. She said how that would be nice.

Mr Flower cried when I said goodbye, but that were only to be expected. I gave him my red jester hat, for a gift and to wear, as he rather was fondness for it. Still, he was very sads though, and I were too.

We leave on the morrow, veryearlytime, before even the mushrooms are up.

Epilog

'I thinky it's from Aelinor,' said Strawberry, all happiness giddilys. 'It must be. She said she would lettery me!'
'Ah,' purred Mr Cat. 'And, are you happily with it? Do you like it?'
'Gosh, I most certainly am! It's more than wonderful! It's very very beauteous and beautiful. I wept when I opened the little box it came in. My giddinessly, it just about saved my very life, Mr Cat. Do you know I had a summons from the palace yesterness? I had nothing to show... until this earlytime when the delivery came.' Strawberry was smiling without stopping. 'I am amazed that Aelinor has made a hat so beautifulness. How clevery she is!'
It was coloryed with pastels. The head, the main part of the hat, was a plain box shape, circley and sky blue. The hat was hung with fluffies, spanglys, glistenys twinkling, petite sparkles, and shimmerys. The short hem of the hat was gorgeousy stitched with tiny Scarlet Weeping Red bows, and Brillianty Blue fingerslips sewn with Unumbered Tears. It was an extremely pretty and cluttered hat.
'Kind of a shame to waste it on Plumcake,' smiled Mr Cat. 'But, I'm very gladness that you are pleased with it.'
'Thankily dear,' said Strawberry, recalling the genuine gratitude and affection she had felt for him when he had rescued her from the pickle during the palace dinner.
'Ah, thinkily 'twere nothing at all. 'Tis friendship, dearily. And you knowed I never did like Plumcake.'
Strawberry was quizzical when he said that, but Mr Cat zinged a whisker, and stalked off.
He wandered o'er the Lush Meadow. He made his way to the Weeping Tree, and climbed into its welcoming branches. He snoozed contentedness, other side up.

When Strawberry answered the summons to the palace, she was feeling eager and excites. She loved the hat, and she was certain Plumcake would be thrilled by it; and now she was wondery whether indeed 'twere from Aelinor, or some other kind benefactor? Had Mr Cat been hinting that he had crafted it? It actually wouldn't surprisey her so much if he had. Despite his often pompousness he did have a caring heart, and some talents with colorys. How sweet and lovely whichever 'twere.

She knelt and presented the hat to the queen.

Plumcake glanced at it for a moment, then waved Strawberry away without so much as a thankily. Strawberry felt awfulness by the rudeness of Plumcake. Then she felt cross. *How ungrateful and spoiled she is!* she thinkied to herself.

Mustard took the hat from her. 'Very nicely done,' he smiled. 'Thankily, Mustard,' she replied, recollecting herself. She addressed the queen: 'Twere my very great pleasurey, Your Majesticnessly!' and she curtsied long and low.

C'est fini
(pour l'instant)

*

'Oh, really, Mr Cat, how marvellous! I always hoped it would fly. What will you call it?' asked Mr Flower, scaling the rocky tor to reach his friend.

Mr Cat's whiskers bristled. He stood astride the crags, holding his Curlystick aloft. He launched it into the sky, as Mr Flower came up and stood alongside him. It span out into a wide curve above the forest, and then span back on itself, for a few moments, before falling into the trees.

'I shall call it *Boomarung*,' he replied.

He felt quite pleased with how the demonstration had gone. The Boomarung had flown nicely, and a fair way.

'I am now calculating trajectories and sub-dividing velocities,' he informed Mr Flower, as they descended towards the forest. 'The entire flight is in the wrist.'

'I suppose we shall have to find another Curlystick.'

'Oh, would you, Flower? Thank you, how kind of you. I can't be expected to do everything. Fetching sticks is hardly my forte. I have importants considers to muse on. I'll wait here for you,' Mr Cat said, and settled on a warm rock, and seemed to Mr Flower to fall into an instant snooze.

'Oh,' said Mr Flower.

*

Strawberry tweeked the Gismo and swirled the Twirliswirl. They waited a few moments, but nothing happened. She tried again.

Aelinor frowned. 'Try the Thingummijig,' she suggested.

Strawberry crossed to the desk and looked inside its little draw. She took the Thingummijig out with a smile of triumph for having found it so well. It was a long curly one.

She came back to the console, and clipped the Thingummijig onto a power point. Spaceyship was delighted! It got all purrily and hummed, and one or two of the console lights blinked on then off again.

'Yay!' said Strawberry, and clapped her hands together. She was wearing her sky blue leather gloves. Not the ones with the tiny flowers stitched at the cuff.

She was terrifically pleased with all the many nice stuffs

Aelinor had gotted her for Spaceyship. Spaceyship seemed pleased too. It was making many other noises such as clacks and clicks, smalls beeps and ta-dums. The Interdimensional Star Vault was thrumming gentles. It was still a quite long way from being ready, but now there was power coursing through its machinerys.

'So you actually weren't to do courier work then?' Strawberry asked, sitting on the plump red sofa. Aelinor sat next to her.

'In fact 'twere a real expedition to the Tall Mountains, so as we might have discoveryed the Crooked Stair which the Old Giants builded,' quoth I.

'Giddiness! And did you?' she asked.

'No. We weren't abled since the Crooked Stair being builded by the Old Giants was only a nice story. There was no stair builded in the mountains. We looked quite thoroughly. We climbed rocks and steeps, crags and cliffs, and peered into every way up we could. There is no Crooked Stair tearfully to must tell. We did find a lovely cave though! It had a very tall entrance, and it were like a wide cavern within. They had some few pretty animal colorys on the walls, and hand prints. There was a short rickety ladder against a wall at the back of the cave, which was beneath what seemed to be a chimney.' I told.

'Oh,' she musilyed. 'That sounds lovely. How terribly sads about the Crooked Stair. It really was a nice story. Was there a fire beneath the chimney?'

'Oddly enough, there weren't. Only a small empty wooden box,' I replied.

*

'You may think that being so awfully clevery would be quite nice,' said Mr Cat suddenly, breaking the sultry silence which had hung with the warming breezes o'er the breakfast table. Weren't actually a proper breakfast table, but it were a table, and had breakfast paraphrenalias; toasts, and jam, marmajam, blancmanges, cups, and tea, and plates.

Mr Flower paused from nibbly toast and regarded his friend.

'I do!' he said.

'Hm. As well you might.' Mr Cat poured himself a tall cup of tea.